THE KEY OF GREEN

Were Adam's eyes the green of paradise?

DEREK JARMAN, "Green Fingers," in
Chroma: A Book of Color

Blue and green dehumanize nature
more than anything else does.

FRIEDRICH NIETZSCHE, *Daybreak*

Sentences (1) and (2) are equally nonsensical, but any speaker of English will recognize that only the former is grammatical.

(1) Colorless green ideas sleep furiously.
(2) Furiously sleep ideas green colorless.

NOAM CHOMSKY, *Syntactic Structures*

Contents

Acknowledgements

The many people who offered advice about specific points or directed me to books and essays beyond my ken are thanked in the endnotes. For more general support I am grateful to the John Simon Guggenheim Memorial Foundation for a year of fellowship support and a generous subvention for the color plates, to the Huntington Library and the British Academy for a short-term fellowship, and to the following individuals: Robert Aldwinckle, Jonathan Bate, Gordon Davis, Elizabeth Harvey, Patricia Tatspaugh, and Julian Yates.

B.R.S.

INTRODUCTION

About Green

For the twenty-first century "green" has emerged as a keyword on the order of "gender," "sexuality," "nation," "race," and "ethnicity"—words that dominated looking, listening, reading, and critical thinking during the last third of the twentieth century.[1] How "green" may change these other keywords remains to be seen. "Green" has power to upset. For a start, it lacks an easily fixable meaning. Trees, the most ubiquitous species of living things larger than we are, provide a finite, visible origin for the term, but "green" covers a vast sweep of mental territory. In Scott Slovic's definition, "green studies" embraces not just texts that explicitly engage the natural world but "the scrutiny of ecological implications and human-nature relationships in any literary text, even texts that seem, at first glance, oblivious of the nonhuman world."[2] "Green" is not a thing; it is a relationship. "Gender," "sexuality," "nation," and so forth are nouns—they really do seem to *be there*—whereas "green" is part noun, part adjective, part adverb, part verb. One can shop green, build green, vote green, think green. What is "green" in these cases? An adverb describing *how* one can shop, build, vote, think? A noun specifying *what* one can shop, build, vote, think? An adjective describing *who* is doing the shopping, building, voting, thinking? "Green" upsets syntax because it upsets any easy relationship between subject and object. "Green" invites us to consider that subjects, especially *thinking* subjects, don't exist apart from the objects amid which they live, move, and think.

For all its brave newness, "green" in these multiple senses has a history. To Shakespeare and his contemporaries, the horizon of *green, greene, gréne, grene* was broad enough to include

- leaves, especially bay leaves, especially bay leaves wound around a poet's brow,
- greenwood, greensward, greenhouse,
- the village green,
- verdigris, litharge of lead (PbO), and quicksilver "ground with the pisse of a yong childe" to make an emerald-green dye,
- the suit of "flaming greene like an Emerald" that St. George is supposed to have worn when, en route to England, he stopped off in Egypt and was crowned king there,
- a table covering for conducting legal business (the Board of Greencloth, the green baize of the House of Commons), playing card games, and shooting pool,
- green phantasms in "Perspective-Houses," where, according to Francis Bacon, the inhabitants of New Atlantis produce "*all* Colourations *of* Light. *All* Delusions *and* Deceits *of the* Sight, *in* Figures, Magnitudes, Motions, Colours: *All* Demonstrations *of* Shadows,"
- greenhead and greenhorn,
- "the greene-ey'd Monster," and
- "Good is as visible as greene."[3]

The last of these greens is John Donne's in "Communitie," a poem printed with Donne's amorous verse in 1633. Donne's speaker begins with the commonly held proposition that we must love good and hate ill. But what about "things indifferent"? These we have to "prove" or try out, "As wee shall finde our fancy bent." Take women. Nature made them neither good nor bad, so we must use them all: "If they were good it would be seene, / Good is as visible as greene, / And to all eyes it selfe betrayes." Green is so visible, it turns out, not just because it is everywhere to be seen in greenwood and greensward or because the speaker is a greenhead full of youthful desire but because women are green goods, pieces of ripening fruit that the speaker can devour one after another: "Chang'd loves are but chang'd sorts of meat" (sig. FF3v). "Communitie," like "greene," turns out to mean several things at once: qualities that all women hold in common (*Oxford English Dictionary,* hereafter referred to as *OED,* "community" I.2), the social communion of men with women (I.3), perhaps a particular woman branded as a common prostitute (†10), certainly a society of men living together in a single place (II.7.b) like Hart Hall, Oxford, or Lincoln's Inn and affirming their group identity by exchanging misogynist poems, and, subsuming all the other meanings, commonness and ordinariness (I.†5).

It is the commonness of green in English culture of the sixteenth and seventeenth centuries that has inspired this book. The color green is certainly not the key to all mythologies in early modern England—it does not function as, say, "the raw" and "the cooked" do in Claude Lévi-Strauss's analyses of the native cultures of Amazonia[4]—but it does provide a key, in multiple senses of the word. Like a long metal bit precisely fitted to the wards of a bolt, the key of green picks one of the locks that shut us off from the past. It gives us access to a surprisingly wide range of cultural experience on the other side, and like the coded key to a map it helps us interpret what we find there. In part, *The Key of Green* is a cultural history like Michel Pastoureau's *Blue* and Amy Butler Greenfield's *A Perfect Red*,[5] but it is time-specific (in this case to the 125 years between 1575 and 1700) in a way more akin to Herman Pleij's laying out the palette of the Middle Ages in *Colors Demonic and Divine*.[6] As a cultural history, *The Key of Green* considers the thematics of green in poetry, plays, and ethical writings. (In this regard I have been anticipated by Linda Woodbridge's wonderfully suggestive chapter "Green Shakespeare" in *The Scythe of Saturn*.[7]) But cultural history also includes landscaping and gardening, tapestries and painted cloths, bed curtains and clothing. The copper salt called verdigris, sap-green made from buckthorn berries, and the hydrous silicate of iron and potassium known as terre-vert figure in a material history of green that merges into social history (gentlemen were advised not to work with smelly pigments like verdigris and sap-green), alchemy, painting theory, and optics. Brilliant examples of this broader cultural history of color have been provided by John Gage and Philip Ball.[8] Green also helps us listen to the past. Like the key of G major, say, with its distinctive system of pitches and harmonics, the key of green invites a distinctive mode of listening.

Passion and Perception in Renaissance Culture: the subtitle to this book brings together three key words. "Perception" is the most fundamental. Before Descartes, thinking color, like thinking anything else, was a whole-body experience. Donne's reference to "fancy" as the power that shapes men's perceptions of women assumes a model of cognition that commanded virtually universal assent until the 1650s. In the story that Donne and his contemporaries told themselves about what was happening whenever they looked or listened, it was fancy that took the synesthetic fusions of "the common sense" and the *imagines* of imagination and memory and delivered up the result, in the form of *phantasmata,* for judgment.[9] Thomas Wright in *The Passions of the Mind in Generall* (1601, 1604, 1621, 1630) was not the only Renaissance thinker to locate judgment, not in the head, but in the heart. As Wright tells the story, *phantasmata* sent from the brain in the form of aerated spirits cause the heart either to dilate or to contract, changing the balance among the body's fluids. The result is felt by the perceiver as passions of one sort or another. Only then, when sensations have been felt throughout the body, does the perceiver begin to put words to what he or she is experiencing.

"The Passions," Wright declares, "not vnfitly may be compared to greene spectacles, which make all things resemble the colour of greene; euen so, he that loueth, hateth, or by any other passion is vehemently possessed, iudgeth all things that occur in fauour of that passion, to be good and agreeable with reason."[10] If you were a speaker of Middle English or early modern Scots and were vehemently possessed with love, you could even say that you "greened" this or that object, this or that person. Donne's greenhead speaker in "Communitie" *greens* the green fruits he picks and eats. Wright's word "passion" both is and is not a synonym for the word that we would use, "emotion." Emotion in the sense of an agitation or disturbance of the mind dates from the 1660s; emotion as a feeling as opposed to an act of cognition is much later still, dating only from the early nineteenth century (*OED,* "emotion" 4.a, 4.b). Instructed by Freud, we think of emotion as an energy that acts *on* the material body; for Donne and his contemporaries, passion was a biochemical state that arises *from* the material body. An emotion is, for us, a *response* to an act of cognition; for Donne and his contemporaries passion was the *impetus* for an act of cognition. It was Descartes' error, as Antonio Damasio and others have argued, to discount "the *feeling* of what happens."[11] Descartes may have devoted an entire treatise to *The Passions of the Soule* (1649, English translation 1650), but proper objects of knowledge for Descartes, Hobbes, and most subsequent philosophers are required to be clear and distinct, not sullied with passions. Green provides a focus for putting the passion back into looking, listening, reading, and thinking.

Most of the time I have preferred the much-debated term "Renaissance" to its competitor "early modern" for four reasons. First, most of the ideas about color entertained by Donne and his contemporaries derive quite directly from Plato, Aristotle, Pliny, and other Greek and Roman authorities. Color theory in the sixteenth century took their ideas as major reference points. Second, the palette within which Donne's contemporaries worked as dyers, weavers, painters, and poets did not extend much beyond the same four hues that Pliny attributes to the Greek painter Apelles: black, white, red, and ocher ("tawny" was the equivalent in early modern English). Green was notoriously difficult to make and notoriously fugitive in the presence of light and air. Third, a decisive shift in ideas about color occurred in the 1660s, when Isaac Newton's experiments with light refracted through prisms demonstrated a physics of color that still obtains today. Fifty years earlier Johannes Kepler had demonstrated the geometry of light rays with respect to the human eye. Between them Kepler and Newton produced a distinctively modern account of color and vision that makes "early modern" a descriptor more apt for the later seventeenth century than for the hundred years before.

There is a fourth reason for "Renaissance": my conviction that a rebirth is possible in our own time.[12] The so-called linguistic turn in criticism since the late 1960s has made us super-subtle readers of texts. We are acutely aware that every phoneme, every word, every statement, every speech act, every discourse results from acts of marking and that the grounds for those acts of marking are ultimately arbitrary. Color challenges these regimes of reading and thinking. Is green a text? Obviously it can be: /griːn/ results from the marking of certain phonetic differences, the word "green" is the sign that speakers of English have agreed to give to one set of light-effects as distinguished from other sets, and "green" as a concept figures in several distinct discourses of color (at least eight by my calculation in chapter one). For all that, green resists being put into words. Is color a physical property of objects? Or a sensation of light-sensitive nerves? Or a combination of both?[13] To experience green, you need space, time, and a human body, but not necessarily words. The methodologies that have dominated academic criticism since the late 1960s—structuralism, new historicism, deconstruction, and Lacanian psychoanalytical theory—rigorously objectify the texts under study. Aesthetic response, sense experience, and emotion—the main concerns of criticism in the quarter century preceding the linguistic turn—have been regarded as retrograde and politically suspect, as "false consciousness" in the face of contemporary political preoccupations. Green invites us to engage the culture of Renaissance and early modern England in terms not limited to black marks on white paper and, in the process, to reconfigure our thinking in the present. *The Key of Green* takes its place in what Patricia Clough has identified as "the affective turn" in cultural studies.[14]

The Key of Green is aligned with a second change in critical direction, the recent turn from language to the body. After self, woman, sodomy, nation, and race it was inevitable that the human body would become an object of study in new historicism. The social constructedness of physiological knowledge has been demonstrated in a series of landmark books by Nancy G. Siraisi, Gail Kern Paster, Andrea Carlino, Jonathan Sawday, and the contributors to David Hillman and Carla Mazzio's *The Body in Parts.*[15] The focus in these studies of the body as an object, as a physical entity, has been given a subjective dimension in Michael Schoenfeldt's *Bodies and Selves in Early Modern England* and Gail Kern Paster's *Humoring the Body.*[16] With respect to cognition, *The Key of Green* shares certain interests with Mary Thomas Crane's *Shakespeare's Brain* and Ellen Spolsky's *Word vs. Image: Cognitive Hunger in Shakespeare's England,* but it differs from these and other attempts to apply cognitive science to fictional texts by insisting on a model of perception based on Aristotelian philosophy and early modern physiology rather than contemporary brain research.[17] Emboldened by arguments made by scientists like Richard L. Gregory in *Eye and Brain,* I am proceeding on the assumption that the mind processes sensations, not only via a series of off/on nerve signals but via an interlayering of analogues.[18] As far as existing books are concerned, *The Key of Green* has perhaps closest affinities with phenomenological studies like Angus Fletcher's *Colors of the Mind,* James Elkin's *The Object Stares Back,* George Lakoff and Mark Johnson's *Philosophy in the Flesh,* Barbara Stafford's *Visual Analogy,* Charles Altieri's *The Particularities of Rapture,* and Teresa Brennan's *The Transmission of Affect.*[19] What I share with these authors is a conviction that all human knowledge is embodied knowledge and hence *felt* knowledge.

The specific ways in which human bodies are positioned vis-à-vis the larger world vary from culture to culture and era to era, as David Howes demonstrates in *Sensual Relations: Engaging the Senses in Culture and Social History.*[20] In that respect, *The Key of Green* participates in a third turn: from the body to the ambient world. My concern with perception is shared with Jonathan Bate in *The Song of the Earth,* Robert N. Watson in *Back to Nature: The Green and the Real in the Late Renaissance,* and Timothy Morton in *Ecology without Nautre: Rethinking Environmental Aesthetics.* Like Watson, I believe that new protocols of thought in the later seventeenth century touched off an epistemological crisis. In Watson's view, "the green" of nature, which had once seemed so immediate, became ever more estranged in the face of a scientifically calibrated "real," producing in Shakespeare's *As You Like It,* Marvell's garden and mower poems, metaphysical and cavalier lyrics, seventeenth-century Dutch paintings, and the religious poetry of Thomas Traherne an anxiety about the relationship of sense experience to truth and a nostalgia for "unmediated contact with the world of nature."[21] Urbanization and cross-cultural contact incident to trade and colonization, as Watson points out, heightened this sense of alienation. In *The Key of Green* I likewise attend to the interface between

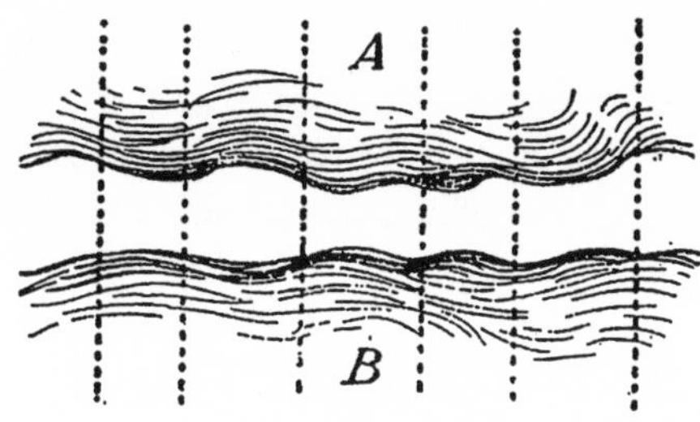

Figure 1. From Ferdinand de Saussure, *Cours de linguistique générale* (Geneva, 1916)

human perceivers and what Watson calls "the green," but what I find there is not a chronological progression from *within* to *without* to wishing again to be *within* but a volatile border or frontier full of plant forms larger than humans, animals with staring eyes, creatures of fantasy that combine the bestial and the human—the kind of liminal space that Donne and his contemporaries knew as antic work, grotesquerie, verdure, and boscage. (Examples can be seen in plates 4, 17, and 19.) Green criticism in these pages attends to changing figure/ground relationships in which the figure is human and the ground is green. Morton catches these dynamics in his description of "a poetics of *ambience*" that does not necessarily require an entity called "nature." The Latin word *ambitus,* Morton observes, gestures toward surroundings—but without specifying just what is there. Ambience "suggests something material and physical, though somewhat intangible, as if space itself had a material aspect—an idea that should not, after Einstein, appear strange. . . . Ambient poetics could apply as easily to music, sculpture, or performance art as it could to writing."[22]

How to attend to figure and ground at the same time: there's the rub. Ferdinand de Saussure's linguistics has trained us to attend to the distinctions between *this* figure and *that* figure, but the place where figure meets ground remains vague, blurry, elusive, and—to some people at least—disconcerting. A diagram published in Saussure's *Course in General Linguistics* shows how marks of meaning are made amid continuous waves of sound and thought. (See Figure 1.) The letter A in Saussure's image designates "the indefinite plane of jumbled ideas"; the letter B, "the equally vague plane of sounds" (2.4.1).[23] Vertical lines indicate the cuts, the difference-markings that speakers make amid the chaos of thoughts and the plenitude of sounds. Saussure himself attended to the waves as well as to the lines, and so did Derrida, but critics with less imagination have limited their focus to the lines. That shift in attention has had the effect of removing the human body from the transaction. The sentient, moving body is in the waves. With the removal of the body has come a denial of what it feels like to be immersed in those waves, what it feels like to make those marks with voice and with hand. It is hard to go swimming in a hairsuit.

An alternative to such asceticism is provided by Michel Serres, who locates the origins of meaning, like the origins of life, in the ocean. To Aristotle, at the point of origin of Western philosophy, water presented itself as changing shades of green.[24] And so it does to Serres. He begins his version of *Genesis* adrift "in the green and stagnant waters of the Sargasso Sea, at a mysterious spot where thousands of tiny sparks, all shapes and all colors, were glimmering crazily in the early morning light."[25] Countless bottles floating in the water, each one bearing a message, catch Serres' visual attention, while his ears hear the "acute and cacophonic carillon" made by the bottles' collisions with one another. On a raft of those message-bearing bottles Serres makes his way to shore. And it is there, on the litoral/literal edge, that I locate myself as a writer. At the place where waves mark, erase, and mark again the place on which I stand, meaning is not something I make alone. Meaning moves toward me; I move toward meaning. At the shore, standing on a quay that extends a short way out into the waves, I realize the situatedness of what I know.

At the same time, I am not afraid to speak and write in first person: the green that I see, name, and know may be reflected off the waves, but still that green is *mine*. What I know is not a third-person fact but a first-person phenomenon. In paying attention to *how* I know, I am following lines of inquiry set forth by Edmund Husserl, Martin Heidegger, and Maurice Merleau-Ponty.[26] The basic premise of phenomenology as practiced by these philosophers is simple enough: you cannot know anything apart from the way in which you come to know it. As Lyotard argues, that premise applies to history as well as knowledge in the present.[27] Phenomenology in the work of Merleau-Ponty and other phenomenological critics of the 1950s and '60s was universalizing in its assumptions about how the human body knows what it knows. By contrast, the version of phenomenology I am pursuing here attempts to be historically relative and politically aware. Such a way of knowing recognizes the embodiedness of historical subjects and attends to the materiality of the evidence they have left behind at the same time that it acknowledges the embodiedness of the investigator in the face of that evidence. Historical phenomenology attends to ground as well as figure, to waves as well as lines. It recognizes the ambient quality of knowing-in-place-in-time. In that respect historical phenomenology can claim affinities with "green" criticism in more familiar, more explicit forms. Taking a cue from Morton, the practice of historical phenomenology might be called "ambient poetics."

To find your bearings in the pages that follow, you may want to go first to the open door in plate 1, near the center of the book. From there, you can proceed in several ways. You might want first just to wander through the Green Gallery without reading any of the text—the equivalent of going to a museum show and choosing not to read the placards alongside the pictures. It is perfectly possible to use the Index of Images at the back of the book and find your way directly to parts of the text that discuss particular images. (Almost all of them make more than one appearance in the text.) Or you may want to start with the text and return to the Green Gallery now and again. If so, please do begin with chapter one, "Light at 500–510 Nanometers and the Seventeenth-Century Crisis of Consciousness," which puzzles over green as a phenomenon and lays out the big issues.

Chapter two, "Green Stuff," takes on the material history of green, beginning with the green furnishings that sixteenth-century people of certain means seem to have enjoyed having around them and proceeding through climate and flora, land forms, Aristotle's physics of color, pigments and dyestuffs, alchemy, ancient and modern theories of vision, and Galenic psychology as demonstrated in Robert Peake's portrait of Princess Elizabeth (plate 10) and Isaac Oliver's portrait of Sir Edward Herbert (plate 11). Chapter three, "Between Black and White," is concerned with "thinking" color. Here is where you will find the most vigorous critique of color-blindness in modern and post modern theory. The dominant psychoanalytical theorists of the twentieth century, Freud, Jung, and Lacan, are much more attuned to light versus dark than they are to hues. Aristotle's black-to-white spectrum of colors offers a way of arranging sixteenth- and seventeenth-century thinkers—philosophers, medical writers, scientists, and ethical writers as well as poets—along a continuum from those most attuned to the body at the black end to those most in denial of the body at the white end.

The implications of pre-Cartesian psychology specifically for looking are the subject of chapter four, "Green Spectacles." Horace's famous line "*ut pictura poesis*" provides the occasion for examining the varying relationships between seeing and wording in several set pieces of ekphrasis—accounts of creation in Genesis and Ovid, Britomart's rescue of Amoret from the House of Busyrane in *The Faerie Queene*, the painted destruction of Troy in Shakespeare's *Lucrece*, Crashaw's instructions to the painter in "The Flaming Heart"—as well as in a series of tapestries woven by the Sheldon workshops between 1590 and 1615 and in a rare surviving set of painted cloths at Owlpen Manor, Gloucestershire. "Listening for Green," chapter five, not only considers some famous instances in which writers say they can hear colors but examines the acoustic equivalents of antic work and grotesquerie in the form of sounds that spin away from logocentric exactitude. Varying musical settings of Psalm 23 ("The Lord is my shepherd . . . he maketh me to lie down in green pastures") figure in a survey of changing ideas about the relationship between words and music. As a site where green materials and looking and listening subjects converge, the theater forms a natural focus for the last chapter, "The Curtain between The Theatre and The Globe." All ten surviving scripts that Shakespeare's company produced at The Curtain during their sojourn there (1597–1599) pull woven hangings into the stage action, suggesting a visual dynamic in which arrases, tapestries, traverses, hangings, and curtains engaged imagination and fantasy in ways that might undo as well as anticipate and confirm the power of words. Some things you might do with green beyond the covers of this book are suggested in the brief afterword, "Coloring Books."

CHAPTER ONE

Light at 500–510 Nanometers and the Seventeenth-Century Crisis of Consciousness

One hesitates to disturb Andrew Marvell in his four hundred years of solitude, but stanza six of "The Garden" takes place in a "mean while" that you and I still occupy, a time in between the Fall (reenacted in stanza five) and death (anticipated in stanza seven). Here we are:

> Mean while the Mind, from pleasure[s] less,
> Withdraws into its happiness:
> The Mind, that Ocean where each kind
> Does streight its own resemblance find;
> Yet it creates, transcending these,
> Far other Worlds, and other Seas;
> Annihilating all that's made
> To a green Thought in a green Shade.[1]

Not just a thought. A *green* thought. What a thought! What? Green, a *thought*?

Ordinarily we think of green as a quality that objects possess. "What is green?" Christina Rossetti asks in her children's rhyme. The answer: "the grass is green, / With small flowers between." Or green is leaves, shiny bright. Or a hopping frog.[2] If we stop and recall our last physics course, we may consider that it is not objects that are green but light rays. Modern physics knows green as particles of energy moving at 186,000 miles per second (in a vacuum—air slows them down) in waves of a certain length. The particles of energy are called photons; the length of the waves in which they move is measured in units of one billionth of a meter, or, nanometers. What people in many cultures call green occurs in waves measuring between 500 and 510 nanometers.[3] What, then, is a green thought? The physiological effect of light rays at that particular frequency striking the retina of the human eye? The psychological effect of those light rays as named by the perceiver's language and narrated by the perceiver's culture? Green, *grün, vert, verdi, verde, viridis,* πράσινος, हरित: as definite as these terms may seem, how can we be sure they are synonyms?

Not every language has a name for light rays at 500–510 nanometers. As part of the World Color Survey begun in 1976, anthropologists have presented informants in various cultures with a standardized chart of color chips and asked them to circle groups of colors they can name. The starting point for color discrimination in all cultures seems to be the binary between white and black. But that is a distinction of brightness, not hue—at least to *us.* Contemporary science recognizes three scales for measuring color: hue (dominant wavelength), saturation (intensity, relative freedom from admixture of white), and value (tone, reflectance, degree of lightness).[4] The simplest model for separating hues, according to the World Color Survey, begins with isolating red + yellow as one hue and green + blue + black as another. A more complicated scheme isolates red from yellow from black but still regards green + blue ("grue" in the researchers' terminology) as a single entity. Separation of green from blue comes next, but often that separation is not firm. The word for blue in modern Welsh, *glas,* spills over into green (*gwyrrd*) in one direction and into gray and brown (*llwyd*) in the other.[5] According to the World Color Survey scheme, the isolating and naming of orange and violet come last.[6] The human eye is able to distinguish millions of color nuances—perhaps as many as seven and a half to ten million—but most cultures get along with just seven or eight basic terms.[7] The notion of stages in color discrimination, as if the whole thing were an evolutionary process, has been called into question, but the fact remains that different cultures see and name colors differently.

How, then, to turn Marvell's "green thought" into words? To judge from the accumulated commentary on "The Garden," readers have never been able to decide. The standard editions in which most readers today encounter Marvell's poem register this confusion. The introduction to Marvell's selected poems in *The Norton Anthology of English Literature* displays appreciative reticence about what Marvell's green might mean: "One of his most remarkable figures—the phrase 'To a green thought in a green shade' from 'The Garden'—derives its power from the unanalyzable suggestiveness the entire poem invests in the term 'green.'"[8] In their Oxford edition, Frank Kermode and Keith Walker bring to the poem a thoroughgoing Neoplatonism that turns "annihilating . . . shade" into something far more definite, a brief for cognitive thought over sense experience: "making the created world seem as nothing compared with what can be imagined by the retired contemplative."[9] On the face of it, such an interpretation seems plausible in light of Marvell's education at Cambridge in the 1630s, when Neoplatonist thought flourished there.[10] Other commentators—David Norbrook and H. R. Woudhuysen in *The Penguin Book of Renaissance Verse,* for example—read "green" as "young, youthful, raw, inexperienced, fresh, tender, immature, unripe."[11] More circumspect is Nigel Smith's gloss of "green thought" as "an original thought about nature and the garden, made under the influence of the garden (that is, contemplative activity while sitting under the shadow of a bush or tree in the garden)."[12]

If readers have remained perplexed, the reason may have less to do with Marvell's coyness than with the radical things that happened to green soon after "The Garden" was written, which most scholars believe was the early 1650s, when Marvell was resident in the household of Thomas, 3rd Baron Fairfax of Cameron, at Nun Appleton, Yorkshire.[13] Eighteenth-century readers seem to have been notably indifferent to the poem's charms. The three editions of Marvell's collected works printed in 1726, 1756, and 1776 give pride of place to Marvell's political poems and prose writings, relegating "The Garden," without comment or annotation, to "Carmina Miscellanea." All three editions present the text as no more than a translation of Marvell's Latin poem "Hortus."[14] "Hortus" itself is presented as a minor work that serves to demonstrate Marvell's "great Facility of writing in the *Latin* Tongue."[15] Edward Thompson, editor of the 1776 edition, writes off poems like "The Garden" as "the warm effusions of a lively fancy, . . . very often thrown off in the *extempore* moment of their conception and birth."[16] And besides, who wants to imagine himself in a garden *alone?* "There is no sublime rapture without reciprocation," Thompson observes apropos the coolness of Marvell's coy mistress (sig. ooo1v).

It was new ideas about nature in Romanticism that prompted nineteenth-century readers and writers to give Marvell's green thought a second thought. Percy Bysshe Shelley's Prometheus follows Marvell's speaker in annihilating what's already made in favor of something the poet himself makes in dialogue with nature. Prometheus "will watch from dawn to gloom / The lake-reflected sun illume / The yellow bees in the ivy-bloom" and from such sensations create "Forms more real than living man."[17] If anyone in particular, Alexander B. Grosart can be credited with rescuing "The Garden" from its eighteenth-century oblivion. Grosart's *The Complete Poems of Andrew Marvell* (1872) begins, not with Marvell's political verse, but with "Poems of the Country," among which "The Garden" figures prominently. Although no specific gloss is provided for the phrase "green thought," Grosart's preface leaves no doubt about how "green" is to be interpreted. "Fundamentally, the Poetry of Marvell is genuine as a bird's singing, or the singing of the brook on its gleaming way under leafage," Grosart rhapsodizes. "There is the breath and fragrance of inviolate Nature in every page of the 'Poems of the Country' and 'Poems of Imagination and Love.'"[18] The images of bird, brook, and leafage may have been inspired specifically by "The Garden," but the category "Poems of the Country" (as opposed to country-house poems) is a nineteenth-century invention. For Grosart and his Victorian readers, "green thought" shapes up as an herbal antidote to red-brick thought in a coal-cinder shade.

Disparities among these interpreters—eighteenth-century editors in their indifference to "The Garden," nineteenth-century readers in their enthusiasm for "nature," twentieth-century scholars in their need to draft the poem into a philosophy—suggest that Marvell in his own mind, in his own time, was somewhere else entirely. Even if the garden at Nun Appleton House survived today in the form that Marvell knew it, how can we be sure that we would be able to see its greenness in the ways Marvell saw it in the 1650s? For a start, we would not be able to know that greenness from a digital image, no matter how many pixels per inch. We would have to move through the space ourselves. "Green thought" is ambient thought: it happens in the course of movement through space and time. And it happens, not in black and white, but in color. Marvell enacts in "The Garden" a mode of perception that we may now be in a better position to appreciate than at any time since the 1650s.[19]

The Scandal of Color

Jacques Derrida, in his attempt to frame "the truth in painting" in four trial essays, one on each side of the subject, recognizes color as a "power," a "force," an "insolence" that threatens to overwhelm the stability of the graphic line.[20] Derrida begins, on the first of the frame's sides, with the fundamental ambivalence about color in Western philosophy, in particular the ambivalence registered in Kant's notion of color as "pure presence" that can be experienced either as vibrations in the ether or, paradoxically, as a nonsensory, nonsensual reflection of form (76–77). On the frame's second side a 1975 exhibition of drawings by Valerio Adami entitled The Journey of Drawing gives Derrida his cue for approaching the truth of painting through time, through a series of "tr" words (travail, trajectory, traversal, transformation, transcription, trace, etc.) that leave their mark in the *trait* of a graphic line. In setting up a contrast between line and color, Derrida is in fact reviving a distinction between *disegno* (design) and *colore* (color), and their relative merits, that goes back to the fourteenth century.[21] The more recent drawings in Albani's Journey, Derrida reports, hold color in check: "The rigor of the divide between *trait* and color becomes more trenchant, strict, severe, and jubilant as we move forward in the so-called recent period. Because the gush of color is held back, it mobilizes more violence, potentializes the double energy: first the full encircling ring, the black line, incisive, definitive, then the flood of broad chromatic scales in a wash of color" (172). The color is "transgressive": it refuses the strictures of the line. Between the black line and the flood of color Derrida imagines a "contract" being drawn up—but a contract that "only binds by leaving the two agencies in their autonomy" (172). If black lines constitute a text, color figures as an anti-text, an excess. In an essay inspired by Derrida's book, Stephen Melville specifies the reasons for color's deconstructive potentiality: "Subjective and objective, physically fixed and culturally constructed, absolutely proper and endlessly displaced, color can appear as an unthinkable scandal."[22]

Any attempt to deny that scandal, to cover it up, to black-and-whitewash it with words is doomed to failure. Color is not an object out there in space, waiting to be named; it is a phenomenon, an event that happens between an object and a subject.[23] *Phenomenon* was a word just coming into English usage in the early seventeenth century. Bacon deploys it in *The Advancement of Learning* (1605) to distinguish how things *appear* to be from how they *are*. To say that the earth revolves around the sun, Bacon observes, "is not repugnant to any of the *Phainomena*"; it is just wrong with respect to the facts.[24] Bacon's contrast between deceptive sensation and *real* knowledge runs deep in Western philosophy. Kant has fixed this contrast in terms that make immediate sense to us today. Kant's *Critique of Pure Reason* (1781, 1787) turns on a distinction between *phenomenon* and *noumenon*, between appearances and *das Ding-an-sich*, the thing-in-itself.[25] *Phenomenon* and *noumenon* are both participles, but the emphasis in *noumenon* falls on past tense: a *noumenon* is an object, something that "has been thought." The emphasis in *phenomenon* falls, by contrast, on present tense, on something that is happening now: a *phenomenon* is a subject-object relationship, something "being thought."

With color there is no "thing-in-itself." Color asks to be thought about, not as an object to be observed or as a text to be read, but as a transaction to be experienced.[26] That transaction happens within three coordinates—space, time, and body—which are, in fact, the fundamental coordinates of all human experience. The "where" of color in "The Garden" resists framing. In stanza one, Marvell contrasts the "short and narrow verged Shade" of the soldier's palm, the politician's oak, and the poet's bay with the ampleness of the space he occupies: "While all Flow'rs and all Trees do close / To weave the Garlands of repose." The operative word here is "shade." The full panoply of that word's available meanings in 1650 seem to be called into play. The shade of "The Garden" is an effect of light, a spot sheltered from the sun (*OED,* "shade" III.9.a), a place of social isolation (III.9.b), an epistemologically dubious visual field of apparitions and shadows (II.5.b), a state of only partial illumination (I.1.a), a representation of such a state (I.3.a), possibly a diffusion of (green) light possessing a particular value or saturation (I.4.a, earliest citation from Locke, 1690). Common to all these meanings is a sensitivity to *modulated* light—emphatically *not* the full daylight, the florescent evenness, the halogen intensity favored by the Enlightenment.[27] All of the trees, fruits, and flowers that Marvell's speaker notices in the course of the poem are subsumed within a shade, within "this lovely green" (stanza 3). Green in "The Garden" is the flood, the line-obliterating wash of color, that Derrida describes in *The Truth in Painting.*

Color-time in "The Garden" is no less ample. It can be measured in the iambs of "this lovely green," in the tetrameters of "How could such sweet and wholesome hours / Be reckon'd but with herbs and flow'rs?" (stanza 9), in the eight-line periodicity of the stanzas, in the minutes it takes the speaker to traverse the poem's imagined landscape and the reader to traverse the words, in the dark-green time/thyme that "th'industrious Bee" computes minute by minute and hour by hour amid the garden's floral sundial (stanza 9), in the hues and values revealed as the sun makes its diurnal progress through the garden's "fragrant Zodiack" (stanza 9), in the human life span whose end is awaited as the speaker's birdlike soul glides into the boughs "And, till prepar'd for longer flight, / Waves in its Plumes the various Light" (stanza 7), in the epochs referenced via Daphne's laurel (stanza 4) and the Garden of Eden (stanza 8). Modern understandings of color vastly extend these measures of time in two directions: diminishingly toward nanometers and expansively toward light-years. For twenty-first-century readers, at least, there is a "when" to the green in

Marvell's "The Garden" that extends from billionths of a second to millions of years. The midpoint in that span is the year 1650, Common Era.

For all his praise of repose, the "who" of Marvell's poem is a body in motion. At first, the speaker need not take a step for ripe apples to drop around his head, for clusters of grapes to crush their wine against his lips, for nectarines and peaches to force themselves into his hands. Almost precisely in the middle of the poem, however, the speaker recapitulates the biblical Fall of man: "Stumbling on Melons, as I pass, / Insnar'd with Flow'rs, I fall on grass" (stanza 5). Adam's fall is experienced by Marvell's speaker as a fall into green. The speaker's physical trunk may now be supine, but his mind and his soul move as if they were active bodies in their own right. His mind heaves like the ocean: it creates, it annihilates (stanza 6). His soul casts the body's flesh aside as if throwing off a garment: it glides into the boughs, it sits and sings, it whets and combs its wings (stanza 7). "Exstasie" is John Donne's term for this out-of-body but from-the-body experience. What first leaves the bodies of the speaker and his lover in John Donne's poem of that name is not their souls (that doesn't happen until two stanzas later) but shafts of light issuing from their eyes: "Our eye-beames twisted, and did thred / Our eyes, upon one double string."[28] It is perhaps this felt quality of vision as a casting forth of light from the viewer's eyes that explains the flight of Marvell's bird-soul into the garden's green shade.

The so-called extramission theory of vision has its origin, for Western thinkers at least, in Plato's explanation of color as the mixing in air of two beams of fire, one issuing from the viewer's eyes and one from the object being viewed. Aristotle argued that color was carried in one direction only, on light reflected off objects, but versions of Plato's extramission theory commanded the assent of Cicero, Euclid, Ptolemy, and Al-Kindī and were not refuted to the satisfaction of most serious thinkers until the optical experiments of Kepler, Descartes, Huygens, and Newton in the later seventeenth century.[29] As wrong as it may be with respect to the thing-in-itself, the extramission theory is, as Bacon would say, not repugnant to the phenomena. Plato's theory actually does make sense of what vision *feels* like. We experience vision as being directed *at* or *to* something: we decide (or so we think) where to cast our gaze. James Elkins, in *The Object Stares Back,* provides a brilliant argument against this too-easy assumption. By their color and pattern, Elkins demonstrates, objects in the natural world positively demand that we look at them in certain ways.[30] The experience of color thus remains a transaction between subject and object—a transaction that happens within the coordinates of space, time, and the human body. The preferred postmodern term "subject" fails to do justice to the active involvement of the body in these transactions. A subject, after all, is thrown (*iactus*) under (*sub*) an external power of some sort. "Viewer" (from the Latin *videre,* to see) is neutral, but still too passive. More accurate is the word "perceiver." The *per* in perceiver catches the "through" quality of the experience of color. To *per-ceive* color is, literally, to "through seize" color.[31]

Garlands of Repose Woven in Silk

The ambient green of Marvell's garden has an almost contemporary indoor counterpart in the Green Closet at Ham House, near Richmond, Surrey (plate 1). When William Murray, boyhood friend of the future Charles I, refurbished Ham House in 1637–1639, he turned this roughly 15 × 15-foot room into a space for displaying small paintings, miniature portraits, and probably small sculptures as well. Murray took his inspiration from the "Cabbonett Room" at Whitehall Palace in which Charles I displayed his own collection of small works of art. Similar intimate spaces for viewing small paintings, prints, drawings, and curiosities were designed by Inigo Jones for St. James' Palace, Oatlands Palace, Somerset House, and the Queen's House at Greenwich.[32] A 1655 inventory describes the Ham House room as furnished with "Hanginges of greene stuffe," together with "A couch[,] a chaire, two stooles and a carpet of the same stuffe" (19). The green silk fabric that lines the walls today is copied from green damask used in a 1672 refurbishment. Also present in the room are copies of the "six green sarsnet curtaines fring'd" (sarsnet is a fine, soft silk) mentioned in a 1679 description—curtains that could be drawn over the pictures to protect them from light and dust (23) and, one imagines, to heighten the effect of revelation when they were whisked open. Andreas von Einsiedel's photograph of the room (plate 1) shows these curtains pulled back on the far left, revealing seven of the paintings hanging on the far wall.

Something of the dramatic effect that such curtains make possible can be witnessed in the autobiography of Edward Herbert, 1st Baron Herbert of Cherbury, who tells the story of being invited about 1610 to the Earl of Dorset's London house, "where bringing mee into his Gallery and shewing mee many Pictures hee at last brought mee to a Frame covered with greene Taffita and asked mee who I thought was there and therewithall presently drawing the Courtaine shewed me my owne Picture."[33] The im-

Figure 2. William Larkin, *Portrait of Edward Herbert, 1st Lord Herbert of Cherbury* (1609–10). Oil on panel. Original image, 21⅘ × 19 inches (55.9 × 48.8 cm). (Photo by Geoffrey Shakerley. © Charlecote Park, Warwickshire / National Trust Photographic Library / The Bridgeman Art Library.)

age, Herbert reports, had been procured by Dorset from the artist William Larkin, from whom Herbert had commissioned a portrait of himself a few years before. That original likeness, Herbert reports, he had given to Sir Thoms Lucy before departing on a trip to the Low Countries and France with Aurelian Townsend in 1608—a gesture of homosocial bonding that Dorset was repeating as he revealed the copy to Herbert. The original portrait hangs today at Charlecote Park, the Lucy family seat in Warwickshire (figure 2). As Herbert makes clear, the green taffeta curtains in Dorset's gallery, unlike the green sarsnet curtains at Ham House, covered only the frame containing Herbert's portrait. That was the more usual arrangement in the seventeenth century, as documented for the Earl of Arundel's gallery at Somerset House in 1619 and for Charles I's gallery at Wimbledon Palace.[34] Lady Olivia in *Twelfth Night* alludes to the same conventions of display—and the same dramatic effect—when she offers to pull aside her mourning veil and show Viola/Cesario her face: "we will draw the Curtain, and shew you the picture. Looke you sir, such a one I was this present: ist not well done?"[35] In Hans Holbein's 1533 group portrait known to history as *The Ambassadors,* what the parted green curtain reveals is the passion of Christ (plate 2). In Catholic tradition it was customary to shroud the crucifix during Lent and unveil it on Easter. The specifically English location of Holbein's portrait may be signified by the fact that the curtain is green. Green was the favored color for this shroud in southeast England.[36] Green curtains, it is worth noting, figure in the backgrounds of Holbein's portraits of Sir Thomas More and Erasmus.[37]

From outdoors to indoors to gallery to green curtain to portrait: the assemblage of space, time, and bodies traced in Herbert's anecdote can be experienced today in the Green Closet at Ham House. Twenty-two of the gilt- and ebony-framed paintings still hanging on top of the green damask are among the 57 works known to have been hanging in the Green Closet in 1677. Of those 57 works, 38 were framed in ebony versus 19 in gilt, showing a marked preference for firm black lines to separate the images from the field of green even as that field provided the continuity from image to image.[38]A miniature portrait of Queen Elizabeth attributed to Nicholas Hilliard (plate 3) hanging in the room today illustrates the effect. Hilliard's likeness of the queen shares wall space with other miniatures and with two locks of hair. Across the damask's foliated green the viewer's eyes move from image to image, from the synecdoche of hair to the synecdoche of painted face in the same way the viewer's mind, were she acquainted with the owners of those faces and wisps of hair, would move from memory to memory. An impression of ebony and gilt framing is likewise provided by the carved doorway that gives access off the wood-paneled Long Gallery. Von Einsiedel's photograph of the Green Closet catches this quality of frames-within-a-frame—a quality not unlike the architectural frontispieces that provide access to sixteenth- and seventeenth-century books and the curtained openings within which "discovery" scenes were staged in London's theaters. To pass through the double doors is to enter a variegated green shade. All the senses of "shade" adumbrated in "The Garden" are called into play here: shelter from the sun, social seclusion, a visual field of apparitions and shadows, modulated illumination, representations (in the paintings) of modulated illumination, plus several different values and saturations of light at 500–510 nanometers.

Color in the Green Closet is no less a function of time. Light from the north-facing windows (it was likely Murray who sealed up a second, east-facing window in his 1637–1639 refurbishment) bathes the space in the sort of even light that Vitruvius had recommended for viewing artwork.[39] "Two window Curtaines of White damusk fring'd," mentioned in the 1679 inventory,[40] were likely designed to produce the steady and invariable light that Wotton, taking his cue from Vitruvius, recommended for displaying works of art. Von Einsiedel's photograph (taken on September 21, 2007, the autumn equinox, at 10:30 a.m. GMT) reveals, however, how the spring-to-autumn sun at a latitude of 51.46°N wreaks havoc with Vitruvius's Mediterranean prescriptions, as sunbeams reflect off the gilding, shimmer on the polished wood, trick out the leaf patterns in the damask, and highlight now this painting and now that one in the course of the sun's diurnal movement around three of the room's four walls. To perceive the pictures, a body has to leave behind the frame of the doorway and move into, through, and about the room. Ninety seconds would be sufficient for a quick walk round; minutes or even hours would be required to stop and view each painting in the way Marvell's speaker stops to consider features of the garden landscape in the precisely numbered stanzas of the first printing of "The Garden." In *The Elements of Architecture,* Wotton describes galleries as spaces "appointed for gentle Motion" (sig. A4v); the Green Closet, a recess off the Long Gallery, would figure then as a place of repose.

Compared to space and time, it is the ambulatory human body in the Green Closet that remains the most elusive factor in this particular experience of green, and not just because a barrier prevents visitors to Ham House today from going more than a few feet beyond the door. Originally this room was not just a *green* cabinet; it was *William Murray's* cabinet. As a place of repose and contemplation amid objects that Murray had chosen, the Green Closet figures as an English equivalent of an Italian *studiolo, camerino, stanzino, scrittorio,* or *grotta* like Federico da Montefeltro's *studiolo* in Urbino or Isabella d'Este's in Mantua. With origins in both medieval monastic cells and in ancient painted chambers being excavated in Renaissance Rome, such spaces figured, according to Stephen J. Campbell, as sites for playing out conflicted impulses in Renaissance culture: on the one hand the impulse to collect rare objects and display one's wealth to the world, and on the other the impulse to retreat from the world's cares and devote oneself to reading, meditation, and cultivation of the humanist self.[41] To Campbell's view, the *studiolo* and its objects might function as synecdoche, allowing their creators to show to select visitors (one thinks here of the Earl of Dorset taking Edward Herbert into his gallery) visible signs of a self that might be hidden from the world at large. Stories on the walls and the books that might be read amid those painted images made a room like the Green Closet, in Campbell's words, "an instrument for thinking" (46). The green couch, the green chair, the two green-cushioned stools included in the 1655 inventory of the Green Closet suggest that looking and reading might be accompanied by a third activity: intimate conversation. The thoughts fostered by the images and books in a *studiolo* (and by the conversations those images and books might inspire) were specifically *felt* thoughts: "even as the emotions continue [in the fifteenth and sixteenth centuries] to be regarded as something to be held at bay, as potentially inimical to the self," Campbell observes, "it is also apparent that they increasingly claim a place for themselves, that it is they—the emotions—that present what is most distinctive about individual selves" (46). Ultimately it is a self—an imagining, thinking, impassioned self—that Marvell's green garden and Murray's Green Closet adumbrate.

Thinking Outside the Black Box

If, as Stephen Melville suggests, color is an unthinkable scandal, why try to think it? Why try to speak about it? "Color has not yet been named," Derrida observes in *The Truth in Painting*.[42] What truth, then, can there be in color? Why isolate the status of color in 1650—indeed, the status of one color in particular—and turn it into an object of study when there are so many more compelling objects of study in view, objects like the political revolutions of 1642 and 1660, the consolidation of capitalism, the institutionalization of science, the expansion of empire, the reification of "race" as a way of classifying people, shifts in the ways sexuality was aligned with gender? There are two compelling reasons.

The first is registered by Derrida in his observation that "color has not yet been named." Color forces us to consider the limits of language and the extent to which we can say that all meanings are textual meanings. "Il n'y a pas de hors-texte"—except, perhaps, for color.[43] Wittgenstein is famous for emptying out the content of color names. In notebooks that he kept while resident at Oxford in 1950, Wittgenstein occupied himself, among other things, with color and with Shakespeare. How is it, Wittgenstein wonders, that people learn the meaning of color names?[44] In everyday life, after all, we are surrounded by "impure colours," and yet we have formed a concept of "*pure* colours" (3.59) and given them precise names. Green is Wittgenstein's favorite example. Some people consider green to be a primary color, located between yellow and blue (3.26), whereas Wittgenstein himself sees blue and yellow as "opposites" (3.26), so that "green is one special way-station on the coloured path from blue to yellow" (3.40). But perhaps that seems so only because schematic color wheels tell him blue and yellow are opposites (3.26). In a later notebook Wittgenstein presses such questions to their logical limits:

> What is there in favor of saying that green is a primary colour, not a blend of blue and yellow? Would it be right to say: "You can only know it directly by looking at the colours"? But how do I know that I mean the same by the words "primary colours" as some other person who is also inclined to call green a primary colour? No,—here language-games decide. (1.6)

Green-as-seen and green-as-named remain two separate entities, the first a matter of "sensations," the latter "a premature simplification of logic" (3.71–75).[45]

Wittgenstein approaches Shakespeare with a similar skepticism about categories. Shakespeare in Wittgenstein's view is a "phenomenon" who resists being placed according to criticism's usual reference points: "one can only place him by placing him wrongly."[46] In one particularly rich passage Wittgenstein brings together color, the major and minor musical scales, and Shakespeare's characters. To think of a dramatic character as a fixed entity, to say that a particular character belongs to the minor mode or the major, is to make the same mistake as assuming that individual colors have a fixed character independent of their context: "The fact that green has such and such an effect as the colour of a table cloth, red another, licenses no conclusion about their effect in a picture" (84e). What is needed in all three cases—color, music, and Shakespeare—is an approach that acknowledges the difference between sensations and the premature simplifications of words. "In philosophy," Wittgenstein concludes, "it is not enough to learn in every case *what* is to be said about a subject, but also *how* one must speak about it. We are always having to begin by learning the method of tackling it."[47]

The cultural implications of the disjunction between color-sensing and color-naming are vast. Wittgenstein delights in postulating a society in which everyone is red-green or blue-yellow color-blind (1.77) or belongs to a totally color-blind tribe (3.128) who ridicule "normal-sighted" people on the stage (3.285). No less interesting to him would be a culture in which people have a different "geometry of colour" than we do (1.66, 3.86, 3.154) and can think about colors only in terms of the shapes in which they naturally occur (3.130), or a culture that knows colors that western cultures don't know (3.42) or a culture that doesn't recognize orange (1.78) or brown (3.123). Clearly, when we try to talk about color, something is "left over." Color presents an extreme instance of Derrida's "supplement."[48] There seem to be three ways of confronting the resulting aporia. Do we sense more than we can say? Do we sense only what we say? Or do we somehow do both, say what we sense and sense what we say?

Such language games point us to the second reason for studying color. Color makes it impossible to separate subject from object. Is color a property of the object? (Aristotle thought so.) A quality in the subject's perception? (Kepler, Descartes, and Newton demonstrated as much.) Or a function of both? (That seems to be the case in Marvell's garden.) Derek Jarman, in the first of the three epigraphs to this book, imagines green as a primal experience: "Were Adam's eyes the green of paradise? Did they open on the vivid green of the Garden of Eden? God's green mantle. Was green the first colour of perception?"[49] Before Adam starts naming things, green is there, in the vegetation, in his eyes. The expulsion from Paradise becomes, in Jarman's view, the banishment of Adam and Eve to a comparatively colorless world:

> Remember them as you buy a dozen Granny Smiths. There were few colours in the wilderness. At that time God hadn't even set a rainbow begging for forgiveness. If he had, Adam would have returned it to the sender, for he missed the colours of Eden . . . violet and mallow (mauve), buttercup, lavender and lime. (63; ellipsis original)

Attempts to restore the garden, beginning with the labors of Cain and Abel, give us "green fingers" (North Americans would say "a green thumb") but not the perception, the "seizing-through," that was possible with Adam's green eyes (64).

Nietzsche, in the second epigraph to this book, sees green in startlingly different terms. Far from conjoining humankind with the natural world, green (along with blue) dehumanizes the natural world. Pliny, in his *Natural History,* claims that the famous Greek painter Apelles used only four colors: black, white, red, and yellow.[50] Nietzsche, noting the absence of green in Apelles' palette, infers that the Greeks saw the natural world in terms that dissolved the boundary between subject and object. Instead of blue they saw deep brown, a variant of Apelles' black: "they used the same word . . . to describe the colour of dark hair, that of the cornflower, and that of the southern sea."[51] With respect to green and yellow, they used "the same word for the colour of the greenest plants and that of the human skin, honey, and yellow resins." It was this "*deficiency*" [*Mangel*]—Nietzsche's word and Nietzsche's emphasis, not mine—that gave the Greeks "the playful facility" to see gods and demigods in the natural world, to project human forms onto natural objects (182–83, 1:266). Such phrases as "the wine-dark sea" would seem, from evidence of the World Color Survey, to indicate that the ancient Greeks, like the Anglo-Saxons, were more sensitive to value than to hue—red wine and the deep sea are both dark[52]—but Nietzsche goes on to set up a model of color perception in which human subjects and natural objects exist in a dynamic, evolving state:

> Every thinker paints his world in fewer colours than *are actually there,* and is blind to certain individual colours. This is not merely a deficiency. By virtue of this approximation and simplification he introduces harmonies of colours *into the things themselves* [*in die Dinge hinein*], and these harmonies possess great charm, and can constitute an enrichment of nature (183, 1:266; original emphasis).

In acknowledging the power of human imagination to transform "the things themselves" Nietzsche in effect rejects Kant's distinction between *noumenon* and *phenomenon.*

The result is not just knowledge of an "object perceived" but pleasure [*Genuss*] in that object and in the act of perception itself. "Perhaps it was only in this way that mankind first learned to take *pleasure* in the sight of existence," Nietzsche speculates. "[E]xistence, that is to say, was in the first instance presented to them in one or two colours, and thus presented harmoniously: mankind then as it were practised on these few shades before being able to go over to several" (183, 1:266, original emphasis). The process that Nietzsche describes here is in fact borne out by the World Color Survey. The most basic distinctions in the world's languages, as we have noted, seem to be among black, white, and red. All other discriminations follow from these. Color vision, according to J. D. Mollon and other biologists and psychologists, probably evolved in human beings in just this way: first the ability to distinguish bright from dark, then a sensitivity to light rays at 510–570 nanometers (the green-to-yellow range), then a sensitivity to rays at 650–700 (the red-to-violet range), and much later, a sensitivity to rays at 400–450 (the blue range).[53] In the conclusion to his disquisition on color, Nietzsche challenges us to recapitulate, in ourselves, this evolutionary process: "And even today many an individual works himself out of a partial colourblindness into a richer seeing and distinguishing: in which process, however, he not only discovers new enjoyments [*neue Genüsse*] but is also *obliged to give up and relinquish* some of his earlier ones" (183, original emphasis). Among those enjoyments-to-be-relinquished is the comfort of holding back at the black-framed door and taking stock of the black-framed objects in the distance—but refusing to enter the green shade that beckons within.

Discourses of Color

When two Danish anthropologists showed up on Bellona Island in Polynesia in 1971 and pulled out the plastic color chips used in the World Color Survey, one of the native informants volunteered, "We don't talk much about colour here."[54] That has not been the case in the West. Thinkers since Plato and Aristotle have had plenty to say about color. Drawing on the work of John Gage in *Color and Culture* and *Color and Meaning*, David C. Lindberg in *Theories of Vision from Al-Kindi to Kepler*, Nicholas Pastore in *A Selective History of Theories of Visual Perception 1650–1950*, and the writers who contributed to Alex Byrne and David R. Hilbert's *Readings on Color*,[55] I believe that seven discourses of color can be distinguished, seven different ways of turning color into words:

- metaphysics
- physics
- chemistry
- botany
- physiology
- geometry
- psychology

In practice, the seven discourses end up overlapping, but the starting place in each case is different. Although each of the discourses finds its origins in Greek and Roman thought, the seven kinds trace out a rough chronology that begins with Plato and ends with Newton's successors in the twentieth and twenty-first centuries.

A rainbow effect seems to be in Plato's mind when he describes in *Timaeus* the mixing of fire from the eyes with fire from objects: "The penetrating motion itself consists of fire, and as it encounters fire from the opposite direction, then, as the one fire leaps out from the eyes like a lightning flash and the other enters them but is quenched by the surrounding moisture, the resulting turmoil gives rise to colors of every hue."[56] All those hues seem to be present in a visual effect that Plato calls "bright-

and-brilliant" (λαμπόν τε καὶ στίλβον).[57] Plato's metaphysics of light and fire seems less disconnected from quotidian experience when we consider that value, brightness versus darkness, seems to be the starting place for color discrimination in the 110 languages included in the World Color Survey as well as in writings by the ancient Greeks and the Anglo-Saxons. Plato's metaphysical take on color has demonstrated remarkable staying power. It is reconciled with Aristotle's materialism in Plotinus, is dilated in Ficino, inspires Kepler's appreciation for the non-corporeal subtlety and speed of light, and ultimately informs Descartes' insistence that true objects of knowledge should be clear and distinct.[58]

Like Plato, Aristotle recognizes light as the medium that carries color to the human eye, but he explains color in terms of physics, as a function of the materiality of objects and the no less present materiality of air. "Transparency" (διαφάνεια) is Aristotle's term for the light-transmitting materiality that objects and air share in varying degrees of density.[59] The chemistry of color, a concern with pigments and with mixing, is no less materialist. Pliny the Elder identifies the four-color palette of Apelles and his contemporaries with four specific substances, three of them associated with specific geographical places. Philemon Holland's 1634 translation enhances the grittiness of Pliny's Latin text: "Of all whites they had the white Tripoli of Melos; for yellow ochres they took that of Athens: for reds, they sought no further than to the red ochre or Sinopie ruddle in Pontus: & their black was no other than ordinarie vitriol or shoemakers black."[60] One consideration that recommended Apelles' four-hue palette to systematizers in the Middle Ages and Renaissance was its accord with the four elements of earth (black), water (white), air (yellow), and fire (red) and the four bodily humors of black bile, white phlegm, yellow bile, and blood.[61] It was the physics of color, the association of certain colors with the four elements and their inherent properties of dry or wet, cold or hot, that informed the botany of color. Thomas Browne, in his chapter "Of the Blacknesse of Negroes" in *Pseudodoxia Epidemica* (1646), might pronounce it "no easie probleme to resolve, Why grasse is green?" but the treatise *On Plants* attributed to Aristotle observes that "Greenness must be the most common characteristic of plant life" (827.b.18–19) and finds the reason in "concoction," the slight heat generated by the plants' taking of nourishment out of earth and water. Green is "the intermediate color between that of earth and water," as can be witnessed in tree leaves, which grow out of the plant's white pith and break through its blackish bark.[62] Various values and saturations of green in leaves and stems, not to mention various hues in flowers and fruits, serve practical botanists like

Rembert Dodoens, John Gerard, William Lawson, and Hugh Plat as major markers of difference between one plant and another.[63]

In Galen's physiology, changing proportions among the human body's four basic fluids—black bile, white phlegm, yellow bile, and red blood—produce distinctive "complexions" that can be discerned as skin tones. Blood in particular can produce almost instantaneous changes in the form of blushes and pallor. Zirka Z. Filipczak has pointed out how sensitive sixteenth-century painters were to the color effects of humors on the skin.[64] To Pliny's eye, the internal source of these changes is one of the things that distinguishes humankind from animals: "For in other creatures, which (as we haue said) do alter their hue, it is an outward colour that they take from the reflection of certain places neer vnto them, man alone hath this change from within himselfe."[65] This rudimentary physiology of color took a radical turn in seventeenth-century anatomies of the eye and continues today in the brain-mapping of neuroscience. Euclid's interest in the paths traveled by light rays (he believed that the source of those rays was in the eye, not in objects out in the world) inaugurated a geometrical discourse of color that was continued by Kepler, Descartes, and Newton.

It was a fusion of physics, geometry, and physiology in the work of these three seventeenth-century thinkers that produced the dominant discourse about color that still obtains today. Color is not color without a human perceiver. Unresolved is the question of what, or perhaps who, is doing the perceiving.[66] "My Soul into the boughs does glide" (stanza 7): Marvell's name for the part of himself that inhabits the green shade is the English equivalent (from Old English *sàwol,* origin uncertain) for what the speakers of Latin called *anima* and the Greeks called ψυχή, or *psyche.* (The root meaning of the Latin and the Greek words is "breath.") Aristotle may have begun a systematic investigation of the elusive perceiving entity that goes by these names, but it was in the late sixteenth century that the enterprise finally acquired a name: *psychologia.*[67] To these seven long-established discourses of color—metaphysics, physics, chemistry, botany, physiology, geometry, and psychology—I propose the addition of an eighth:

- historical phenomenology

This approach incorporates the other seven discourses but qualifies their claims of universal truth by attending to historical and cultural differences. An explosion of fire tempered by tears, the flight of the bird-soul into a bough, the color of Adam's eyes, the dehumanization of the natural world: for the perceiver light at 500–510 nanometers is not the same in all times and all places.

In the history of color—or more precisely in the history of Western ideas *about* color—the seventeenth century represents a decisive turning point. Thomas Kuhn's notion of "paradigm-shift" is not inappropriate here, since what changed was not just ideas about color but the whole frame of reference for thinking about color and investigating its properties.[68] In John Gage's summation, "The seventeenth century saw the most thoroughgoing and far-reaching changes in the European understanding of color as a physical phenomenon."[69] At the beginning of the seventeenth century, most thinkers still described color in essentially Aristotelian terms, as the effect of differing material transparencies ranged between black and white. Substances were thought to present "true" colors; the rainbow, only "apparent" colors. By the end of the century, as a result of Newton's experiments, colors—all colors—were understood to be an effect of light. Black and white, since they did not involve the refraction of light rays, were no longer regarded as colors. Furthermore, color could have no existence outside the human eye: color results only when refracted light rays converge on the retina. Fundamentally, nothing in this physical-geometrical-physiological-psychological model of color perception has changed across the past three hundred years. The perceiver doesn't seize through; he or she is seized on. In 1650, twenty-two years before Newton first began to report his findings, the situation was altogether less certain.

On the Rack in 1650

The paradigm shift in conceptions of color during the seventeenth century is symptomatic of a larger shift in thought about thought. According to the model of the mind that Marvell and his contemporaries inherited from Aristotle, Galen, Avicenna, Averroës, St. Augustine, and Aristotle's scholastic disciples, all knowledge begins with sense experience. In Aristotle's own words, "no one can learn or understand anything in the absence of sense, and when the mind is actively aware of anything it is necessarily aware of it along with an image, for images are like sensuous contents except in that they contain no matter."[70] The route from the senses to the intellect was not, however, the direct electrical connection between sense organs and brain mapped by modern physiology—the electrical workings of the nerves were not demonstrated until the late eighteenth century and were not widely accepted until the nineteenth. Rather, a circuit through the heart via the vaporous fluid *spiritus* was imagined to act as the body's internal communication system.[71] As a result, sensation was a whole-body experience.

A green thought would have involved not just the stimulation of the retina by waves of light at 500–510 nanometers and the brain's matching up this sensation with the concept "green" but also (1) the fusing of the sensation with reports from the other senses by the faculty known as common sense, (2) the referral of this enhanced sensation to the combinatory powers of the faculty known as imagination or fantasy, (3) the transmission of the resulting kinesthetic sensation to the heart, and (4) the excitation there of the body's four humors according to whether the heart dilated in desire or contracted in avoidance. The perceiver experienced this rush of humors throughout the body as passion of one sort or another. Only *then* did ratiocination come into play. So strong was the effect that reason or judgment could be, quite literally, overwhelmed. In *The Passions of the Mind in General* (1601, 1604, 1621, 1630), Thomas Wright accepts the epistemological necessity of imagination and the passions even as he counsels the reader how to moderate them. Wright describes how imagination, in a state of passionate desire, "putteth greene spectacles before the eyes of our wit, to make it see nothing but greene, that is, seruing for the consideration of the Passion."[72] In another place he compares the working of the passions to the raging of the sea. Without the passions, the soul is a calm sea; stirred by the passions, it is a "raging gulfe, swelling with waues, surging by tempests, minacing the stony rockes, and endeauoring to ouerthrow Mountaines" (sig. E6).

Within Marvell's lifetime (1621–1678), more than thirty books with "passions" in the title were published in England.[73] Three books published in a single year, 1650, indicate how conflicted these accounts of passion and imagination could be. Competing for a buyer's attention on the booksellers' racks in 1650—the very year Marvell took up residence at Nun Appleton House—were the first English-language installment of Marin Cureau de La Chambre's multivolume anatomy of *The Characters of the Passions* (La Chambre was court physician to Louis XIII), René Descartes' *The Passions of the Soule* (the French text had been published just the year before), and Thomas Hobbes's *Humane nature: or, The fundamental elements of policie. Being a discoverie of the faculties, acts, and passions of the soul of man* (this volume was the second in a three-part study of body, man, and state that Hobbes had been working on for ten years). Passion and imagination figure in these three books in radically different ways.

According to La Chambre, some of the spirits that course through the nerves can, like Marvell's bird-soul, actually leave the perceiver's body: these spirits "are fluid bodies, they disperse and steal away with the least agitation, they penetrate everywhere, and no resistance can stop them; and although as they are Organs of the Soul, they love to be always with her; yet as they are subtil and loose bodyes, which have a great affinity with the air, their first inclination is to deliver themselves from the prison wherein they are, and to leave the mixture of those gross and impure things, to unite themselves to their like."[74] The contrast with the model of the mind set in place by Descartes' *The Passions of the Soule* could hardly be sharper. Where La Chambre imagines a perceiver so passionately engaged with the world around him that spirits leave his body, Descartes insists on a perceiver who keeps an objective distance between himself and the objects he observes.

Descartes' reputation as the chief engineer of radical rationalism has been persuasively challenged by Lilli Alanen. Descartes does, after all, recognize passions as "thoughts" (*pensées*).[75] Nonetheless, it is only about 250 words into the English translation of *The Passions Of the Soule* that Descartes gets to the fundamental proposition that "soul" consists in what is left over when everything attributable to "body" has been subtracted. To distinguish soul from body "will not be found a very hard task, if it be taken notice of, that what we experimentally find to be in us, and which we see are in bodies totally inanimate, ought not to be attributed to ought else but the body; and contrarily, that all which is within us, and which we conceive cannot in any wayes appertain to a body must be imputed to our soul."[76] Hence, Descartes draws a firm distinction between two sorts of "apprehensions" (in French, *perceptions*): those caused by the body and those caused by the soul (sig. B11v). Although he takes account of apprehensions caused by the body, Descartes regards only apprehensions caused by the soul as grounds for secure knowledge. Primarily this is because apprehensions caused by the soul are active, the result of acts of volition, whereas apprehensions caused by the body are passive, the result of "some peculiar motion of the spirits" (mouvement particulier des ésprits) almost always coupled with "some emotion made in the heart" (de quelque émotion qui se fait dans le coeur) (sig. C10, 3:989).[77] It should come as no surprise that Descartes' interest in green is limited to his *Optics* and *Meteorology* (both 1637), where color figures as a problem in geometry. Mathematics, as Descartes insists, offers the most exact language for dealing with the physical world.

In *Humane Nature*, Hobbes tells the story of a man, supposedly blind since birth, who claimed to have been cured at the shrine of St. Albans. The Duke of Gloucester, who happened to be in the city at the time, "to be satisfied of the truth of the Miracle, asked the man What Colour is this? who, by answering, It was Green, discovered himself, and was punished for a Counterfeit."[78] On several counts this story shapes up as an exemplary fable. Hobbes uses it, in the immediate context, to distinguish two kinds of knowledge, sense and science. "Both of these sorts are but *Experience;* the former being the experience of the effects of things that work upon us from *without,* and [the latter] the experience men have from the proper use of *names* in Language" (sig. D6; original emphasis). The counterfeit blind man could claim to have sense experience of green, but not "knowledge of the *truth of Propositions,* and how things are called" (sig. D6; original emphasis). Hobbes's understanding of sense experience is radically reductive. We attribute color and shape to objects outside us, Hobbes observes, whereas in reality color and shape are "but an *Apparition* unto us of the *Motion,* agitation or alteration which the *Object* worketh in the *Brain,* or spirits, or some internal substance of the head" (sig. B5; original emphasis). Fantasy or imagination is nothing more, therefore, than "*conception remaining, and by little and little decaying from and after the act of Sense*" (sig. B10; original emphasis). Cognition, for Hobbes, *is* imagination—but imagination understood in an altogether literal way, as the recording of images in tissues of the brain. As for science, Hobbes recognizes the arbitrariness of names—there is no inherent reason why green should be "green" or red should be "red" (sigs. C7–C7v)—even as he affirms that scientific knowledge arises from the proper use of names in language, that is to say, from propositions, or "two appellations joyned together by . . . *is*" (sig. D2v).

The operation of the passions in Hobbes's scheme is no less matter-of-fact than the operation of imagination. Motions from an outside object that reach the brain are registered as conceptions; motions that reach the heart are registered as passions, but only as passions of two basic sorts. Those that help "the motion which is called *Vital*" are felt as delight, contentment, or pleasure; those that hinder, as pain, hatred, or tedium (sigs. D11–D12). When he goes on to give these two sorts of passions a political application—pleasure can result from one's imagined power over another person, hatred from one's imagined subjection (sigs. E8–E14)—Hobbes confirms that passions function in a biological way, as life-preserving mechanisms, something close to instincts. The subtitle to *Humane Nature* declares that Hobbes's investigation of the faculties, acts, and passions of the soul is being conducted "according to such Philosophical Principles as are not commonly known or affected." Those principles, it turns out, are a thorough-going materialism conjoined with a thorough-going rationalism.

The paradigm shift that was underway in the mid-seventeenth century can be appreciated by comparing how La Chambre, Descartes, and Hobbes each sorts out knowledge into two basic kinds. These binary divisions amount to three competing projects in structuralism *avant la lettre*—and invite three acts of deconstruction on our part. La Chambre, acting on advice from Plato, imagines knowledge as a form of light. An image of an external object formed in the imagination operates like a luminous body: "it multiplies in all the parts of the Soul, it enlights them and excites after them those [parts of the soul] which are capable to be moved" (sig. D8v). The luminous result figures as "the middle, or horizon of spiritual and corporal things" (sig. E1). Greater or lesser degrees of light create two kinds of knowledge: either "clear and distinct" or "obscure and confused" (sig. E1). The former sort La Chambre assigns, not just to the understanding, but to the senses, the imagination, and the understanding working together; the latter he assigns to the appetite and "all the other powers, which have a natural knowledge of their objects, and of what they are to do" (sig. E1).

Where La Chambre imagines a horizon of greater or lesser light between soul and body Descartes insists, as we have seen, on a clear separation. For Descartes, there are two kinds of apprehensions, those caused by the soul and those caused by the body. "Clear and distinct" knowledge results only from volitions of the thinking soul. Hobbes's fundamental distinction follows from his anecdote about the blind *poseur* who claims to see green. "By this we may understand," he says, "there be *two kindes* of Knowledge, whereof the *one* is nothing else but *Sense*, or Knowledge *original* . . . ; the *other* is called *Science*, or knowledge of the *truth of Propositions*, and how things are called; and is derived from *Understanding*" (sigs. D6v–D7; original emphasis). Sense or science: Hobbes has dismissed imagination entirely and has reduced the passions, La Chambre's grand subject, to the lowly status of appetites or instincts.

And now for the three acts of deconstruction. La Chambre's casual reference to "natural knowledge" calls into question just how different base "appetite" is from the grand passions to which La Chambre's devotes two hefty tomes. Descartes, for his part, draws a distinction between body knowledge and soul knowledge that turns out to depend, literally, on the pineal gland. Better La Chambre's twilight "horizon" than Descartes' "very small kernel" (une petite glande) suspended in the innermost brain in such a way that the least motions of the animal spirits cause it to move (sig. C4v, 3:977). With respect to Hobbes's distinction between "sense" and "science," one always has to suspect separations that alliterate. In sum: where La Chambre, Descartes, and Hobbes see structures, a postmodern critic is apt to see contradictions and anxieties. In the suggestive terms provided by Alan Sinfield, the relationship of sense experience to reason constitutes a major "fault line" in the seemingly solid edifice of seventeenth-century culture.[79] Mind, soul, passion, reason: the availability of diverse ideas about these matters on booksellers' racks in 1650 helps to explain the fascination—and the elusiveness—of Marvell's green thought. At the moment Marvell was writing, an older model of subjective knowledge, known through the body, was being challenged by a newer model of objective knowledge, known through the exercise of reason. In that state of indecisiveness about the psychology of perception Marvell's "The Garden" figures as a symptomatic text and green as an exemplary test case.

It should come as no surprise that it was in the seventeenth century that *consciousness,* that indispensable word in the story we tell about ourselves, was coined and put into circulation. Before consciousness there was *conscience,* literally "*with* knowledge." With what? With whom? The modern meaning of conscience as "moral sense" (*OED,* "conscience" II) insinuates the presence of other people, one's cultural peers, so that conscience becomes knowledge with others. However, before *conscientia* made it into Middle English as *conscience,* there was *inwit,* (*OED,* "conscience" etymology), in particular, the faculty of common sense that fuses sensations and distributes them through the body via *spiritus.* The core of conscience is thus *inward* knowledge, what one knows with(in) oneself (*OED,* "conscience" I). Edward Herbert invokes both senses, the moral and the sensate, in his treatise *De Veritate* (On Truth; 1645)—but he begins with *sensus,* with sense experience:

> Conscience is the common sense of the inner senses [*Conscientia est sensus communis sensum internorum*]. It springs from the faculty which is conscious [*à facultate illa quae conscit oriunda* (sig. N4v)], through which we examine not only what is good and evil, but also their different degrees, according to their value or reverse, by means of the high authority of the Common Notions, with the aim of reaching a decision concerning what we ought to do.[80]

"Common notions" is Herbert's term for "Whatever is believed by universal consent" (116), a body of beliefs that Herbert regards, not as cultural constructions, but as "natural instinct" (117). *Inwit → conscientia → conscience → consciousness:* the addition of *-ness* in this progression turns a cognitive process into a personal state of being. With consciousness, a perceiver both knows and knows that she knows.[81] Philip Massinger's character Camiola catches this self-reflexive quality in the earliest use of *consciousness* cited in the *Oxford English Dictionary.* In *The Maid of Honour,* a tragicomedy probably acted at the Red Bull Theatre in the 1620s, Camiola refuses to act on her admiration for her suitor and social superior Bertoldo. Why? he asks her. "The Consciousnesse of mine owne wants," she replies.[82] If there is still perhaps a moral edge to Massinger's usage, by the end of the century the term has come to mean, in Locke's definition, "the perception of what passes in a Man's own mind."[83] "What passes" there, even for Locke, is more than rational propositions. Later in the treatise, Locke distinguishes three distinct sorts of knowledge: intuitive, demonstrative, and sensitive. Consciousness belongs to the third sort. We know fire not just because we see it or have it pointed out to us but because it will cause pain if touched. Sensitive knowledge recognizes "particular external Objects, by that perception and consciousness we have of the actual entrance of *Ideas* from them" (sig. MM2v; original emphasis). The "with" in *consciousness* conjoins the "I"-who-thinks with the "I"-who-feels.

Passion's ~~Slave~~ Salvé

What does it mean for Marvell's speaking "I" to say that his "Soul" leaves his body? What connects the observing "I" with this entity called "Soul"? Stanza six of "The Garden" would seem to establish that fixed reference point in "Mind." It is the mind that withdraws into its happiness: "The Mind, that Ocean where each kind / Does streight its own resemblance find." It is the mind that observes the soul in flight. The mind doesn't apprehend the soul as a philosophical idea; it senses the soul as a visible, tactile, audible image, as a bird that glides, sits, sings, whets, combs, and waves its wings in the ambient light. Implicitly at least, what connects mind to soul is imagination, the mind's capacity to take remembered sensations and use them to represent objects that are not physically present: "Yet it creates, transcending these, / Far other Worlds, and other Seas" (stanza 6). "Soul" is one of those physically absent though experientially present objects created by "Mind."

Marvell's image of the mind as an ocean invites multiple interpretations. A Platonic reading would stress the principle of sameness that aligns objects in the world with the ideas of those objects already implanted in the mind. Earlier in "The Garden," the speaker says he will carve on trees, not the names of lovers, but the trees' own names. Nigel Smith finds an allusion here to the mystical "doctrine of signatures," whereby "God put into each piece of creation a distinct sign, which was the true name of that object" and into Adam's mind "a mental impression of each signature so that we would be able to name and hence know every object in creation."[84] Most modern editors cite another alternative in the form of vulgar error number 3.24 in Sir Thomas Browne's *Pseudodoxia Epidemica,* the notion "That all Animals of the Land, are in their kinde in the Sea" (sig. Y1). Such glosses enhance readings that find in "The Garden" a transcendence of "the rational contemplative" (Frank Kermode and Keith Walker's phrase) over the "pleasure[s] less" of the first line in the sixth stanza.[85] A third interpretation of "ocean," however, provides a smoother segue to the lines that follow: "Yet it creates, transcending these, / Far other Worlds, and other Seas." Thomas Wright is not the only Renaissance writer to seize on the image of ocean waves for describing the wash of passion through the body's sinews. Othello, his blood put to boil by Iago's insinuations, compares his own state of mind "to the Ponticke Sea, / Whose icie Current, and compulsiue course / Neu'r keepes retyring ebbe" (F 1623, 3.4.456–57). Iago's warning, uttered a few minutes earlier, is still ringing in the audience's ears: "Oh, beware, my Lord, of iealousie, / It is the greene-ey'd Monster, which doth mocke / The meate it feeds on" (3.3.169–71). What turns green in Othello's case is not his eyes but the shade he sees with his eyes. Jealousy is a "monster" because it serves *monstrare,* to show, to demonstrate (*OED,* "monster" etymology). The words "mock" and "meat" gesture toward the story, familiar from Pliny the Elder, about the four classical Greek painters who competed for mastery. "Zeuxis for proofe of his cunning, brought vpon the scaffold a table, wherein were clusters of grapes so liuely painted, that the very birds of the aire flew flocking thither for to bee pecking at the grapes."[86] The green-eyed showman both feeds the eye and starves the eye.

To perceive the world through green spectacles is to perceive the world with passion—passion that is not limited to jealousy. Searching out precedents for "a green Thought in a green Shade," many of Marvell's editors have cited a passage from an anonymous late-sixteenth-century play, *The Raigne of K. Edward the Third,* in which a *green* thought is an *amorous* thought. When King Edward chances to encounter the Countess of Salisbury in the course of his Scottish wars, he conceives a passion for her that all his lords cannot mistake. "I might perceive his eye in her eye lost," Lodovick tells another courtier, "His eare to drinke her sweet tongues vtterance."[87] When the king asks Lodovick to write a letter to the countess on his behalf, he suggests they retreat to a "sommer arber": "Since greene our thoughts, greene be the conuenticle" (2.1.61, 63). Similarly, the speaker in Marvell's "The Mower's Song" says that Juliana has planted in his mind "thoughts more green" than the meadows he mows.[88] In Middle English, *gren* was not just a name for an object or a quality; it was an action you could *do. Grenen* was a verb: "to green" was "to desire, long"[89]—and it remained such in early modern Scots (*OED,* "green" v²). James VI of Scotland, I of England favors the verb in several of his poems. His short treatise on Scots verse includes a poem about a man who cannot sleep: "That nicht he ceist, and went to bed, bot greind / Zit fast for day, and thocht the nicht to lang."[90] In another poem, James himself confesses, "Scarce was I yet in springtyme of my years, / When greening great for fame aboue my pears / Did make me lose my wonted chere and rest" (19). In none of these passages do Plato's love-inspiring ideal forms seem to be anywhere in the neighborhood. How can green as passionate desire accord with green as the rational contemplative? That, ultimately, is the subject of this book.

Green spectacles, the green-eyed monster, greening for fame: it is perhaps fear of green that explains why so many upright people in early modern England chose to wear black.[91] An intense chromophobia is registered in the terms Phillip Stubbes uses in *The Anatomy of Abuses* to excoriate lords of misrule. The "wilde-heds" of a parish, according to Stubbes, choose a grand captain for their high jinks, who in turn chooses for his retinue twenty, forty, sixty, or even a hundred "lustie Guttes like to him self" and furnishes them "with his liueries, of green, yellow or some other light wanton colour."[92] Stubbes's antic associations of green and yellow make the yellow stockings of Malvolio, that "deu'll a Puritane," look all the more outrageous.[93] In contrast, Stubbes praises black as "a good, graue, sad, and auncient colour."[94] With respect to color, as to so much else, the Stoic vein in the Roman edifice gratified Christian eyes. Pliny the Elder, in his *Naturalis Historiae,* divides colors into two sorts—and helps us understand Stubbes's preferences: "All colors," he says, "be either sad [*austeri*] or liuely [*floridi*], and those be so either naturally, or by artificall mixture".[95] Naturally, as a post-republican living in decadent times, Pliny prefers *austeri* colors to *floridi* colors and prefers pigments that are pure to those that are mixed. He goes on to provide—and to denigrate—a catalog of expensive pigments fetched from as far away as India. "Vert d'Azur" (Holland's translation for *armenium*) and "Verd de terre" (*chrysocolla*) are among them.[96]

For portraying passion, *colores austeri* are not enough, as Apelles himself has to confess in John Lyly's play *Campaspe,* acted before Queen Elizabeth by the boys of St. Paul's School during Twelfth Night festivities in the early 1580s. Pliny's story of how Apelles, commissioned by Alexander the Great to paint a portrait of Alexander's mistress Campaspe, falls in love with his subject becomes a graceful way for Lyly to flatter the fifty-year-old queen. Grace is indeed the issue. In the course of a visit to Apelles' studio, Alexander tries to show off his knowledgeability by observing that "four colours are sufficie[n]t to shadow any countenance."[97] Not so, counters Apelles. In Phidias's time that may have been true, but not now. In those days men had "fewer fancies and women not so many favors" (3.4.101–2; sig. D2). Black eyebrows but yellow hair, one attire for the head but another for the body: these fashions demand an extended palette. "For as in garden knottes diuersitie of odours make a more sweete sauour, or as in musicke diuers stringes cause a more delicate consent, so in painting, the more colours, the better counterfeit, obseruing blacke for a ground, and the rest for grace" (3.4.107–11; sig. D2). "Grace" is that ineffable quality beyond the reach of art—and according to Lyly's Apelles it consists in color.[98]

In an earlier exchange, Campaspe has identified "color" as an effect that can be heard as well as seen. When Apelles first tries to insinuate his passion, Campaspe replies, "I am too young to vnderstande your speache, thogh old enough to withsta[n]d your deuise: you haue bin so long vsed to colours, you can do nothing but colour" (3.1.15–17; sig. C2). The colors Campaspe alludes to here are not the pigments on Apelles' palette but the "colors" of rhetoric, those verbal appeals to passion that help an orator sway his listeners. Derrida's distinction between graphic line and the wash of color seems useful in understanding how rhetoricians of antiquity, the Middle Ages, and the Renaissance understood the functions of *colores rhetorici.* The graphic line is to logical proof what colors are to passionate persuasion. The court cases recounted in Seneca's *Controversiae* include example after example of what one modern translator calls "a method of interpreting the facts that was to the advantage of the speaker."[99] According to one of Seneca's authorities, Asinius Pollo, a *color* in this sense can be defined as "putting more than was required in the narration and less than was required in the proofs" (4.3). Like grace in Apelles' painting, color in rhetoric is a supplement, something beyond the graphic line of logical argument. In the works of medieval writers, Andrew Cowell has argued, the colors of rhetoric are associated with the body, an entity that is susceptible to color in the form of cosmetics, dyed fabric, and the taints and tints of desire.[100]

The green in Marvell's "The Garden" is "lively," not "sad." Raymond Williams makes a useful distinction between the past-tense, always-already quality of structures of *thought* and the present-tense, provisional quality of structures of *feeling:* "if the social is the fixed and explicit—the known relationships, institutions, formations, positions—all that is present and moving, all that escapes or seems to escape from the fixed and the explicit and the known, is grasped and defined as the personal: this, here, now, alive, active, 'subjective.'"[101] The verbs in stanza seven of "The Garden"—sliding, casting aside, gliding, sitting, singing, whetting, combing, waving—suggest that consciousness within Marvell's green shade is mobile and tactile. It involves touching. In the ocean of his mind, the speaker experiences green thought as a rush of spirits that leave the body, as the feel of air on the skin in the act of gliding, as muscles gripping the bough, as singing in the throat, as music in the ears. Postmodern models of interpretation are ill equipped to address sensations like these. Deconstruction, new historicism, even Lacanian psychoanalytical theory are tools for analyzing markings of difference, regimes of power, the tyranny of signifiers in fine, structures of thought. Thus Rei Terada, in *Feeling in Theory: Emotion after the "Death of the Subject,"* presents emotion as a function of textuality. S ≠ s: Ferdinand de Saussure's formula for representing the arbitrariness of language, where S = Signifier and *s* = signified, becomes for Terada a formula for locating emotion in the gap between language and the language user. Emotion is said to consist in the ≠ of Saussure's formula: "A living system is self-differential; only self-differential entities—'texts'—feel."[102] Where does this get us with green? Is green a text? Can green do the feeling?

A more promising model has been presented by Eve Kosofsky Sedgwick and Adam Frank in *Touching Feeling: Affect, Pedagogy, Performativity.* Touch, as Sedgwick and Frank observe, undermines the binary between active and passive on which poststructuralist protocols depend. There is a dynamic, tactile basis to "feel." Its earliest meaning in the *Oxford English Dictionary* is "to examine or explore by touch" ("feel" v., I), from whence the more abstract meaning "to perceive, be conscious" (II) was derived. Shakespeare puns again and again on "feel" as "perceive" and as "experience by touch." "You see how this world goes," Lear taunts the blinded Gloucester. "I see it feelingly," is Gloucester's reply" (F 1623, 4.5.143–45). The contrast here between seeing and feeling points up the quasi-active quasi-passive quality of "feel," a quality that is registered in the dictionary's third meaning ("To be felt as having a specified quality; to produce a certain impression on the senses [*esp.* that of touch] or the sensibilities; to seem") but is implicit in the other two senses as well. Feeling is an experience that the subject receives from without but knows from within. What Sedgwick and Frank pursue in *Touching Feeling* is precisely what green thought demands: a model of interpretation that can register *shades* of difference. Models based on *binary* difference can never be more than variations on black and white. "We don't want to minimize the importance, productiveness, or even what can be the amazing subtlety of thought that takes this form," Sedgwick and Frank concede. "But it's still like a scanner or copier that can reproduce any work of art in 256,000 shades of gray."[103]

For reading green, the method I am proposing is historical phenomenology. Robert Cockcroft, in *Rhetorical Affect in Early Modern Writing,* points out that two orders of feelings are involved in any encounter between a twenty-first-century reader and a sixteenth- or seventeenth-century text: feelings attributed to personae in the text and feelings engaged in readers. Because the two sets of feelings—those in the text and those in the reader—are culturally conditioned, what a postmodern reader feels about a text may be entirely different from what an early modern reader felt. But feelings the postmodern reader most certainly will have.[104] Cockcroft demonstrates the truth of that proposition by isolating the emotions—not always acknowledged—that inform the analyses of several post-structuralist critics, including Stephen Greenblatt, David Norbrook, Germaine Greer, Lisa Jardine, Terry Eagleton, Harold Bloom, and Catherine Belsey (83–116). Taking a different cue from classical rhetoric, Daniel M. Gross has insisted that passions are neither the indices of individuality that Romanticism has made them out to be nor the biological givens that contemporary brain science assumes but cultural constructions that perform certain kinds of social and political work.[105] Historical phenomenology offers a way of restoring two things that have been missing from criticism since the 1970s: sense experience and emotional response. In place of the universalizing assumptions that marked new criticism as a method of reading and liberal humanism as a controlling ideology, new historicism insists on the historical contingency of sense experience and the constructedness of verbal meaning. In a move beyond new historicism and deconstruction, historical phenomenology recognizes a continuity between intellect and other ways of knowing.

Descartes may recognize passions as "thoughts," but since Descartes, the ideal has been *transparency* of thought. With respect to the ambient world, we have been helped in that project by prosthetic devices that extend human senses and amplify them. Some of those devices—telescopes and microscopes—have been available since the sixteenth century; some—radar and digital technology—were invented more recently. With respect to the inner world, Harvey (in his demonstration of the hydraulics of blood circulation), von Helmholtz (in his investigation of the electrical workings of the nerves), and Freud (in his application of hydraulics and energy transfers to the psyche) have applied the same ideal. The prostheses in these cases have included not only microscopes, galvanometers, X-rays, and the high-frequency sound waves of computerized tomography scans but the binary difference marking in Saussure's linguistics. "All that is I see"—along with Gertrude, that is the story we tell ourselves (*Hamlet,* F 1623, 3.4.123). When we say so, we, like Gertrude, fool ourselves. What does the world look like, sound like, feel like if we change the story? If we unapologetically put on Wright's green spectacles? If we set in place a green filter between our eyes and what we tell ourselves we are seeing? That vision, that altered vision, is the subject of this book.

Computing Time

The availability of conflicting books on the passions by La Chambre, Descartes, and Hobbes during Marvell's lifetime proves the truth of Raymond Williams's contention that "no mode or production and therefore no dominant social order and therefore no dominant culture ever in reality includes or exhausts all human practice, human energy, and human intention."[106] Residual, dominant, and emergent elements all come into play in what Williams calls the "practical consciousness" of everyday life (125). Does the *practical* consciousness implied by "The Garden" constitute a *crisis* of consciousness? The final stanza, I confess, has always left me feeling disoriented:

> How well the skillful Gardener drew
> Of flow'rs and herbes this Dial new;
> Where from above the milder Sun
> Does through a fragrant Zodiak run;
> And, as it works, th' industrious Bee
> Computes its time as well as we.
> How could such sweet and wholsome Hours
> Be reckon'd but with herbs and flow'rs!

It is that computing bee that gives me pause. At the very least, the speaker introduces here an awareness of lapsed and elapsing time that was absent from the "happy Garden-state" of the previous stanza. The editors of the *Norton Anthology of English Literature,* seconding Kermode and Walker, insist that the entire garden is not just the place of sensuous delights it has seemed up till now but a sundial, a device for calibrating time. Nigel Smith anticipates eighteenth-century Deists—or rather, has Marvell anticipate eighteenth-century Deists—in observing that the gardener "in a secondary sense . . . is God the clockmaker." James Reeves and Martin Seymour-Smith favor a paraphrase that is more abstract still: "Time itself could not exist without the actions of Nature."[107] All of these commentators find an objectifying turn in the final stanza, an act that enables the mind to get its analytical bearings before leaving the garden behind. If that is the case, Marvell anticipates the objectifying turn in Hobbes's *Humane Nature* and delivers us to our rational twenty-first-century selves. Or perhaps he does not. It is not, after all, the binary tick-tock of a mechanical clock that computes time in Marvell's garden but an animated body (the bee) whose movements may have a *telos* (gathering golden pollen from the dark green thyme). But those movements defy any linear logic. Time in "The Garden" is a function of space and bodies—and light. Marvell among the bees is a poet, not a philosopher. The soul-as-bird as well as those ambient bees may derive from Plato's *Ion.* "Poets tell us that they gather songs at honey-flowing springs," Socrates says, "and that they bear songs to us as bees carry honey, flying like bees." True enough, "for a poet is an airy thing, winged and holy, and he is not able to make poetry until he becomes inspired and goes out of his mind and his intellect is no longer in him."[108] As for Socrates, his feet are planted on the ground.

If there was indeed a crisis of consciousness in the mid-seventeenth century, it has yet to be resolved. The philosophical principles that Hobbes adduced in 1650 as "not commonly known or asserted" are anything but that today. They constitute the very principles that inform structuralism, deconstruction, and those versions of cognitive theory that regard the human brain as a particularly sophisticated computer. It is these rationalist principles that have blinded us to any concept of green beyond the effect of light on the retina at 500–510 nanometers—or at least have made us reticent to talk about any other concept but that. As an investigation of passionate perception in Renaissance culture, *The Key of Green* offers a cure for color blindness. As such, it stands as a critique of the prejudice against sense experience and emotional response that certain modes of post-modern criticism seem to need. Prejudice is "prejudging," making up one's mind in advance *not* to be seduced by passion.

Francis Bacon, in *The Advancement of Learning,* warns against the artificial separation of domains of inquiry: "generally let this be a Rule, that all partitions of knowledges, be accepted rather for *lines & veines,* then for *sections and separations:* and that the continuance and entirenes of knowledge be preserved. For the contrary hereof hath made particular Sciences, to become barren, shallow, & erronious: while they haue not bin Nourished and Maintained from the common fountaine" (93; original emphasis). Acute semiosis is one result of this narrowness and malnourishment. In terms of Bacon's agenda, *The Key of Green* belongs to that branch of natural philosophy Bacon calls "HVMANE PHILOSOPHY OR HVMANITIE" (93). For this branch of knowledge in particular Bacon cautions against too hasty a partition into body and mind. "I doe take the consideration in generall, and at large of HVMANE NATVRE, to be fit to be emancipate, & made a knowledge by it self." Bacon declares, "chiefly in regard of the knowledge concerning the SYMPATHIES AND CONCORDANCES BETVVEEN THE MIND AND BODY, which being mixed, cannot be properly assigned to the sciences of either" (93–94).

Onward (like a conquering army) and upward (like an ambitious courtier or merchant) may be the directions implied by the *Advancement* in Bacon's title, but backward is the actual direction that thought has taken in the four centuries since Bacon wrote his treatise. The "*lines & veines*" in Bacon's metaphor imply that knowledge is like a boulder or a mountain; the thinker can see the lines and veins only by stepping back from the object. Marvell, confronted with his living green subject, moves in the opposite direction: into, around, about. Let us follow him there.

CHAPTER TWO

Green Stuff

When Philip Howard came into his inheritance as 13th Earl of Arundel in 1580, he ordered a full inventory of the contents of Arundel Castle in Sussex to be drawn up. The castle's furnishings had been assembled over a period of four hundred years by the Fitzalan family, the new earl's progenitors on his mother's side, although many of the items in the inventory must have dated from the 1540s and the 1570s, when the twelfth earl had rebuilt the castle's living quarters. Hard goods in the inventory—bedsteads, cupboards, tables, chairs, "forms" (benches), stools, andirons, chamber pots—are surprisingly sparse by modern standards. What dominates the list instead are sundry fabrics: wall hangings, window cloths, carpets, bed curtains, valences, quilts, counterpanes, bolsters, pillows, cushions. For each of the castle's twenty principal rooms, these items outnumber the pieces of wooden furniture on the order of four to one. Even then, beds and stools are apt to be described in terms of the hangings or cushions that come with them.

Take, for example, the room specified as "Lord Lumleyes Chambre," named for Philip Howard's uncle, who retained a life interest in the Arundel estate even though he had no children to challenge Howard's inheritance:

> Item, i peece of hanging of the vii planetts. Item, i olde windowe-clothe of parke-worke. Item, i bedd of crymson taffata, with v curtyans, and valens thereto, and one counterpointe of the same stuffe lined with fusti˜. Item, i fetherbed and boulster, ii pillowes of tike [ticking, pillows stuffed with feathers], i pallet-case of canvas, ii white rugges for blanckets, and

> one woole bedd of white canvas. Item, i little quishio˜ of wrought velvett. Item, i joined stoole. Item, i closestoole and ii chamb˜ pottes.[1]

Thanks to the thoroughness of the earl's Yeoman of the Garderobe, Thomas Cowper, and three commissioners sent down from London, we know not only the furniture that the Earl of Arundel, his family, and his guests used but the palette of colors among which they sat, talked, wrote things down, ate, had sex, slept, defecated, and, on occasion, died. No doubt about it, the most visually striking thing in Lord Lumley's Chamber must have been that crimson-caparisoned bed with its taffeta curtains, valence, and padded counterpane "of the same stuffe." Red, present throughout the inventory, emerges as a prominent color: twelve furnishings are explicitly described as crimson, red, or russet, not to mention the fields of red that, judging from the series of portraits by William Larkin in the Suffolk collection, figured in a dozen "Turkey carpets" of various sizes.[2] But the color most frequently encountered in the Arundel Castle inventory is green.

Listed, item by item, are a carpet of green cloth for the cupboard in the Square Chamber, another green carpet for the table in the Dancing Chamber, green-silk curtains for the bed in the King's Chamber, yet another green carpet in the Cage Chamber, eight hangings of green cloth in the gallery, green window cloths in Percy's Hall, a completely green suite of bed fabrics plus a green window cloth and a green cupboard cloth in the adjoining Percy's Chamber, hangings of green cloth plus a green bed canopy and a green cupboard cloth in the upper chamber in Beaumond's Tower, a green silk quilt in the Receiver's Chamber, a green window cloth in the chamber-next-the-gate, and one final green carpet in the chamber-next-the-hall-end. Less obvious perhaps from the written inventory but just as prominent in the visual experience of the castle would have been the green subjects represented in tapestries and embroideries: the "park work" found in Lord Lumley's chamber and two other rooms (most likely tapestries representing the fenced-off forests in which the Fitzalans, the Lumleys, the Howards, and other aristocratic families hunted deer), the ten "verdures" (tapestries ornamented with representations of trees or other vegetation [*OED*, "verdure" 3]), the three hangings of "okes and white horses" in the Square Chamber, the five hangings of "brode leaves" in the chamber-next-the-gate, the five hangings of "oke leaves and Matravers knotts" in the King's Chamber (presumably designs that interlaced oak leaves with the coat of arms of Philip Howard's grandfather, Henry Fitzalan, who held the title Baron Maltravers before becoming

12th Earl of Arundel). Some sense of these woven versions of flora and fauna can be witnessed in an early-sixteenth-century tapestry from Flanders that hangs today in Cotehele House, Cornwall (plate 4). All told, the Arundel inventory specifies no fewer than 39 separate objects colored green, most of them large objects like wall hangings, carpets, and window curtains.

Those 39 instances of green in the Arundel inventory amount to more than three times the number of crimson, red, and russet objects that caught the appraisers' eyes. The contrast with other colors is sharper still: there are just four instances of blue in the inventory, four of black, three of gold, two of silver, two of yellow, one of "tawny." Except for the upper chamber in Beaumond's Tower, where the specified color is green throughout, every room in Arundel Castle accommodated multiple colors. However, the sheer number of objects colored green, their expansive sizes, and their conspicuous positioning on walls, windows, table tops, and floors suggest an ambience in which green functioned as the matrix against which other colors stood out as isolated elements.

The high proportion of green stuff in the 1580 Arundel inventory was not, it seems, atypical, even for households smaller in size and further down the social scale. Catherine Richardson's survey of 1,430 probate inventories made in Kentish towns between 1560 and 1600 reveals that soft furnishings were most usually described as green, sometimes as green only and sometimes as green in combination with other colors. Where color is specified, 15 out of 17 chairs are described as green, 49 out of 70 cushions (plus 7 more of green and another color), 8 out of 15 window curtains (plus 3 of green and another color), 23 out of 111 bed curtains (plus 48 of green and another color), and 5 of 28 valences (plus 11 of green and another color). Bedding itself (sheets, coverlets, and counterpanes) were usually described as white (66 instances out of 104), but sometimes as green (9 instances) and sometimes as green and another color (4 instances).[3] "The wals of our houses on the inner side," William Harrison reports in his "Description of England" prefaced to Holinshed's *Chronicles,* are either paneled in oak or else "hanged with tapisterie, arras worke, or painted cloths, wherin either diuerse histories, or hearbes, beasts, knots, and such like are stained."[4] According to Paul Hentzner, who visited England from Silesia in 1598, "their beds are covered with tapestry, even those of farmers."[5] If the Arundel inventory is any indication, these commonplace bed hangings were woven with leaves, plants, and trees. The inhabitants of Renaissance England—at least those wealthy enough to possess a bed—did their sleeping, dreaming, copulating, and dying within green enclosures.

"One counterpointe of the same stuffe": the Arundel inventory employs the word "stuff" in its most basic sense as the material out of which something is made (*OED*, "stuff.," *n.* II), but the word fits the context in other ways, too. Stuff can mean woven material in particular (II.5.a–b), movable property in general (I.1.g), furnishings proper to a place or thing (I.1.h), and, as I have just demonstrated in my analysis of the inventory, material for literary elaboration, substance as distinguished from form (II.3.d), as well as the compositions that result from that literary elaboration (III.7.a).[6] Toward the end of this chapter, I connect green stuff to persons, in the sense of "capabilities or inward character, figuratively what a person is made of" (II.3.b)—although in the case of green the situation is not just figurative. By the end of the chapter, I hope green will have come to seem "matter of an unspecified kind" (III.6.a). Skeptical readers may wish to note that "stuff" in early modern English could also mean worthless ideas, discourse, or writing, as in "Stuff and nonsense!" (III.8.b).

"Green stuff" involves all eight discourses of color that were outlined in chapter one: metaphysics, physics, chemistry, botany, physiology, geometry, psychology, and historical phenomenology. As such, the *stuff* in "green stuff" extends beyond the material objects that have claimed meticulous and sustained attention in books like Patricia Fumerton's *Cultural Aesthetics,* Margreta de Grazia, Maureen Quilligan, and Peter Stallybrass's anthology *Subject and Object in Renaissance Culture,* Anne Rosalind Jones and Peter Stallybrass's *Renaissance Clothing,* Jonathan Gil Harris and Natasha Korda's anthology *Staged Properties in Early Modern English Drama,* and Linda Levy Peck's *Consuming Splendor.*[7] As all these authors realize, physical objects from the past hold such fascination for us precisely because of their connection with the subjects who owned them, displayed them, used them. The objects figure as visible, graspable synecdoche for men and women who have disappeared forever. No wonder we turn such objects into fetishes, particularly when a Plexiglas barrier in a museum or a country house lets us see—but not touch—them. Harris and Korda, adapting a phrase from Arjun Appadurai's *The Social Life of Things,* refer to the "life histories" of objects. "The significance a particular object assumes," Harris and Korda explain, "derives from the differential relation of its present context to its known or assumed past, and assumed future, contexts" (18). All the objects on display in the Green Gallery near the center of this book have life histories of that sort: they imply a psychological connection with long-dead subjects, and they invite a corresponding psychological connection with us. Taking "stuff" in all its plenitude allows us to get at those two psychological connections. In the process, we can avoid two common mistakes: (1) confusing our connection as perceivers in the present with the original owners' connection as perceivers in the past and (2) pretending that our connection does not exist or isn't important. "Green stuff" is the *content* of Marvell's "green thought." Let us begin with the ambient green of England's earth.

"Is not their Clymate foggy, raw, and dull?"

The late sixteenth and early seventeenth centuries in northern Europe may have come down in the history of weather as "the Little Ice Age," but then as now, the Gulf Stream endowed Great Britain with a climate remarkably milder and wetter than the climate across the English Channel. As if to counter the Constable of France's scoff in *Henry V* about England's climate, Hentzner reports to his readers on the Continent that, quite the contrary, England's climate "is moist and temperate at all times, and the air never heavy" (62).[8] Modern climatology knows the weather pattern prevailing over most of Great Britain to be a "marine coastal climate," a pattern of moderate temperatures and ample moisture that is also to be found along the coasts of Oregon, Washington State, British Columbia, and certain parts of New Zealand.[9] Actually, "climate" does not just mean "average weather." The Greek word κλιμα originally referred to a zone between two specific latitudes—that is to say, a "clime"—that includes not only temperature and rainfall but also the plants and animals that typically go with those temperatures and that amount of rainfall (*OED*, "climate" *n.* etymology).[10] According to statistics kept by the Meteorological Office of the British government, the average temperature in England for the period 1971–2000 was 13.1°C (55.58°F) and the average annual rainfall was 838.0 millimeters (32.99 inches).[11] The mean temperature in 1600, during the Little Ice Age, may have been just 1°C less than that and rainfall perhaps 5 percent less.[12] What this configuration of temperature and rainfall produces, then and now, is a remarkably lush and green clime.

"Verie fruitfull" is Harrison's description of the clime between latitude 50.04°N and 55.46°N (vol. 1, sig. K5v). A quarter of the land, Harrison reports, is given over to pasture; Hentzner estimates it to be a third.[13] What this means in visual terms is described by Thomas Platter, another foreign visitor to England, who made his way from Dover to London through the countryside of Kent in 1599: "There are many slopes or hills in England bare of trees and having no springs, covered with a delicate short turf, which makes good pasturage for the sheep, hence great herds of snow-white sheep graze on them, and they all have very soft and more delicate skins than any other sheep."[14] The assemblage of slopes, hills, and sheep in Platter's description suggests a green cubist landscape with clustering white dots—something that might, in a later century, have been painted by Cezanne.

It had not always been so. According to ancient testimony, Harrison reports, England and Wales "haue sometimes beene verie well replenished with great woods & groves." Now, however, you can ride ten or twenty miles in some places and see few, if any, trees except for stands kept as windbreaks (vol. 1, sigs. T3–T3v). The destruction of forests was the result, according to Harrison, of a number of factors: the need for arable fields, the greed of owners who are still enclosing land for grazing, and the recent demand for oak timbers for ostentatious houses unknown in earlier times. Notable stands of woods still existed in some places, however, including the Forest of Arden.[15] It was the open green expanses—"champian country" it was usually called, after the level and open *campagna* outside Rome and the vineyards and farms of Champagne in France—that typically delighted Renaissance eyes the most. John Norden, in *The Surueyors Dialogue,* refers to the well-husbanded fields of Taunton Dean in Somerset as "the *Paradice of England.*"[16]

The green surround within which the inhabitants of early modern England lived their lives was extended by Thomas Trevelyon's imagination to the entire cosmos. Both versions of Trevelyon's folio-size book of pictures and designs, the one in the Folger Shakespeare Library (datable to 1608) and the one formerly in the Wormsley Library (dated 1616), contain images of Ptolemy's scheme of the universe.[17] In the Folger Shakespeare Library version, "The natuere [*sic*], course, colour, and placing of these seuen Planets according to Ptolemie" (plate 5), the earth in the center is colored a bright, deep green, while a bright, less-saturated yellow-green washes over the rest of the universe: the orbits of the planets (the moon, Venus, Mercury, the sun, Mars, Jupiter, and Saturn), the three spheres beyond (the stars, the crystaline firmament, and the Prime Mover), even "the Abitude of God And Alle the Electe" in the outermost sphere. Why green as the color of the cosmos? The sky, after all, never appears to be that color. That Trevelyon's choice was not eccentric is suggested by the so-called great pavement still to be seen in the sanctuary of Westminster Abbey. Installed by Odericus of Rome and dated 1268 in an inscription, the mosaic represents the cosmos as interlaced circles of green and purple porphyry stones robbed from classical ruins in Rome, intermixed with gray Purbeck marble from the channel coast, yellow-hued limestone from Italy, greenish Genoese serpentine, and other stones. Green hues predominate.[18] Discourses of color specific to Trevelyon's time and place suggest other possible answers for representing the cosmos as green. Trevelyon's verbal discriminations among the "colours" of the various planets—the "Lead colour" of Saturn, the "temperate, faire, and bright" aspect of Jupiter, the "firie colour" of Mars, "the Well of pure light" presented by the sun, the light "cleare; yea mor bright then Jupiter" displayed by Venus as morning star and evening star, the "somewhat shining, but not verie bright" aspect showed by Mercury, the curiously undescribed light of the moon—are in fact discriminations among degrees of value or brightness. A system in which the sun figures as "the well of pure light" presents a metaphysics of color in which the difference in value between the two greens in Trevelyon's image counts most, not the differences in hue or saturation. With respect to physics, green in Aristotle's spectrum occupies a middle position between black and white—a situation that explains, in chemical and botanical terms, why leaves spring from the white pith of trees and their blackish bark, as we observed in chapter one. Perhaps in Trevelyon's scheme, green radiates from the earth as the central point in the circular geometry of the cosmos. The temperateness of green may indicate the artist's physiological and psychological state as an observer who attempts to see the whole.

Landscape with Figures

Introduce to the land a shaping human presence, and you have a landscape. Amusingly varied in its pronunciation according to the earliest printed citations—"landtschap" (the original Dutch), "lantskip," "landskip," "lantskop," "launce-skippe"—the word entered early modern English in the 1590s as a technical term for painted representations of land forms, flora, and sometimes fauna (*OED*, "landscape.," *n.* 1.a–b), from whence it quickly became a word for the features themselves (2.a, 3). Present in both of these senses is the Germanic verb *schaffen*, to create, to fashion, to shape. And that takes a human being, whether the landscaping is being done with paints, brushes, and drafting tools or with picks, shovels, and grafting tools. The position of human figures within the green matrix can be gauged according to several regimes of geometry.[19]

At closest range are the eyes that stare out from behind leaves and branches in sculpted representations of "the green man," still to be found in cathedrals, parish churches, and other medieval buildings all over Great Britain. Clive James's *The Green Man: A Field Guide* lists more than two thousand such carvings in England alone.[20] The origins of the green man can be traced either to the hunting-and-gathering prehistory of *Homo sapiens*—or to 1939. It was Julia Hamilton Somerset, Lady Raglan, writing that year in the journal *Folklore,* who coined the name "the green man." It is that recent. The connections Lady Raglan made among (1) carved faces on medieval capitals, bosses, bench ends, and tombs, (2) figures in folk festivities like Jack-in-the-green, Robin Hood, and May-lords, and (3) traditional inn signs depicting a green man have, since 1939, proved irresistible to searchers for Jungian archetypes, purveyors in the heritage industry, advocates of environmental consciousness, even the men's movement.[21] Versions of the green man have been found not only in Europe but in Africa, the Middle East, Central America, and central, southern, and eastern Asia.[22] Roman origins for the European examples are illustrated in Kathleen Basford's classic study, *The Green Man.*[23] As arresting as they may be to modern eyes, carvings of faces leering through leaves and branches were already obsolete by 1600. None were carved on the capitals and bosses of English churches after the mid-fifteenth century, even if they continued to appear on tombs into the eighteenth century as *memento mori.* (To be fair, very few English churches were built between 1500 and 1660.) After the iconoclasm of Edward VI's reign, many people would have regarded such carvings as relics of a past time in at least three respects: (1) as vestiges of the Catholic religion, (2) as avatars of folk festivities like Robin Hood plays, lately under attack, and (3) as reminders of a time, not so distant, when the green of England, like the Isle of Anglesey in *Sir Gawain and the Green Knight,* was full of dangers. The third of these considerations was probably the strongest.

In Norden's *The Surueyors Dialogue* (1607, 1610, 1618, 1738), the authority figure is asked by his naive pupil about the state of Britain "at the beginning, when it was first peoplet." He paints a distinctly inhospitable picture. "A very desert and wildernes," the master surveyor replies, "ful of woods, fells, moores, bogs, heathes, and all kind of forlorne places: & howsoeuer we find the state of this Island nowe, records doe witnes vnto vs, that it was for the most part an vniuersall Wildernes, vntill people finding it a place desolate, and forlorne, beganne to set footing heere." In time, the new arrivals learned how to cut down trees, root up weeds, cultivate useful plants, and wall themselves off from wild animals and human enemies. Among the wild animals in this natural clime, Norden lists bears, boars, bulls, and wolves—the first three of which, let it be noted, supplied traditional names and emblems, along with the green man, for sixteenth-century inns and ale houses. The wild animals began to disappear, Norden reports, "when their shelters, great woods, were cut downe, and the Country made more and more champion" (sig. Q4v). In the beginning was not "the paradise of England" but a "universal wilderness." Carvings of the green man kept the memory alive, and only the shaping presence of human civilization held the wilderness at bay.[24]

An image of Britain's early human inhabitants is provided by the Flemish artist Lukas de Herre, a Protestant refugee in England from 1567 to 1577, in one of the several surviving manuscripts of his "Corte beschryuinghe van Engheland, Schotland, ende Irland."[25] Like a Baedeker guide, William Camden's Latin *Britannia* (1586, 1587, 1590, 1594, 1600, 1607; first translated into English in 1610) told early-modern visitors like Hentzner all they needed to know about Britain's history and culture. Hentzner was not the only visitor to have drafted passages from Camden into the account of his own travels, as if he had found out the information on the spot by himself.[26] Editions of *Britannia* published in Frankfurt in 1590 and 1610 were aimed at a Continental market—which included Hentzner. Camden's description of the Picts (literally, "the painted") cannot have been de Heere's direct source (the first edition of *Britannia* dates from ten years after his departure from England), but de Heere's depiction of the two Picts shown in plate 6 closely matches Camden's verbal picture. Verses from the fourth-century Roman poet Ausonius are quoted by Camden to establish that "Like to greene mosse with gravell rewes between, / The Britans Caledonian are all be painted seen."[27] Blue predominates in de Heere's depiction of the right-hand figure, but the left-hand figure displays a green snake on his right arm and a circular green design on his right kneecap, and both figures are firmly planted in a swath of mossy green and gravelly yellow and brown. "Caledonian" locates the figures beyond the northern horizons of Camden's world, in Scotland. Several hundred miles to the west, across the Irish Sea, wild men were still to be found in the sixteenth century, and they were clad in green. Four figures are shown in de Heere's drawing of "Irish men and women" (plate 7). From left to right are arranged an "Edel-vrouwe" or noblewoman, a "Burghers vrouwe" (what Jonson and Middleton would have called a "citizen's wife"), and two male representatives of "Wilde Iresche," one wearing soldier's garb, the other wrapped in a full-body mantle, both bare-legged and barefoot like Captain Thomas Lee in Marcus Gheerhaerts's 1594 portrait of the soldier of fortune who had spent his career fighting for England's interests in Ireland.[28]

The positioning, postures, and coloring of de Heere's four figures are telling. Closest to the viewer and visually dominant with his red breastplate, probably made of thick leather, is the soldier, who further establishes his dominance by grasping a large, albeit sheathed, sword. The two female figures on the left, despite their difference in social station, wear gowns of a similar cut (the noblewoman's is blue, the citizen's wife's is pink), and they hold hands. Seemingly farthest from the viewer, thanks to the soldier's spatial, chromatic, and gestural prominence, is the mantle-clad man. De Heere has colored this mantle green, as one might expect from Randle Holme's description of wild Irishmen in heraldry: "The Habit of these kind of wild People, is to go bare headed, their Mantle about their shoulders, which they call a Brackin, or Irish Mantle."[29] *Bracken* in Holme's time could mean either a type of tartan plaid worn by Scottish Highlanders and the northern Irish (*OED*, "bracken" n^2) or a type of fern ("bracken" n^1 1.a) and the brownish hue the plant presents when it is turning (1.b). The brownish-green wash in de Heere's drawing suggests it is the second of these possibilities that is in play here. Spatially, chromatically, and politically, de Heere's mantle-clad wild Irishman constitutes the green ground out of which the other three figures emerge.

Red breastplate, gold trim, blue cloak, sword and scabbard: it is easy enough to read the man on the left.[30] What exactly can be read in the right-hand figure's green mantle? That, for English writers and readers, was the problem. Edmund Campion, in his history of Ireland, describes such garments as being, physically, of a piece with a green land that is so wet and lush that it rots the few domesticated animals that feed upon it. Sheep are few, Campion reports, "and those bearing course fleeces, whereof they spinne notable rugge mantle."[31] The ragged edges of the mantle in de Heere's drawing catch the coarseness of the wool from which the garment has been woven. It is the "monstrously disguising" potentialities of the Irish mantle that drive Edmund Spenser's spokesman Irenaeus to two pages of rant in *A View of the Present State of Ireland.*[32] Iranaeus will concede that such garments were used by the ancient Romans and that in raw, cold climates like Ireland's, a mantle gives its itinerant wearer housing and bedding as well as clothing, but the Irish mantle also functions as "a fit house for an Out-law, a meet bed for a Rebell, & an apt cloake for a thiefe" (sig. D1). For rebels in particular, a mantle is useful for hiding out:

> [W]hen he still flyeth from his foe, & lurketh in the thicke woods & straite passages, waiting for advantages, it is his bed, yea and almost as his houshold stuff. For the wood is his house against all weathers, & his Mantle is his couch to sleepe in. Therein he wrappeth himself round, & coucheth

> himselfe strongly against the gnats, which in that countrey doe more annoy the naked Rebels, whilst they keepe the woods, & doe more sharply wound them then all their enemies swords, or speares, which can seldome come nigh them. (sig. D1v).

Amid Ireland's dense forests, the mantle's green hue thus functions as camouflage. All in all, Irenaeus deplores the Irish mantle not for what it shows but for what it does *not* show. Unlike other forms of clothing, unlike the garments worn by de Heere's noble lady and citizen's wife, a green Irish mantle is not legible. What is under it escapes surveillance. The wearer of a green mantle can disappear into the savage landscape from which he takes his elusive, changeable character.

Altogether more hospitable were the gardens of England. Like ale house signs depicting the green man, the design of gardens in Renaissance England kept primeval memories alive, but in perspective, at a safe distance. Francis Bacon's essay "Of Gardens" is altogether typical of these designs in imagining a garden as modulating between the civilities of the dwelling house and a series of ever wilder green horizons.[33] In his essay "Of Gardens," Bacon gives green a central place. Bacon envisions an ideal garden of 30 acres (he confesses he is thinking in "*Prince-like*" proportions), to be divided into three parts as one moves outward from the house: first "a *Greene*" of four acres, then "the *Maine Garden*" of twelve acres, and finally "A *Heath* or *Desart* in the Going forth" comprising six acres.[34] Eight additional acres are allotted to gardens on either side of the house, four on one side and four on the other. Four acres, twelve acres, six acres, eight acres, one viewer: these are the figures in Bacon's landscape. The open green space next to the house serves—literally, physically, psychologically—to *frame* the main garden. "The *Greene* hath two pleasures," Bacon observes. "The one, because nothing is more Pleasant to the Eye, then Greene Grasse kept finely shorne; The other, because it will give you a faire Alley in the midst, by which you may go in front upon a *Stately Hedge,* which is to inclose the *Garden*" (141; original emphasis). In effect, green in Bacon's scheme combines the pleasant affect of the color itself with the intellectually satisfying geometry of hedges, walkways, and alleys.

With respect to the actually existing gardens of his day, Bacon's interpolation of a green lawn between the house and the main garden represents an innovation. Bacon ridicules "the Making of *Knots,* or *Figures,* with *Divers Coloured Earths* . . . that lie under the Windowes of the House" as nothing better than "Toyes," something better suited to fancy pastry-work (141). Most gardens of the sixteenth and early seventeenth centuries favored such designs, however, because they extended the artfulness of the house outward, inviting an ambler to move by degrees from art to nature in the progression from house to knot garden to meadows to woods. Each of these spaces came equipped with its own mythology, which inspired the pageants staged there on the occasion of royal visits.[35] The effect of Bacon's advice, or at least the taste for which he spoke, can be appreciated by comparing Robert Smythson's plat of Ham House and its gardens ca. 1609 with John Slezer and Jan Wyck's design of ca. 1671–1672, which is being used to reconstruct the garden today. On the house's sun-facing south side, Smythson's plat shows three huge rectangles that shape the garden's flowers, shrubs, and fruit trees into an interlaced diamond pattern on the left, fourteen parallel rows on the right, and an interlocked series of octagons converging on an oval in the center.[36] In the same location today can be seen a green lawn that gives onto a loosely geometrical "wilderness" of trees in the distance. Plane geometry survives in the two smaller gardens that flank the house on the east and west, just as Bacon advises. Andrew Marvell's garden, with its green expanses, its fountain, its fruit trees, and its geometrical dial, implies the same variety amid the same dominant hue. In Bacon's ideal garden, in Marvell's fictional garden, in the reconstructed gardens at Ham House, the perceiver is invited to appreciate, by degrees, his or her distance from the wilderness of trees, bushes, briars, and thorns just at the horizon line. Bacon's "heath or desert," extended on occasion into the hunting park beyond, was close enough for most of Marvell's contemporaries.

The Natural History of Green

Before there were test tubes there were trees; before there were labs there were forests. It was not until a year after his death that Francis Bacon's *A Naturall Historie* was published. If Bacon's *Essayes or Counsails* (1597, expanded in 1612 and 1625) can be considered "the lawn," or approach to knowledge, and his systematic works like *The Advancement of Learning* (1605) the main garden, then his *Natural History* (1627) shapes up as a desert, heath, or forest. Indeed, the main title bestowed on it when it was published the year after Bacon's death was *Sylva Sylvarum* (literally, *Forest of Trees*). In classical Latin, *silva* might mean not only woodland or, in the plural, the trees that make up that woodland but the raw material of a literary work (*OED*, "silva" 1, 3, 5). In more ways than one, then, *silva* is green stuff. Collections of occasional verse like Statius's *Silvae* (first century of the Common Era) and Ben Jonson's "The Forrest" (1616) provide one inspiration for poems as tongues in trees, but the botanical writings of Aristotle's pupil Theophrastus are probably the ultimate precedent for thinking about objects of knowledge as trees and systems of knowledge as forests. John Maplet's *A Greene Forest, or a Naturall Historie* (1567) regards the products "of Natures tempering and dighting" in just this way.[37] The book's three sections offer alphabetically ordered descriptions of (1) minerals and stones; (2) herbs, shrubs, and trees; and (3) brute beasts, fowls, fishes, worms, and serpents. Knowledge, in Maplet's view, is alive and growing. Theophrastus, he reports, lamented the limitations of human life when "the mother of all such greene things as grewe vpon the earth multiplieth euerie ech day with increase, and diuersitie of many kinds and playeth the prodigall his parte" (sig. E4).

William Rawley, editor of Bacon's *Sylva,* apologizes in his preface that the volume may seem "an Indigested Heap of Particulars."[38] But that was Bacon's intent. Readers of the book, so Rawley reports, were desired by Bacon "no wher to depart from the Sense, and cleare experience; But to keepe close to it, especially in the beginning" (sig. A2). Nonetheless, Bacon has ventured probable causes for the things he describes, so that readers "would not think themselues vtterly lost, in a Vast VVood of *Experience,* but stay vpon these *Causes,* (such as they are) a little, till true *Axiomes* may be more fully discouered" (sig. A2v). Bacon worries that readers may not be able to see the *silva* for the *silvae.* What *Sylva Sylvarum* purports to offer its readers is an exercise in radical induction, an exploration that begins with individual trees and proceeds to map out the terrain of natural history from there. Knowledge in Bacon's forest begins, just as Aristotle says it should, with sense experience, proceeds through causes, and ends with axioms.

Several of the thousand numbered experiments in *Sylva Sylvarum* establish that color, for Bacon as for most of his contemporaries, was material stuff. Experiment 291 presents different colors as inherent qualities of different metals, which the application of water (in solutions), chemicals (in putrefaction), and heat (in vitrification) will reveal: "*Metalls* giue *Orient* and *Fine Colours* in *Dissolutions;* As *Gold* giueth an excellent Yellow; *Quick-Siluer* an excellent Greene; *Tinne* giueth an excellent Azure; Likewise in their *Putrefactions,* or *Rusts;* As *Vermilion, Verdegrease, Bise, Cirrus,* &c. And likewise in their *Vitrifications*" (sigs. K8v–L1). The items in the last list are artists' pigments, "vermillion" being a red pigment, "verdigris" a green, "bice" a brownish gray, and "ceruse" a white. Bacon seems to be thinking in artistic terms throughout the experiment, since he invokes the three variables recognized in Renaissance treatises on painting: hue, value, and saturation.

Bacon is apt to lose twenty-first-century readers, however, when he begins to talk about the reasons for the color-producing effects in metals. He speaks of metals as if they were living things. "By their Strength of Body," Bacon says, "they are able to endure the Fire, or Strong Waters, and to be put into an Equall Posture; And againe to retaine Part of their principall Spirit; Which two Things, (Equall Posture, and Quicke Spirits) are required chiefely, to make *Colours* lightsome" (sigs. K8v–L1). "Equal posture" is easy enough: Bacon seems to be specifying the relative strength of metal particles vis-à-vis fire, water, and other chemicals (*OED,* "posture" *n.,* 2.a). "Quick spirits," however, give metals a dynamism and volatility that would seem to belong to animals possessed of the power of motion. When Bacon describes certain colors as "lightsome," he refers to not just perceived brightness in the viewer's eye but movement through the air. Bacon speaks about light in a thoroughly material, almost tactile way, especially in his systematic comparison between how sound waves and rays of light move in waves. According to Bacon, there are thirteen modes of "consent of visibles, and Audibles" (sigs. K1v–K2), that is, thirteen ways in which their motion through a medium is the same or similar, and twenty-three "dissents" (sigs. K2v–K4v). The need for a medium in both cases (air or water) is especially crucial to experiment 873, in which Bacon inquires why the water of the sea (often read as green, as prompted by Aristotle's treatise *De Coloribus*) "looketh *Blacker* when it is moued, and *Whiter* when it resteth."[39] The reason, according to Bacon, has to do with the motion of the water refracting the light in the air: "the *Beames* of light passe not Straight, and therefore must be darkened; whereas, when it resteth, the *Beames* doe passe Straight" (sig. GG4). The same effect is noted in another experiment, this time demonstrating the effect of water in magnifying the size of objects as well as the intensity of light: "There is no doubt, but *Light* by *Refraction* will shew greater, as well as *Things Coloured*" (sig. CC1v).

In effect, Bacon considers color within two analytical frameworks: as a property of material objects like metals and as a property of light traveling through the media of air and water. For that double perspective, Bacon is indebted ultimately to Aristotle's remarks on color in *De Anima* (*On the Soul* 418.a–b) and *De Sensu* (*On Sense and Sensibilia* 439.a-b).[40] What Aristotle envisions in these texts is a thoroughly material but surprisingly dynamic world in which the boundary between solid-seeming objects and the air or the water that surrounds them is not so firm as it might appear. Indeed, color marks the spot where less transparent bounded bodies meet the more transparent substances of air and water. Transparency is a potential present, to varying degrees, in all kinds of objects—in marble as in air. That potentiality in objects is activated by fire "or something resembling fire," which is not to be imagined, in modern terms, as energy hitting objects from some external source—the sun, say—but as a material medium that "contains something which is one and the same with the substance in question" (*De Anima* 418.b.14–20).

To Aristotle's analytical eye, the edge between solid-seeming objects and transparent-seeming air and water is neither hard nor rigid. When the transparency of fire meets the transparency of this or that object, the result is color: "it is manifest that, when the transparent is in determinate bodies, its bounding extreme must be something real; and that colour is just this something we are plainly taught by facts—colour being actually either at the limit, or being itself that limit, in bodies" (*De Sensu* 439.a). What we see when we look out into the world, according to Aristotle, is not, then, discrete objects but color. That, according to Helkiah Crooke in his medical encyclopedia *Microcosmographia* (1615, 1616, 1618, 1631, 1634, 1651), is what "All Authors which euer writ of the Sight, haue determined with one consent."[41] Later in the same chapter Crooke insists that "Colours are another thing then the light" (sig. NNN3). Colors work upon the light, as we may observe in a looking glass, which receives the colors brought to it by enlightened air. "So also the greenenesse of Trees and Medowes doth appeare in such bodyes as are opposite vnto them, which could not be except the colour should worke vpon the Light" (sig. NNN3). Marvell's green-thinking persona is one such body: the garden's reflected green colors his very person.

In terms of the three color variables—hue, value, and saturation—Aristotle's theory, like Plato's, gives primary attention to value, or brightness. Indeed, hues are explained as a function of brightness. Different colors, Aristotle explains in *De Sensu,* result from different ratios of white to black, just as different concords in music result from different ratios of high sounds to low (439.b.15–440.a.19). Aristotle understands white to be the effect of light and black the effect of darkness. To range other colors along a spectrum of brightness, from white at one end to black at the other, seemed only natural. It was left to Aristotle's system-happy disciples to reconcile this scheme with the four elements, the four bodily fluids, and the four temperaments. If black equals earth and white equals fire, all the other colors can be understood as different combinations of fire, air, water, and earth. Black (full darkness) and white (full brightness) form the poles of a spectrum within which all other colors are explained as varying combinations of black and white.

In the minds of most Europeans, this remained the usual schema well into the seventeenth century, when experiments by Descartes, Huygens, and Newton established the red-to-violet spectrum that was there to be seen in the rainbow all along.[42] The persistence of Aristotle's model in the face of such patently contradictory evidence can be better understood, perhaps, by the World Color Project's demonstration that a distinction between white and black—in effect, between bright and dark—is the fundamental matrix within which human beings, in most of the world's cultures, distinguish hues. Aristotle considers three theories about how black and white combine to form other colors: (1) through juxtaposition of black bits and white bits in fixed ratios, (2) through varying superpositions of black over white and white over black, and (3) through true mixtures in which black loses itself in white and vice versa. Without really favoring one theory over the others, Aristotle organizes the spectrum thus:

μέλαν | φαιόν | κυανοῦν | πράσινον | ἁλουργόν | φοινικόν | ξανθόν | λευκόν

That is to say:

black | gray | deep blue | leek-green | violet | crimson | yellow | white[43]

Robert Fludd, writing on the colors of body fluids in the early seventeenth century, was among the first to map this spectrum as a circle.[44] Gray could be considered part of black, Aristotle says, and/or yellow part of white. Either way, green occurs at or near the middle of the spectrum.

Sap-Green, Verdigris, Verditer, Sinople, Samargd

When, in *Twelfth Night,* Olivia has drawn aside the curtain of her mourning veil and opened to view "the picture" of her face, Viola's reaction is appreciative but skeptical. "Ist not well done?" Olivia asks, as if her face *were* a painted portrait. "Excellently done," Viola quips, "if God did all." Olivia retorts, "'Tis in grain sir, 'twill endure winde and weather" (F 1623, 1.5.224–27). It might be specifically to her red lips that Olivia is referring, since the phrase "in grain" derives from the belief that *Coccus ilicis,* the dyestuff for a brilliant fade-resistant scarlet, was a seed or berry and not an insect (*OED,* "grain" *n.*[1] III.10), but in general, "in grain" colors in Shakespeare's time were distinguished from other colors as being fast-dyed, as having thoroughly penetrated into a fabric's fibers. Olivia's concern with fixity is not surprising in an age when most colors were, as the technical term has it, *fugitive*. If color in Aristotle's *De Sensu* and *De Anima* is contingent on physical variables (color happens only in the presence of fire or something like fire), color in early modern household furnishings, garments, drawings, and paintings was even more so. The range of hues available today in any well-equipped paint store and the stability of dyes that color contemporary clothing, fabrics, and carpets stand in sharp contrast to the limited range and corruptibility of early modern pigments and dyestuffs.[45] Analine dyes, derived from coal tar and commercially produced beginning in the 1860s, have, literally, *made* that difference.[46]

Particularly in England's marine coastal climate, it was ironic that green should be so prominent in the landscape and so hard to achieve in pigments and dyes. Sources for good greens were few. The three terrains in Maplet's green forest—minerals, plants, and animals—exhaust the possible sources of dyestuffs and pigments in the sixteenth and early seventeenth centuries. In the case of green, only two sources were readily available: vegetable matter and copper salts. To judge from Nicholas Hilliard's "A Treatise Concerning the Arte of Limning" (1598–1603) and Henry Peacham's *The Art of Dravving with the Pen, and Limming in Water Colours* (1606), connoisseurs in the early seventeenth century were aware of the organic and mineral origins, the grittiness, even the smells of colors in a way that their counterparts a hundred years later were not. "Limning," the usual Renaissance term for drawing and painting with colors dissolved in water, gum, or egg, is presented in both treatises as an accomplishment worthy of a gentleman. Hilliard describes it as "sweet and cleanly to vsse."[47] As colors "fit for limning" he dismisses "all ill smelling coullers [and] all ill tasting" (88). Among those obnoxious colors are a remarkable number of greens: "*verdigres, verditer, Pinck, Sapgrene*" (88). Peacham is more tolerant. "Vert-greace," he explains, "is nothing else but the rust of brasse, which in time being consumed and eaten with Tallow turneth into greene, as you may see many times vpon fowle candlesticks that haue not beene often made cleane."[48]

When Olivia assures Viola that the hues she sees are all "in grain," there is an implicit assumption that they might *not* be so. Color, Olivia implies, might be something alienable, alien, and alienating. To early modern eyes, color was alienable because, with human-made objects as with nature, color was impermanent. The fading flowers of seduction poems ("Gather ye Rose-buds while ye may"[49]) had their counterparts in the fading flowers embroidered on cushions. Vegetable dyes in particular were susceptible not only to losses in saturation but to changes in hue. Even well-cared-for tapestries like the Mortlake version of *Hero and Leander* (plate 23) now show evidence of greens that have turned bluish. Small tapestry panels and cushion covers produced by the Sheldon workshops in Worcestershire in the late sixteenth and early seventeenth centuries display deep, true greens on the reverse sides, but a pale blue on the fronts, due to exposure to sunlight over the past four centuries.[50] The effect may result from the fragility of organic dyes like sap-green or from sun-induced degradation in yellow overdyes that once made blue underdyes appear green. Sir William Petty, in an account of dyeing published by the Royal Society in 1660s, ranked all dyestuffs under just three headings: red, yellow, and blue.[51] Green is conspicuously absent.

Philip Ball notes that "the humanistic concern to match colors to nature placed a greater demand on green than on any other color" (115). It is understandable, then, that the introduction of a supposedly stable green, verdigris—Peacham calls it "the purest greene that is"—caused great excitement in the fifteenth century, especially among painters in oils, such as Bellini, Raphael, Tintoretto, and Veronese.[52] Within a surprisingly short time, however, the shortcomings of verdigris had become apparent: greens derived from copper salts are apt to turn brown. A substitute for verdigris was found near Verona, on Cyprus, and at certain places in France in the form of terre-verte, or celadonite, a silicate of iron and potassium (*OED,* "terre-verte" etymology). As the sources of terre-verte indicate, color might seem to English eyes not only alienable but alien. Pliny, in his account of the Apelles' palate, taught readers to disdain far-fetched pigments, even as they fetishized them. Geoffrey Whitney's version of the emblem "*In colores*" takes over the main idea from Andrea Alciati—different colors suit different human temperaments—but Whitney adds two things: a focus on the dyer as a technician and a defense of English dyestuffs. It was only in later editions of Alciati's *Emblematum Liber* that the original woodcut showing nine temperaments coordinated with nine colors became the image of a dyer at work that Whitney not only copied but made the occasion of the emblem's verses: "The dier, loe, in smoke, and heate doth toile, / Mennes fickle mindes to please, with sundrie hues"[53] (figure 3). Whitney's second addition was a whole new set of verses that defend England from the disdain of strangers who come from countries richer in dyestuffs:

> But say we lacke, their herbes, their wormes, their flies,
> And want the meanes: their gallant hues to frame.
> Yet Englande, hath her store of orient dies,

134 *In colores.*

To Edwarde Paston. *Esquier.*

Figure 3. Woodcut from Geoffrey Whitney, *A Choice of Emblemes, and Other Deuises* (1586). Shown actual size, $3\frac{1}{2} \times 3\frac{7}{8}$ inches (8.9×9.8 cm). (Reproduced by permission of the Folger Shakespeare Library.)

And eeke therein a DYER most of fame,
Who, alwaies hathe so fine, and freshe, a hewe,
That in their landes, the like is not to vewe.
(sig. R4)

If the allusion is to the polymathic courtier-poet Sir Edward Dyer, Whitney has anticipated by as much as a decade Shakespeare's praise of "A man in hew all *Hews* in his controwling."[54]

Alienable and alien, color could also be seen as alienating. Viola distrusts the colors she sees in Olivia's face. The portrait looks excellently done, but only "if God did all." Richard Haydocke, in his translation of Paolo Lomazzo's *Tratatto dell'Arte de la Pittura* (1584), makes the curious decision to omit Lomazzo's section on pigments and to put in its place "*a briefe Censure of the booke of Colours, where I haue also taken occasion to vse a word or two, concerning* the Artificiall Beauty of Women, for those good I haue published it."[55] At first blush, Haydocke's choice seems provincial if not downright bizarre. Instead of information about the pigments and binders that Raphael, "Leonard Vincent," Correggio, "Michael Angel," Titan, and other Italian artists have actually used—sap-green, verdigris, verditer, and the rest—the reader gets analyses of the vegetable, mineral, and animal substances that women apply to their faces. These include "sublimate" (described as a distillation of salt, quicksilver, and vitriol), white lead, alum, lemon juice, oil of Tartary, rock-alum, salnitrum, and camphire. All of these substances, it should be noted, are either bleaching agents or corrosives that induce blush-like redness. To Haydocke's view, and presumably that of his readers, the status of color in Lomazzo's original text and in Haydocke's substitution is the same. Color in both cases is antipathetical to living flesh: "For it is certaine, that all Paintings and colourings made of minerals or halfe-minerals, as iron, brasse, lead, tinne, sublimate, cerusse, camphire, iuyce of lemons, plume-alume, salt-peeter, vitrioll, and all manner of saltes, and sortes of alumes . . . are very offensiue to the complexion of the face" (sig. MM2).

The object-like quality of color is never more apparent than in heraldry. Colors in heraldric blazons are not just colors: they are rare and expensive *stuff*.[56] "Value" in color takes on new meaning. Yellow is not yellow, but "or" (gold). White is not white, but "argent" (silver). Black is not black, but "sable." Red is not red, but "gules" (from the Latin *gola,* or throat, around which it was fashionable in the twelfth century to wear a fox fur collar). Blue is not blue, but "azur" (the color of lapis lazuli or ultramarine, both fetched from "beyond the sea"). In this context, "vert" (the common French word for green, as in grass) was something of an embarrassment. Two verbal ploys remedied the situation. One was to take over the term *sinople,* which originally seems to have designated a red, *rubrica Sinopica,* that came from Sinopis on the Black Sea.[57] The other strategy was to associate "vert" with the emerald or "smaragd," as it was often called from its Latin name *smaragdus.* Gerard Legh, in *The Accedence of Armorie* (1562, 1568, 1576, 1591, 1597, 1612), does just this. Citing the authority of Isidore of Seville's seventh-century *Etymologiae,* Legh declares "this stone passeth all other colours in greennes, either of tree, hearb, or grasse of the fielde."[58] Held up to the sun, a smaragd "rayseth of it selfe a beame in the ayre" (sig. B4v). In a chapter of *A Greene Forest, or a Naturall Historie* titled "Of the Smaradge," Maplet notes the same effect and reports further that an emerald, when cut and polished, "sheweth a man his liuely Image, wherevpon the valiant Caesar had no greater delight, than in looking on this, to see his Warriours fight, and to behold in the Smaragde which of them went best to worke, and was moste actiue" (sigs. D4v–D5). Whether Caesar looked at battles *on* the smaragd or *through* the smaragd, the green affect would have been the same. Legh sums up the opinion of "all authors" in declaring that green "is much comfortable to the sight of man, and of all colours moste ioyfull to the hart" (sig. B4). For his part, Hilliard describes the emerald as "the most perfect greene on earth growing naturally, or that is in any thinge, or that is possible by Arte to make" (108).

Legh's double perspective on green—it is both a physical substance and a psychological affect—is altogether typical of how colors are written up in Renaissance treatises on painting. Lomazzo insists that painting does not "onely expresse the outward formes of things; but also discouereth certaine inward passions; . . . as it were laying before our eies, the affections of the mind, with their effects" (sig. HH5v). To green, Lomazzo attributes "a pleasurable sweeteness" (sig. KK2v). By the time Whitney adapted Alciati's emblem "*In colores,*" the associations of particular hues with particular passions had become commonplace. Thus Whitney's translation of Alciati's Latin verse identifies black with mourning, white with purity, yellow with greed and jealousy, "tawny" with disappointment, red with soldiers' bravery and boys' shame (and here the affects begin to shade into social types), blue with mariners, violet with prophets, and "*medley, graye,* and *russet*" with "the poore and meaner sorte" (sig. R3v). Green figures in Alciati's and Whitney's spectrum in an implicitly middling position, after black and white, as if all the succeeding colors were generated out of it: "The *greene,* agrees with them in hope that liue; / And eeke to youthe, this colour we do giue" (sig. R3v). In his own account of green, Lomazzo takes over from Ludovico Dolce's 1565 dialogue on color a consideration of whether the use of boughs, herbs, and green fabrics in funeral rites indicates sadness or hope.[59] (It is hope, of course.) Mentioned in Lomazzo's section on green is the custom among the ancient Persians and Romans of burying an emerald with a noble lady. Isabella d'Este, Marchioness of Mantua, is reported to have owned a smaragd that was found in the tomb of Cicero's daughter.

Hunting the Green Lion

In experiment 327 of *Sylva Sylvarum,* Bacon again speaks of metals as if they were living, growing things. Prepare, he advises the reader, a temperate heat that can "*Disgest,* and *Mature*" the metal, apply the heat so that "the *Spirit of the Metall be quickened,*" be careful that "the *Spirits doe spread themselues Euen,*" ensure that none of the spirits escape into the air, give the process time enough, and, if you have chosen the right metal to work with, the result will be . . . gold."[60] The trouble with alchemy, Bacon says in the preface to the experiment, is not the physical feasibility of transforming base metals into gold—"The *Worke* it selfe I iudge to be possible" (sig. M6v)—but the ill-considered means that experimenters have used and the vain theory in which they have grounded their labors. Too much heat, not enough time, the wrong metal: these are the logistical reasons alchemy has failed. As for the received theory, it is "full of vnsound Imaginations" (sig. M6v). Bacon's experiment 327 is designed to purge alchemy of "Vanities" taken over from astrology, natural magic, superstitious interpretation of divine scripture, "Auricular *Traditions*" (not only oral but occult), and supposed testimonials by ancient authorities (sig. M6v). And yet these syncretic elements are the very thing that ensured alchemy's hold on the imaginations of poets, playwrights, and visual artists. Seventeenth-century scientific thinkers like Bacon, Boyle, and Newton may have tried to provide alchemy with a strictly physical rationale, but it was the quicksilver quality of alchemy, its mercurial capacity to dissolve metallurgy into botany into astrology into magic into hermeneutics into history into Platonic philosophy into spirituality that gave alchemy such staying power well into the seventeenth century. Technology and spirituality: for us, those are radically separate discourses. In seventeenth-century alchemy, they coalesced.[61]

In addition to being an amalgamation of discourses, medieval and Renaissance writings about alchemy, according to Gareth Roberts, can be analyzed as a set of rhetorical strategies (obscurantist code, metaphor, paradox), as a repertory of narratives (dream vision, discipleship to a master, conflict ending in violence, parricide and incest), and as a pattern of recurrent images (sowing-growth-harvest, marriage between a red man and a white woman, copulation-conception-gestation-birth).[62] Among those images, one of the most common is "hunting the green lion." That is the code phrase Newton preferred in the notes he made about his alchemical experiments.[63] Graphic realizations of the green lion are to be found in various printings and manuscript copies of "The Rosary of the Philosophers," a text that was first printed in German at Frankfurt in 1550, translated into English at Lübeck in 1588, and transcribed in a number of manuscripts, of which British Library MS Add. 29,895 is among the earliest. An inscription of ownership and marginal notes in the same hand identify one of the surviving manuscripts, currently owned by the British Library, as having belonged to someone named John Clark. Plate 8 shows how Clark's manuscript adapts the German book's image of the green lion devouring the sun. "I am the true grene and goulden Lyon, without cares," the caption reads. "In me all the Secretts of the philosophers are hidden."[64] The manuscript's twenty illustrations are designed to function as visual focal points for meditation, like the beads in a rosary or the illuminations in a book of hours, guided by the written text.[65] Less than a recipe book for how to turn base metals into physical gold, "The Rosary of the Philosophers" invites the reader to turn base flesh into spiritual gold—or rather, to do both at the same time.

The pursuer of knowledge, according to the poem, needs to read the book over and over again in order to come to know "the principall state of humane things, & the most seacrett treasure of all the seacretts of the whole woorld" (fol. 2). This secret treasure of knowledge, emblemized in the philosopher's stone, operates on three levels at once. The author speaks of knowledge as "colors," indeed, as colors that can be touched and felt: "the philosophers wold never have Labored and studdied to expresse such diversities of cullers, and the order of them, unlesse they had sene and felt them. . . . Therefore let your exercise and labor be used in nature because our stone is of an Animal, of a vegetable, and of a mynerall substance" (sigs. 3v–4). Next to this passage, Clark has drawn not one but two pointing fingers. To Clark, as to other readers of early modern English, "animal" meant spiritual, by way of Latin *anima.*

In mineral terms, the green lion devouring the sun signifies the precise moment when the spirits of the metal are freed from dross and begin to coalesce into gold. In *The Mirror of Alchimy* (1597), attributed to Roger Bacon, the sequence of colors in the process is specified as first black (putrefaction), then red and white (coagulation), and finally green (concoction).[66] The color produced by quicksilver, as Bacon observes in experiment 291, is "an excellent green." In vegetable terms, green signifies growth. The "vegetable soul" that mankind was imagined to share with both plants and animals includes reproduction. Maplet cites Girolamo Cardano to the effect that metals "are nothing else but the earths hid & occult Plants, hauing their roote, their stock or body, their bough & leaues."[67] If metals, like plants and animals, possess souls or spirits, then the transmutation of base metal into gold becomes a form of growth not unlike what happens with plants. George Ripley's *The Compound of Alchemy* (1591) describes the production of gold as fertilization, gestation, and birth in hermaphroditic images that combine male sperm with female menstruation:

> In the time of this said proces naturall,
> While that the sperme conceived is growing,

> The substance is nourished with his owne menstruall,
> Which water only out of the earth did spring,
> Whose colour is greene in the first showing. . . .

This menstrual fluid, not just the vitriol that catalyzes metals, is truly "the blood of our greene Lyon."[68] In "The Rosary" and the texts it inspired, Adam McLean explains, "the physical process became a mirror for soul development, and the inner content of soul experiences became projected upon outer processes in the laboratory or the natural world" (117). Thus the warning in the proem: "Be thou therefore of one mynd and opinion in the work of nature . . . , for our Art is not effected with the multitude of things: And though the names thereof be divers and manifold, yett it is allwaies one onely thing, and of one thing: . . . Therefore it is necessary, that the Agent and patient be one thing" (sig. 3v).

The green lion presents an especially suggestive instance of Michel Foucault's claim that the distinctive *èpistême* of the sixteenth and seventeenth centuries, the distinctive paradigm for ordering knowledge of all sorts, was analogy.[69] Alchemical writings like "The Rosary of the Philosophers" bracket together forms of knowledge that we in the twenty-first century find altogether disparate—metallurgy, botany, human physiology, psychology, spirituality—and regard them as "always one only thing." Even our distinction between subject and object—"agent" and "patient" in the terminology of the "Rosary"—shape up as two aspects of a fundamental unity. Foremost among the ancient authorities claimed by alchemists and ridiculed by Francis Bacon was "Hermes Trismegistus," whose corpse was supposed to have been found clutching a "smaragdine table"—that is, an emerald tablet—on which was inscribed the fundamental propositions of occult philosophy. Among the inscriptions on that green tablet was an epigram encrypting Foucault's analogical principle: "That which is beneath is like that which is above: & that which is above, is like that which is beneath, to worke the miracles of one thing."[70] That Hermes = Mercury = mercury = quicksilver = an excellent green is coincidence enough to detain the most enlightened skeptic. Under the aegis of Hermes' epistemology, to know metals is to know plants is to know the human soul. And to know all three, at the moment of transmutation, is to know green.

Perhaps it is alchemy that finally explains why Trevelyon would imagine the entire cosmos as green (see plate 5). A section in the Wormsley manuscript includes a section entitled "The greene Dragone: For Joyners and Gardeners." The image of a green dragon with red ears, red and yellow wings, red legs and feet, and a red tail, holding a pink glove in its mouth, presides over the ensuing forty leaves, which illustrate "some thinges for ioyners, and Gardeners, as knotes, and Buildings, and Morysies, and Termes, With many other thinges to serue their Vse very well" (2:573). An alchemical inspiration is possible. Like all the assemblage of objects that Trevelyon depicts in this section, a "term" combines "animal," vegetable, and mineral elements. A human head emerges out of a stone pillar, which typically is placed to mark the borders of a garden (*OED,* "term" *n.* V.15). A "term" becomes a "herm" when the head of Terminus, the god of boundaries, becomes the head of Hermes, the god of boundaries transgressed (*OED,* "herma").[71] Ultimately it is a fascination with the phenomenon of transmutation itself—mineral, botanical, spiritual—that explains why images out of alchemy suddenly glint in writings by so many and so diverse Renaissance writers, including Andrew Marvell.[72] As Lyndy Abraham points out, Marvell joined the household of Thomas, Lord Fairfax, just when his employer had retired from public life and set himself the task of translating François Foix de Candale's commentary on Hermes Trismegistus's *The Pymander.*[73] "No white nor red was ever seen / So am'rous as this lovely green": does Marvell imagine here, beyond lovers' blushes, the red sun married to the white moon?[74] That way madness lies, think many modern readers. If so, the way thither passes through Bacon's *Sylva.*

The Eye's Green Apple

Scientific reasons for the central position of green in Aristotle's spectrum have been provided by modern neurophysiology and psychophysics. Each human retina contains two sorts of photoreceptors: rods and cones. The 120 million rods (so called because of how they look under a microscope) absorb light waves across the entire visible spectrum, but the chance of light being absorbed is greatest for waves at about 475–525 nanometers, in the range that English speakers identify as "blue" and "green." Since any activation of the rods triggers the same response in the optic nerve, regardless of the wavelength of the light, rods register distinctions only between light and dark—that is, distinctions in value. Distinctions in hue are triggered by a different set of receptors: the cones. The retina's five to seven million cones (again, that's what they look like when seen through a microscope) are clustered at the focal point opposite the eye's lens. There are, in fact, three different sorts of cones, all of them sensitive to light waves across the visible spectrum but each of the three sorts most susceptible to light waves at different frequencies.

S-cones respond most readily to light waves at about 440 nanometers, in the range identified in the English language as "blue"; M-cones, by light waves at 535 nanometers, in the "green-to-yellow" range; and L-cones, by light waves at about 565 nanometers, in the "yellow" range. Secondary processing follows these excitations and alters the signals that are relayed via the optic nerve to the brain. Positive and negative afterimages (red after green, yellow after blue, white after black), color discrimination, and color constancy all have their effect on how the brain "reads" the signals. Thus, red results when green-to-yellow signals produced by the M-cones are subtracted from yellow signals produced by the L-cones.[75] It takes negative green to make positive red.

The curve shown in plate 9 demonstrates how much more sensitive the L-cones at 565 nanometers are in comparison with the M-cones at 535 nanometers and, even more remarkably, in comparison with the S-cones at 440 nanometers. Reading the spectral chart from left to right, it is easy to see how red "events" emerge out of a green-to-yellow matrix. Red demands to be noticed in a way that blue and green do not. At the same time, red needs green to enforce its demand. Many neuroscientists, biologists, and psychologists believe that two sets of cones, one sensitive to green and the other to red, were the first to evolve in primates—in effect, making green and red the first colors to evolve out of black-and-white vision.[76] The reason for this evolutionary turn is suggested by a story that Robert Boyle tells in *Some Uncommon Observations about Vitiated Sight* (1688). An 18- to 20-year-old gray-eyed gentlewoman, Boyle reports, lost her vision as a result of medically induced blisters on her neck and other parts of her body. Although her sight eventually returned, the young woman could no longer see colors. When she walked in the meadows, she told Boyle, she did not see green but "an odd Darkish Colour."[77] When she kneeled down to pick violets, "she was not able to distinguish them by the Colour from the neighbouring Grass, but only by the Shape, or by feeling them" (sigs. S6–S6v). Without color vision, the dappled light reflected off leaves and grass would make it very hard for human eyes to distinguish fruit from foliage, target from scan, figure from ground. Searching for a "final cause" for his informant's misfortune—the title of the entire volume is *A Disquisition about the Final Causes of Natural Things*—Boyle asked her whether she was troubled by "Female Obstructions," to which she replied not now, but "formerly she had been much subject to them, having been obstinately troubled with the Greensickness" (sig. S6v). No comment from Boyle, who just by asking the question seems to have imagined that greensickness, far from making one see the world through green spectacles, might make it impossible to see green—or any other color, for that matter. Findings of the World Color Survey bear out the hypothesis that green and red were the first colors to impinge on human vision; among the world's languages it is red that tends to get named first, after black and white. By comparison, red's evolutionary counterpart green and its evolutionary successor blue are so unremarkable that they can remain fused as "grue."

Rods and cones were not, of course, available to Andrew Marvell and his contemporaries as explanations for how color happens in the eye and the brain. As early as 1611, Johannes Kepler demonstrated the geometry of vision: light beams from objects in the world are refracted through the lens of the pupil—the "apple" of the eye, it was called in early modern English (*OED*, "apple" *n.* A.7.a)—to become inverse images on the retina at the back of the eye. Though the presence of color is of course assumed, Kepler's geometry can totally be charted in black and white, as witness not only Kepler's verbal descriptions but the engraved diagrams in Descartes' *La Dioptrique*, published 33 years later. It was not until 1801 that the English scientist Thomas Young hypothesized that color vision results from different sorts of receptors in the eye that are sensitive to different ranges of light waves.[78] In the meantime, the two conflicting theories about the physics of vision—rays sent out from the viewer's eyes to objects versus rays sent from objects to the viewer's eyes—entailed two conflicting stories about the physiology of color.

Plato's explanation, as we noted in chapter one, actually combines the two theories. According to Plato, rays of fire from the eyes meet rays of fire from objects in the midst of daylight to form "a single homogeneous body aligned with the direction of the eyes."[79] The resulting "body of fire" transmits the motions of whatever it encounters and whatever encounters it "to and through the whole body until they reach the soul" (45c–d). The mixing of the two fires happens in midair. Different colors are said to result from two factors: the relative strengths of the two beams of fire and the differing effects of moisture, both in the ambient air and inside the eyes. If the "parts" of the rays coming from objects is the same size as the "parts" of the rays coming from the eyes, the result is transparency—no color at all (67d). If the incoming parts from objects are smaller than the outgoing parts from the eyes, the result is dilation, producing a perception of white. If the incoming parts are larger than the outgoing parts, the result is contraction, producing black. Between white and black—the same two poles recognized by Aristotle and by most cultures around the world today—Plato ranges all the other colors, which vary according to the intensity of the fire and the degree of moisture present in the air or inside the eyes. All hues seem to be present in what Plato calls a "bright-and-brilliant" quality in objects, a value rather than a hue proper (68a). Hues themselves—red, orange, purple, violet, gray, amber, beige, cobalt blue, turquoise, and green, in that order—are the products of a less intense type of fire, something intermediate between white and bright-and-brilliant. Thus green results when fire from the eyes, mixed with fire from daylight, is filtered through the eyeballs' moisture (producing red), vivified by additional bright-and-brilliant (producing orange), and tempered by blackness resulting from contraction of the pupils (producing green) (68b–d).

Fire and water are likewise determinants of color in Aristotle's explanation. Passages in Aristotle's *Historia Animalium* (The History of Animals) and his treatise *De Generatione Animalium* (On the Generation of Animals), supplemented by a book devoted to eyes in the *Problemata* attributed to Aristotle during the sixteenth and seventeenth centuries, all assume that different colors are perceived when fiery beams reflected from objects penetrate the watery content of the eyeball in different ways. Just as color in objects results from the varying degrees to which matter can be penetrated by fire, so the sensation of color within the eye depends on the varying ways in which the eye's internal fluid is penetrated by fire. Among the organs of sensation, Aristotle points out, only the eye "has a bodily constitution peculiar to itself."[80] The organs of touch and taste are part and parcel of the body itself; the organs of smell and hearing are passages in the body. The eye, by contrast, is its own entity, even though it communicates with the brain via direct passages: "the eye is the purest part of the liquidity about the brain drained off through the passages which are visible running from them to the membrane around the brain. A proof of this is that, apart from the brain, there is no other part in the head that is cold and fluid except the eye" (*De Generatione Animalium* 744.a.8–10).

Even before it is struck by fiery beams from objects, the eye itself possesses color. In *Historia Animalium,* Aristotle carries out a quick cross-species comparison of eyes and comes to this conclusion: "Of the eye the white is pretty much the same in all creatures; but what is called the iris differs. In some it is black, in some distinctly blue, in some greyish-blue, in some greenish; and this last colour is the sign of an excellent disposition, and is particularly well adapted for sharpness of vision."[81] Green irises are best because they indicate a density of water within the eye that is just right for receiving fiery beams from without. Blue eyes have too little liquid in them and therefore are too much moved by the light. Dark eyes have too much liquid and are moved too little. "The sight of the eye which is intermediate between too much and too little liquid is the best, for it has neither too little so as to be disturbed and hinder the movement of the colours, nor too much so as to cause difficulty of movement" (*De Generatione Animalium* 780.a.22–24). Just as green in objects results from a middling transparency, in which the elements of earth and fire are present in equal ratios, so the sensation of green within the eye depends on a tempering of fire and water.

In short, green-colored eyes see best, and green is what they like to see. Among the questions raised in book 31 of the treatise known as "Aristotle's Problems" is why vision deteriorates when we gaze on objects of other colors whereas "it improves if we gaze intently on yellow and green objects, such as herbs and the like."[82] The answer is to be found in the density and elemental composition of green objects: "Now green things are only moderately solid and contain a considerable amount of moisture; they therefore do not harm the sight at all, but compel it to rest upon them, because the admixture of their colouring is suited to the vision" (959.a.34–37). The version of this question and answer that was anthologized in the handy octavo *The Problemes of Aristotle, with other Philosophers and Physitians* (which went through 17 editions between 1595 and 1704) sums up a now forgotten commonplace: "the greene colour doth meanly move the instrument of the sight, and therefore doth comfort the sight: but this doth not black nor white colour, because their colours doe vehemently stir and alter the organ and instrument of the sight, and therefore make the greater violence: but by how much the more violent the thing is, which is felt or seene, the more it doth destroy and weaken the sense."[83] Perhaps Adam's eyes *were* the green of paradise.

That within which Passingly Showeth

The transparency that Aristotle locates at the surface of all forms of matter was recognized by Renaissance observers on the surface of human skin. Lomazzo, in his *Tratatto,* distinguishes quantity or proportion as the "matter" of painting from the "form" imparted by "colours answerable to the life" (sig. B3). A convincing portrait requires not only matter but form, not only quantity but color. It is well and good for a painter to get the quantity right. "But when unto this proportioned quantity he shall farther adde colour, then he giveth the last forme & perfection to the figure, insomuch, that whosoever beholdeth it may be able to say: this is the picture of the *Emperor Charles* the fift, or of *Philippe* his sonne, it is the picture of a melancholie, flegmaticke, sanguine, or cholericke fellowe, of one in love, or in feare, or a bashfull young man &c" (sig. B3v). That is to say that color communicates the sitter's passions. Lomazzo contrasts the "pleasurable sweetenesse" of green with the "tarditity, musing, melancholie, &c." of dull earth colors, the "courage, prouidence, fierceness and boldnesse" of red, the vigilance, grace, and sweetness of gold, yellow, light purple, and other bright colors, and the "ioy, mirth, delight, &c." of rose, light green, and bright yellow (sig. KK2v).

When Lomazzo praises color as being able to represent "the true difference" not only among beasts, birds, and fish but also among men of different countries and conditions, he has in mind external appearances as well as "all the passions of their mindes, and allmost the very voyce itselfe" (sig. HH5v). The sitter's passions show up not just in skin tone—a ruddy complexion for a sanguine temperament, say—but in the hues, values, and saturations of the setting and the props. Any attempt to fix *the* meaning of a color (green = hope, green = love-longing, green = jealousy) misses the complexity of the situation.[84] Differing configurations of sitter, setting, and props, realized in multiple combinations of hue, brightness, and intensity, open up a dazzling range of possibilities. Two English portraits dating from the early seventeenth century can show us some of green's manifold valences.

In 1603, James VI and I's daughter Elizabeth sat for a portrait by Robert Peake (plate 10). According to an inscription on the canvas, she was seven years old at the time. Since no royal payment to Peake is recorded, it is likely that Elizabeth's portrait and a companion piece showing Henry, Prince of Wales, in the company of Sir John Harington were commissioned by Lord and Lady Harington of Exton, who were appointed by James to look after Elizabeth when he ascended the English throne in 1603.[85] Sumptuous interiors with draperies, cushioned chairs, and Turkish carpets were more common in late-sixteenth-century English portraits than exterior landscapes, but for Elizabeth's outdoor surroundings, Peake may have found precedent in Nicholas Hilliard's small portrait of George Clifford, 3rd Earl of Cumberland (1590?), dressed to the hilt as the Queen's Champion and holding down a patch of green turf, as well as in Marcus Gheeraerts the Younger's large-scale portrait of Captain Thomas Lee (1594), shown bare-legged and ready for action amid the wild Irish country where he had recently seen military action.[86] The green landscape within which Princess Elizabeth contemplates the viewer may be intended to represent the Harington estate at Combe Abbey, Warwickshire.[87]

The organization of the space is curious, though. If, to a modern eye, it seems to lack the depth provided by geometrical perspective, it may be that another kind of perspective governs the point of view. Leonardo da Vinci (Haydocke's "Leonard Vincent") distinguishes *prospettiva lineale* (the system of sight lines that now counts as "perspective," pure and simple) from *prospettiva di colore* from *prospettiva spedizione*. It is the third sort, which is concerned with the "dispatch," or relative clarity, of the things and people being represented, that constituted in Leonardo's eye a painter's genius.[88] Lomazzo, in his *Tratatto,* explains what "color perspective" entails. In his managing of color, Lomazzo observes, a painter "expresses" two things: "First the colour of the thing whether it be artificiall or naturall: which he doeth with the like colour, as the colour of a blewe garment with artificiall blewe; or the greene colour of a tree with a like greene. Secondly he expresseth the light of the sunne, or any other bright light apte to lighten or manifest the colours" (sig. B4). That is to say, he expresses value as well as hue.

In Peake's portrait of Princess Elizabeth, perspective *di colore* and perspective *spedizione* are much more prominent than perspective *lineale.* Elizabeth stands on a very solid-looking patch of dark green. Behind her the landscape presents itself, not as the continuous plane we would expect in perspective *lineale,* but as two horizontal bands: one that stretches from the dark green foreground to a river in the middle distance, the second from the river to a misty blue horizon visible only at the right. What should occupy the horizon line is masked for the most part by the green boughs of trees. Although perspective *di colore* determines the varying degrees of golden light on the leaves—those in the foreground display more gold flecks of light than those further back—the boscage has a certain foreshortening effect with respect to Elizabeth's upper torso and face, making her seem as if she were standing a few feet in front of a verdure tapestry. If there is a vanishing point, it is situated, not at the horizon line, but behind Elizabeth's eyes—an effect that heightens the sense of Elizabeth's presence.

One could say, indeed, that the boscage has much more to do with putting the sitter across to the viewer than it does with situating her in an actual landscape, at Exton or elsewhere. The activities shown in the landscape point toward the destiny that Elizabeth realized ten years later, on February 14, 1613, when she married Frederick, the Elector Palatine—a union celebrated by John Donne in "An Epithalamion, or mariage Song on the Lady *Elizabeth,* and *Count Palatine* being married on *St. Valentines* day." As was customary, Donne, in his verses, puts the bride and groom to bed. Their sexual union he imagines in alchemical colors, but with the usual genders reversed: "Here lyes a shee Sunne, and a hee Moone here, / She gives the best light to his Spheare, / Or each is both, and all."[89] The park-work character of the bed curtains may be indicated in Donne's comparison of the bed to "the Arke / (Which was of soules and beasts, the cage, and park)" (sig. Q8) and in the way he locates, outside the closed curtains, himself and his readers, who "As Satyres watch the Sunnes uprise" (sig. R1v). Sexual energies also animate the landscape in Peake's portrait, where gender distinctions divide the green space vertically as land forms divide it horizontally. On the left, two female figures converse in a summer bower; on the right, male figures mounted on horses compete in a tournament, an activity that does for courting human males what parading their feathers does for courting peacocks.[90] The scenario anticipates *The Two Noble Kinsmen* by Shakespeare and John Fletcher, in which Emilia discusses with Theseus's bride-to-be Hippolyta how reluctant she is to give up female companionship and marry. Hippolyta's knowing reply perhaps alludes to greensickness as a condition deemed to be peculiar to pubescent young women who have not yet found release from their longing for love.[91] Hippolyta says she can no more credit Emilia's resolve not to marry "Then I will trust a sickely appetite, / That loathes even as it longs."[92] In the event, Emilia does marry. Her suitors compete for her possession in a tournament. The left and right scenes in Peake's portrait of Princess Elizabeth are offered not so much as depictions of what one might have seen happening in Exton park as suggestions of Elizabeth's inner life.

So, too, the water and the dominant green. Through its perspective *spedizione,* Peake's palette conveys the seven-year-old princess's unripeness, the coolness and moistness of a body that will be warmed at sexual maturity. In a pair of poems by Edward Herbert, greensickness figures as something not to be regretted but celebrated. "The Green-Sickness Beauty" of Herbert's verses is to be found, not in the sexually mature young women usually diagnosed in early modern medicine, but in prepubescent girls like Princess Elizabeth. Beams of the rising sun seem fairer in their first blush than in their later red, Herbert's "I" observes, and a budding rose smells sweeter than a blossom with petals fully opened.

> So in your green and flourishing estate
> A beauty is discern'd more worthy love,
> Then that which further doth it self dilate,
> And those degrees of variation prove,
> Our vulgar wits so much do celebrate.[93]

Herbert's connoisseurship of female beauty depends on knowledge that ripeness will come in due course, that the warm blood will "give at last a tincture to your skin," but in the meantime, he appreciates the here-and-now vitality of "the green-sickness beauty." Similar sentiments inform Donne's astonishingly misogynist poem "Communitie."

It is in a melancholic's posture that Edward Herbert, he of the portrait revealed from behind green taffeta by the Earl of Dorset, confronts us in Isaac Oliver's miniature of ca. 1613–1614 (see plate 11). Reclining in tournament gear beside a wooded spring, Herbert's image remains one of the most arresting Renaissance English portraits. It deserves fame likewise as one of the most arresting portrayals of Renaissance English green. By my calculation, green pigments occupy at least 50 percent of the portrait's $7 \times 8\frac{7}{8}$–inch surface. Add to this the represented objects usually understood to be green—the grass next to the spring, tree shoots and small plants, the blue-hued landscape in the distance—and the total rises to something like 65 percent. One might say that green, as much as the person of Edward Herbert, provides the stuff for Oliver's artistic elaboration.

Scholarly commentary on the portrait has recognized two roles for the recumbent Herbert: chivalric knight and melancholic philosopher.[94] The valorous deeds that the portrait conveys are suggested by Herbert's tournament costume as well as by the armor, plumed helmet, and caparisoned horse that a squire attends in the middle distance. In his autobiography, Herbert makes much of his installation as Knight of the Bath by the newly arrived James VI and I. Herbert describes the investiture in detail: the Earl of Shrewsbury's putting on of Herbert's right spur, the ritual bathing the night before the ceremony, the procession from St. James to Whitehall, the gown of purple satin and the pledge of white silk and gold worn on the left sleeve by all the newly installed knights "vntill they have done something famous in Armes or till some Lady of honor take it of and fasten it on her sleeue saying I will answer hee shall prove a good Knight."[95] Herbert did not have to wear his knot for long. "A principall Lady of the Court and certainly in most mens opinion the handsommest tooke mine of and said she would pledge her honor for myne" (38).

As for the role of philosopher, the device on Herbert's shield, a red heart emerging with sparks from golden flames (or are they golden wings?), and the inscribed motto "Magica Sympathia" have been connected by Roy C. Strong to Herbert's best known piece of writing in his own time, his treatise *De Veritate* (1624, 1633, 1639, 1645, 1656), as well as to various emblems of winged hearts, like the heart rising out of a book in George Wither's

Figure 4. Nicholas Hilliard, *Portrait of Henry Percy, 9th Earl of Northumberland* (1594–98). Watercolor on vellum. Original image, 10⅛ × 6¾ inches (25.7 × 17.3 cm). (© Rijksmuseum, Amsterdam / The Bridgeman Art Library.)

Figure 5. Isaac Oliver, *Portrait of an Unknown Man in a Black Hat* (1590–95). Watercolor and body color on vellum laid on card. Shown actual size, 4⅞ × 3⅜ inches (12.4 × 8.9 cm). (The Royal Collection, © 2007 Her Majesty Queen Elizabeth II.)

Emblemes (1635).[96] The effect of Herbert's affecting the philosopher is suggested by one of Jaques's poses in *As You Like It*. Two of Duke Senior's cohorts describe how they came upon Jaques in the forest lamenting the death of a deer. "The melancholy *Iaques*," as he apostrophized the dying deer, "lay along / Vnder an oake, whose anticke roote peepes out / Vpon the brooke that brawles along this wood" (F 1623, 2.1.26, 30–32).[97] Philosophy, with feeling, likewise accounts for the greenwood trees that shelter Henry Percy, 9th Earl of Northumberland, in Nicholas Hilliard's rectangular miniature of 1590–1595 (figure 4), the unknown black-hatted young man in a rectangular miniature by Oliver of the same date (figure 5), and Democritus in one of the woodcuts by Christof le Blon that adorn the title page to the third and later editions of Robert Burton's *The Anatomy of Melancholy* (1628, 1632, 1638, 1651, 1652, 1660, 1676; see figure 6). The situation of all these figures—Herbert included—is captured succinctly in "The Argument of the Frontispiece," added to the fourth edition of Burton's *Anatomy* (1632): "Old *Democritus* vnder a tree, / Sittes on a stone, with booke on knee." Democritus, whose theory that all matter is composed of atoms carries the notion of "anatomy" about as far as it can go, is flanked by images of "Iealousye" and "Solitarinesse."[98] Percy, the unidentified young man in a black hat, and Democritus share with Herbert an untied collar, the better to sigh withal. In all four cases, the subjects' proximity to earth suggests the cool, dry qualities of black bile and the melancholic humor that black bile was thought to induce. The elevated situation of all four figures relative to other planes in the landscape suggests their philosophical detachment.

Knight and philosopher, however, hardly exhaust the valences of green

Figure 6. Frontispiece of Robert Burton, *The Anatomy of Melancholy* (1638), detail. Engraving by Christof le Blon. Shown actual size, $2\frac{7}{8} \times 3\frac{3}{8}$ inches (7.3 × 8.6 cm). (Reproduced by permission of the Huntington Library, San Marino, California.)

in Oliver's portrait of Herbert. Indeed, the portrait gives material witness to green stuff in all its varieties. Considering its dominant hue, the panel could almost count as green stuff in an inventory of movable goods. Who commissioned Oliver's portrait of Herbert, where the owner kept it, to whom he or she showed it: answers to all of these questions remain undocumented. The diminutive size of the portrait—smaller than a sheet of copy paper—suggests, however, that it was intended for viewing in intimate circumstances, either alone or on an occasion like the one Herbert describes when the Earl of Dorset pulled back the curtain and displayed a replica of the portrait Herbert himself had commissioned from William Larkin. Another copy of the Larkin portrait was ordered, Herbert reports in his autobiography, by "a greater person then I will here nominat" who kept it "in her Cabinet" (60). That personage may have been Queen Anna (144–45).

More intimate—and greener still—were the circumstances in which Herbert discovered a third copy of his portrait, this time in the possession of the wife of Sir John Ayres. Lady Ayres had managed to find a copy and "get it contracted in to a litle forme by Isaac the Painter [Isaac Oliver] according to his manner and afterwards, caused it to bee set in gould and Enamiled and soe wore it about her neck soe lowe that shee yet hid it vnder her brests" (60). Something of Oliver's manner can be witnessed in the miniature of Herbert as the recumbent knight-philosopher. When Lady Ayres looked at Herbert's image it seems to have been with the "green spectacles" that Thomas Wright describes in *The Passions of the Mind in General.* Her wit could see nothing but green—"that is," according to Wright, "seruing for the consideration of the Passion."[99] In a word, Lady Ayres *greened* Edward Herbert:

> Coming one daye into her Chamber I sawe her through the Courtaines lying vpon her bed with a wax Candle in one hand and the Picture I formerly mentioned in the other. I coming therevpon somewhat boldly to her shee blew out the Candle and hid the Picture from mee; My selfe therevpon being Curious to know what that was shee held in her hand got the Candle to bee lighted againe, by means whereof I found it was my Picture shee looked vpon with more earnestnesse and Passion than I could haue easily beleiued especially since my selfe was not ingaged in any affection towards her (61).

How he happened to be in Lady Ayres's bedroom Herbert does not say.

With respect to landscape, Oliver's portrait replicates the geography of Hilliard's portrait of Thomas Percy, Oliver's of a young man in a black hat, and Burton's of Democritus. The philosopher-knight in Oliver's portrait of Herbert is situated somewhere in between the ascetic isolation of Hilliard's Percy and the comparative sociability of Oliver's black-hatted young man and Le Blon's Democritus. Hue and value in the Herbert portrait define three distinct planes: the bright yellow-green on which Herbert reclines, the truer and cooler green of the middle distance, and the soft blues of the far distance. (According to the principles of perspective *spedizione,* these soft blues should be read as green.) The last of the three planes recedes in three sequential waves: first woods that alternate with open spaces, then a river with a three-masted ship, and finally a castle-keep with a mansard roof.

All of these features may refer specifically to a landscape that Herbert praises in his autobiography. In 1608, the 25-year-old Herbert decided to make up for lost time, leave behind his wife and three young children, and travel abroad—something he had been too young to do before he was married at the age of fifteen. Against his wife's understandable objections, he set out for France with his friend Aurelian Townsend. Among the pair's many pleasurable pursuits in France, Herbert singles out for special mention the time they spent with Henri, Duc de Montmorency and Constable of France, at two of his estates, one at Chantilly and the other at Merlou, five or so miles away. Montmorency's Chantilly estate boasted "a greate and strong Castle" (occupied today by the Musée Condé) that straddled several islands in the River Nonette, an interior "sumptuously founded with hangings of silke and gould, rare Pictures and Statues," and excellent fishing. But it was the adjoining forest, "sett thick both with tall trees and vnderwoods" (47), that impressed Herbert the most.

The green lion may also be lurking in Oliver's painted woods. The "Sympathia" emblazoned on Herbert's shield is a key concept in his treatise *De Veritate,* "On Truth." *Sym* + *pathia* is, literally, "passion with," a concept that aligns Herbert's philosophy with both Foucault's *èpistême* of analogy and the rush of spirits through the body that Herbert and his contemporaries knew as passions. Cognition, in Herbert's account, is a process of working out conformities between external objects and the mind's myriad "faculties," or predispositions, for perceiving shape, quantity, movement, time, color, and other qualities.[100] Analogy provides the basis for Herbert's epistemology to such a degree that he can declare, "We are not only *like* elements, vegetables and brutes in virtue of heat, cold, movement, walking, desire, hunger, thirst, animal cunning, and sleep, but we *are* ourselves elements, vegetables and brutes" (170; emphasis added). As the catalog of qualities in this quotation suggests, Herbert's model allows ample play for emotions (*adfectus*) in acts of perception. The particular affect of Sympathia, of conformity across categories, is "joy" (177).

Seeing Herbert's gaze as a lover's gaze suddenly brings out the red of that flaming heart on the shield, the red feathers of the helmet, the red stripes of the attendant squire's costume. Red, as Lomazzo notes in his *Trattato,* communicates "courage, prouidence, fiercenesse and boldnesse by stirring vp the minde like fire" (sig. KK2v). Those qualities figure in counterpoint to the "pleasurable sweeteness" (sig. KK2v) of the portrait's dominant green and contrast with the water that gushes, most suggestively, from a spring just beneath Herbert's head. (Modern commentators seem to have missed the force of this water by seeing a flowing stream where Oliver has clearly painted an active fountainhead.) Legh, in *The Accedence of Armorie,* catches the same equipoise when he specifies what the combination of green and red means in heraldry. Alone, vert "signifieth ioyfull loue, bountifull minde, and gladnesse, with continuance of the same." Combine vert with "Sanguine," and the affect is "to laugh, and weepe at once" (sig. B4v).

Like his poet-brother George, "who was not exempt from passion and Choler" (9), Edward Herbert freely confesses in his autobiography to being a passionate person. The young Edward admires his language tutor's composure under provocation: "Though yet I confesse I could neuer attaine that Perfection, as being subject euer to Choller and Passion more then I ought and generally to speake my mynde freely and indeed rather to imitate those, who, having fire within doores chuse rather to giue it vent then suffer it to burne the house" (15). One particular passion that Herbert approaches and avoids again and again—a passion hot and moist rather than hot and dry—is lust. In a summary statement toward the end of his autobiography, he tries to dismiss that particular passion, but then has to confess, "If I transgressed sometimes in this Kynde It was to avoyd a greater ill, as abhorring any thing that was against Nature" (101). That greater ill could be masturbation; more likely it is sodomy. Herbert's painted portrait, for all its cool moist green, for all its trappings of melancholic sequestration, for all its darts of fire, portrays a physiologically balanced temperament such as Herbert locates in the Duc de Montmorency's estates, in "the Groves near *Merlow* [*sic*] Castle":

> You well compacted Groves, whose light & shade
> Mixt equally, produce nor heat, nor cold,
> Either to burn the young, or freeze the old,
> But to one even temper being made,

Upon a Grave embroidering through each Glade
An Airy Silver, and a Sunny Gold,
So cloath the poorest that they do behold
Themselves, in riches which can never fade,
While the wind whistles, and the birds do sing,
While your twigs clip, and while the leaves do friss,
While the fruit ripens which those trunks do bring,
Sensless to all but love, do you not spring
Pleasure of such a kind, as truly is
A self-renewing vegetable bliss.

(sig. E3v)

An actual forest, the physiological effects of blood ("burn the young") and phlegm ("freeze the old"), a park-work tapestry interwoven with silver and gold threads, and the generation of fruit end in a "vegetable bliss" that anticipates the "lovely green" of Marvell's "The Garden" (sig. I1) and the "vegetable Love" of "To His Coy Mistress" (sig. E2). Herbert's sonnet celebrates a balanced temperament that the author himself confesses never to have achieved in life, and it does so through complex engagements with green.

Chemical analysis would doubtless indicate which of Hilliard's green pigments his pupil Isaac Oliver has used in Herbert's portrait: cedar green, verdigris, pink mixed with bice, pink mixed with massicot, sapgreen, fleur-de-lis green. Too much attention to hue, however, would miss the variations in value and intensity that characterize Oliver's ways with green. Roy C. Strong finds in the brightness of Oliver's colors a retro quality that connects his portrait of Herbert to Hilliard's brilliantly colored miniatures of the 1590s rather than with the lifelike tones of early-seventeenth-century painting on the continent, as exemplified in Oliver's miniature of his wife Elizabeth Harding. Strong attributes this discrepancy to Oliver's need to satisfy Herbert's old-fashioned tastes rather than please himself.[101] Strong's clear preference for the more subdued palette of the Harding portrait speaks to a tendency in art history, with respect to the Renaissance period at least, to value rationalized perspective in the management of space and to prize ever greater degrees of verisimilitude in rendering naturalistic effects of light and color. Brightness is something we are not equipped to see—or at least to talk about even if we see it. Oliver's portrait of green, in all its varieties of hue, value, and intensity, offers the viewer a purchase on the world in which linear perspective is not the only way to organize space and verisimilitude of light is not the main thing that color communicates. Green in Oliver's portrait is over-determined: it is more than the sum of its material parts. Green figures as movable goods, as a matrix for viewing the primary visual subject, as landscape, as the point where the mineral, the vegetable, the animal, the human, and the spiritual sympathetically converge, as the midpoint in the spectrum between black and white, as a physiological state, as the impetuosity of desire, as inward character, as pigment, as material for artistic elaboration—and in that plenitude as "matter of an unspecified kind."

CHAPTER THREE

Between Black and White

1 | 0. Look out for the marked term, warn critics of a certain stripe. In any binary, one term functions as the standard against which the other term is marked as "different," and that can be dangerous. One is one because it isn't zero, and one, as the unmarked term, is suspect. Alexander Pope, like most Enlightenment writers, habitually thinks in such contrasts.[1] In epistle 2 of *An Essay on Man* (1734) Pope confronts the ethical ambiguities that attend human actions: "This *Light* and *Darkness* in our Chaos join'd, / What shall divide? The *God* within the *Mind.*"[2] Otherwise, the mind is like "some well-wrought Picture" in which light and shade are mixed. The mind is not, however, the only place in which God is seated as a judge.

> If white and black blend, soften, and unite
> A thousand ways, is there no black and white?
> Ask your *own Heart,* and nothing is so plain;
> 'Tis to *mistake* them, costs the *Time* and *Pain.*
> (sig. D1v)

Tell that to Frantz Fanon.[3] Aside from its political dangers, black/white binarism is ambiguous with respect to color. Since Newton's experiments with prisms in the 1660s, we have come to think of white light as the presence of all colors and black as the absence of any color.[4] By the criterion of *colore,* then, white would seem to be the standard. Consider, however, the marks made with black ink on white paper as drawn lines, scripted letters, or letterpress. By the criterion of *disegno,* the marked term is black.[5]

That vertical line separating 1 from 0 and "black" from "white": just what is *there*? In Ferdinand de Saussure's structuralist linguistics, it is a "cut made from the mass of thought," a cut that can be rendered graphically as the bar used in algebra[6] (see figure 1). For Derrida the line separating "black" from "white" is less definite. Most famously it is an aporia, an undecidable reading in philology ("you are to blame" versus "you are too blame" is a good example from early modern English) or an unsolvable problem in philosophy (Socrates loved to lead his students to such impasses). More frequently, Derrida refers to the space between 1 and 0 as *jeu,* as play. To talk about that space of play, he says, one must turn to *assemblage,* to an "interlacing," a "weaving," a "web."[7] Elsewhere he characterizes the space of play as an "enfolding" and connects the word *hymen* (membrane, marriage) in Stéphan Mallarmé's short piece "*Mimique*" with the words *hymn, huphos* (textile, spider web, net, a verbal text), and *humnos* (a weave, the weave of a song). "The hymen is thus a sort of textile," he suggests. "Its threads should be interwoven with all the veils, gauzes, canvases, fabrics, moires, wings, feathers, all the curtains and fans that hold within their folds all—almost—of the Mallarméan corpus."[8] Wings and feathers, fabrics and curtains: one thinks of Marvell's soul, waving in its plumes the various light, and the Earl of Dorset's curtain, veiling Edward Herbert's portrait until just the right moment. In effect, Derrida refuses Saussure's bar and embraces the shadowy chaos that inspires in Pope both fear and a sneer. Ultimately it is the binary logic of Enlightenment thought, expressed in the caesurae of rhymed couplets as well as in logical oppositions like "black" and "white," that Derrida is resisting. But Enlightenment thought is not *all* thought, not even all Western thought before the 1960s. Between black and white, thinkers in the century and a half before Pope were apt to see, not a bar, but a continuum. And what filled that continuum was not chaos but color.

Line, Shadow, Color

Nicholas Hilliard, in his *Treatise Concerning the Arte of Limning* (ca.1598–1603), acknowledges the primacy of line over the two other elements of his technique, shadowing and color: "the principal p[ar]te of painting or drawing after the life," he declares, "consisteteh in the truth of the lyne."[9] And to prove his point he instances a drawing of Queen Elizabeth made with only four strokes of the pencil. A man might cast a shadow on a white wall, Hilliard says, but it would take an outline of that shadow sketched on the wall in coal to capture "the countenance" (84). Hilliard takes pains, indeed, to distance himself from all shadow effects. For him, the key considerations in "limning" are line and light. His most famous sitter agreed. Receiving Hilliard for the first time, Queen Elizabeth said she had noticed how artists of different nations "shadowed" their works differently. The Italians, reputed "to be cunningest, and to draw best," do not use shadows. (Elizabeth had been sketched by Federico Zuccarro during his visit to England in 1575, but clearly she had not read Richard Haydock's 1598 translation of Lomazzo's *Tratatto dell'arte de la pittura,* where Titan's ways with colored shadows are singled out for praise.[10]) Indeed, Her Majesty affirmed, "best to showe ones selfe, nedeth no shadow of place but rather the oppen light" (84). Hilliard could not have agreed more. Shadows are produced, he informed the queen, when an artist works in a studio with only a single source of light from a window, and the result is "a grosser lyne, and a more aparant lyne" (86) that produces a three-dimensional embossed effect not necessary in works like his, designed to be seen close at hand. Satisfied with this exchange, Elizabeth "therfor chosse her place to sit in for that porposse in the open ally of a goodly garden, where no tree was neere, nor anye shadowe at all, saue that as the heauen is lighter then the earth, soe must that littel shadowe that was from the earthe" (86).

As for color, Hilliard notes that "some authors, sayeth, ther are but toe cullers, which are black and whit, because indeed in whit and black all things are or maye be in a maner very well Discribed" (88). One can see that, he claims, in "grauen portraiture" (88), and he specifically cites Albrecht Dürer and Hendrik Goltzius. If Hilliard speaks here for other viewers, the lines delineating the walls, the clothing, the flesh, and the bed curtains in Goltzius's double portrait of Tarquin and Lucrece (figure 7) could be read as descriptions or "writings down" (*de* + *scriptere*) of hues. Certainly in heraldry books, lines drawn in various patterns were read as indications of distinct colors. Figure 8 shows a chart of these black-and-white "colors" as provided in Randle Holme's *The Academy of Armory* (1688, 1693, 1701). Newton, while experimenting with prisms and light in the 1660s, carefully examined engravings like Goltzius's to determine whether black lines on white paper might "seem colured at a distance" or whether color might seem to be present in "verges of shadows"—as if color effects might result from the vibration of black and white.[11] To Newton's skeptical eye, no such color effects were present. Were they present to eyes like Hilliard's? Noting that some authors say that black and white are not colors at all, Hilliard treats black and white as the stuff of shadowing and lightening, which he sees as less important than line but more important than color. The hundreds of black lines in Goltzius's depiction of the rape of Lucrece—the result of hundreds of cuts into a copper plate—have

Figure 7. Hendrik Goltzius, *Lucrece and Tarquin* (ca. 1585). Original image, 8⅜ × 9⅝ inches (21.5 × 24.8 cm). (Collection of the author.)

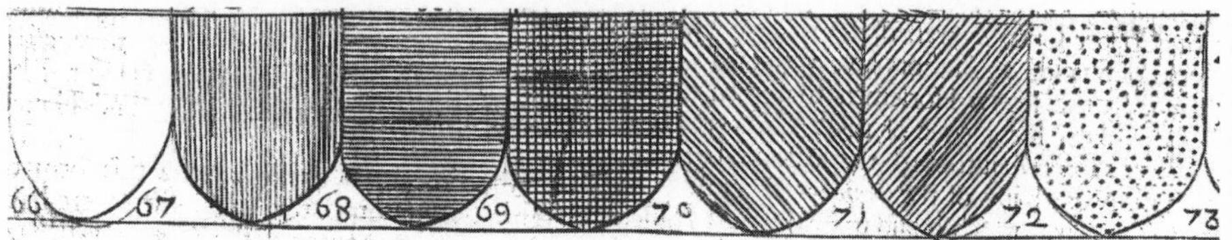

Figure 8. from Randle Holme, *The Academy of Armory* (1688). Original image, 1⅛ × 6¼ inches (2.9 × 15.9 cm). (Reproduced by permission of the Huntington Library, San Marino, California.) Key: 66 = silver, 67 = red, 68 = blue, 69 = black, 70 = green, 71 = purple, 72 = gold.

much more to do with shadow than with color. The lines define Lucrece's darkened bedroom, a space in which the only sources of light are reflections through the open doorway to the left (Lucrece and Tarquin's just-finished banquet, an event removed in time as well as space) and the lurid light cast on the bodies by the implied spectator, who seems to have intruded into the scene with a candle or a lamp. As for Hilliard, the primacy of line and shadow over color can be observed in all of his portraits of Elizabeth, including the one displayed in plate 3, against the floriated damask of the Green Closet at Ham House—a color field that replicates the garden setting in which Hilliard says he first took Elizabeth's likeness. (By the time he painted this particular portrait, however, Elizabeth was in her sixties and was content to have earlier exemplars of herself copied from art, not nature.) Portraits by other artists confirm that black and white were what Elizabeth's court most liked to wear.[12]

Black earth, white light: the coordinates within which Elizabeth chose to situate herself for the first of Hilliard's portraits are familiar from sonnets of the 1590s: Astrophil's "blackest face of woe" (sonnet 1) when confronted with "*Stella,* Starre of heauenly fier" (song 8, "In a groue most rich of shade"), Spenser's declaration to Elizabeth Boyle that "Dark is the world, where your light shined neuer" (sonnet 8), Daniel's lament that when Delia frowns "my liues light thus wholy darkned is" (sonnet 20).[13] Shakespeare's "man right faire" and "woman collour'd il" take their places within these black/white coordinates.[14] What happens between the coordinates, at the edge of the marking, where black line meets white paper, where black coal meets white wall, where colored ill meets right fair? Saussure inserts a cut. Derrida insinuates play. What Aristotle and his Renaissance successors imagined was a range of colors, varying according to greater and lesser degrees of white combined with black:

black | gray | blue | leek-green | violet | red | yellow | white

As we have had occasion to observe several times already, something like the same perception is still registered by speakers of many of the world's languages, who distinguish color primarily in terms of "dark" versus "bright."[15] In sonnets of the 1590s, the space between black and white is filled most frequently with the other two hues in Apelles' four-color palate, with the red of lips and the golden-yellow of hair.[16] In a move beyond these four colors, the man right fair in Shakespeare's sonnets is said to have "all hues in his controlling" (20.7), although red blushes might be what the speaker mainly has in mind. To this familiar colorscape of black, white, red, and yellow Queen Elizabeth's chosen spot in the garden adds an ambient green.

Amid that distinctive Renaissance blazon of colors, Hilliard adopts a pose familiar from Sidney, Spenser, Daniel, and Shakespeare. For the artist, confronted with the beauty of his sitter, "it hehoueth that he be in hart wisse, as it will hardly faill that he shalbe amorous, (and therfore fittest for gen̄t:) for whoe seeth an exelent precious stone, or diserneth an exelent peece of musike with skill indeede, and is not moued aboue others with an amorous Ioye and content then the vulger" (76). Hilliard's modern editors expand "geñt:" to "gentlemen." How gentle*women* might respond is perhaps indicated by the reported conversation with Queen Elizabeth. Or perhaps she is an exception among her sex. Also in question is just how "the vulgar" would respond. With joy and contentment "below" that of a gentleman? With joy only and no contentment? With contentment and no joy? With indifference? With hostility? The gentleman's equipoise of passion and self-possession Hilliard formulates as "an affectionate good Iugment" (76). Lyly's Apelles, confronted with Alexander's mistress in *Campaspe* (and with Queen Elizabeth herself when the comedy was performed at court) affects just that passionate detachment. Or is it detached passion?[17] Hilliard and Apelles are not afraid to green the subjects they paint, even as they temper that greening with good judgment. They keep the green in line.

The pre-Newtonian spectrum of black to white may be false to the physics of refraction, but it is true to the phenomena of perception. Black, white, and the colors in between provide a suggestive way to align and compare changing ideas since the sixteenth century about the-entity-that-perceives and changing valuations of imagination and reason during the seventeenth-century crisis of consciousness.

Psychology Noire

In a curious reversal of cinema, the history of psychology begins in color but ends in black and white. For Plato, as we have seen, vision occurs when streams of fire projected from the eyes of the observer mingle with daylight to form a homogenous "body of fire" that connects the observer's eye with objects round about. Different colors are said to result from different interactions between the fire that penetrates the eyeballs and the moisture inside, as moderated by dilation and contraction of the pupils. The entity towards which these colored light rays move as they course through the seer's body is ψυχή, or *psyche*—a combination of breathed sounds that happens also to mean "breath" (*OED*, "psyche" etymology). Thus, a speaker of ancient Greek enacted *psyche* even as he or she spoke it. We are, then, being etymologically precise when we observe that color is a *psychological* phenomenon. What is this entity that is doing the perceiving of color and the speaking about it? How can we account for it in λόγος, in *logos*, in discourse? In English at least, "psychology," like "consciousness," is a seventeenth-century invention. The modern Latin term *psychologia* had been used by Melanchthon and other sixteenth-century German writers to distinguish study of the soul from *somatologia,* study of the body (*OED,* "psychology" endnote).[18] By the sixteenth century, of course, "soul" (via the Latin *anima,* which also means "breath" or "spirit") had acquired its Christian penumbra. It was not until the mid-eighteenth century that "mind" displaced "soul" as what it is that psychology turns into words, numbers, and graphs (*OED,* "psychology" 1.a). In the seventeenth century, before that shift in terms, the psychology of color still concerned the soul and entailed fundamental questions about the relations of soul to body, reason to passion, perceiver to object, and experience to words.[19] Let us begin in living color, with Plato and Aristotle and their differing ideas about "soul."

For Plato, *psyche* is a universal principle in which individual human beings participate by the very fact of their existence. According to *Timaeus,* an individual's *psyche,* like the world's *psyche,* combines three elements: sameness, difference, and the indivisibility and changelessness that Plato calls Being.[20] The operations of *psyche* as described in *Timaeus* seem to be identical with the operations of reason. Whenever *psyche* comes into contact with something, it decides what that thing resembles or differs from, producing "firm and true opinions and convictions." When, on the other hand, *psyche* concerns itself exclusively with sameness, the result is "understanding and knowledge" (*Timaeus* 37.b–c). Thus all green sensations are to be referred, by the principle of sameness, to the Idea of Green. The observer doesn't just see green; he *knows* that it is green that he sees.

Lest there be any doubt that *psyche* = reason, Plato concludes his account of understanding and knowledge with this not-so-friendly warning to anyone who would contradict him: "And if anyone should ever call that in which these two arise, not soul but something else, what he says will be anything but true" (*Timaeus* 37c). Aristotle, in his treatise *On the Soul,* did not mind defying this warning. For Aristotle, *psyche* is a thoroughly embodied affair. It is what makes a living thing take nutrition, sense, think, and move.[21] *Psyche* has substance; it is form-in-matter (414.a). *Psyche* is "the actuality of a certain kind of body" (414.a). As such, it cannot be imagined apart from the body: "Hence the rightness of the view that the soul cannot be without a body, while it cannot *be* a body; it is not a body but something relative to a body. That is why it is *in* a body, and a body of a definite kind" (414.a). To be fair, Plato recognizes three "kinds" of soul: one situated in the head (the soul that thinks), one in the chest (the soul that contains "those dreadful but necessary disturbances" of pleasure, pain, boldness, fear, anger, expectation, "unreasoning sense perception," and "all-venturing lust" [*Timaeus* 69.d–e]), and one in the diaphragm (the soul that has appetites for food and drink [*Timaeus* 70.e]). But Plato is careful to distinguish the immortality of the soul-in-the-head from the mortality of the soul-in-the-chest and the soul-in-the-diaphragm. The neck functions as "an isthmus . . . to keep them apart" (*Timaeus* 69.e). Aristotle preserves this tripartite scheme by recognizing three sorts of "psychic powers"—(1) nutritive, (2) appetitive-sensory-locomotive, and (3) thinking (*On the Soul* 414.a)—even as he insists that human beings share their nutritive soul with plants and their nutritive and appetitive-sensory-locomotive souls with animals. Color, for Aristotle, functions like shape and motion: it gives form to a body, it makes a body what it is. As such, color is part of the living-form-in-matter that, for Aristotle, constitutes *psyche.*[22]

These competing ideas of *psyche,* one derived from Plato and one derived from Aristotle, were played out in the gray matter, and in the speech, of Renaissance men and women. An episode in Book 2 of Edmund Spenser's *The Faerie Queene* (first published in 1590) recounts, in graphically physical terms, the story that Renaissance men and women told themselves about how sensations become ideas. Sixteenth- and seventeenth-century readers, not provided with the explanatory footnotes or endnotes of modern editions, enacted in their reading of canto 9 the very epistemology that the House of Temperance bodies forth in its disposition of rooms.[23] After touring the lower quarters, Sir Guyon and Prince Arthur are escorted up into the castle's high turret, which is constructed according to Renaissance ideas about the brain. Three chambers compose the tower, one devoted to things future, one to things present, and one to things past. The first chamber, inhabited by a figure named Phantastes, is "dispainted all within, / With sundry colours, in the which were writ / Infinite shapes of things dispersed thin," including things "such as in the world were neuer yit," as well as things "daily seene, and knowen by their names, / Such as in idle fantasies doe flit."[24] Sounds as well as images fill the room: "And all the chamber filled was with flyes, / Which buzzed all about, and made such sound, / That they encombred all mens eares and eyes" (2.9.51.1–3). In the second chamber, presided over by "a man of ripe and perfect age" (2.9.54.2), the colors and shapes become pictures of "memorable gestes, / Of famous Wisards" (2.9.53.3–4), while the buzzing sounds become words. Spenser's catalog of the room's contents begins with visual images, with "picturals / Of Magistrates, of courts, of tribunals" (2.9.53.4–5)—but merges into political institutions—commonwealths, states, policy, laws, judgments, decretals—before turning into words, "All artes, all science, all Philosophy, / And all that in the world was aye thought wittily" (2.9.53.8–9).

In the third chamber, "th'hindmost roome of three" (2.9.54.9), gests, picturals, and words are committed to the keeping of memory. Memory is thus located behind the chamber of fantasy in the front and the chamber of understanding in the middle. "Ruinous and old" (2.9.55.1), the chamber of memory is "hangd about with rolles, / And old records from auncient times deriu'd" (2.9.57.6–7) and is presided over by Eumnestes, "an old oldman, halfe blind" (2.9.55.5), who orders an agile young servant to fetch him documents. Despite its vital activity, there is an unsettled and unsettling disorder to Spenser's chamber of memory that contrasts sharply with the clear and pristine images of "gestes" of wise men and "picturals" of social institutions that cover the chamber of understanding's walls. There is a teleological progression, of course, in Spenser's movement from past to present to future, from inchoate colors and sounds to painted picturals to inscribed texts, but Spenser is exquisitely sensitive to what comes *before* cognition: the colors, the thinly dispersed images, the buzzing sounds that have not yet become characters, deeds, and words. Spenser's knowledge is ambient knowledge: to know what they come to know, Sir Guyon and Prince Arthur must traverse the three rooms in the tower just as Marvell traverses the garden.

In the course of the seventeenth century, the chamber of Phantastes was visited less and less often. "The Allegory," John Hughes opines in his 1715 edition, "seems to be debas'd by a mixture of too many low Images, as Diet, Concoction, Digestion, and the like."[25] John Upton, in his 1758 edition, identifies Spenser's Alma with "mind,"[26] but Spenser's Latin name for her means "nourishing" or "kind." Thomas P. Roche, Jr., and other recent commentators are surely right to identify *alma* with *anima*, the Latin word for "soul" and for "breath"—but they reduce the sundry colors of Spenser's description to stark black and white when they preempt the play of sense experience with logos-heavy footnotes.[27] If Spenser's Castle of Alma were an actual structure somewhere in the English countrywide—Arundel Castle, for example—it would have undergone radical renovations in the eighteenth century when Alma/Anima/Psyche/Soul moved out and Mind moved in. At Arundel (we surveyed a sixteenth-century inventory of the interior's "green stuff" in chapter two) Thomas, 8th Duke of Norfolk, considered demolishing the old castle entirely and replacing it by an up-to-date neoclassical house to designs by James Gibbs, the architect of St. Martin's-in-the Fields in London and the Radcliffe Camera at Oxford. In the event the duke devoted his decorating energies to Worksop Manor in Nottinghamshire and contented himself at Arundel with refacing the south range with red brick and inserting regular sash windows, giving the long hall a centrally placed front door under a pediment, knocking out the north range to open up the view, and planting grass in the castle's now breached quadrangle. These alterations took place around 1718, at just the moment John Hughes was bringing Enlightenment to Spenser's dark conceit.[28] The effect at Arundel would have been similar to Hughes's effect on Spenser: a rationally organized, primarily horizontal space would have replaced the original castle's organic, primarily vertical accretion of rooms, large windows placed at regular intervals would have let in light, remaining vestiges of the old structure would have been framed as "picturesque" amid the new sweeping vistas of lawns. The neo-Gothic appearance of Arundel Castle today dates to a complete rebuilding carried out by the 15th Duke of Norfolk between 1877 and the beginning of World War I.[29]

When in the eighteenth century Mind became the entity-that-perceives, what happened to Soul? She (and by now Soul was definitely a "she") took refuge amid the stained glass of the Church, and there, for many people, she remains today. (In German, the ur-language of Romanticism, it is still *der Geist,* "the spirit," that does the knowing.) In the meantime, psyche took on a new identity as a stand-in for consciousness. In little over a hundred years, psyche has received in the pages of Freud, Jung, Lacan, and their disciples an intensity of analysis that rivals if not exceeds the prior two thousand years of writing about psyche/anima/soul. For all that saturated attention, the results are surprisingly lacking in color. The three entities in Freud's tripartite psyche are distinguished from one another primarily by value, by degrees of darkness and light. The id, Freud explains in the third of his *New Introductory Lectures on Psycho-Analysis* (1933), "is the dark, inaccessible part of our personality."[30] In Freud's verbal description, "the psychical personality" first shapes up as a mineshaft or a tube. As for the id, "we picture it as being open at its end to somatic influences, and as there taking up into itself instinctual needs which find their psychical expression in it, but we cannot say in what substratum" (73). The ego, by contrast, is turned outward toward the light of the world and functions as "the medium for the perceptions arising thence" through "the system *Pcpt.-Cs,*" or perceptual-conscious system (75). Dreams may give us our primary access to the id, but the colors of those dreams find their origins, not in the somatic substratum touched by id—that remains a place of darkness—but in the perceptions of the conscious ego.[31] The very few analyses of color that Freud provides in *The In-*

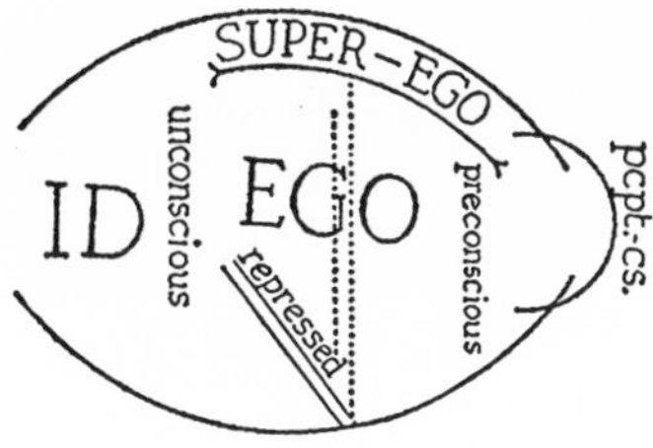

Figure 9. Sigmund Freud's model of the psyche, rotated 90 degrees clockwise, from *New Introductory Lectures on Psycho-analysis* (London,1933).

terpretation of Dreams (1900) link the colors to something the dreamer has seen in the waking world. The id remains in the dark.

Why not red for the impetuous id? Why not angry yellow? Why not orange? For the superego, why not a cool blue? For the ego caught in between, why not merging colors as red, yellow, orange, blue, green, and violet compete for dominance? In one startling passage in his lecture on the psychical personality, Freud briefly entertains such an image. But first he supplies a black-and-white diagram (figure 9). What seemed earlier to be a mineshaft or a tube becomes in this sketch an egg—or, turned on its side, as it is in figure 9, an eye ball. In either case, the id communicates with interior darkness through an open end, while the *Pcpt.-Cs.* communicates with the outer world through a circular protrusion that looks remarkably like the cornea of an eye. Within the oval, ego occupies a middle position, connecting spaces designated as "preconscious" and "unconscious" that are likewise embraced by the super-ego, which "as heir to the Oedipus complex . . . has intimate relations with the id" (23:79). From the colors, movement, and sounds of the *pcpt.-cs.* the superego remains more remote than the ego, but not so remote as the id. Once he has presented the drawing, Freud realizes that black lines on white paper cannot wholly account for the workings of the dynamic energy system he has been imagining: "We cannot do justice to the characteristics of the mind by linear outlines like those in a drawing or in primitive painting, but rather by areas of color melting into one another as they are presented by modern artists. After making the separation we must allow what we have separated to merge together once more" (79). What "modern artists" could Freud have had in mind in 1933? Böcklin? Monet? Cezanne? Schiele? Freud's vagueness points up how much more important value is than hue to his model of the psyche.

A similar black-to-white axis defines Jung's concept of "the shadow." To retrieve the shadow from the personal unconscious, Jung explains in *Aion: Researches into the Phenomenology of the Self* (1948), "involves recognizing the dark aspects of the personality as present and real."[32] Jung's black-to-white axis, like Freud's, is vertical. The shadow exists, not behind or beyond, but below: "Closer examination of the dark characteristics—that is, the inferiorities constituting the shadow—reveals that they have an *emotional* nature, a kind of autonomy, and accordingly an obsessive or, better, possessive quality" (8). Emotion in Jung's account preserves the seventeenth-century sense of passion as something that happens *to* a person, as something that possesses *him* rather than something he possesses. A vertical black-to-white axis governs even those passages in Jung's writings on archetypes that give explicit attention to color. Against the fixed coordinates of black and white, color most often figures in these writings as a circle. When Miss X, a 55-year-old American, came to work with Jung in 1928, he encouraged her to paint a series of 24 pictures which, under Jung's suggestion, moved from quasi-representational images toward more abstract, brightly colored mandalas, or circular representations of the cosmos, that Jung interpreted in light of Buddhist tradition, alchemy, and Jakob Böhme's Gnostic book *XL Questions concerning the Soule* (1620; English translation 1647). Jung advised Miss X "not to be afraid of bright colors, for I knew from experience that vivid colors seem to attract the unconscious."[33] (Freud's unconscious, by contrast, seems color-phobic.) Four particular hues in Miss X's paintings are allied by Jung, via Böhme, with "the four orienting functions of consciousness": blue with thinking, red with feeling, green with sensation, and yellow with intuition (335).

The importance of visual imagination in Lacan's three stages of psychic development would seem to promise more scope for color than Freud's enclosed ovoid of id-ego-superego or Jung's shadow. Individuation for Lacan is initially a visual experience, as the child perceives in a mirror its physical separateness from its mother's body and from the world at large. Lacan's description of that moment reads, however, like a freeze-frame from a black-and-white film of the 1940s. Lacan calls attention to the imperfectly coordinated motions, the "flutter of jubilant activity," that lead to the six-month-old's fixation on its image in the mirror, but the emphasis falls on form, on *disegno,* on what Hilliard would call the truth of the line: "For the total form of his body, by which the subject anticipates the maturation of his power in a mirage, is given to him only as a gestalt . . . in which, above all, it appears to him as the contour of his stature that freezes it and in a symmetry that reverses it, in opposition to the turbulent movements with which the subject feels he animates it."[34] The disjunction between the child's underdeveloped motor control over his body and its fascination with the image in the mirror shows up, Lacan claims, in the disconnected limbs and exoscopic organs painted by Hieronymus Bosch (78).

More blatantly black and white is the symbolic order that drafts the body image into language. That "I" in the mirror does not speak: it *is spoken* into being by other people, by the things they say to the "I," by the words and the structure of the language they speak, by the fundamental algorithm that governs all speaking and writing: S/s, the Signifier over the signified.[35] Even the Real, the intuited state of being that Lacan posits beyond language, remains a matter of line. A strikingly graphic image in Lacan's "Presentation on Psychical Causality" (1946) gestures toward the post-linguistic object of Lacan's version of psychotherapy: "when we begin to glimpse the operative meaning of the traces left by prehistoric man on the walls of his caves, the idea may occur to us that we really know less than him about what I will very intentionally call psychical matter. Since we cannot, like Deucalion, make men from stones, let us be careful not to transform words into stones" (132). The cave paintings at Lascaux, discovered just six years before Lacan's lecture, are drawn in earth pigments of black, gray, and brown. Bosch is among the very few painters—just six by my count—who make the index to Lacan's complete *Ècrits.* (The others are Pieter Brueghel, Salvador Dalí, Francisco José de Goya, Leonardo da Vinci, and G. D. Tiepolo, all of whom are cited in connection with *disegno* features of their work like grotesque figures.)

When it comes to the entity-that-perceives, we dwell by and large in a world of black and white—or at least we are told that we do. We were first delivered to this unfortunate pass by certain seventeenth-century thinkers.

Various Light

It was perhaps at Cambridge in the 1630s that Andrew Marvell's soul acquired its agility. In stanza 6 of "The Garden," the speaker's soul casts aside the body's "vest," glides into the boughs of a fruit tree, sits there and sings, preens its wing feathers, "And, till prepar'd for longer flight, / Waves in its Plumes the various Light."[36] When Marvell matriculated at Trinity College, Cambridge, in 1633—a few weeks shy of turning thirteen—a group of theologians at Emanuel College were just beginning to make a stir by tempering the strictures of Puritanism (for which Cambridge University was infamous) with broader, more tolerant ideas derived from classical philosophy, particularly from Plato.[37] A. Rupert Hall is surely right that "the Cambridge Platonists" as a unified school of philosophy is a twentieth-century invention (Ernst Cassirer wanted an Academy on the Cam to match Ficino's on the Arno), but Benjamin Whichcote, Nathaniel Culverwell, and John Smith at Emanuel College, and later, Henry More and Ralph Cudworth at Christ's College, taught an eclectic blend of ideas that gave the soul, the entity-that-perceives, a latitude that John Calvin would have found dangerous and Hobbes and Locke would have preferred to forget.[38] "Latitudinarian" is, in fact, the group name that these Cambridge dons were given when their philosophical ideas were put into action vis-à-vis the many competing religious sects in seventeenth-century England. Whichcote and company were inclined to give a wide berth to differing opinions on liturgy and church government. And they were eclectic in their philosophizing.

Plato may provide the common denominator among Whichcote, Culverwell, Smith, More, Cudworth, and their disciples, but in formulating a theory of knowledge, each writer engages a range of other ancient authorities—Aristotle alongside Plotinus, Democritus alongside Seneca, the Jewish Kabbalah alongside Galen—and proceeds with a syncretic insouciance that is largely oblivious to internal contradictions. In their muddle, the Cambridge Platonists help explain why Renaissance philosophy does not figure, by most accounts, as one of the great epochs in the intellectual history of the West. Rosalie Colie's summation concerning Marvell seems altogether just: "If Marvell is 'something' philosophically, then I think he is simply a generalized Neoplatonist of the sort most seventeenth-century poets were, half conscious of the implications of such 'system' as that belief had, half reliant upon its empirical usefulness to poets of any philosophical allegiance. It was easy, then, for the middling-thoughtful man to be Platonist: in fact, it was difficult for him not to be."[39] The result of such middling thoughtfulness, with respect to sensation, imagination, passion, and reason, can be witnessed in the gloss-resistant green of Marvell's garden—and in the broad range of opinions about perception that seventeenth-century thinkers entertained.

How to do justice to these diversities of opinion about perception without dividing them into "wrong" (scholasticism) and "right" (empiricism)—that is to say, into black and white? Cues for addressing this expansive variety are provided by Henry More, one of the younger Cambridge Platonists and one of two (the other is Cudworth) who thought of himself as a philosopher rather than a preacher. More's first major publication was *A Platonick Song of the Soul* (1647), in two parts: "Psychozoia; or . . . A Christiano-Platonicall display of LIFE" and "Psychathanasia or the Immortality of Souls, especially MANS SOUL."[40] In "Psychozoia," More

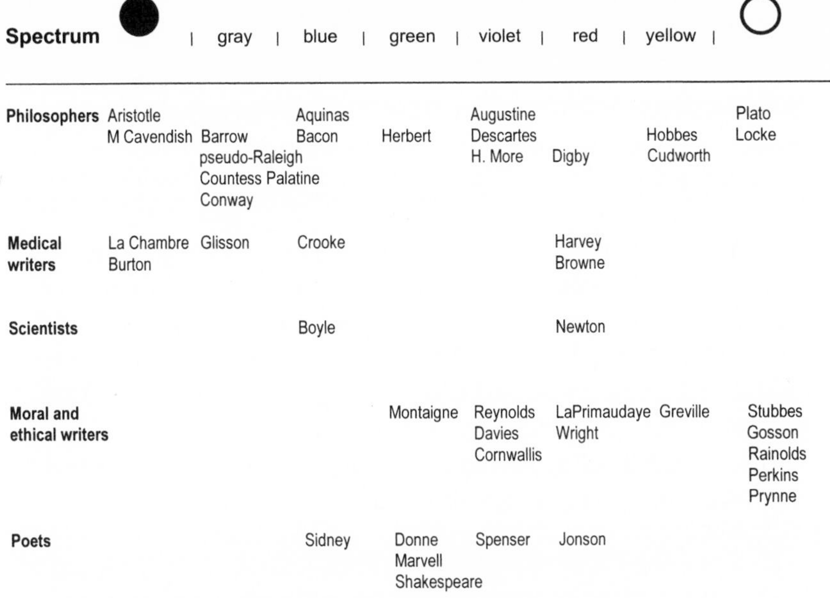

Figure 10. Spectrum of sixteenth- and seventeenth-century thinkers

seizes on the rainbow, "that gay discoloured Bow," as a metaphor for the diffusion of divine light down the great chain of being, the links of which are imagined in this case to be "vast discoloured Orbs" that reflect the light of the sun in varying degrees, depending on their proximity to that ultimate source of light (1.2.8.1–9). Unlike the rainbow that Queen Elizabeth grasps in her right hand in Isaac Oliver's famous portrait at Hatfield House, Hertfordshire (all hues, indeed, in her controlling), More's rainbow does not concentrate power but disperses it. More uses color to make carefully graded distinctions. Like Aristotle, like most European thinkers before Newton, like speakers of most of the world's languages, More imagines a spectrum that extends from black to white.

That spectrum can help us in sorting out the various positions on perception that were taken during the seventeenth-century crisis of consciousness (see figure 10). Chromatic theory from Aristotle to Newton held that colors result from varying combinations of black earth with white light. Aristotle's and Plato's very different conceptions of the psyche define the ends of a continuum along which seventeenth-century philosophical, medical, scientific, ethical, and literary writers can be ranged according to how much scope they give to embodied imagination versus abstracting reason.[41] The materiality of Aristotle's psyche suggests placement at the black/earth end; the fiery qualities of Plato's psyche, placement at the white/light end. If black and white constitute polarities, they do so in terms different from those we are used to making: matter versus idea, Becoming versus Being, even body versus mind. Instead, differing combinations of these binaries are at play at *every* point on the continuum, including the ends. Henry More stands as a case in point: a Platonist who accepts the metaphysical existence of Ideas, More can at the same time embrace a thoroughgoing materialism with respect to sensation, imagination, and the formation of knowledge. A materialist philosopher like Hobbes, by contrast, can accept the embodied nature of the soul but be much more interested in "the truth of propositions" than in the process of sensation. Not least among the attractions of the spectrum model, for me at least, is the centrality it recognizes in the middling thoughtfulness of green.

On certain key points all of these sixteenth- and seventeenth-century writers are substantially in agreement:

- ensoulment is the fundamental principle of life
- a distinction is to be drawn between soul and body
- all knowledge begins with sense experience
- a vaporous *spiritus* provides the human body's internal communication system
- sense experience activates bodily passions
- a distinction is to be drawn between passion and reason

That is to say, all of these thinkers could have joined Sir Guyon and Prince Arthur on their tour of the House of Temperance and found nothing there to surprise them. All of them accept the fluid nature of perception. How they deal with that fluidity is another story. Each of the six points of agreement among the writers in figure 10 also functions as a point of contention that divides the writers into hues, to wit:

- the number of souls a person possesses, three (nutritive, sensitive, rational) or one (rational)
- the precise relationship of the rational soul to the body
- the relative importance of sense experience in the formation of knowledge
- the amount of attention that should be given to *spiritus* as a material bodily system
- whether one accepts or rejects the passions as forms of knowledge
- the status of reason vis-à-vis sense experience and passions

If we read the spectrum from left to right, from black to white, we in effect recapitulate the paradigm shift in seventeenth-century accounts of consciousness.

We should realize, however, that very few of these writers can be said to represent a pure hue. For comparing, say, La Chambre (black) with Descartes (violet) with Hobbes (white), it is tempting to invoke Raymond Williams's notion of residual, dominant, and emergent elements of culture.[42] Thus La Chambre rehearses ideas about perception grounded in Galenic physiology and Aristotelian psychology—ideas that had been maintained for 1,500 years but were rapidly being challenged, revised, and discarded at the time La Chambre was writing. Descartes, pursuing a rationalist agenda but nonetheless giving passions their epistemological due, could be regarded as the one writer among the three who speaks for a dominant model of perception that allowed the readers of the second printing of Richard Crashaw's collected poems (1670) to thrill to "the sweetly---killing Dart" of light that pierces Saint Teresa's body at the same moment Newton was carrying out his experiments with prisms.[43] Finally, Hobbes defines an emergent rationalism that in turn became dominant in the eighteenth century, when passions that one formerly would have *suffered* became sensibilities that one makes a decision—a rational decision—to *cultivate.*[44]

Black

Other than La Chambre, whose ideas about the soul's capacity to leave the body we noted in chapter one, the extreme black end of the spectrum is anchored by Robert Burton and Margaret Cavendish. Black? Burton helps us understand why. In the ever-proliferating pages of successive editions of *The Anatomy of Melancholy,* Burton's spokesman Democritus Junior enacts how the world is experienced by a man whose *spiritus* is flooded with black bile. His account "Of the Inward Senses" early in the proceedings describes the kind of images that dominate the melancholic's fantasy or imagination, "monstrous and prodigious things, especially if it be stirred up by some terrible object, presented to it from common sense, or memory." Imagination works most forcibly in poets and painters, "as appeares by their severall fictions, Antickes, Images."[45] What these productions have in common is their location in the creator's imagination. "*Antike* work," according to Edward Phillips's *The New World of English Words* (1658), is "a Term in painting, or Carving, it being a disorderly mixture of divers shapes of men, birds, flow'rs, *&c.*"[46]

Just such fictions, antics, and images dominate Margaret Cavendish's *The Description of a New Blazing World* (1666), although one could hardly attribute them to black bile. The third-person protagonist in this fictional narrative is a duchess who sounds very much like Cavendish herself. Among the highlights of the duchess's adventures are passage via the North Pole to another world revolving around another sun, encounters there with people whose complexions range from azure to deep purple to grass-green to scarlet to orange and whose bodies take the forms of bears, worms, fish, birds, flies, ants, geese, spiders, lice, foxes, apes, jackdaws, magpies, parrots, satyrs, and giants, according to their professions and social functions, an extended philosophical dialogue with the other world's empress on questions of matter, spirits, form, color, and the skewed false impressions offered by microscopes and telescopes, and an episode in which the Empress of the Blazing World sends her soul to join the duchess' soul in inhabiting the body of the duke back in *this* world, so that the three souls—the empress's, the duchess's, and the duke's—are able to carry on delightful conversations among themselves.[47]

Modern editors have done the Duchess of Newcastle a huge disservice by severing *Observations upon Experimental Philosophy* from *The Description of a New Blazing World* and publishing them as separate books.[48] The juxtaposition of rational argument and fanciful fiction is precisely what Cavendish is *about* in this publication, as she makes clear in the preface to *A New Blazing World.* The first part of the book, *Observations,* is cast as a work of "reason"; *A New Blazing World,* as a work of "fancy." By distinguishing fancy from reason, Cavendish insists that she is not marking the black/white, wrong/right binary that readers might expect. Indeed, fancy and reason, to Cavendish's view, are two different forms of rationality: "mistake me not, when I distinguish *Fancy* from *Reason;* I mean not as if Fancy were not made by the Rational parts of Matter; but by *Reason* I understand a rational search and enquiry into the causes of natural effects; and by *Fancy* a voluntary creation or production of the Mind, *both* being effects, or rather actions of the rational part of Matter."[49] One mind, multiple capacities, two different but complementary deployments of those capacities.

Gray

Writers in the gray range try more systematically than Margaret Cavendish to reconcile reason and fancy, but they do so in more materialist terms, by granting matter the power to shape perception in certain ways or by enduing matter itself with perceptive functions. Close to Cavendish in her boldness to take on "mechanical" thinkers like Descartes and Hobbes is Anne Conway, a protégé of Henry More who took More's eclectic Platonism in unexpected directions. In *The Principles of the Most ancient and Modern Philosophy concerning God, Christ and Creation, that is, concerning the Nature of Spirit and Matter* (1692) Conway argues that the generation and production of ideas requires two principles, spirit and body. These Conway identifies with male and female, as well as with light and darkness. The creation of children requires both male and female: "In the same way, the internal productions of the mind (namely the thoughts which are true creatures according to their kind and which have a true substance appropriate to themselves) are generated. These are our inner children, and all are masculine and feminine; that is, they have a body and spirit."[50] For Plato, in the *Symposium,* the production of such intellectual offspring is ostensibly a metaphysical affair, since it is presumed to happen between two males.[51] Conway's version of Plato's idea draws imaginative force from "the conjunction and cooperation of male and female" (38). Knowledge for Conway requires a body—and, by implication at least, a body that knows erotic arousal.

"Animate materialists" might be the best name to apply to Isaac Barrow, Francis Glisson, and the unknown author of *Raleigh's Sceptick.* All of them resolutely refuse the body/mind binary that had always informed Western philosophy but that took on new epistemological importance in the seventeenth century as practitioners of the new science aspired to an "objective" view of the matter and the energy in the world around them—and within their own bodies. Published by William Bentley in 1651 as one of two books attributed to Raleigh, *Sir Walter Raleigh's Sceptick* presents a radically materialist view of perception and truth. According to the author of this text (whoever he may actually have been), "the instruments of Sence" *determine* just what it is that the imagination conceives: "That very object which seemeth to us White, unto them which have the Jaundise, seemeth Pale, and Red unto those whose Eyes are bloud-shot." Indeed, differently shaped eyes present a different reality. The long and slanting pupils of goats, foxes, and cats "do convey the fashion of that which they behold under another form to the imagination, than those that have round Pupils do."[52] With respect to the eyes of insects at least, "Raleigh" anticipates here the findings of modern science.

More radical still are the animate views of matter proposed by the mathematician Isaac Barrow and the physician Francis Glisson. Like Henry More, his Cambridge contemporary, Barrow was enthusiastic about Descartes' rational orientation toward the physical world but could not accept Descartes' rigid distinction between matter and spirit. For Barrow, proof of the extension of spirit into matter was provided by magnetism.[53] With respect to light and color, Barrow's physics required a distinction between *lux* as the light source and *lumen* as the light effect produced by the refraction and diffusion of light rays off the surfaces of objects and particles in the air before light rays reach the perceiver's eye.[54] In his lectures on optics at Cambridge (published in 1669), Barrow attempted a mathematical description of these refractions and diffusions. Among his auditors at Cambridge was Isaac Newton, who later assumed Barrow's professorship. The magnetism that, for Barrow, demonstrates the presence of spirit in matter is endowed with specifically human qualities in Francis Glisson's *De Natura Substantiae Energetica, seu, De vita naturae* (1672). Glisson projects onto the material world attributes commonly accepted as belonging to the human soul (or souls): not just motion, as Barrow believed, but perception and appetite.[55] The ultimate source of these powers is affirmed to be God, but Glisson imagines all three to be diffused in matter, even below the level of human consciousness.

Blue

So far, so bizarre. Only with blue do we begin to encounter writers whose opinions about perception we can recognize as common sense, in the modern understanding of that phrase as opinions everybody accepts as given. But the emphasis has to fall on "begin." Francis Bacon, Helkiah Crooke, and Robert Boyle, in their separate fields of natural philosophy, medicine, and optics, advance arguments that remain current in twenty-first-century science, but they also take into account qualifying factors of embodied subjectivity that writers on the *other* side of the green divide—Descartes, Browne, Newton—tend to discount or ignore entirely. As we observed in chapter one, Bacon's all-encompassing concept of "Learning" is capacious enough to include "the human sciences" as well as the natural sciences. Any such division into the human and the natural, moreover, is false to what Bacon insists are "the SYMPATHIES AND CONCORDANCES BETVVEEN THE MIND AND BODY, which being mixed, cannot be properly assigned to the sciences of either."[56] On the other hand, one consequence of this premise was Bacon's belief that minerals, like humans, could copulate and produce offspring—in the most desirable case, gold.

Crooke's account of common sense in the section on the brain in *Microcosmographia* invites comparison with Descartes' account of the intellect. There are two sensitive faculties, Crooke explains: one external and one internal. Where many thinkers would have distinguished five external senses (vision, hearing, smell, taste, touch) from five internal senses (common sense, imagination, fantasy, estimation, memory), Crooke contrasts the singular objects of sense experience (a thing seen, a thing heard, etc.) with the "common or manifold" objects of common sense. In Crooke's model it is "the Primary or *Common sense*" that actually does the thinking:

> this is it which alone maketh the differences of Images as wee call them or Abstracted Notions. She sitteth in the substance of the Braine as in a throne of Maiesty beholding the Formes or Ideas of all things vnder her feet. This is shee that discerneth betwixt sweete and bitter, and distinguisheth white for sweete. This common sense Aristotle compareth to the center of a circle, because the shapes and formes receiued by the outward senses are referred or brought heereunto as vnto their Iudge and Censor.[57]

Descartes' image of the *res cogitans* sitting in the brain like a spectator in a theater may at first seem similar, but Crooke's *Common sense* deals directly with sense experience, with colors (white), tastes (sweet), and colors-tastes (white-sweet), in a way that Descartes' more fastidious intellect does not.[58] The physical brain, in Crooke's estimation, is a complex of tissues with different "temperaments" (hot or cold, moist or dry) and "conformations" (structures) where mental experiences of all kinds quite literally *take place*. The brain may be "the Pallace of the Rational Soule," but the soul uses all of the physical resources available to her, bringing forth "mixt actions by the mediation of the animall spirit" (sig. oo6v). These actions include imagination and memory as well as ratiocination.

Robert Boyle's *Experiments and Considerations Touching Colours* (1664) is often cited as a precursor of Newton's experiments with prisms,[59] but Boyle pursued interests in the subjective experience of color that engaged Newton hardly at all. The space of Newton's investigations was the air; Boyle's included the perceiver's body. As proof that colors are not inherent in objects, Boyle adduces instances when color is perceived in the absence of objects, for example, in dreams or as a result of a blow to the head. Take, for instance, the lady who was talking with some friends when "upon a sudden, all the objects, she looked upon, appeared to her dyed with unusual Colours, some of one kind, and some of another," all of them "bright and vivid" or the ingenious man who claimed that the first sign of infection with the plague is the patient's seeing objects, particularly clothes, "beautifi'd with most glorious Colours, like those of the

Rainbow" or the lady of unquestionable veracity who told Boyle that after a fall "the Images in her Hangings, did, for many daies after, appear to her, if the Room were not extraordinarily darken'd, embellish'd with several offensively vivid Colours, which no body else could see in them."[60] It is the embodiment of color that allows Boyle, later in his book, to attack the usual attribution of black skin to hot climates and to locate blackness no deeper in the body than the epidermis or outer skin (sig. M2) and to speculate that its cause is "some Peculiar and Seminal Impression" (sig. M1), what more recent science knows as genetics. Boyle delights in noting that black people in Africa think white skin so abhorrent that they treat albinos as witches and refuse Europeans permission to be buried on their lands (sigs. M3v–M4).

Green

The midpoint on Aristotle's spectrum is occupied by two writers who think with their bodies as well as their brains and are not afraid to say so. That one of those thinkers is Michel de Montaigne will come as no surprise to modern readers. The other, Edward Herbert, has been written out of the history of philosophy. The systematic attention that Herbert gives to sense experience in his treatise *De Veritate* (*On Truth;* 1624, 1633, 1649, 1659) still seemed smart to Thomas Reid and other philosophers of the Scottish "common sense" school of the mid-eighteenth century, but the main plot line in the history of Western philosophy has cast Herbert's concerns as a residual diversion alongside the emergent rationalism of Hobbes and Locke.

In his essay on the materialist philosophers Democritus and Heraclitus (Book 1, essay 50), Montaigne acknowledges that "soul," the entity-that-perceives, embraces functions "of a lower and meaner Form" as well as "those of a Nobler Note" and insists that one has to pay attention to both sorts of functions in order to "discover" the soul completely and understand her "as she moves her own natural pace."[61] What we know, Montaigne maintains, are not objects out there in the world but our subjective experience of those objects—experience that has color, texture, and taste: "Health, Conscience, Authority, Knowledg, Riches, Beauty, and their contraries, do all strip themselves at their entring into us, and receive a new Robe, and of another Fashion, from every distinct Soul, and of what Colour, Brown, Bright, Green, Dark and Quality, Sharp, Sweet, Deep, or Superficial, as best pleases them, for they are not yet agreed upon any common Standard of Forms, Rules, or Proceedings" (sigs. PP6v–PP7). Elsewhere, in his "Apology for Raimond de Sebonde" (2.12), Montaigne anticipates Wittgenstein by insisting that the relationship between color sensation and color names is unprovable, the ultimate scandal. With respect to color Montaigne sides with the skeptics: "Why shall not they be allow'd, say they, as well as the Dogmatists, one to say Green, another Yellow, and even of those to doubt?" (sig. U4).

It was during his second sojourn in France between 1619 and 1625, as James I's ambassador, that Herbert wrote and published in Latin his treatise *De Veritate, prout Distinguitur a Revelatione, a Verisimili, a Possibili, et a Falsi* (*On Truth in Distinction from Revelation, Probability, Possibility, and Error;* Paris, 1624). The book's contemporary importance is suggested by the three later editions of the Latin text published in London in 1633, 1645, and 1659—and by Locke's singling out Herbert's positions for attack. A French translation, probably by Marin Mersenne, was published at Paris in 1639 and found a generally approving but critical reader in Descartes.[62] What troubled both Descartes and Locke was Herbert's argument that we know external objects only because those objects correspond to preexisting internal counterparts in *sensus,* which Herbert's twentieth-century translator renders—accurately, in my view—as "consciousness." In any act of perception, Herbert argues, three elements must be considered: (1) objects existing independently of the mind, (2) subjectivity, and (3) the media through which objects and faculties are brought into "conformity." Faculties are "aroused" or "awakened" by objects. The reciprocal movement of objects and faculties results in *sensus,* in apprehension or cognition.

In keeping with the equal attention he gives to objects, subjectivity, and media, Herbert recognizes four classes of truth: (1) truth of the thing-in-itself (*veritas rei*), which is unchangeable and absolute; (2) truth of phenomena (*veritas apparentiae*), as objects present themselves to the senses; (3) truth of concept (*veritas conceptus*), whereby external objects and internal perception are brought into conformity; and (4) truth of intellect (*veritas intellectus*), or reason. Where many of his peers—Descartes, for example—would locate ultimate truth in what the intellect perceives, Herbert takes a more contextual view, and he regards reason as the *least* certain form of truth: "We must notice, then, that the deliverances of natural instinct attain the first degree of certainty; those of the internal ways of apprehension the second; those of the external class the third; and those of discursive reasoning the fourth only; for being dependent on the others it is exposed to a greater number of conditions, and is furthest removed from the soul or principle of proof."[63] Here, several centuries too early, are the grounds for Kant's *Critique of Pure Reason* and the phenomenological writings of Husserl, Heidegger, and Merleau-Ponty.

Violet

It is in the range of violet that light begins to dominate earth. In epistemological terms, *veritas rei,* the truth of the-thing-in-itself, begins to obscure bodily sensations of the thing—a process that culminates in Freud's deeply buried id, Jung's shadow, and Lacan's prelinguistic self. Objective proof, not subjective experience, emerges as the criterion for what is worth knowing. In that spectral shift Henry More, René Descartes, Edward Reynolds, Sir John Davies, and Sir William Cornwallis occupy key positions.

More's psyche is even more alacritous than Marvell's soul. Capable of extending himself into space, the psyche plumbs the dark depths of the universe and "lifts herself unto the azure sky," all the while leaving the perceiver's body unmoved: "The soul about it self circumgyrates / Her various forms" ("Psychathanasia," 1.2.42.2; 43.2–4). At first blush, More seems green. The medium he chooses for *A Platonick Song of the Soul* are the nine-line stanzas of *The Faerie Queene,* a poem to which More's ears were attuned by his father reading aloud to the family on winter nights.[64] If *A Platonick Song of the Soul* is philosophy, its appeal is not only to reason but to visual and aural imagination. Just as Spenser's Alma occupies three chambers in a tower with three distinct kinds of furnishings, More's Psyche disposes herself in three woven "films," or veils, that drape downward from heaven to earth ("Psychozoia," 1.1.39.8). An individual's psyche is, in More's view, a particular embodiment of Psyche the World Soul. Both macrocosm and microcosm are in More's view when he describes the distinctive weavings associated with Physis (nature), Arachne (sense perception), and Semele (knowledge). These personalities represent the three souls—nutritive, sensitive, and rational—that most westerners thought of themselves as possessing.

The veil of Physis is described by More as a park-work tapestry of the sort inventoried at Arundel Castle, but animated in this case with the buzzing sounds from Spenser's Chamber of Phantastes:

> The first of these fair films, we *Physis* name.
> Nothing in Nature did you ever spy,

> But there's pourtraid: all beasts wild and tame,
> Each bird is here, and every buzzing fly;
> All forrest-work is in this tapestry . . .
> ("Psychozoia" 1.1.41.1–5).

Thinner and finer is the weave of Arachne's spiderweb of the senses. In the midst of the web sits Haphe, or Touch, "the centre from which all the light / Dispreads, and goodly glorious Forms do flit / Hither and thither" (1.1.49.2–4). The space of that flitting More imagines in several ways: now as a "shining mirour" in which Psyche "sees / All that falls under sense" (1.1.50.1–2), now as a weaving ("All sensible proportions that fine twist / Contains" [1.1.55.8–9]), now as "a just Diapason / For every outward stroke" (1.1.56.7–8). The thinnest weaving of all belongs to Semele, she who loved Jupiter's light so much that she was consumed by his fire. Semele's very name suggests the kind of knowledge that More is ultimately celebrating. What the soul knows, in More's scheme, *is* a simile, a correspondence of sense experience to ideas—to Ideas that Really Exist. The transition from Physis's park-work tapestry to Arachne's web/mirror to Semele's rapturous knowledge is a process of revelation and clarification that finds parallels in the flight of Marvell's bird-soul, in the three chambers of Spenser's Castle of Alma, in St. Paul's declaration "For now we see through a glasse, darkly: but then face to face."[65]

Henry More's initial enthusiasm for Descartes' *Principia Philosophiae* (1644) was tempered as More came to realize what it ultimately meant for Descartes to limit extension in space only to bodies, to material substances. On December 11, 1648, a few months after the publication of *A Platonick Song of the Soul,* More wrote to Descartes to disagree. Why, he asked the French philosopher, shouldn't the soul be able to extend itself into space? Descartes' letter in reply, dated February 5, 1649, is polite but firm: "Commonly when people talk of an extended being, they mean something imaginable. . . . Nothing of this kind can be said about God or about our mind; they cannot be apprehended by the imagination, but only by the intellect. . . . So we clearly conclude that no incorporeal substances are in any strict sense extended."[66] One notes the distinctions: "mind," not "psyche"; "intellect," not "imagination." In a letter to another of his English correspondents, William Cavendish (it was into his body that his wife Margaret imagined her soul to transmigrate in *The Blazing World*), Descartes locates quite precisely in the human body the sensations that More thinks that he feels in the azure sky. "I am convinced," Descartes writes to Cavendish, "that hunger and thirst are felt in the same manner as colours, sound, smells, and in general all the objects of the external senses, that is, by means of nerves, stretched like fine threads from the brain to all the other parts of the body" (3:274). So much for Arachne's cosmic web.

Descartes' position in the spectrum of seventeenth-century thought is more complicated than it is often made out to be.[67] On the one hand, Descartes' criteria for objects of knowledge, as we noted in chapter one, are two: (1) clarity and (2) distinctness. In *Principles of Philosophy* (1644) he gives these twin criteria precise definitions: "A perception which can serve as the basis for a certain and indubitable judgement [*sic*] needs to be not merely clear but also distinct. I call a perception 'clear' when it is present and accessible to the attentive mind. . . . I call a perception 'distinct' if, as well as being clear, it is so sharply separated from all other perceptions that it contains within itself only what is clear."[68] On the other hand, Descartes accepts acts of imagination and passion as "thoughts." Where Aristotle and scholastic thinkers posited three souls—vegetative, animal, and rational—Descartes assumes only one. In such a move he was anticipated by Aquinas. Descartes begins his treatise on *The Passions of* the *Soule* (note the definite article) in established Aristotelian fashion, by attending first to the body. Then he turns to his true subject: "there remaines nothing in us, which we ought to attribute to our Soul, unless our thoughts."[69] Those thoughts or "apprehensions," as we noted in chapter one, are divided into two sorts: those caused by the body and those caused by the soul (sig. B12). Descartes' appreciation for both sorts of thoughts is indicated in several of the many letters he exchanged with Princess Elizabeth, daughter of Elizabeth, Queen of Bohemia, whose portrait as a young woman appears as plate 10.

By anyone's standards, Elizabeth, Princess Palatine (1618–1680) was a serious-minded person. To judge by her correspondence and the books she inspired, she was especially interested in the passions: how they connect soul with body, how they are experienced in day-to-day living, how they color rational judgment, how they impinge on the duties of rulers to their subjects. Meeting Descartes while both of them were living in The Hague, Elizabeth read his *Meditations on First Philosophy* and put to him some pressing questions that led first to an exchange of letters and ultimately to *The Passions of the Soul,* which is dedicated to her. In his letters to Elizabeth, if not in his treatise, Descartes betrays a candor and irony that one might not expect from the ruler-wielding creator of Cartesian coordinates. If Princess Elizabeth wishes to understand the union of the soul with the body, Descartes writes in a letter dated June 28, 1643, she has to do more than *think* about it; she has to *live* it: "I can say with truth that the chief rule I have always observed in my studies, which I think has been the most useful to me in acquiring what knowledge I have, has been never to spend more than a few hours a day in the thoughts which occupy the imagination and a few hours a *year* on those which occupy the intellect alone. I have given all the rest of my time to the relaxation of the senses and the repose of the mind" (3:227, emphasis added). Be that as it may, Descartes' collapsing Aristotle's three souls into one figures as a strategic move in the shift from soul to mind as the entity-that-perceives.

On matters epistemological, Descartes was not Elizabeth's only correspondent. It was at her behest that Edward Reynolds published *A Treatise of the Passions and Faculties of the Soul of Man* (1640, 1647, 1650, 1651, 1656, 1658), which offers a more sanguine account of the workings of passion, fantasy, and imagination than Descartes' *Passions.* Written in the 1620s, the treatise was not published until 1640, ten years after Reynolds had succeeded John Donne as preacher at Lincoln's Inn. In 1660, he became Bishop of Norwich. Reynolds acknowledges the disasters that ensue when passions anticipate reason rather than serve under reason's direction, but he also recognizes the usefulness of passions "for the heating and enlivening of Vertue, for adding spirit and edge to all good undertakings, and blessing them with an happier issue."[70] In the course of his treatise, Reynolds, like La Chambre and Descartes, devotes whole chapters to individual passions, including love, hatred, desire, delight, sorrow, hope, boldness, fear, and anger.

Even more remarkable is the scope Reynolds gives to "fancy" or imagination. The office of imagination is twofold: to assist the understanding and to stimulate the will (sigs. C4v–D1). With respect to the understanding, fancy has a "double prerogative": in the form of *phantasmata* it captures the "quicknesse and volubilitie" of thoughts, even as it fixes objects for meditation by the understanding. By "thoughts," Reynolds means "those springings and glances of the heart, grounded on the sudden representation of sundry different objects" (sig. D3v). Reynolds's model of perception, like Thomas Wright's, accommodates the heart as well as the brain, passion as well as reason. Quickness of apprehension might seem to be the work of reason, Reynolds acknowledges,

> yet the Imagination hath indeed the greatest interest in it: For, though the Act of Apprehending be the proper worke of the Vnderstanding, yet the forme and qualitie of that Act . . . namely, the lightnesse, volubilitie, and suddennesse thereof, proceeds from the immediate restlesnesse of the

> Imagination; as is plaine, by the continuall varietie of Dreames and other Fancies, wherein the Facultie is the principall worker. (sigs. D4–D4v)

Reynolds's emphasis on quickness, lightness, volubility, suddenness, variety anticipates Marvell's green thought. "The Imagination," Reynolds concludes, "is a Facultie boundlesse, and impatient of any imposed limits, save those which it selfe maketh" (sig. D4v).

To be sure, Reynolds never loses sight of Plato's metaphysic of light in placing the faculty of understand "above" the passions and the workings of imagination. He frequently likens understanding to the irradiating of objects by the sun. Nonetheless, the human capacity for knowledge requires, in Reynolds's scheme, darkness as well as light. As Aristotle observes with respect to conveyance of light through the medium of air,

> there is required a mixture of Contraries in the Ayre; it must not bee too light, lest it weaken and too much disgregate or spread the sense; nor yet too dark, lest it contract and lock it up: But there must be a kinde of middle Temper; cleerenesse of the Medium for conveyance, and yet some degrees of Darknesse for qualification of the Object. Even so also the Objects of mans Understanding must participate of the two contraries, *Abstraction* and *Materiality.* (sig. KKK2; original emphasis)

As for the Countess Palatine herself, to judge from her dealings with Descartes and Reynolds, she belongs in the black-to-gray range of the spectrum, along with Margaret Cavendish and Anne Conway. At least she prompted Descartes and Reynolds to take positions that are greener than one might otherwise have expected from a professional philosopher and an Anglican bishop.

The nimbleness and alacrity that Reynolds attributes to the soul is no less palpable in Sir John Davies' advice in verse on how to know oneself. *Nosce Teipsum* (the complete text was published in 1599, 1602, 1608, 1619, 1622; only excerpts were published in 1653), subtitled *An Oracle Expounded in Two Elegies,* offers an account of perception that celebrates the soul's sensuously physical alacrity as it moves through the world even as Davies keeps a steady gaze on the metaphysical status of truth. Davies' soul possesses all the quickness and volubility of Marvell's, Henry More's, and Edward Reynolds's as it plumbs the depths of creation, soars into the sky, sweeps across oceans from China to Spain. Davies' recurrent metaphors for the soul in flight are extension (1.438, 1.441), disembodied freedom (1.509 ff.), embracement (1.525), and fire (1.539).[71] Davies' soul gathers knowledge through the senses, but she transforms that knowledge—"sublimates" is Davies' alchemical word (1.538)—into a pure essence that is all her own: "For though our eyes can nought but Colours see; / Yet colours give them not their powre of sight" (1.325–26). *That* power belongs to the soul. Mankind is the "horizon" between angels and the rest of creation (1.881–84). As such, the soul is situated in the human body like a sunbeam in the ambient air. Winds (is Davies thinking of passions?) do nothing to change that diffusion:

> Still resting whole, when blowes the Aire devide;
> Abiding pure when th'Aire is most corrupted;
> Throughout the Aire her beames dispersing wide,
> And when the Aire is tost, not interrupted;
> So doth the piercing *Soule* the bodie fill. . . .
> (1.913–17)

In Davies' verse, in its imagistic richness as well as in its argument, the Aristotelian body embraces Christian Platonism.

A deeper hue of violet can be witnessed in the books of essays (1600, 1606, 1610, 1616, 1617, 1631, 1632) that Sir William Cornwallis modeled on Montaigne's. Cornwallis maintains Montaigne's willingness to take up almost any subject and bring to that subject a genial skepticism. About words, for example. In an astonishing anticipation of Lacan, Cornwallis seems to imagine a time before there was speech and to question the capacity of speech to connect members of speech communities:

> If we were now, as wee were once, though speach should bee superfluous for all should have beene good, and I thinke then, all knowledges should have seene trueth in a like quantitie) yet it had not beene so daungerous: for our vices are the Ocean, our wordes the Barkes transporting, and trafficking sin with him, and imperfection with imperfection: so that multitudes, and Assemblies (where talke turnes the minde outward) are as perillous to an honest minde, as to receive education in a Bordello.[72]

Unlike Montaigne, however, Cornwallis believes that knowledge through reason is possible. To the soul and to the body belong two distinct kinds of knowledge, reason and affection (sig. X7). "It is Affection that hath skil of colours, and hath set up the estimation of White and Red" in amorous poetry and painting (sig. o5). As for green, Cornwallis regards it as "a colour of the Soule" and associates it with the "fantasticness" of youth: "It is Greene Thoughtes in Greene yeares, or at the farthest, greene Thoughts in a seare Substance" (sig. N1). Through the exercise of reason, "fantasticness" matures into wisdom, resolution, and constancy. Green ripens, first into violet and then into red.

Red

The account of the brain that Thomas Browne, Doctor of Physic, offers in *Nature's Cabinet Unlock'd* (1657) brings us to a more matter-of-fact position in which the workings of sensation, common sense, fancy, imagination, memory, and the passions are still being acknowledged even as primary attention is turned to the body as a physical entity subject to empirical investigation. What *really* matters in perception, so this shift in attention implies, happens in the brain, not in the limbs, the sinews, or the heart. Thus Browne locates "the Animal faculty," or workings of the soul, in particular ventricles or "bellies" of the brain.[73] Spirits may retain in Browne's account their origins in the heart and may be "made more lucid, like to celestial flames of fire" by their passage through the arteries, but their "receptacles" are located in the anterior cavities of the brain (sig. o6v). In sum: the brain is "the treasure of the animal spirits: therefore by right the brain is the noblest of all members; whose excellency if *Aristotle* had known, he would never have written the nobility and dignity of the heart" (sig. o8v).

Browne's empiricism with respect to perception is anticipated by William Harvey, in his account of the circulation of the blood, and seconded by Isaac Newton, in his account of the workings of light on the retina. Realizing that his mechanical explanation of how the heart pumps blood through the veins is not going to work very well with received ideas about *spiritus* circulating from brain to heart and back again, Harvey carefully states at the outset of *Exercitatio Anatomica de Motu Cordis et Sanguinis in Animalibus* (1628) that "the blood that has Spirit is no lesse blood." No one denies, Harvey says, that blood being pumped through the veins toward the heart is "imbued with Spirits." The same is true of blood being pumped from the heart through the arteries: "Albeit the blood in the *arteries* do swell with greater store of Spirits, yet those Spirits are to be thought inseparable from the blood, as those which are in the *veins;* and that Blood and Spirit make one body, as whey and butter in milk, or heat and water in warm water, by which the *arteries* are fill'd, and the distribution of which body from the *heart* the *arteries* do perform, and this body is nothing else but blood."[74] Harvey is thus careful to preserve *spiritus* as the body's intercommunication system. Even Thomas Willis, whom a recent biographer has credited with relocation of the soul from heart to brain in anatomical investigations of the 1660s, could not get along without *spiritus* as an explanation for cognition.[75] Newton, in his 1671 report to the Royal Society about his experiments over the previous five years, is similarly conservative. He provides precise measurements of apertures, prism sizes, and widths of bands of light but refuses to speculate on what happens beyond the retina. In effect, Newton limits himself to the *noumena* of physics as distinct from the *phenomena* of vision. "Whoever thought any quality to be a *heterogeneous* aggregate, such as Light is discovered to be," Newton exclaims. "But, to determine more absolutely, what Light is, after what manner refracted, and by what modes or actions it produceth in our minds the Phantasms of Colours, is not so easie. And I shall not mingle conjectures with certainties."[76]

In moral and ethical writers the distancing tactics of Browne, Harvey, and Newton translate into a stoical sense of dislocation in which soul and body present themselves as two distinct, indeed adversarial, entities. Pierre de La Primaydaye's *The French Academie* (1580; published in English in 1586, 1589, 1594, 1601, 1602, 1605, 1614, 1618) includes standard accounts of the five external senses, the five internal senses, *spiritus,* the passions, the brain, and cognition. The frame within which this information is presented, however, constantly invites the reader to abstract the soul from the body. Like Aquinas and Descartes, La Primaudaye collapses Aristotle's three souls—vegetative, sensitive, and intellectual—into one, but he describes the workings of this all-inclusive soul primarily in terms of reason—and hence describes it as largely clueless about its vegetative and sensitive functions. "Because there is no nature in us more high and excellent then our soule," he remarks, "none can know it as it is, but onely the creator that made it, especially that reasonable part of the soule, wherein the image of God is more lively, and shineth more cleerely then in the rest." If God can know the human soul in a way that the human soul cannot know itself, one would think that a human soul could know its vegetative and sensitive workings. Not so. "But because there is no part in us above that, we cannot perceive and know how it useth the internall senses, with their vessels & instruments."[77] I know, La Primaydaye says, and I know that I know, but I can never really know *how* that I know. Here are the beginnings of Freud's id, Jung's shadow, and Lacan's prelinguistic "I"/eye.

The red line separating soul from body is registered in the very design of Sir Kenelm Digby's *Two Treatises* (1644): one concerning "*the nature of bodies,*" the other "*the nature of mans soule.*" Having met and conversed with both Descartes and Hobbes during a sojourn in Paris in the 1630s, Digby took advantage of political exile in France during the Interregnum to complete his attempt to combine Democritus's atomist theory of matter with Aristotle's common sense psychology and Descartes' rigorous empiricism. The result is a vertiginous cobbling together of materialism and idealism that is always threatening to fall apart under the reader's feet. Digby's atomist explanation of sensation would put him in the blue range. Despite his admiration for Descartes, he criticizes the French master's account of sensations as blows or strokes against a "kernel" suspended in the brain. Instead, Digby argues that atoms of the thing being perceived actually enter the perceiver's body through pores in the sense organs, intermixing themselves with the spirits, and making physical contact with the brain. These material presences Digby calls "tinctures."[78] In Digby's account of memory little "similitudes" are imagined to be "wheeling and swimming about" in the watery caves of the brain (sig. NN3).

This materialist bias prompts Digby to accept, despite his acquaintance with contemporary experiments with light (sig. MM1v), an explanation of color that comes straight out of Aristotle. Color is thus a property of objects, varying according to the penetrability of objects' mass and surface reflectivity (sig. KK3), while varying presentations of color result from different proportions of white to black.[79] Digby may be much more interested than Descartes in the material bases of sensation, but he seconds Descartes and Hobbes in positing three sequential stages of knowledge-formation—"apprehensions," "enunciations," and "discourse"—that quickly turn sensation into words and words into propositions. Not surprisingly, books figure in Digby's judgment as the greatest of human achievements (sig. YY2). Like Descartes, Digby can think about thinking without a body: "Nay, if all the beautifull fantasmes, which fly about so nimbly in our braine, be nothing else but signes vnto in [*sic*] our soule, of what is without vs; it is euident, that though peraduenture she would not without their seruice, exercise that which by errour we missename *Thinking;* yet the very same soule and thinker might be without them all: and consequently, without braine also" (sig. FFF4v). Take away the body, and you still have "a *substance,* a *thinker,* an *Ego,* or *I,* that in it selfe is no whit diminished, by being (as I may say) stripped out of the case it was enclosed in" (sig. FFF5; original emphasis).

The principles of interpretation implied by such a statement are worked out in Digby's *Observations on the 22. Stanza in the 9th. Canto of the 2d. Book of Spencers Faery Queen,* published the same year as *Two Treatises.* The "frame" of Alma's Castle, a circle atop a quadrilateral atop a triangle, is praised for the way it articulates the relation of soul (a perfect circle) to body (an imperfect figure) via the four humors (a quadrilateral). Digby reads Spenser's verse first by apprehending Spenser's images, then by giving those images names, finally by turning words into rational propositions.

Yellow

Sense experience recedes even further in the yellow philosophizing of Fulke Greville, Thomas Hobbes, and Ralph Cudworth. All of them devalue sense experience in favor of "higher" modes of knowing. For Greville in "A Treatie of Humane Learning" (probably written in the 1620s, published 1633) sensation and imagination are inherently corrupt. Greville's verse account of how mankind comes to know the world and what it *does* with that knowledge rehearses the usual Aristotelian-Galenic model of perception in which sense experience is processed by imagination, imbued with passions, stored in memory, referred to judgment, and acted upon by the will. At every stage, corruption of the flesh clouds the possibility of clear understanding and right action. Sense, "Mans first instructor," is the most deceptive faculty of all, precisely because it seems to the perceiver to be perfect, "So that by iudging Sense herein perfection, / Man must deny his Natures imperfection."[80] This tainted knowledge is passed along, insuring that each stage falls short of truth. False colors give Greville his conceit for charting this progression. Imagination is "so shadowed with selfe-application / As makes her pictures still too foule, or faire" (10.7–8). Memory, deceived by this "disguis'd intelligence" (14.3), yields no "Images" (14.4) suitable for instruction. Understanding may be possessed of "generall truths; yet haue they such a staine / From our corruption, as all light they lose" (15.4–5). The denigration of color continues in Greville's critique of what thinkers, writers, and statesmen do with this corrupted knowledge. Color and shadow give Greville the images he needs to portray art in the service of pernicious political power,

> where wit serveth might,
> To shake diuine foundations, and humane,
> By painting vices, and by shadowing right,
> Which tincture of Probabile prophane,
> Vnder false colour giuing truth such rates,
> As Power may rule in chiefe through all Estates.
> (41.1–6)

For Greville, as for his friend Sir Philip Sidney, the true end of poesy is delightful teaching, an enterprise that involves not only clear vision but regulation of the body's passions. Poesy, in Greville's account, is a framing of

Ideas-with-a-capital-I, "Which in a glasse, shows Nature how to fashion / Her selfe againe, by ballancing of passion" (114.7–8). Greville's mirror lacks the brilliance of More's. Touch stops at the cold glass.

Where Greville sees corruption, stain, and tincture, Thomas Hobbes sees necessity. After 1,800 years of Aristotle, how else to begin an epistemology than with sense experience? Hobbes's radical move in *Humane Nature* (1650, 1651, 1684) and *Leviathan* (1651, 1680; Latin translation, 1676, 1678, 1681) is to deny that there *is* any other reality than what the senses perceive. "*Whatsoever accidents* or *qualities* our Senses make us think there be in the *World*," Hobbes declares, "they be *not* there, but are *seeming* and *apparitions* onely."[81] Color figures as a case in point:

> [T]he things that really *are* in the world without us, are those *motions* by which these seemings are caused. And this is the *great deception of the Sense*, which also is to be by Sense *corrected:* for as Sense telleth me, when I see *directly*, that the Colour seemeth to *be* in the Object; so also Sense telleth me, when I see by *reflection*, that Colour is not in the Object. (sigs. B9v–B10; original emphasis)

Such a claim would seem to place Hobbes solidly at the black-to-gray end of the spectrum, in the company of Burton, La Chambre, Margaret Cavendish, and Francis Glisson. Where Hobbes parts company with these body-centered materialists is his argument that the stuff of thought is words—a "linguistic turn" three hundred years *avant la lettre*. For Hobbes, as we noted in chapter one, imagination is no more than a fading sense impression, "a Conception by *little* and *little decaying*, or growing more *obscure*" (sig. C1v), as he defines it in *Humane Nature*. These conceptions are situated by Hobbes, not in "soul," but in "mind" (sig. C4). What fixes conceptions in the mind is words—or rather "marks" that men make to distinguish one conception from another (sig. C11). Hobbes did not need Derrida to tell him that marks come before voices: "A *name* or appellation therefore is the *voice* of a man *arbitrary*, imposed for a *mark* to bring into his minde some conceptions concerning the thing on which it is imposed" (sig. C11). From there the way ahead is clear: from sensations to conceptions to marks to propositions to syllogisms to science, defined by Hobbes as "knowledge of the *truth of Propositions*" (sig. D6). The foundation of science may rest in "*motions* by which these seemings are caused," but Hobbes is primarily interested in what happens next, when seemings have become words.

The deconstructive implications of Hobbes's propositions were not lost on contemporaries like Ralph Cudworth. Cudworth's positions as Regius Professor of Hebrew at Cambridge from 1645 to 1688 and Master of Christ's College from 1654 gave him plenty of time to work on disproving what he called "the *Atheistical System* of the World" as argued by Democritus and Hobbes. In that atheistic system, Cudworth complains, "sensible *Ideas* of Light and Colours . . . seem plainly to be nothing else but our own *Phancies, Passions,* and *Sensations* however they be vulgarly mistaken for Qualities in the Bodies without us."[82] In place of that, Cudworth set out to demonstrate *The* True *Intellectual System of the Universe* (emphasis added), an enterprise that had realized barely a quarter of the projected scheme when Cudworth published in 1678 the 590,000 words he already had on hand. If sense experience were the only foundation of knowledge, Cudworth wonders, how would we ever arrive at abstract concepts? Hobbes's answer is straightforward enough: through marks, voices, names, words, propositions, syllogisms. Cudworth, however, cannot let go of the conviction that there is more to things than how they seem to us. Democritus and latter-day atomists ought to know that, he says. How else could they conceive of atoms, things that cannot be seen? "And had not these Atheists been Notorious Dunces, in that *Atomick Philosophy* which they so much pretend to, they would clearly have learn'd from thence, That *Sense* is not *Knowledge* and *Understanding,* nor the *Criterion* of Truth as to *Sensible* things themselves; it reaching not to the *Essence* or *Absolute Nature* of them, but only taking notice of their *Outside,* and perceiving its own *Passions* from them" (1.4.1, sig. ZZZ1). On the contrary, reason and understanding "[discover] to us that there is nothing in the Objects themselves like to those forementioned *Sensible Ideas;* and resolves all Sensible Things into *Intelligible Principles*" (1.4.1, sig. ZZZ1). Reading a page or two of any book, Cudworth claims, will demonstrate as much. Does every single word correspond to "a *Phantasm,* or *Sensible Idea*" (1.4.1, sig. ZZZ1v)? Of course not. Take, for example, "God." Who has seen the intelligible principle for which this word stands? Hobbes's words, in Cudworth's critique, have their limits.

White

The ascent toward out-of-body, brain-only enlightenment in Greville, Hobbes, and Cudworth reaches its apogee in Puritan polemicists on the residual right and John Locke on the emergent left.

To misogyny and homophobia on Phillip Stubbes's professional résumé, add chromophobia. Presented as a traveler's account of a trip to dystopia, Stubbes's *The Anatomie of Abuses . . . in a Verie Famous Ilande Called Ailgna* [read *Anglia*] (1583, 1584, 1585, 1595)[83] puts into the mouth of his spokesman Philoponus descriptions of clothing in a, literally, dazzling array of colors: hats with crowns "nowe blacke, now white, now russet, now red, now gréene, now yellowe, now this, nowe that, neuer content with one colour, or fashion two dayes to an ende" (sig. D7v), topped by "a great bunche of feathers of diuerse and sundrie colours" (sig. D8); doublets "pincked and laced with all kinde of costly lace of diuers and sundry colours" (sig. E2v); "gay" ("bright or lively-looking, esp. in colour" [*OED*, "gay," 3]) hosen or pants (sig. E3v); shoes, "wherof some be of white leather, some of black, and some of red: some of black veluet, some of white, some of red, some of gréen" (sig. E4); coats and jerkins "diuerse in colors" (sig. E4v); cloaks "of dyuerse and sundry colors, white, red, tawnie, black, greene, yellowe, russet, purple, violet, and infynite other colors" (sig. E6v): boot-hosen or leg-coverings "wrought all ouer, from the gartering place vpward, with nedle worke, clogged with silk of all colors, with birds, foules, beasts, and antiques purtrayed all ouer in comlie sorte" (sig. E7). Not so in former times, eighty to a hundred years before, "when men went clothed in black, or white frize coates, in hosen of Huswyues carzie of the same colore, that the shéep bore them" (sig. E1). ("Carzie," or kersey, was a coarse wool fabric [*OED*, "kersey," 1].)

Among the colors favored by the denizens of Aiglna, it is green in particular that drives Stubbes to distraction. Take, for example, Lords of Misrule. On holidays in Aiglna "all the wilde-heds of the Parish" will elect a captain whom they treat as a king by casting themselves as the king's court. "Then euerie one of these his men, he intresseth with his liueries, of greene, yellow or some other light wanton colour" (sig. P2). The retinue deck themselves out in scarves, ribbons, laces, gold rings, and bells and parade around the parish as hobby-horses, dragons, and other "Antiques" (sig. P2), accompanied all the while by pipers and drummers. On Mayday, Whitsuntide, and other holidays the young men and maidens of the parish, accompanied by older men and wives, betake themselves "to the woods, groues, hils & mountains, where they spend all the night in plesant pastimes, & in the morning they return bringing w^{t} them birch & branches of trees" (sig. P3v). Their "cheifest iewel" is a Maypole with strings from top to bottom "sometime painted with variable colours" (sig. P3v). As the severity of his judgments might indicate, Stubbes would prefer a black-and-white world. Better still would be an all-white world. To Philoponus's descriptions of chromatic riot in Ailgna, his interlocutor Spudeus makes this response: "As in a *Camelion* are said to be all coulours, saue white, so I think, in these people are all things els, saue Uertue and christian sobrietie" (sig. F5). Among others of Stubbes's ilk—John Rainolds, William Perkins, and William Prynne—there are doubtless shades of difference. But who wants to know that much about white?

White, it appears, was John Locke's favorite color. "*Whiteness*" comes first in the list of "*Ideas*" that Locke uses as examples in his treatment "Of *Ideas* in general, and their Original" in Book 2, chapter 1, of *An Essay concerning Humane Understanding* (1690, 1694, 1695, 1700, 1706, 1710, 1715, 1721, 1726, 1731, 1735, 1741, 1748). Next in order come "*Hardness, Sweetness, Thinking, Motion, Man, Elephant, Army, Drunkenness,* and others"—a suggestive list in which Hannibal seems to be a ghostly presence.[84] Later on in *Humane Understanding,* Locke narrates a scene of writing that establishes, once and for all, how ideas can exist without a body to think them. The date is July 10, 1688, and Locke is sitting or standing at his desk, paper before him, pen in hand. Looking around the room, or out the window, he can see water. The very fact that he is writing down his thoughts prompts Locke to consider that ideas exist outside the thinker's own person: ideas, he comes to realize, exist *among* people. Knowledge may begin with sensation—near the beginning of *Humane Understanding* Locke devotes several pages to disproving Edward Herbert's notion of innate principles of perception—but writing changes sensations into something quite different.

Writing seems to be an intimate, entirely personal act: "Thus I see, whilst I write this, I can change the Appearance of the Paper; and by designing the Letters, tell before-hand what new *Idea* it shall exhibit the very next moment, barely by my drawing the Pen over it." Once the marks have been made, however, Locke feels a sense of estrangement from the thoughts that moments ago were *his:* "they are not barely the Sport and Play of my Imagination, when I find, that the Characters that were made at the pleasure of my own Thoughts, do not obey them: nor yet cease to be, whenever I shall fansie it, but continue to affect my Senses constantly and regularly, according to the Figures I made them." On paper, the thoughts exist whether the writer would have it so or not. Another person can read them, and they will then become *that* person's thoughts. The sense experiences that inspired the markings on paper have disappeared. Locke concludes: "if we add, that the sight of those shall, from another Man, draw such Sounds, as I before-hand design they shall stand for, there will be little reason left to doubt, that those Words, I write, do really exist without me, when they cause a long series of regular Sounds to affect my Ears, which could not be the effect of my Imagination, nor could my Memory retain them in that order" (sig. SS4v). Ideas that have been inked on paper take on a life—or rather a nonlife—of their own.

Where Hobbes talked about "conceptions," Locke talks about "the materials of Reason and Knowledge," "*the materials of thinking*" (sig. F3; original emphasis). These materials, he explains, come in two sorts: (1) sensation and (2) reflection (sigs. F3–F3v). Sensation apprehends particulars; reflection transforms particulars into propositions (sig. TT1v). In both cases, the materials that Locke has in mind are paper and ink. In his attack on Herbert, Locke ridicules supposedly universal principles that turn out to be "Doctrines, that have been derived from no better original, than the Superstition of a Nurse, or the Authority of an old Woman" (sig. E1). Children accept these doctrines as truths, "for white Paper receives any Characters" (sig. E1). In effect, Locke imagines the mind to be a blank piece of paper on which experience is written. As traces on that paper propositions have greater staying power than sensations.

In the scene of writing in Book 4, chapter 11, Locke is reminded by some water that lies in his line of vision that yesterday he also saw water and that "water" still exists. About the colored bubble on yesterday's water, however, Locke is less certain:

> [I]t will also be equally true, that a certain number of very fine Colours did exist, which at the same time I saw upon a bubble of that Water: But being now quite out of sight of both the Water and Bubles too, it is no more certainly known to me that the Water doth exist, then that the Bubbles or Colours therein; it being no more necessary that Water should exist to day, because it existed yesterday, than that the Colours or Bubbles exist to day, because they existed yesterday, though it be exceedingly much more probable, because Water hath been observed to continue long in Existence, but Bubbles, and the Colours on them, quickly cease to be. (sig. TT1v)

To affirm that water exists—a proposition—is thus easier than to affirm that colors exist—an evanescent sensation. It is no more *necessary* that water exist than colors, but much more *probable.* Ultimately Locke's criterion of truth is a proposition's lasting power: "For names being supposed to stand perpetually for the same *Ideas;* and the same *Ideas* having immutably the same Habitudes one to another, Propositions, concerning any abstract *Ideas* that are once true, must needs be eternal Verities" (sig. TT2). "Habitudes" have everything to do with habits and nothing to do with habitation. Locke's verities have been blanched of sensation in a stroke of black ink.

From black to gray to blue to green to violet to red to yellow to white: the spectrum of thought about thought in sixteenth- and seventeenth-century England invites several general observations. First of all, the spectrum cannot be read from left to right chronologically. Textbook histories of philosophy may plot the triumph of scientific empiricism in the seventeenth century, but one of the latest writers, Margaret Cavendish, occupies the left end of the spectrum in the company of a sixteenth-century practitioner of Galenic medicine, while John Locke at the right end shares space with one of the earliest, most intemperate writers, Phillip Stubbes. All told, Raymond Williams's observation seems just: at a given cultural moment one can identify residual, dominant, and emergent ideas existing simultaneously. And often within the works of a single person. If one writer in this group deserves an award for "Most Confused," it is probably that atomist Christian Platonist Aristotelian empiricist, Sir Kenelm Digby. Point number two: medical writers, with their professional interest in the human body, tend to occupy the black end of the spectrum; moral and ethical writers, with their anxieties about the human body, the white end. Harvey and Browne, the two seeming exceptions among the physicians, both recognize that cognition necessarily involves the body, even if they choose not to locate precise functions in particular organs and tissues. Among the moral and ethical writers, only Montaigne occupies a position infraviolet. A third general observation concerns the scientists. If Bacon and Crooke are drafted into this group, it is remarkable how many of them (only Newton stands outside) are situated in the blue range. Finally, one cannot escape noticing how all of the women in this survey gravitate toward the black end. As diverse as their departure points and strategies may be, Margaret Cavendish, the Countess Palatine, and Anne Conway never seem to have forgot that thought happens in place, in time, in a body. As for the poets and playwrights, their provisional places on the spectrum will become clearer in the chapters that follow.

"This *Light* and *Darkness* in our Chaos join'd, / What shall divide?" For such a task, as Pope knew, God comes in handy, especially when he has been internalized as "The *God* within the *Mind*." In the absence of God, Saussure can fill in, even though he makes no guarantees that his divisions are true and lasting. But why not embrace the chaos? Where Pope sees chaos it is just as possible to see capaciousness. The spectrum of thought about thought that we have surveyed in this chapter suggests three conclusions:

- the relationship between this body that I can see and touch (and sometimes hear, smell, and taste) and the thoughts that I have constitutes the great paradox of being human,
- an entity-that-perceives may always seem present to me but its names and its nature (ψυχή, *anima,* mind, *Geist*) are not the same in all times and all places,
- my knowledge of the world about me is more nuanced, more responsible to the other inhabitants of that world, and hence more livable when I stop drawing lines between subject and object.

True objectivity, Donna Haraway has argued in her feminist critique of science, is not to be found through microscopes, telescopes, and digital technology but through a frank acceptance of the capacities, the limitations, the situatedness of the perceiver who uses those devices: "objectivity turns out to be about particular and specific embodiment and definitely not about the false vision promising transcendence of all limits and responsibility. . . . Feminist objectivity is about limited location and situated knowledge, not about transcendence and splitting of subject and object. It allows us to become answerable for what we learn how to see."[85] Historical phenomenology accepts that political challenge, and it finds in Edward Herbert, Margaret Cavendish, the Countess Palatine, and other seventeenth-century thinkers viable alternatives to the disembodied epistemologies of our own time and place.

CHAPTER FOUR

Green Spectacles

Ut pictura poesis: no Renaissance commonplace was more common than the claim that poetry is like a picture. In early modern English, as Lucy Gent reminds us, "picture" was an extraordinarily capacious word. It could refer not only to painting and sculpture but to tapestry, heraldry, embroidery, marquetry, *imprese,* emblems—and things made out of words: "It could mean, in short, anything to do with a visual image, though not necessarily a visible image; a poet's description could be a picture, too."[1] The best known source for the idea that picture and poetry are alike was Horace's epistle to Piso and his sons, known to history as Horace's "Ars Poetica." "As Painting, so is Poësie" goes the passage in Ben Jonson's translation, published in 1640.[2] It was an idea that had curiously strong appeal until eighteenth-century aestheticians like Shaftesbury and Lessing sorted out the arts according to distinctions among media—words versus paint versus musical tones versus body movements.[3] Most people still accept these distinctions as common sense.

That was hardly the case in the seventeenth century. Plutarch's version of an observation originally made by Simonides of Keos—"*Poema pictura loquens, pictura poema silens*" (poetry a speaking picture, picture a silent poem)—commanded such wide assent that Philip Sidney is exceptional in labeling it only a metaphor.[4] Horace, for his part, keeps the tenor and the vehicle distinct. In the ensuing passage that explains his famous phrase, Horace sets in place three variables—space, light value, and time—that quite clearly are being taken over from one domain, painting, and are being applied to another domain, poetry. If poetry is like painting, it is because the reader of poetry, in act an act of judgment, makes it so. Here is the complete passage in Jonson's translation:

> As Painting, so is Poësie. Some mans hand
> Will take you more, the neerer that you stand;
> As some the farther off: This loves the darke;
> This, fearing not the subtlest Judges marke,
> Will in the light be view'd: This, once, the sight
> Doth please; this, ten times over, will delight.
> (539–43)

In Horace's formulation, poetry and painting are alike because perception of both happens within coordinates of space, light value, and time. About space and time it is easy enough to agree. But light value? What does the perception of poetry have to do with light value?

Jonson can help us get our bearings. Among his own collection of commonplaces, *Timber,* Jonson includes a version of Horace's famous dictum: "*Poetry,* and *Picture,* are Arts of a like nature," Jonson writes.[5] But Jonson's reasons for why that is the case are not Horace's. Quoting Plutarch's tag about poetry as a speaking picture and picture as "a mute Poesie" (609), Jonson locates the similarity between the two art forms in a common act of mimesis: "For they both invent, faine, and devise many things, and accommodate all they invent to the use, and service of nature" (609–10). Light value comes into play when Jonson proceeds to distinguish the two entities he has just conflated: "Yet of the two, the Pen is more noble then the Pencill. For that [the pen] can speake to the Understanding: the other [the 'pencil' or paintbrush] but to the Sense" (610). Horace's original *sententia* has been altered to read "As picture is to sense, so poesie is to understanding." Jonson's word "speake" specifies just what it is that finally makes poesy superior: words. By this account, St. John got it wrong. In the beginning was sensation; in the end is the word.[6]

In plotting a progression from sensation to verbal judgment, Jonson is doing no more, of course, than repeating the main accounts of perception that we surveyed in chapter three. Along the spectrum of seventeenth-century writers (see figure 10), the superiority Jonson accords to words would probably place him in the red range, in the company of Browne, Harvey, Newton, and Digby. And yet in the very next entry in *Timber,* Jonson grants picture not only chronological and ontological primacy over poetry ("Picture is the invention of Heaven: the most ancient, and most a kinne to Nature") but power that goes beyond words ("it doth so enter, and penetrate the inmost affection . . . as sometimes it orecomes the power of speech, and oratory" [610]). Jonson's ambivalence about the relationship between picture and poetry—his assumption, on the one hand, that acts of perception begin with sensation but end with words and his acknowledgment, on the other, that picture possesses a power that can disable words—stands as yet another sign of the seventeenth-century crisis of consciousness. However intently Jonson and his contemporaries wanted to believe that poems are pictures and pictures are words, there remains the physical fact that black lines and colored pigments on the one hand and words on the other are not the same stuff at all. A certain configuration of line and color may gesture toward the same thing that a certain word does, but colors don't *name* things. Words do that. Bodies of perceivers occupy the place of *ut* in Horace's formulation. *Ut* is part conjunction, part preposition: it with-joins and before-positions. And so it is with the perceiver implicit in Horace's metaphor, now closer to the sensation, now farther away, now loving the darkness ("Haec amat obscurum" [380]), now passing judgement in full light ("Judicis argutum quae non formidat acumen" [381]), now looking just once, now coming back again and again to consider. That perceiving body is not, like the air, transparent. It refracts the spectacle through the eye's green apple before the spectacle becomes words in utterances of mouth or hand. "Like" happens in the space between spectacle and speech. Bodies occupy that space. Bodies make the "like."

The ambience in which Renaissance men and women looked at pictures and read books made Horace's maxim immediately plausible. Recent histories of "the book" (note the singular)—Lucien Febvre and Henri-Jean Martin's *The Coming of the Book* (1976), Elizabeth Eisenstein's *The Printing Revolution in Early Modern Europe* (1983), Adrian Johns's *The Nature of the Book* (1998), John Barnard and D. F. McKenzie's *The Cambridge History of the Book in Britain*, vol. 4 (2002), Roger Chartier's *Inscription and Erasure* (2007)—tend to assume a "reader" (note the singular) who is absent in body, unlocated in space and time, sedentary in posture, totally absorbed by the printed text he holds in his hands.[7] He never yawns, he never lets his mind wander, he never even looks around. Should he have done so, there would have been plenty to distract him in the spaces where sixteenth- and seventeenth-century men and women actually did much of their reading: gardens like Marvell's (see chapter one) and "cabinets" or "closets" like William Murray's at Ham House (see plate 1). The interplay of visual objects and printed texts in spaces like the Green Closet at Ham House produced, according to Stephen J. Campbell, a "semiotic virtuosity" in which texts might provide "a poetic and metaphoric commentary on objects in the collection."[8] That virtuosity could, it seems to me, operate in the other direction as well, as images in the room informed texts in hand. In England at least, the ambience in such spaces was usually provided by folds of woven fabric in the form of tapestries, hangings, painted cloths, bed curtains, needlework cushions, and carpets.[9] These woven artifacts figure as physical, period-specific versions of the *assemblage*, the interlacing, the weaving, the infolding that Derrida finds in the space between one letter and another. They give us reference points for understanding how Renaissance men and women walking, sitting, and reclining within arbors and chambers might have taken printed texts in hand and read them. Ambient reading in such spaces encouraged constant—and constantly varying—interplay between the verbal and the visual.

The space between seeing something and saying something about that seeing can be charted in several ways. A series of spectacles will engage our senses and challenge our understanding in this chapter, a series of scenes of perception as imagined by painters of pictures, weavers of woolen threads, and "painters" and "weavers" of words. When the stuff of the imagining is words, and not pigments or threads, the result is *ekphrasis*, a "picture" in the sense of poetic description. As one of the tropes in classical rhetoric, ekphrasis has generally been taken to be nothing substantial, a form of ornament.[10] Here I take various forms of ekphrasis to be evidence of how men and women ordered their perceptions in the seventeenth century. Exploring the relationship between sensation and speech in each of these cases can help us appreciate what the seventeenth-century crisis of consciousness meant specifically for visual experience.

Two Archetypal Stories

Ut comes out of one's mouth easily enough, but the process whereby visual sensations become verbal summations is not so straightforward as these two simple sounds might suggest. That process can in fact be narrated in several ways. There are two archetypal stories between which all other stories—early modern, modern, postmodern—can be ranged. Both of these ancient stories acknowledge that passions intervene between seeing and speaking. At one extreme is Plato's story: a comedy in which the sensing protagonist overcomes obstacles to right understanding but, through the exercise of reason, arrives at the story's climax in an act of recognition. According to Plato's principle of sameness, the *psyche* matches sensations to ideas that are already present in the ocean of the mind. The only effect that Plato mentions in connection with this act of matching is love (ἔρως, *erōs*), a desire to possess the thing being recognized—love of physical beauty in the case of the senses, love of wisdom in the case of the soul.[11] Aristotle's story admits unpredictability and the possibility of tragedy: it accepts that the protagonist's knowledge depends on sensation, on imagination, on passion—experiences that are subject to ἁμαρτία (*hamartia*), or miscalculation, and to περιπετεα (*peripeteia*), an outcome that may run counter to what the protagonist expects. Recognition (ἀναγνώρισις, *anagnorisis*), as described in Aristotle's *Poetics,* involves multiple affects. Recognition figures, along with *peripeteia,* as "the most powerful means tragedy has for swaying our feelings."[12] *Erōs* is not among those feelings.

Plot, character, thought, verbal expression, music, spectacle: among tragedy's six elements, Aristotle regards plot as primary. You can have a tragedy without characters, he says, but you cannot have a tragedy without a plot (*Poetics* 1450.a.25). Plot is to tragedy what line drawing is to painting: "the most beautiful pigments smeared on at random will not give as much pleasure as a black-and-white outline" (1450.b.38–39). Is character, then, color? Not quite. For Aristotle, line and color are not the distinct phenomena they are for Renaissance art critics preoccupied with *disegno* versus *colore,* and for Derrida preoccupied with *The Truth in Painting.* Color happens, Aristotle explains in his treatise *De Sensu,* when transparent light penetrates finite objects to varying degrees and thus determines the visible limits of those objects.[13] Characters function as the locus of feeling in tragedy, particularly in those moments when the black-and-white plot line takes an unexpected turn and the characters on that trajectory suddenly recognize something or someone, making them realize the finite limits of their being. The result is "a shift from ignorance to awareness" (*Poetics* 1452.a.31) that involves, on the part of the characters, a shift in the "state of happiness or unhappiness" (1452.a.33) and, on the part of those who watch, the experience of pity (ἐλέον, *eleos*) and fear (φόβον, *phobos*) (1449.b.27). Recognition for Aristotle may involve words—"O god— / all come true, all burst to light!"[14]—but the more important result is the feelings those words encode.

In between Plato's story at one extreme and Aristotle's at the other, we can discern various strategies for representing and directing the transformation of visual experience into words. Let us begin with the creation of the world.

Chaos and Cosmos

"Of bodies chang'd to other shapes I sing": the opening lines of Ovid's *Metamorphoses* (George Sandys's translation; 1626, 1628, 1632, 1638, 1640) establish the poem's focus on the instability of bodily stuff.[15] The climactic last word in the Latin original is *corpora*, bodies. A paradigm for the place of bodies in Ovid's design is provided, as Lynn Enterline has argued, by the description of Arachne's tapestry in Book 6.[16] Having been taught the art of weaving by no less an artist than the goddess Pallas, Arachne is foolish enough to challenge her teacher, disguised as an old woman, to a contest. Skirts tucked up to their waists, both contestants set to work. Both can capture the subtleties of the rainbow, "Wherethrough a thousand severall colours shine, / No eye their close transition can define" (6.65–66; sig. Z1v). They differ, however, in their choice of narrative subjects and in the ways they dispose those subjects in the picture space. In framing their narrations, and in that act relating spectacle to words, Pallas and Archne choose radically different strategies. Pallas chooses heroic deeds performed by the gods; Arachne chooses rapes committed by the gods on mortal women.

Pallas sets off her narrative subjects by placing at the tapestry's four corners what Sandys calls "little Rounds" (sig. Z2), each containing a warning story about the metamorphoses that await mortals who presume to challenge the gods. Ovid's Latin describes these corner elements as four "contests" (*certamina*) that are "clear in color, set apart like little seals" ("clara colere suo, brevibus distincta sigillis") (6.85–86).[17] The outermost edges of her tapestry Pallas encircles "with the peaceful olive" ("circuit extremas oleis pacalibus oras") (6.101). Ovid's description of Pallas's rondels is perhaps the inspiration for the emblems and mottoes that often surround the narrative subjects in Renaissance tapestries. *Spring* from the suite of four seasons tapestries woven by the Sheldon Workshops in Worcestershire (one of the four is dated 1611) and preserved today at Hatfield House offers an example (see plate 12). Presided over by outsized figures of Venus and Cupid (just beyond the upper left frame in the detail in plate 12), the visual field is teeming with flora and fauna out of verdure and *mille fleurs* tapestries of a century earlier, tapestries like the one shown in plate 4. Amid these plants and animals, human figures pursue fishing, hunting, and other seasonal activities. Surrounding the whole ensemble are rondels of allegorical figures, each identified in a Latin inscription. The detail from the tapestry's lower right quadrant, shown in plate 12, includes across the bottom emblems of "SUBMOVENDAM IGNO-

RANTIAM" (Ignorance must be dispelled) with the figure of a sphinx, "TEMERITAS" (Rashness), with a charioteer driving two horses, "INVIDIA SIBI MA[GNUM] TORMENTUM" (Jealousy is a great torment), with a frenzied, bare-breasted female figure, "CONCORDIA INSUPERABILIS" (Invincible Concord), with a three-faced, six-armed conqueror, "DIVES INDOCIUS" (Ignorant Dives), with the rich man of Luke 16:19–31 arriving in Hell, and "HAUD INVISTA VINDICTA" (Not unjust revenge) with a raven being stung by the scorpion it has seized in its beak.[18] Pallas would have approved.

In place of Pallas's ethically instructive rondels, Arachne uses intertwined plant motifs to frame the stories she weaves: "About her web a curious traile designes, / Flowres intermixt with clasping ivy twines" (6.127–28; sig. Z2v).[19] A gloss provided by Sandys, on the spot, in the margins, does not let these plant forms go unremarked. "Well suting." Sandys exclaims, "with the wanton Argument: Lasciviousnesse Hieroglyphically presented by Ivy" (sig. Z2v). A note in the appended commentary expands this refusal to see flowers as flowers and ivy as ivy. Having woven the rapists and the raped "to the life," Arachne "incloseth the web with a traile of Ivy, well suting with the wanton argument and her owne ambition. Worne in garlands at lascivious meetings; and climing as ambitious men, to compasse their owne ends with the ruine of their supporters" (sig. Zb3). Within a border filled with flowers and ivy, as Enterline observes, the human figures of Arachne's tapestry fade into the weaving just as so many figures in Ovid's poem fade into the landscape.[20] The contest is won by Pallas, of course, and Arachne is punished by being turned into a spider. Needless to say, a spider's web, like Arachne's borders, is devoid of words and ethical content.

In the fifteen books of Ovid's *Metamorphoses,* as in the Sheldon tapestries at Hatfield House, the background for bodies changed to other shapes is a color field of green. Charles Paul Segal has called attention to the groundedness provided by sylvan scenery in Ovid's dizzily episodic narrative. Secluded groves, quiet water, cool shade, soft grass, the occasional outcropping of rocks or the depths of a cavern provide a unity of place that is much more apparent than any unity of time.[21] Graphic evidence of this green continuity is to be found in the engraved plates that accompany each book in the 1632, 1638, and 1640 editions of Sandys's translation. Some are signed by Franz Cleyn, the artist who designed tapestries for the Mortlake Workshops, and Salomon Savery, the engraver. Each plate presents a unified landscape that accommodates, in one synoptic view, all the metamorphoses that unfold for the reader, one by one, in narrative time.

Figure 11. Franz Cleyn (designer) and Salomon Savery (engraver), plate for Book 1, *Ovid's Metamorphosis Englished, mythologiz'd, and represented in figures* (1632). Original image, $9\frac{1}{2} \times 6\frac{3}{4}$ inches (24.5×17.3 cm). (Reproduced by permission of the Huntington Library, San Marino, California.)

Figure 11, for example, displays the myriad interchanges between landscape and human figures in Book 1, beginning in the lower right and moving counterclockwise in a spiral toward the center: Prometheus's creation of man out of clay and water, the knocking back to earth of the warring giants from whose blood springs up a new race of men, Lycaon at the very moment of being turned into a wolf and cast out by Jupiter from human habitation, Deucalion and Pyrrha after the flood covering their faces and casting the bones of their parents over their shoulders to produce a new generation of men, the mountainous bulk of Python, killed by Apollo's arrows, Daphne eluding Apollo's rape by being turned into a laurel tree, Pan lulling Argus to sleep so that he can to rescue Io from her heifer's body, Syrinx becoming the reeds that compose Pan's pipe. Daphne's story in particular illustrates how tenuous the border is between human figures and the green ground out of which they emerge and into which they return. Sandys's translation catches the subjective dimension of Daphne's transformation. We not only see from the outside how hair turns to leaves and arms to branches; we get to feel from the inside the sensations of limbs growing numb, body becoming bark, legs turning into roots:

> Forth-with, a numnesse all her lims possest;
> And slender filmes her softer sides invest.
> Haire into leaves, her Armes to branches grow:
> And late swift feet, now rootes, are lesse then slow.
> Her gracefull head a leavy top sustaynes:
> One beauty throughout all her forme remaines.
> (1.547–551; sigs. B2v-B3)

In effect, Daphne dissolves into "the pathlesse Woods" ("nemora avia") that were her haunt before Apollo singled her out (1.479; sig. B2).

An etiology for Ovid's landscape is set in place by the account in Book 1 of how the world was formed:

> The Sea, the Earth, all-covering Heaven vnfram'd,
> One face had Nature, which they *Chaos* nam'd:
> An vndigested lump, a barren load,
> Where jarring seeds of things ill-joyn'd aboad.
> (1.5–9; sig. A1)

Those "jarring seeds" ("discordia semina") were able to grow only when "God, the better Nature" composed the strife ("Hanc deus et melior litem natura diremit") by imposing form on the stuff of creation, specifically by separating fire from air from earth from water (1.21–23; sig. A1). And,

Sandys insists, by giving names to the stuff of creation. What makes the concord among the four elements possible, according to Sandys's commentary, is Love-with-a-capital-L, which Sandys, seizing on Ovid's singular *deus,* identifies with the Judeo-Christian God. Sandys will admit that Ovid, by failing to specify where chaos came from in the first place, "seemes to intimate the eternitie of his *Chaos:* yet appeares in the rest so consonant to the truth, as doubtlesse he had either seene the Books of *Moses,* or receaved that doctrine by tradition." Thus, Sandys points out, Ovid designates God as the creator of the world, "and by that word *Commanded* [*diremit*] so often reiterated, that hee made them by his Word only" (sig. C2). The books of Moses, let it be remembered, were thought to include Genesis.

In Genesis, the powers that turn chaos into cosmos are first Word then Light: "And God said, Let there be Light: and there was light" (1:3). According to the Gospel of John, "In the beginning was the Word, and the Word was with God, and the Word was God" (1:1). To arrest the turbulent motion of the discordant seeds of chaos, Sandys inserts first God's Word and then his own. Sandys's running commentary is anything but running: he uses it to fix the fugitive figures who course through Ovid's landscape. Through her transformation, Daphne, for example, becomes pure form and a name: "*Daphne,* almost overtaken, invokes the deities of the River and Earth, to devoure or transforme that beautifull forme which had so much indangered her: who assistant to distressed virtue, convert her into a lawrell; (expressed in her name) the image of her beauty and chastity: innobled by her lover with addition of honours" (sig. E1v). That is to say, Daphne's beautiful form becomes the laurel tree's beautiful form, which becomes the sign or name of (male) victory and power. In effect, Sandys sets up in the opening pages of his translation a three-part paradigm that defines how perception proceeds throughout all that follows: first a visual image, then a verse narrative, finally a prose commentary that fixes the meaning.

As resourceful and ingenious as Sandys may be in his commentary on *Metamorphoses,* Ovid's green stuff is much more resistant to form than the Bible's. To be sure, Genesis describes the creation of plant life in terms of seeds: "And God said, Let the earth bring forth grasse, the herbe yeelding seed, *and* the fruite tree, yeelding fruit after his kind, whose seed *is* in it selfe, vpon the earth: and it was so" (1:11). The description of the Garden of Eden in Genesis 2:8–14, however, provides much more detail about the four rivers that flow out of the garden than it does about the garden itself. Such attention to water is not surprising, perhaps, in an account that imagines the preexisting stuff of God's creation as water and darkness rather than as jarring seeds. About the Garden of Eden, we know only this: "And the Lord God planted a garden Eastward in Eden; and there hee put the man whom he had formed. And out of the ground made the Lord God to grow euery tree that is pleasant to the sight, and good for food: the tree of Life also in the midst of the garden, and the tree of knowledge of good and euill" (2:8–9).

Illustrations of Genesis in seventeenth-century Bibles show how deeply language is implanted in the Garden of Eden. A copy of the 1616 printing of the King James Bible in the Huntington Library (the first edition was published in 1611) has been professionally limned throughout. The depiction of the Garden of Eden in plate 13 imbues the entire landscape with the force of a Hebrew inscription דחדח (an approximation of Yahweh or Jehovah) figured as a dazzling gold burst of light that parts gray clouds of darkness. "The tree of knowledge of good and euill," with its yellow- and red-dappled fruit amid dark green leaves, is entwined with banderoles that specify just what that knowledge is: "CREATED·GOOD·AND·FAIRE·BY·BREACHE·OF·LAWE·A·SNARE." (Banderole, rather than ribbon or banner, seems to be the right word to designate the media that carry these words. [*OED* "banderol(e)," 1, 2.] As a flag on a ship or a streamer on a knight's lance, a banderole, in early modern usage, served as a marker of identity.) The chromatic force of "fair" as "light as opposed to dark" (*OED* "fair" *a.* II.6) is perhaps emphasized by the virulent purple of the serpent whose body is twined about the trunk of the tree and is threaded through another banderole that reads "DVSTE·FOR·TO·EATE·MVST·BE·MY·MEATE." Other banderoles, left and right, give verbal presence to Eve ("DESIRE·TO·KNOWE·HATH·WROVGHT·OVR·WOE") and Adam ("BY·TASTINGE·THIS·TH'EXILE·OF·BLISSE"). The words "desire" and "taste" invite a sensuous as well as moralizing reading of these two human figures. Finally, an additional pair of banderoles give the seventeenth-century viewer/reader a vantage point for placing himself vis-à-vis what he sees and reads. That vantage point embraces the events of the entire Bible, including Christ's sacrifice in the New Testament. "BY·PROMIS·MADE·RESTORD·WE·BE," reads the banner on the left, completed by the banner on the right: "TO·PLEASVRES·OF·ETERNITYE."

The prominent positioning of all these captions never lets the perceiver forget that the visual images have precise verbal meanings. The capital letters and the dots that separate each of the words in the Genesis illustration give the phrases a sculpted solidity that demands notice as a physical presence no less palpable than the pairs of animals that occupy the garden along with Eve, Adam, and the serpent. The words are very much *there* in the landscape. At the same time, however, the image is surrounded by a strap-work design that incorporates foliage, flowers, and fruit recalling the flowers-and-ivy border of Arachne's tapestry in Book 6 of *Metamorphoses.* Except for that, differences between Ovid's green matrix and the Bible's are unmistakable. In place of the swirling action in Cleyn's illustrations for Sandys's Ovid, the illustrator of Genesis in the 1616 King James Bible imposes a rigid symmetry under the aegis of God-as-Word. Under such a regime, there is no danger whatsoever that human figures might merge into the landscape. If Cleyn's illustrations for Ovid read like Arachne's tapestry, the Genesis illustration reads like Pallas's. The banderoles function like the *sigilla* at the edges of Pallas's design: they carry a moral warning. How one should read the strap-work border is altogether less certain.

What we encounter in these two accounts of the creation of the world, Ovid's and the Bible's, and in the seventeenth-century illustrations that accompanied them are two paradigms of knowledge, two ways of relating visual sensation to words. Genesis offers a version of Plato's story in which sensation finds completion in words and in the mental repose that ensues. Completion and repose are just what Ovid's narrative and Cleyn's illustrations refuse. Instead, they enact a version of Aristotle's story in which recognition is always provisional, always grounded in passion. In their own ways, Ovid's Renaissance translators Arthur Golding and George Sandys attempt to redress this situation—Golding by incorporating moralizing judgment in the translation itself, Sandys by giving Ovid's verse its sensuous due but assembling in his commentary every sensible thing about Ovid that had been said since late antiquity. With respect to the creation of the world and to the nature of human knowledge, John Milton offers another sort of compromise.

Milton uses the brief description of creation in Genesis as the stuff of his own much ampler creation. The vantage points from which Milton's Eden is surveyed in Book 4 of *Paradise Lost* (1668, 1669, 1674, etc.) are curiously multiple. In certain places, the reader enjoys a godlike view from beyond and above that encompasses the entire mountaintop garden, its nether reaches, its summit, and its surroundings. In other places, the reader shares the passionate and partial viewpoint of Satan—a view from below—as he tries to penetrate Paradise. A corrective perspective on Satan's descent from heaven is provided by Uriel, "whose eye pursu'd him down / The way he went."[22] In other places still the reader's view is Adam's as he stands atop the garden. The composite of these multiple views reveals a garden composed of four concentric circles of green. The first is an impenetrable wilderness. Satan approaches the border of Eden:

> where delicious Paradise,
> Now nearer, Crowns with her enclosure green,
> As with a rural mound the champain head
> Of a steep wilderness, whose hairie sides
> With thicket overgrown, grottesque and wilde,
> Access deni'd. . . .
>
> (4.132–37)

Then come the ascending shades of an evergreen forest:

> and over head up grew
> Insuperable highth of loftiest shade,
> Cedar, and Pine, and Firr, and branching Palm,
> A Silvan Scene, and as the ranks ascend
> Shade above shade, a woodie Theatre
> Of stateliest view.
>
> (4.137–42)

Then the reader arrives at Adam's viewpoint:

> Yet higher then thir tops
> The verdurous wall of Paradise up sprung:
> Which to our general Sire gave prospect large
> Into his neather Empire neighbouring round.
>
> (4.142–45)

At the topmost circle, bright colors appear against the green:

> And higher then that Wall a circling row
> Of goodliest Trees loaden with fairest Fruit,
> Blossoms and Fruits at once of golden hue
> Appeerd, with gay enameld colours mixt. . . .
>
> (4.146–49)

From wilderness through forest through green wall through orchard one ascends through "pure now purer aire" (4.153) to the *almost* panoptic view commanded by Adam. Between Adam and God intervenes that canopy of flowers and fruits—one fruit in particular. The word "theatre" catches the distinctive quality of Milton's green. To God's view and those of Satan and Uriel, the trees of Paradise look like a wooden theater in which Adam figures as an actor, an Edenic equivalent to the South Bank playhouses to be seen in "long views" of London like Visscher's. To Adam's perspective, on the other hand, the trees compose the platform from which he views the rest of the world. The multiple perspectives entertained in the description of Eden assure that green is simultaneously something one sees from without and within which one sees.

Ovid's *Metamorphoses,* the first chapter of Genesis, and Milton's garden of Eden provide distinctive versions of green that, among them, catch exactly the Renaissance ambivalence about reason and passion. The clarity of vision offered by Milton's cosmos contrasts with the imaginative seductions lurking in Ovid's turbulent chaos. As a reenactment of Genesis, Milton's green is logocentric. Ovid's, by contrast, is logo-fugal: it flees from words. The green matrix in *Metamorphoses* is suffused with the very passions that make Satan, "his face / Thrice changed with pale, ire, envy, and despair" (4.115), a violator of Eden. To the illustrator of Genesis in the 1616 King James Bible, those passions appear purple. Milton's green offers a circumspect vision from the wooden theater on the mountain's top; Ovid's, a dissolution of word and form in the wilderness below. Sandys is altogether typical of Renaissance readers of Ovid in wanting to have it both ways, to give himself up to passion and yet maintain the ironic distance that words make possible.

To Hold the Mirror Up to Nature

Inevitably the silvering has tarnished and the image you see is ghostly dark, but look into a seventeenth-century mirror and you have the strange sensation of looking into the very space in which faces now rotted to the bone once regarded themselves as living presences. Pay attention to what surrounds your face and you will come to see that *how* you see is very different from checking out your image in the steel-edged mirrors favored by postmodern industrial chic. Andreas von Einsiedel's photograph of a late-seventeenth-century mirror hanging at Cotehele House, Cornwall, captures the vertigo that this changed context can induce in twenty-first-century viewers (see plate 14). Painted *putti* hover around the image. Now-faded images painted in the cartouche at the mirror's center superimpose likenesses of Diana and Apollo on the viewer's face. Or is it the other way around? The viewer is cast in an equivocal role. Is she Venus surrounded by little Cupids, or is she chaste Diana? Is he Narcissus gazing at his own image in the watery surface, or is he Apollo, the god of firey light?[23] Contributing to the fluid, layered effect is the fact that the mirror is hung on top of a park-work tapestry. Back away from the mirror, and your image, already insinuated among Diana, Apollo, and *putti,* begins to merge into a field of foliage, flowers, and fruit. Not only mirrors but also portraits in sixteenth- and seventeenth-century England were frequently hung on top of tapestries.

The Long Gallery at Hardwick Hall, Derbyshire, allows us to experience the effect of this arrangement on a grand scale (see plate 15). Many of the furnishings inventoried in 1601 are still to be found *in situ* in Elizabeth Shrewsbury's country house overlooking the coal fields that helped establish her wealth.[24] To walk around the Long Gallery is to experience a visual palimpsest that invites the viewer's eyes to move back and forth between the woven narrative in the tapestries and the painted portraits hung on top. Differences in scale between the two sets of images mean that the viewer, in order to see it all, has to move backwards and forwards as well as sequentially around the walls. Seen from close up, the tapestries, despite their narrative content, function as visual equivalents of Arachne's flower-and-ivy borders. Seen from further away, the portraits disappear into the tapestries' large-scale narratives. In effect, the viewer/reader enacts the scenario described in Horace's *Ars Poetica,* stepping closer and stepping back, moving among shadows and light, looking just once or circling back for repeated study.

In Elizabeth Shrewsbury's time, the High Great Chamber adjacent to the Long Gallery was likewise lined with pictures hung on top of tapestries (see plate 16). On the walls in 1601 were "Sixe peeces of fayre tapestrie hanginges of the storie of Ulisses Eleven foote deepe" (that is, each was eleven feet long), a suite of eight woolen cloths "stayned with frett and storie and silk flowers," a looking glass painted with the arms of England, "Fowre pictures of the fowre partes of the worlde," and portraits of Henry VIII, Queen Mary, Edward VI, Queen Elizabeth, the Duke of Alba, Emperor Charles the Great, Cardinal Wolsey, Cardinal Pole, and Stephen Gardener.[25] Of these elements, the eight painted cloths have disappeared, the mirror may or may not be identifiable with one still in the house, and the surviving portraits now hang in the Long Gallery, but the six tapestries depicting episodes in the story of Ulysses—all 44 expensive feet of them—still line the walls. Woven in Brussels to designs by Michael Coxie and purchased by Elizabeth Shrewsbury from Sir Christopher Hatton's estate in 1587, the tapestries are bordered with interlocked images of leaves, flowers, and fruits, intermixed with human figures. The lower right corner of one of the tapestries, for example, shows a female figure pulling her hair in a state of passion (see plate 17). The image seems to anticipate an anonymous poet's satire of Hero in *The Loves of Hero and Leander a Mock Poem* (1653): "But she poor Lady almost frantick, / As you may see in arras antick & / With hair dishevel'd romes about, / Vowing to find *Leander* out."[26]

Sandys's impulse to read the borders of Arachne's tapestry as an indulgence in lasciviousness is confirmed by designs like this one, in which human figures are disposed amid foliage, flowers, and fruit that are almost as large as they are. In plate 17, the leaf to the female figure's right (is it ivy?) is as large as the figure's chest, while the fruits above are almost as large as her head. Whatever may have been happening at the edges, the effect of the hanging arrangements in the High Great Chamber at Hardwick Hall was physically to insinuate the stories of Henry VIII, Queen Elizabeth, and the other painted notables into the heroic story of Ulysses. It is hard to avoid the thought that these disparate stories would have been *thematically* insinuated as well. When the object on the wall was a mirror like Elizabeth Shrewsbury's "looking glass paynted about with the Armes of England,"[27] the story that was being diffused into the hangings was the viewer's own. The images in Elizabeth Shrewsbury's mirror would have reminded the viewer of her or his exalted place among the arms-bearing families of England.

A similar effect of visual layering was present even in the clothing that framed the wearer's face. Fantastic plant motifs in tapestries, cushions, and bed curtains likewise appeared on clothing. Although the weight of fabrics might be different, woven furnishings and dress fabrics in early modern England shared similar designs.[28] The early-seventeenth-century embroidered jacket from the Burrell Collection shown in plate 18 suggests how green motifs could provide the visual matrix for the presentation of oneself to other people. Almost identical jackets are preserved at the Museum of Costume in Bath and at the Victoria and Albert Museum in London. The V&A example (inventory T.228–1944) is displayed in the British Galleries alongside a portrait attributed to Marcus Gheeraerts the Younger (inventory E.214–1994), which depicts Margaret Laton wearing the very garment. The effect of such garments is to set the wearer's face within a border of plant forms in just the way that faces in painted portraits emerged out of tapestries.

Back away far enough from images in seventeenth-century mirrors and from portraits hung atop tapestries, and you become aware of the visual field within which these images are placed, out of which they emerge—a visual field alive with motion, full of possibilities. The green matrix amid which human stories are enacted in Ovid, Genesis, and Milton was realized, physically and imaginatively, in domestic interiors, tapestries, painted cloths, and book covers. The narratives woven into these fabrics and painted upon them came mostly from Ovid and the Bible. Exploring three particular interiors, different in scale both physically and socially, can help us appreciate a variety of ways in which *ut* might function for a Renaissance reader walking, looking, sitting, reading within them.

Life in Elizabeth Shrewsbury's country house took place amid a colorscape of red, blue, gold, and silver against a background of green. In the High Great Chamber (see plate 16), that green effect can be witnessed, not only in the *Ulysses* tapestries but, above that, in the painted plaster frieze that runs the entire perimeter of the 60×30-foot room.[29] The forestscape in the frieze supplies a continuous setting for otherwise disparate episodes: a boar hunt, Venus chastising Cupid, the four seasons, animals domestic (deer) and exotic (elephants and camels), and the story of Diana and Callisto, which occupies pride of place opposite the main entry doors—a position occupied today by a pair of upholstered thrones with canopy and Turkey carpet, all worked in images of leaves and flowers. The two chairs and the canopy date from sometime after 1626, when Elizabeth Shrewsbury's grandson William and his wife Christian Bruce assumed ownership of the house.[30] William's tutor had been Thomas Hobbes, who died at Hardwick Hall in 1679 and is buried in the nearby village church of Ault Hucknall. In Elizabeth Shrewsbury's time, the room was furnished with a long table that could be draped with two figured carpets, a table with inlay work (this or another similar table is still in the room today), a gilded cupboard, one needlework chair together with its footstool and a foot carpet, three forms or benches, and 16 stools. Needlework coverings and cushions, many of them featuring embroidered flowers, were provided for the forms and stools.[31] One sumptuous chair surrounded by twenty or so less comfortable places to sit suggests the space's use as a public reception room in which Elizabeth would hold court—and, from time to time, look at herself in that mirror painted with all the arms of England.

What the disparate visual elements in Hardwick's High Great Chamber have in common is green. A graphic source for part of the frieze has been identified by Anthony Wells-Cole as a set of hunting prints engraved by Philips Galle (1578)—the two-dimensional stuff for the plasterer's three-dimensional composition.[32] The literary stuff for the Diana and Callisto episode is supplied by Ovid's *Metamorphoses*, Book 3, where the green landscape of Gargaphie is set in place before a single event occurs there. At the far end of the valley, according to Arthur Golding's 1567 translation, is a bower "so vaulted with the leauie trees the Sunne had there no powre." Walled about with flint, the bower favored by

Diana and her nymphs is furnished with a crystal spring "whereof the vpper brim / Was greene with grasse and matted herbes that smelled verie trim."[33] Since Diana, powerful and chaste, was one of Elizabeth Tudor's favorite avatars, it is likely that Elizabeth Shrewsbury chose the motif in anticipation of a royal visit that never happened. Venus chastising Cupid suggests the same motive. The exploits of Ulysses in the tapestries below figure is a male equivalent to the stories of Diana and Venus above. Despite the rationalized perspective in the scenes that these plant and human images frame, despite the cornice that separates plaster frieze from tapestries, despite the focal point provided by the canopied thrones, the overall visual effect of the High Great Chamber is apt to seem diffuse to modern eyes—even to postmodern eyes, trained to appreciate discontinuities and unexpected juxtapositions. Anyone entering the High Great Chamber by the doors opposite the thrones is assaulted by a plenitude of images that divert attention away from any single axis of vision.

On a much smaller scale physically and at a lower order socially is the chamber called Queen Margaret's Room at Owlpen Manor in Gloucestershire. Built in stages between 1450 and 1616, the small manor house owes its survival in a largely unaltered state to a shift in the Daunt family's attentions to their properties in Ireland and to the building nearby of a more up-to-date pile, Owlpen House, in the 1840s. Margaret of Anjou, on her way to defeat at the Battle of Tewksbury in 1471, was about seventy years too early to have stayed in the room now named for her at Owlpen Manor and about two hundred years too early to have enjoyed the painted cloths fitted to the walls of that room.[34] Dating from around 1680, the painted cloths at Owlpen constitute a rare survival *in situ* of a form of wall decoration that was common throughout the sixteenth and earlier seventeenth centuries. Catherine Richardson's survey of 1,430 probate inventories from towns and cities in Kent from 1560 to 1600 turns up 1,191 painted cloths, as compared with only 411 hangings and 357 pictures.[35] On a grander scale, most likely, than any of these examples is a suite of painted cloths depicting four scenes from the life of St. Paul, hanging today in the Upper Chapel at Hardwick Hall. The suite has been attributed to one of Elizabeth Shrewsbury's chief craftsmen, John Ballechouse, and dates from before 1601.[36] The borders to the painted cloths at Hardwick, despite their religious subject matter, present the viewer with the same enticements to imaginative play as the tapestries in the High Great Chamber. The detail in plate 19 shows what might going on in the head of St. Paul, stunned on the road to Damascus by a shaft of light from heaven and thrown from his horse. In a frieze of leaves, flowers, fruit, and vase-like shapes of strap work, a monkey prepares to eat a pomegranate. Although present in royal inventories in the fourteenth and fifteenth centuries and apparently no embarrassment to Elizabeth Shrewsbury, paintings and "stainings" on linen and other fabrics were much cheaper than tapestry work, and it is hard not to catch a note of social condescension (or is it retro taste?) in Falstaff's advice to Mistress Quickly that she replace the old fly-bitten tapestry in her dining room with "a pretty slight Drollery, or the Storie of the Prodigall, or the Germane hunting in Waterworke" or in Falstaff's berating his ragtag regiment for looking "as ragged as *Lazarus* in the painted Cloth, where the Glutton Dogges licked his Sores."[37] ("Water work" refers to the technique whereby earth pigments were bound with water-soluble sizing and thus affixed to the cloth.[38])

In keeping with Falstaff's references to the Prodigal Son and to Lazarus, most surviving painted cloths take up narrative subjects from the Bible rather than classical mythology or romance. The Owlpen set shows scenes from the life of Joseph, he of the coat of many colors, in a continuous landscape of stylized trees, foliage, and flowers backed by conical hills (see plate 20). Shown around the room's four walls in counterclockwise order are Joseph in his multicolored coat receiving his father Jacob's admiration, Joseph being cast into a pit by his envious brothers as a company of Ishmaelite merchants from Gilead pass by with their camels, and Joseph being sold to a group of Midianite traders bound for Egypt. The account of Joseph's life in Genesis 37–50, like the account of creation in Genesis 1, includes only minimal gestures toward the physical setting in which the human events take place: the first reference to Joseph at seventeen years old "feeding the flocke with his brethren" (37:2), Jacob's sending Joseph away from the Vale of Hebron to find his herdsmen brothers in Sechem (37:13–14), the detail that Joseph is "wandring in the field" in Sechem when he is told his brothers have moved elsewhere (37:15), the brothers catching sight of him "afarre off, euen before he came neere vnto them" and deciding then and there to kill him (37:18), and the journeys to, within, and out of Egypt (37:36; 39:1; 41:46, 57; 42:3, 29; 43:15; 44:4, 14; 45:25; 46:1–7; 50:7–9; 57:14). These scant references to the physical surround are more than made up for, however, by land forms in the dreams that Joseph interprets: the brothers' sheaves of wheat making obeisance to Joseph's sheaves (37:7), the vine and grapes in the butler's dream (40:9–11), the cows and the ears of corn in the pharaoh's dream (41:1–7). Seizing on these details, the painter of the Owlpen cloths has provided a green field almost as fecund as Ovid's.

Christopher Simon Sykes's photograph in plate 20 catches the lush green surround within which the four events from Joseph's story emerge out of the cloths' continuous landscape. From the right appear the Ishmaelite merchants "with their camels, bearing spicery, and baulm, and myrrhe, going to cary it downe to Egypt" (37:25). The chair to the right and the table bearing a book and a cabinet for keeping jewels, souvenirs, and miniature portraits suggest what it might feel like to sit down and read in such a setting. Boundaries between words and pictures are not fixed. Rather, words can inform pictures, and pictures can inform words, to produce the state of "semiotic virtuosity" that Campbell describes. As with the Long Gallery at Hardwick Hall, the visual environment in Queen Margaret's Room at Owlpen Manor is layered: pattern upon pattern, story upon story. Until 1927, the room was dominated by a fifteenth-century bedstead that Queen Margaret might plausibly have used, had the Battle of Tewksbury occurred at a more convenient time. How would it feel to dream amid a painted story in which the interpretation of dreams figures so prominently?

On a smaller scale still than Hardwick Hall or Owlpen Manor is the tiny (roughly 9 × 9-foot) painted closet that once formed part of the late-sixteenth-century fabric of Hawstead Place, Suffolk, and now has been reassembled in the Christ Church Mansion Museum at Ipswich (see plate 21). A russet hue separates the emblematic panels from each other, and they are framed in black, but green dominates the landscapes in which each image is placed, and green provides the support for the six horizontal mottos at the top that organize the images into groups of eight or twelve panels each. The sentiments of these superimposed mottoes—"Nuncquam minus sola quam cum sola," reads the one shown in plate 21, "Never less alone than when alone"—suggest the use of the closet as a place for solitary meditation and, through the feminine ending of *sola,* as a place of meditation specifically for a woman. An eighteenth-century visitor to the now-demolished house reported that the painted chamber communicated with a bedroom on the first floor.[39] Hawstead Place was owned by Sir Robert Drury, the death of whose daughter and only heir Elizabeth is commemorated by John Donne in *An Anatomy of the World* (1611) and *The Second Anniversarie* (1612). Use of the painted closet, and perhaps its design, has been attributed to Sir Robert's wife, Lady Ann Drury, a niece of Sir Francis Bacon.[40] Campbell, in his account of Isabella d'Este's *studiolo* in the Palazzo Ducale in Mantua, emphasizes the male identification of most such spaces in the fifteenth and sixteenth centuries and investigates the ways in which the duchess's choices of images and objects reflect a gender-conscious response to that situation.[41] If the same logic is applied to Lady Ann's closet, one cannot escape the chasteness, even austerity, of the room's design.

The temporal direction of Lady Drury's meditations is suggested by the spatial disposition of the panels. As shown in plate 21, the panels closest to the floor depict native plants with the exactitude of a botanical book. Above that bottom rank, the rest of the square panels display emblems with Latin mottoes inscribed on slender banderoles. (On some of the walls smaller panels, rectangular rather than square, continue the plant motifs right up to the band of mottoes and divide the emblems into two tablets or "pages," one on the left and one on the right.) Many of the message-bearing scenes, like their sources in sixteenth- and early-seventeenth-century emblem books, locate the subject in a wooded landscape, as, for example, the man lighting a candle at the tail of a glowworm in the top left panel in plate 21 ("Nil tamen imperti"; "To bestow nothing") or the greyhound licking a hand extended from a tree in the top right panel ("Non fugitiva fides"; "Faithfulness is not fleeting"). In this assemblage, green provides more than visual intricacy for the eyes' delight; it directs the meditator's eyes upward from the plants, those images-without-words, through the images-with-words of the emblems in the middle ranks, to the words-without-images in the mottoes at the top. The visual regime here seems close Pallas's weaving. Perhaps the logotropism that defines the room's perspective is as much a function of Protestant sensibilities as of Lady Ann's gender. The chamber has sometimes been called Lady Drury's *Oratory:* a place in which Ophelia might carry out Hamlet's request "Nimph, in thy Orizons / Be all my sinnes remembred" (F 1623, 3.1.91–92). More clearly, perhaps, than any of the other rooms on our tour, Lady Drury's Oratory presents itself as "an instrument for thinking."[42] Reading in such a setting, what might Ann Drury have made of Donne's extravagant conceits in the pair of poems he wrote to commemorate the first two anniversaries of her daughter's death?

The High Great Chamber and Long Gallery at Hardwick Hall, Queen Margaret's Room at Owlpen Manor, and Lady Drury's closet from Hawstead Place imply three different arrangements for stimulating visual sensations and turning those sensations into words. In all three cases, narrative subjects emerge out of a green matrix: the plaster-work forestscape and tapestries at Hardwick Hall, the continuous landscape in the painted cloths at Owlpen Manor, the green framing of the emblems at Hawstead Place. The insistence with which these visual images point toward words varies from location to location. The logo-tropic impulse seems strongest in Lady Ann's closet, where banderoles in the emblems and mottoes at the top give the images precise verbal meanings. The story of Joseph in the painted cloths at Owlpen Manor certainly *implies* words—the whole long narrative in Genesis, narrative explanations of the four particular episodes that have been chosen for depiction, Joseph's interpretations of dreams—but it does not positively *demand* those words.

Harder still to read are the visual images at Hardwick Hall. For a start, there are so many of them. Furthermore, their relationship to each other seems to have the same fluid, fugitive quality as the images in Ovid's *Metamorphoses.* Just what do the parallel stories of Diana and Hercules in the High Great Chamber *communicate?* Sandys, always ready with a moralization, could probably speak for many Renaissance visitors to the room as he turns the visual experience into words. But moralizations, however learned and subtle, miss the awe, the marveling at power and wealth, that Elizabeth Shrewsbury surely meant to inspire in her visitors. Missing, too, is any delight a spectator might take in ingenious workmanship, the sort of delight registered in Ovid's description of Pallas's and Arachne's abilities to interweave all the colors of the rainbow. Perhaps Nicholas Hilliard gives us our cue when he recommends "an affectionate good Iugment" as the appropriate response to an excellent precious stone, an excellent piece of music, a beautiful person in the flesh, or a painted portrait of that beautiful person.[43] An affectionate good judgment: in that phrase Hilliard invites a greening of what one sees, as long as the greening is tempered by reason. Commentaries like the one Sandys appends to Ovid's verses, banderoles inscribed with words, and mottoes inserted above or below an image provide those black-edged bounds. Where one rests one's gaze—toward the affection end of Hilliard's spectrum or toward the judgment end—remains, however, an open question.

Reading the High Fantastic

Take for example Paris's judgment when confronted with the blandishments of Juno, Pallas, and Venus. Plate 22 shows how the Sheldon Workshops turned *The Judgment of Paris,* as recounted in Ovid's *Heroides* (16.51–88), into an *assemblage* of colors and words.[44] In the Sheldon Workshops' version of *Spring* (see plate 12), human activity has been inserted into a riot of flora and fauna quite without regard to rational perspective. Plants and birds rival the human figures in size, although they are proportionate to the figures of Venus and Cupid that preside over the entire design just to the left of the detail shown in plate 12. Plant forms likewise provide the green matrix for the Sheldon version of *The Judgment of Paris* in plate 22. The narrative event occupies only a small area of the whole, by my calculation only 15 percent of the tapestry's 10½ × 12-foot surface. Far more present to the viewer's eye are the sinuous and sensuous plant forms that modern viewers are apt to write off as a border or a frame. Where modern and even postmodern viewers see superfluous decoration, early-modern viewers saw *something.* They had, in fact, a whole range of names to specify what they were seeing: "antic work," "antique work," "grotesque work," "arabesques," "boscage," "damask work."

Finely discriminated definitions for most of these terms are provided by Edward Phillips in *The New World of English Words, or, A general dictionary containing the interpretations of such hard words as are derived from other languages* (1658). Phillips's definition of "*Antike* work" we have encountered in chapter three: "a Term in painting, or Carving, it being a disorderly mixture of divers shapes of men, birds, flow'rs, *&c.*"[45] Both of the possible etymologies of the term are relevant: "antique" designs of the sort being discovered on the walls of Roman ruins like the Baths of Titus (*OED,* "antic" adj. A.1 + etymology) and "antic" representations, "purposely monstrous, caricatured, or incongruous, of objects of the animal or the vegetable kingdom, or of both combined" (*OED,* "antic" n. B.1 + etymology). Similar, according to Phillips, is "*Grotesch,* (Ital[ian].) a kind of mixt, or confused piece of painting, or sculpture, antick work; hence it is taken for any rude mishapen thing" (R2). The origins of the term "grotesque" are indicated by Patrick Hume in his *Annotations on Milton's Paradise Lost* (1695). Milton's description of the wilderness that Satan traverses on his way to Eden as being "with thicket overgrown, grottesque and wilde" (4.135–36) prompts Hume to this learned gloss: "Full of dark obscure Dens and Caverns: *Grotesque,* Fr[ench]. for dark, and inartificial Paintings and Sculptures, used first in obscure blind Grotto's, of the Fr[ench]. *Grotte,* a Cave, of the mispronounced Lat[in]. *Crypta,* a Cave, an obscure place or recess from the Sun, of the Gr[eek]. Κρύπτω, to hide."[46] Hume's qualifier "inartifical" implies that grotesquerie lacks the finesse of serious art. The place for "*Grotesca,*" according to Sir Henry Wotton in *The Elements of Architecture* (1624) is edges. Vitruvius's strictures on interior decoration in *De Architectura* 7.5 put Wotton into a quandary as to "whether *Grotesca* (as the *Italians*) or *Antique* worke (as wee call it) should be receiued."[47] Vitruvius had lamented that taste in his own day (first century BCE) had turned from "definite representations of definite things" (*ex rebus finitis imagines certae*) like harbors, rivers, fountains, groves, mountains, shepherds, gods, battles, and mythological stories and favored instead monstrosities (*monstra*) like stalks instead of columns, "striped panels with curled leaves and volutes" instead of gables, and "slender stalks with heads of men and of animals attached to half the body."[48] For his part, Wotton is willing to allow artists more scope, although with respect to grotesque work, "I could wish such *medlie* and *motlie* Designes, confined onely to the *Ornament* of *Freezes,* and Borders, their properest place" (sig. N1v).

The other two terms in Edward Phillips's dictionary seem even more appropriate for the Sheldon design: "*Arabesque,* (French) a curious flourishing, or branched work in painting, or Tapestry" (sig. C3) and "*Boscage,* a place set thick with trees, also a term in painting, a picture that represents much wood or trees" (sig. E4). Except perhaps for "boscage," none of these terms are neutral. Present in "antic/antique" is the notion of monstrousness, in "grotesque" a sense of confusion and darkness, in "arabesque" a note of the curious, the exotic, the foreign. All of the terms, as Phillips's subtitle states, "are derived from other languages." Another such tainted word is "damask," the usual descriptor for twilled linen woven in such a way that light catches leaf and flower designs. Damascus was the original source for such goods, as also for silk fabrics woven with elaborate designs, often in a variety of colors (*OED,* "damask" II.3, 4). Knowing that one has to abandon English in order to name the visual experience of such designs helps to explain why Sandys should be so hostile to the "curious traile" of "Flowres intermixt with clasping ivy" that Arachne weaves around the scenes of rape that constitute her narrative subject or why Milton should make a "thicket overgrown, grottesque and wilde" a haunt for Satan.

Montaigne describes the same arrangement in the opening to his essay "Of Friendship" (1.27). I write like a painter, Montaigne begins, setting up what follows as a portrait of his friend Etienne la Boetie. Before a painter starts to work, Montaigne observes, he chooses the fairest place he can find, which Montaigne imagines to be an interior wall (*paroi*). Then the painter works on the picture with all the skill he has. And then "all voyde places about it, he filleth vp with antike Boscage or Crotesko worke; which are fantastical pictures, having no grace, but in the varietie and strangenes of them."[49] Florio's approximation of Montaigne's spelling *crotesques* suggests that, in 1603, the Italian term *grotesco* had not yet been assimilated into English, as it was to become in Phillips's *New World* eighty years later. Florio's addition of the word "boscage" suggests the need for a synonym—and a linkage between that plant-specific term and the more general "grotesque work."

In the psyche of a Renaissance perceiver, antic/antique work, grotesquery, arabesques, boscage, and damask are the stuff of fancy.[50] Spenser's description of the "infinite shapes of things" painted on the walls of the Chamber of Phantastes is just the sort of "disorderly mixture" that Phillips identifies with "*antike* work." Actually, there *is* an order to Spenser's catalog: "Infernall Hags, *Centaurs,* feendes, *Hippodames,* / Apes, Lions, Aegles, Owles, fooles, louers, children, Dames" begins with monsters, then proceeds through animals, and ends with humans.[51] The last item in Spenser's inventory, "Dames," invites us to see in a new light the woman at the border of the *Ulysses* tapestry at Hardwick Hall (see plate 17). The sinister, disturbing quality of antic work—and its association with female imagination—are even stronger in Milton's description of Eve's dream in Book 5 of *Paradise Lost*—or rather in Adam's morning-after rationalization of Eve's dream about tasting the forbidden fruit of the Tree of Knowledge. Not to worry, Adam begins, addressing Eve as "Best Image of my self" (5.95). In the soul, he explains, there are many "lesser Faculties" (5.101) that serve Reason. Second only to Reason is Fancy:

of all external things,
Which the five watchful Senses represent,
She forms Imaginations, Aerie shapes,
Which Reason joyning or disjoyning, frames
All what we affirm or what deny, and call
Our knowledge or opinion; then retires
Into her private Cell when Nature rests.
(5.103–109)

During sleep, Fancy's way with the imaginations is freer. When Nature rests, Fancy goes to work as a second creating Nature, and one of her tricks is to disjoin images from words:

Oft in her absence mimic Fansie wakes
To imitate her; but misjoyning shapes,
Wilde work produces oft, and most in dreams,
Ill matching words and deeds long past or late.
(5.110–113)

Eve's dream, Adam concludes, is just such a work of fancy. The Tree of Knowledge in Eve's dream is an example of fancy's "wild work," not least in the wordlessness of that knowledge. Words are supplied in short order.

How to reconcile Spenser's anxieties about grotesquerie and Milton's antipathy, on the one hand, with the green blandishments of the Sheldon tapestries on the other? The design of *The Judgment of Paris* would, at first blush, seem to encourage free play of the imagination as the perceiver's eye moves around and through the weaving's luxurious plant forms on its way to the narrative subject in the center. Once the perceiver has arrived there, however, it is not just gods in the shape of human bodies that are waiting to be encountered but words. Inscriptions on the strapwork frame supply the words needed to fix the experience in memory. "WHEN PARESE GAVE THE GOLDENE APPEL" reads the caption at the bottom. The inscription at the top cites—incorrectly—book and chapter, if not verse, as if the subject were taken from the Bible: "OVT[ ]OF[ ]OVID [ ]EPE[S]TELS IX CHAPTER." Understanding may reach its goal at the center, but only after the imagination has made its way through a tangle of green thoughts from margin to center, from becoming to being. Sir Philip Sidney charts precisely that course in the tapestry metaphor that figures prominently near the beginning of *The Defence of Poesy* (written 1580–1585, printed 1595): "Nature neuer set forth the earth in so rich tapistry, as diuers Poets haue done, neither with pleasant riuers, fruitful trees, sweet smelling flowers: nor whatsoeuer els may make the too much loued earth more louely" (sig. C1v). Sidney finds in woven hangings just the image he needs to demonstrate the difference between the world delivered to human eyes by nature and the world delivered to human eyes by poets. In sum: "Her world is brasen, the Poets only deliuer a golden" (sig. C1v). What Sidney has in mind is not just prettified images of the rivers, trees, and flowers to be found in nature but "new formes such as neuer were in Nature"—things like "*Heroes, Demigods, Cylops, Chimeras, Furies,* & such like" (sig. C1v). It is, perhaps, the custom of hanging portraits atop tapestries, as in the Long Gallery at Hardwick Hall, that explains Sidney's next maneuver. "But let those things alone and goe to man," he continues (sig. C1v). Has nature ever produced so true a lover as Theagines in Heliodorus's *Aethiopica,* so constant a friend as Pylades in Euripides' *Oresteia,* so valiant a man as Orlando in Ariosto's *Orlando Furioso,* "so right a Prince" as Cyrus in Xenophon's *Cyropaedia,* or "so excellent a man euery way" as Aeneas in Virgil's *Aeneid* (sigs. C1v–C2)? The sequence that Sidney follows here—first rivers, trees, and flowers, then human subjects—implies the same visual regime as *The Judgement of Paris.* Play of fancy with plant forms leads to sharp focus on narrative images and ends with a declaration of ethical meaning.

Sidney provides a fair enough summary, perhaps, about how one follows the linear sequence of lines in a poem. But who is to say, in the case of the Sheldon tapestry, that imagination does not wander away from the narrative subject once it has been found, noted, and named? Paris, after all, was not such a smart judge. He chose Venus, who had promised him Helen of Troy, and there began the Trojan War. What we see in products of the Sheldon workshops is another version of the figure/ground conundrum presented by portraits hanging atop tapestries in the Long Gallery at Hardwick. In both locations, narrative subjects emerge out of a field of green—and, potentially at least, merge back again.[52] In the Sheldon version of *When Paris Gave the Golden Apple,* as in the tapestries and pictures in the Long Gallery, we are confronted not only with two different subjects but with disparities in scale. Foliage, flowers, and fruit in the Sheldon tapestry are huge in comparison with the narrative figures at the center: inevitably the plant forms seem closer to the viewer than Ovid's story does, even though one's distance from the images in feet or meters remains the same. To take in the foliage, flowers, and fruit in a single gaze the viewer has to step backwards; to see the narrative subject in all its detail, the viewer has to do just the opposite, move in closer. These coordinates of body, space, and time are beyond the ken of most postmodern criticism, which is equipped to talk only about the "text" presented by the central image and the verbal texts inscribed above and below it. What to do with the rest of the design? Lacking any narrative content, it can only be relegated to the status of a frame. But can a "frame" really be 85 percent of the whole? Most versions of postmodern criticism need texts, once they have been framed, to remain fixed in space and time at precise distances from the analyst-critic. For Renaissance perceivers, the so-called frame, and the directions to bodily movement encoded in that frame, were part and parcel of visual experience.[53] And so, perhaps, they remain for us if we have eyes to see. The plant and animal forms of antic work and grotesquerie shape up as Renaissance versions of what Derrida characterizes as the "repeatedly folded frontier" between the human and the supposedly nonhuman, "the edge of the *so-called* human" and the "heterogeneous multiplicity of the living" beyond.[54]

Something closer to the fixed-point coordinates preferred by modern viewers can be seen in productions of the royal tapestry works set up by James VI and I in 1619 at Mortlake, Surrey, upriver from London near Hampton Court. The Mortlake version of the meeting of Hero and Leander, probably designed by Franz Cleyn, who drew the plates for Sandys's Ovid, includes trees and plants—but as residual elements in a picture-space that is dominated by the columns, niches, and pedimented door of a round temple, all organized according to rational perspective (see plate

23). The hues, however, tell a different story—or probably once did. The cool blues so prominent in the tapestry's appearance today were probably originally lustful greens. Green, as we learned in chapter two, was usually achieved by overdyeing blue with yellow, and yellow dyes were particularly subject to fading. Antic work, in this as in all Mortlake designs, has been relegated to a precisely defined border that may entice the viewer's eye momentarily but primarily serves to enhance the rational geometry of the entire design. It is tempting to see the Mortlake aesthetic as yet another sign of the shift from "Elizabethan" to "Jacobean" taste that F. P. Wilson and John Buxton have discerned, a shift occasioned in part by Van Dyck's tenure in England.[55] Indeed, Van Dyck has been credited with the border designs for the Mortlake suite *Acts of the Apostles,* after cartoons by Rubens.[56] Cartoons that Franz Cleyn drew for Mortlake tapestries are pasted to the ceiling of the Green Closet at Ham House, just up the Thames from Mortlake.[57] In plate 1, the edge of one of these cartoons is visible above the gilded cornice on the far wall.

To shift one's gaze from tapestries, painted cloths, and painted panels to the printed page was not, in the sixteenth and seventeenth centuries, so disruptive as it might seem today. Plate 20 suggests how tapestries or painted cloths might provide the surroundings for reading a book. As we shall see in a survey of stage directions in chapter six, one of the most frequent fictional locations that might be discovered by drawing back a curtain was a study, often with the character in the pose of a reader, asleep in a chair over a book. And among the productions of the Sheldon workshops were tapestry book covers like the one shown in plate 24. This particular example may have been designed for a Bible, since the central panel presents a be-haloed male figure in robes, kneeling beneath a heavenly burst inscribed "DEUS." The Bible from which the colored image in plate 13 is taken is bound in crimson velvet, with elaborate multicolored embroidery showing, on the front cover, Moses raising the serpent in the wilderness and, on the back cover, Christ on the cross. The spine features eight bands of arabesques centered on Tudor roses worked in gold thread. That such bindings were not necessarily rare, at least for wealthy owners, is indicated by Paul Hentzner, a visitor from Germany who toured Whitehall Palace in 1598. The queen's books, he notes, were "bound in velvet of different colors, though chiefly red, with clasps of gold and silver."[58] Whatever a book's content, the effect of such bindings as a reader took the book in hand would have been the equivalent of the verdure and antic work of tapestries. If an engraved title page were present, framing printed letters with strap work, plant motifs, or antic figures, the reader would have entered the book via an intermediary between the visual fantasy of the cover and the printed words of the text.

Busyrane's Deceptions and Eleutherillida's Marvels

Tension between knowing-through-the-senses and knowing-through-names provides the animating force for the quests recounted in *The Faerie Queene* (Books 1–3 were published in 1590; Books 4–6, in 1596). About sense experience in general, Spenser registers an ambivalence that is altogether typical of his age. He distrusts it even as he represents it in writing, particularly when the experience at hand has been contrived as an act of deception. Two scenes of spectacle in Books 3 and 4 of *The Faerie Queene* shape up as eloquent examples. In Book 3, canto 11, Britomart comes upon the recumbent figure of Sir Scudamour, in despair because his lady Amoret has been taken captive by Busyrane and Scudamour cannot breach the barriers Busyrane has erected and rescue her. The setting and the posture in which Britomart finds Scudamour anticipates by a dozen years Isaac Oliver's portrait of Edward Herbert (see plate 9). The *impresa* on Scudamour's shield is different, but otherwise, the scenes are remarkably similar:

> . . . at last she came to a fountaine sheare,
> By which there lay a knight all wallowed
> Vpon the grassy ground, and by him neare
> His haberieon, his helmet, and his speare;
> A little off, his shield was rudely throwne,
> On which the winged boy in colours cleare
> Depeincted was, full easie to be knowne,
> And he thereby, where euer it in field was showne.
>
> (3.11.7.2–9)

The boy with the colored wings is, of course, Cupid.

After giving Scudamour encouragement, Britomart is able to breach the flames that guard Busyrane's castle and proceed to rescue the captive Amoret by passing through three rooms. The first is hung with tapestries that might have been woven by Arachne: seventeen stanzas are devoted to inventorying the rapes of mortals by the pagan gods. The sinister quality of the weavings is indicated from the start by the narrator's noting (presumably through Britomart's eyes) the gold and silver threads that show themselves through the silk "Like a discoloured Snake, whose hidden snares / Through the greene gras his long bright burnisht backe declares"

(3.11.28.8–9). The borders to the tapestries, which the narrator notices last, outdo Arachne in lasciviousness: they are made up of broken bows and arrows, threaded by "a long bloudy riuer" (3.11.46.8). Presiding over the first room is Cupid, his wings "with sundry colours dight" (3.11.47.6), standing atop an altar of precious stone with a wounded dragon at his feet—a pose that parodies St. George and the dragon from Book 1.

The second room through which Britomart passes is no less sinister. Its walls are covered with pure gold, "Wrought with wilde Antickes, which their follies playd, / In the rich metall, as they liuing were" (3.11.51.5–6). When darkness overtakes the room, Britomart witnesses a masque that begins with the sound of a trumpet, evolves into the sounds and tactile sensations of thunder and a windstorm, intensifies with the addition of the smell of smoke and sulfur, and reaches a climax in a whirlwind that blends what is common among multiple sensations before a grave personage appears "as on the ready flore / Of some Theatre" (3.12.3.5–6). Still there are no words. The grave figure does not, as one might expect, speak like a Prologue, a Chorus, or a Presenter. Instead, he performs a dumb show: "By liuely actions he gan bewray / Some argument of matter passioned" (3.12.4.5–6). The argument turns out to be a Triumph of Cupid in the mode of Petrarch's *Trionfi,* a pageant in which the narrator (speaking for Britomart) is able instantly to identify "*Fancy*" in the painted-feather guise of Ganymede or Hylas (3.12.7.1), "*Desyre*" in an "emrodered Bonet" (3.12.9.1, 6), "*Doubt*" in "a discolour'd cote" (3.12.10.1, 2), etc., leading up to the appearance of a lady whose bleeding heart is being removed from her body by Cruelty and Despight and, finally, the entry of the god himself, who "clapt on hie his couloured winges twaine" (3.12.23.7) over the "rude confused rout" of the subjects who follow in his wake, persons "whose names is [*sic*] hard to read" (3.12.25.1, 2). It is in a third room beyond that Britomart, the next night, finds Amoret (she of the bleeding heart) and rescues her from the spell Busyrane has cast, writing out his charms "With liuing blood" (3.12.31.3) from knowledge inscribed in "wicked books" (3.12.32.2) or perhaps in just one "baleful booke" (3.12.36.3). When Britomart and Amoret return through the first two rooms, the furnishings of those two spaces have "vanisht vtterly" (3.12.42.3), the result of the illumination, the knowledge of the truth, that the reader has attained along with Britomart in the progression through the three rooms.

The distinctively Protestant and English character of this epistemological rite of passage can be appreciated by comparing Britomart's roundtrip traversal of Busyrane's three rooms with Poliphilus's one-way progression through three rooms to reach Queen Eleutherillida in Francesco Colonna's *Hypnerotomachia Poliphili* (1499), translated into English as *The Strife of Loue in a Dreame* (1592). To reach the queen, Poliphilus must move through and beyond three woven hangings, variously referred to as "Curtain," "cloth," and "Arras" by the English translator.[59] Passing through a hanging cloth into the first room, Poliphilus discovers "an other Curtaine of excellent Arras full of Imagerie, as signes, shapes, plants, and beastes, singularly well done" (sig. o1). As his guide pulls aside "the Curtaine," Poliphilus enters the second room, hung about "with discourses and reason marueilously woven, with infinite knottes, bucklinges, tyings, and old fashioned harping Irons, or Hookes, as if they had been fastened and knit together" (sig. o1). So far the progression from "Imagerie" to "discourses and reason" looks very much like the first two chambers in Spenser's Castle of Alma in Book 2 of *The Faerie Queene,* spaces that we traversed in the company of Sir Guyon and Prince Arthur in chapter 3. It is the third room in Poliphilus's progress that reveals the decisive difference between Spenser's English, Protestant sensibility, anxious about false appearances, and Colonna's Italian, Catholic sensibility, thoroughly comfortable in taking visual pleasure.

Queen Eleutherillida's domain, beyond the third curtain, is a large and visually sumptuous courtyard overlooked by a gallery "the roofe whereof, was all painted with a greene foliature, with distinct flowers and folded leaues, and little flying Byrdes, excellently imphrygiated of museacall paynting" (sig. o1v) and lined with palm-wood banquettes covered with green velvet cushions. The banquet, musical entertainment, and dancing that Pophilus enjoys within this space beggar language (not really, of course, since Colonna seizes on the occasion to display his rhetorical skills)—especially, Pophilus confesses, the language of a lover like himself, "who continually suffer in euerie secret place of my burning heart, an vncessant strife" (sig. R2v). Britomart penetrates the three painted and gilded chambers of Busyrane's house in order to discover in their depths a burning heart that needs to be rescued; Pophilus penetrates the three curtains of Queen Eleutherillida's palace to discover in the palace's green courtyard visual delights that make his heart burn all the more ardently. Britomart's progress ends in words; Pophilus's, in a confession of wordlessness. "In truth," Pophilus confides, after pages of ekphrastic ecstacy, "the many maruels in excellency, and varietie vnhard of . . . I am no whit able to describe them, and much lesse worthie to publish them" (sig. R2v).

The ambivalence of the English translator and his readers before Colonna's banquet of the senses is perhaps registered in the fact that the Aldine Press edition of *Hypnerotomachia* (1499), one of the most beautiful

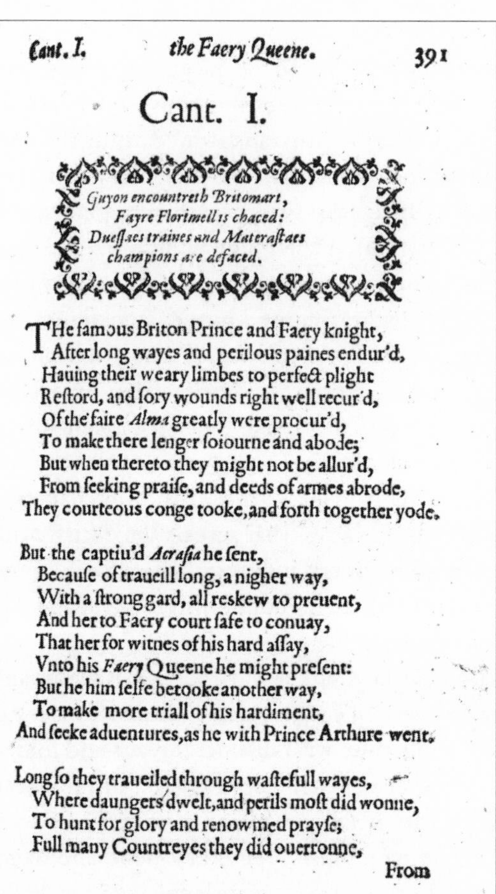

Cant. I. *the Faery Queene.* 391

Cant. I.

Guyon encountreth Britomart,
Fayre Florimell is chaced:
Dueſſaes traines and Materaſtaes
champions are defaced.

THe famous Briton Prince and Faery knight,
After long wayes and perilous paines endur'd,
Hauing their weary limbes to perfect plight
Reſtord, and ſory wounds right well recur'd,
Of the faire *Alma* greatly were procur'd,
To make there lenger ſoiourne and abode;
But when thereto they might not be allur'd,
From ſeeking praiſe, and deeds of armes abrode,
They courteous conge tooke, and forth together yode.

But the captiu'd *Acraſia* he ſent,
Becauſe of traueill long, a nigher way,
With a ſtrong gard, all reskew to preuent,
And her to Faery court ſafe to conuay,
That her for witnes of his hard aſſay,
Vnto his *Faery* Queene he might preſent:
But he him ſelfe betooke another way,
To make more triall of his hardiment,
And ſeeke aduentures, as he with Prince Arthure went.

Long ſo they traueiled through waſtefull wayes,
Where daungers dwelt, and perils moſt did wonne,
To hunt for glory and renowmed prayſe;
Full many Countreyes they did ouerronne,
From

Figure 12. Opening of Book 2, canto 1, from Edmund Spenser, *The Faerie Queene* (1590). Original page size, 7¾ × 5 inches (19.7 × 12.7 cm). (Reproduced by permission of the Folger Shakespeare Library.)

printed books ever produced, presents the classically inspired full-page plates as part and parcel of the book's aesthetic, the printed equivalents of illuminations in manuscripts, whereas the 1592 English translation contains 22 woodcuts of diverse sizes and of no more than serviceable quality, inserted at irregular intervals in the black-and-white blocks of text. By contrast, the first printing of *The Faerie Queene,* Books 1–3, by William Ponsonby two years earlier, contains only one illustration, a full-page woodcut of Redcrosse (or is it St. George?)—but it occurs at the *end* of Book 1, *after* the verbal picture of Redcrosse fighting the dragon and the verbal meaning of that picture have been set in place. Otherwise, Spenser's text is set off by a large-scale, standard-issue printer's ornament on the title page, rectangular printer's ornaments above the titles to each of the three books, and border ornaments that have been assembled into frames around the italicized quatrains that summarize each canto (see figure 12).

The typography, though Spenser probably had nothing to do with it, is eloquent: antic work frames *words*. Ponsonbie's printing of Books 4–6 in 1596 repeats the same graphic design.

What to make of Spenser's epistemology and the reading strategy he offers his readers? The progression from sense experience to common sense to fancy to imagination to passion to judgment to words is common enough. What seems distinctive is Spenser's ambivalence about this process. The "pictures" he provides are full of sensuous, precisely observed details, and yet the knowledge they inspire is suspect from the start. In what, then, does true knowledge consist? Certainly it does not require an abrogation of passion. The original ending to Book 3 in the 1590 edition, before Spenser postponed the reunion of Amoret and Scudamour to Book 4, is a triumph of passion, of bodily pleasure. Scudamour puts his arms around "Her body, late the prison of sad paine, / Now the sweet lodge of loue and deare delight" (3.12.452.3–4). Secure in Scudamour's embrace, Amoret "did in pleasure melt, / And in sweete rauishment pourd out her spright" (3.12.452.6–7). So overcome are both lovers that they do not speak. To the narrator (or to the narrator speaking for Britomart, who is herself "much impassioned" at witnessing this scene [3.12.46a.7]), Scudamour and Amoret look like an ancient statue of "faire *Hermaphrodite*" (3.12.462.46a.2). If this is Platonism, it is not bloodless Platonism.

The nature of true knowledge is to be witnessed, not in the summary verses at the head of each canto, much less in the footnotes of modern scholarly editions, but in the counterpart to the House of Busyrane that Spenser constructs in the extended version of Scudamour and Amoret's story in Book 4. Tell us how you first won the love of Amoret, the assembled company in Book 4, canto 9, ask Scudamour. He found her, he tells them, in the Temple of Venus. Scudamour's description of this place in canto 10 shapes up as a natural foil to the deceptive artifice of the House of Busyrane. What distinguishes the Temple of Venus, in its green garden setting, from the House of Busyrane is finally a matter of light. Venus's altar beggars description, not because of its precious substance or intricate workmanship, but because of its transparency, "Pure in aspect, and like to christall glasse" (4.10.39.7). The emphasis falls on "like." The narrator knows no word to specify the stuff out of which Venus's altar is made: "Yet glasse was not, if one did rightly deeme, / But being faire and brickle, likest glasse did seeme" (4.10.39.8–9). Right knowledge in Spenser requires transparency, a *sensuous* transparency, that the reader of *The Faerie Queene* learns to recognize in the very act of reading. The fact that Scudamour's story of finding Amoret in the Temple of Venus comes *after* the story of losing her later to the House of Busyrane illustrates the epistemological situation exactly: true knowledge is what one once knew and what one can know again, if one learns to see through the delusions—or at least the *possible* delusions—of sense, fancy, and imagination. The resulting knowledge, as the embrace of Scudamour and Amoret testifies so movingly, is passionate knowledge, but it is knowledge from which all hobgoblins have been banished. Knowledge in Spenser consists of sensations that have names and names that take shape as sensations.

The Greening of Troy

Turning over the title page that is emblazoned *Lucrece* (no author's name is specified) and reading through a one-page dedication to the Earl of Southampton signed by "William Shakkespeare," the purchaser of Richard Field's 1594 quarto printing of the poem found herself or himself confronting the typographic assemblage shown in figure 13. On the left, tightly printed in pica italic with proper names in pica roman, is "THE ARGVMENT," the title itself distinguished in great primer capital letters. At the top of the right-hand page appears a standard-issue printer's ornament that Field used in twelve other books, an ornament complete with plant forms metamorphosing into horned satyrs on either side of an enigmatic female face swathed in folds of cloth and crowned with a strap-work headdress that merges into the sinuous plant forms that surround it. The ornament's "antique" qualities, a quick-witted reader might notice, are no less appropriate to the subject at hand than its sensuosity. Below the ornament comes the poem's title, graduated downward from "THE RAPE OF" in double pica capital letters to "LVCRECE." in great primer caps. Then, in a further visual diminution, the poem begins with its first two compact eight-line stanzas, in great primer caps and lowercase.[60] The narrative proceeds on for 44 leaves, front and back, in the same perfectly regular visual rhythm. Four distinct kinds of perception seem called for by this opening's typographic design: (1) transparent logic-centered reading in the argument, (2) play of fancy in the ornament, (3) motto formation in the title, and (4) a combination of all three kinds of perception—logical, fanciful, and summational—in the stanzas. Discrepancies between "The Argument" and the narrative itself (only in the argument is the political outcome of Lucrece's ravishment spelled out) can perhaps be explained by these differences in perceptual appeal. No sooner has the argument provided, *avant la vue,* the kind of moralizing judgment one might expect at the top of an emblem than the ornament entices fancy and imagi-

THE ARGVMENT.

LVcius Tarquinius (for his exceſſiue pride ſurnamed Superbus) after hee had cauſed his owne father in law Seruius Tullius to be cruelly murdred, and contrarie to the Romaine lawes and cuſtomes, not requiring or ſtaying for the peoples ſuffrages, had poſſeſſed himſelfe of the kingdome: went accompanyed with his ſonnes and other Noble men of Rome, to beſiege Ardea, during which ſiege, the principall men of the Army meeting one euening at the Tent of Sextus Tarquinius the Kings ſonne, in their diſcourſes after ſupper euery one commended the vertues of his owne wife: among whom Colatinus extolled the incomparable chaſtity of his wife Lucretia. In that pleaſant humor they all poſted to Rome, and intending by theyr ſecret and ſodaine arriuall to make triall of that which euery one had before auouched, onely Colatinus finds his wife (though it were late in the night) ſpinning amongeſt her maides, the other Ladies were all found dauncing and reuelling, or in ſeuerall diſports: whereupon the Noble men yeelded Colatinus the victory, and his wife the Fame. At that time Sextus Tarquinius being enflamed with Lucrece beauty, yet ſmoothering his paſſions for the preſent, departed with the reſt backe to the Campe: from whence he ſhortly after priuily withdrew himſelfe, and was (according to his eſtate) royally entertayned and lodged by Lucrece at Colatium. The ſame night he tretcherouſlie ſtealeth into her Chamber, violently rauiſht her, and early in the morning ſpeedeth away. Lucrece in this lamentable plight, haſtily diſpatcheth Meſſengers, one to Rome for her father, another to the Campe for Colatine. They came, the one accompanyed with Iunius Brutus, the other with Publius Valerius: and finding Lucrece attired in mourning habite, demanded the cauſe of her ſorrow. Shee firſt taking an oath of them for her reuenge, reuealed the Actor, and whole maner of his dealing, and withall ſodainely ſtabbed her ſelfe. Which done, with one conſent they all vowed to roote out the whole hated family of the Tarquins: and bearing the dead body to Rome, Brutus acquainted the people with the doer and manner of the vile deede: with a bitter inuectiue againſt the tyranny of the King, wherewith the people were ſo moued, that with one conſent and a general acclamation, the Tarquins were all exiled, and the ſtate gouernment changed from Kings to Conſuls.

THE RAPE OF LVCRECE.

FRom the beſieged Ardea all in poſt,
Borne by the truſtleſſe wings of falſe deſire,
Luſt-breathed TARQVIN, leaues the Roman hoſt,
And to Colatium beares the lightleſſe fire,
VVhich in pale embers hid, lurkes to aſpire,
And girdle with embracing flames, the waſt
Of COLATINES fair loue, LVCRECE the chaſt.

Hap'ly that name of chaſt, vnhap'ly ſet
This bateleſſe edge on his keene appetite:
VVhen COLATINE vnwiſely did not let,
To praiſe the cleare vnmatched red and white,
VVhich triumpht in that skie of his delight:
VVhere mortal ſtars as bright as heauēs Beauties,
VVith pure aſpects did him peculiar dueties.

B

Figure 13. "The Argument" and opening stanzas from William Shakespeare, *Lucrece* (1594). Original page size, 6⅜ × 4½ inches (16.5 × 11.5 cm). (Reproduced by permission of the Huntington Library, San Marino, California.)

nation. The title, with its lapidary capital letters, insinuates rape into the play of imagination. The stanzas can then be read as negotiations among these three distinctive ways of knowing.

It is a curious paradox that the rape in *The Rape of Lucrece* is never represented. It happens *beyond* words, in the blank, letterless space at the bottom of signature F1, between the stanza beginning "For with the nightlie linnen that shee weares, / He pens her piteous clamors in her head" (line 680 in modern editions) and the stanza beginning "For shee hath lost a dearer thing then life, / And he hath wonne what he would loose againe" (line 687).[61] The sudden shift to present perfect tense ("hath lost," "hath wonne") gestures toward an act that remains unspeakable. When Lucrece is left alone to make sense of what has happened, the reader witnesses a passage from passion to speech in the second half of the poem similar to what Tarquin has enacted in the first half—but a passage far more fraught, indirect, and convoluted. Lucrece's first course is to take a page or two or three out Seneca's tragedies and declaim a 39-stanza lament. She comes to the realization that it is useless to rail against external causes of her plight—opportunity, time, Tarquin, night—and that only an action on her own part can offer remedy: "This helplesse smoake of words doth me no right" (sig. H1v). *Lucrece* is a narrative poem, after all, so many more words are still to come—two soliloquies, dialogue with her maid, a letter written to her absent husband—but famously, it is a painting of the fall of Troy, occasioned by the rape of Helen, that helps Lucrece find the words she needs and the resolve to follow through on what she has declared in her second lament, "For me I am the mistresse of my fate" (sig. H2v).

The teeming subjects that Shakespeare's narrator notices in the painting suggest a suite of painted cloths rather than an easel picture. Lucrece's looking is impassioned looking. It is not the linear narrative of the fall of Troy that interests her but "A thousand lamentable obiects" (sig. K1v), visible signs of passion. Presenting themselves in turn to her gaze are tears shed by the wives of slaughtered husbands, ashy coals in the eyes of dying soldiers, grace and majesty in the faces of commanders, quickness and dexterity in the movements of youths, the trembling marching of pale cowards, blunt rage in Ulysses' eyes followed by mild glances, Nestor making a gesture with his hand as he speaks through his white beard, the gaping faces of his listeners, one man in the crowd leaning his hand on his neighbor's head, another man swollen and red with anger from having been pushed backwards, still another striking out in rage. Painting, to Lucrece's eyes, figures as metonymy for passions, for grief, despair, pride, eagerness, rage, moderation, anger. Small details take on huge affective power:

> For much imaginarie worke was there,
> Conceipt deceitfull, so compact so kinde,
> That for ACHILLES image stood his speare
> Grip't in an Armed hand, himselfe behind
> Vvas left vnseene, saue to the eye of mind,
> A hand, a foote, a face, a leg, a head
> Stood for the whole to be imagined.
> (sig. K3)

Lucrece's search finds its ultimate object in Hecuba. What Lucrece notices is not Hecuba's body, not even her face, but "her old eyes" staring on Priam's wounds (sig. K3v). The result of such looking is a kind of dialogue between Lucrece and the thousand lamentable objects she finds in the painting.

Line and hue, *disegno* and *colore,* figure in these transactions: "So LVCRECE set a worke, sad tales doth tell / To pencel'd pensiuenes, & colour'd

Figure 14. Jan Muller, "Lucretia's Suicide" (ca. 1590). Original image, 7 × 8⁶⁄₈ inches (18 × 22.5 cm). (Reproduced by permission of the Rijksmuseum, Amsterdam.)

sorrow, / She lends them words, & she their looks doth borrow" (sig. K4v). In effect, Lucrece uses the painting as a mirror in which she can find images of her own passions and endue those passions with words. It is as if she had stepped up to a painted looking glass like the one in plate 14 and had discerned her own image alongside Hecuba's. Lucrece's fusion of looks and words ends in two dramatic acts of touching. In the first, Lucrece finds Sinon in the painting—he was the person responsible for luring Priam onto the battlefield—and scratches his image with her fingernails. In the second gesture, it is her own body that Lucrece touches, as she takes knife in hand, assumes the pose made famous in dozens of Renaissance prints, and sheaths the knife in her breast. She becomes her own spectacle. Jan Muller's version of that event (see figure 14), like Hendrik Goltzius's version of the moments before the rape (see figure 7), heightens the theatricality by framing the action within drapery. Curtains that in Goltzius's image quite certainly belong to the bed become more ambiguous in Muller's image. They figure as bed curtains but also as curtains of the sort that might hide just such a picture as Muller has made—or, in Shakespeare's case, just such a picture as Lucrece has made in imitation of Hecuba. Among the paintings that the German traveler Paul Hentzner noted in Queen Elizabeth's collection at Whitehall Palace was "Lucrece, a Grecian bride, in her nuptial habit."[62] (Muller, in another plate, engraved in the same size and at about the same time, imagined Cleopatra's suicide as taking place within curtains just like these.[63]) Shakespeare's *Lucrece* provides for the reader what the painting of Troy provides for Lucrece: a story in pictures, incitements of fancy, metonymy for passion, verbal cues for putting passion into words. Whatever "The Argument" may say in cramped italic type, the outcome of Lucrece's story is far more ample than "*the state gouernment changed from Kings to Consuls*" (sig. A4v). The experience of *Lucrece* engages four modes of perception, of which summation is only one—and the least important. "What's *Hecuba* to him, or he to *Hecuba*, / That he should weepe for her?"[64]: all of Shakespeare's writings play out that paradox. The stance of passionate identification that Lucrece finds for herself before the painted spectacle of Troy's fall is precisely the stance that spectator-listeners are invited to take before the dramatic spectacles of Shakespeare's plays in performance.

Heartburn in the 1640s

Since the nineteenth century, if not earlier, readers of Richard Crashaw's poem "The Flaming Heart vpon the Book and Picture of the seraphicall saint, TERESA, (As She Is Vsvally Expressed with a SERAPHIM beside her.)" have desperately wanted to identify the "Picture" in question with a famous sculpture of St. Teresa by Gian Lorenzo Bernini (1662). The headnote to Crashaw's poem in *The Norton Anthology of English Literature* seems calculated to make sure that this desire gets perpetuated in twenty-first-century undergraduates:

> The great Italian sculptor and architect Pietro [*sic*] Bernini portrayed a famous mystical experience described in Teresa's autobiography in a stunning baroque statue still in the church of Santa Maria della Vittoria, in Rome. It shows the saint in an attitude of ecstatic, swooning abandonment while a juvenile seraph stands over her, about to plunge a golden arrow into her heart. Crashaw may or may not have seen this statue while Bernini was at work on it (it was installed only after Crashaw's death), but his poem addresses a painter who has produced a picture of this episode conceived much as Bernini presented it.[65]

Figure 15. I. Meslager, *Le Vray portraict de S.te Terese,* an engraving from Richard Crashaw, *Carmen Deo Nostro, Te Decet Hymnus : Sacred Poems* (Paris: Peter Targa, 1652). Shown actual size, 2⅞ × 1⅞ inches (7.3 × 4.8 cm). (Reproduced by permission of the Folger Shakespeare Library.)

Compared with Bernini's sculpture, the picture that actually accompanies the poem in Crashaw's *Carmen Deo Nostro . . . Sacred Poems* (1652)—or rather, the picture that heralds all three of the St. Teresa poems near the collection's end—is bound to seem a disappointment (see figure 15). In place of Bernini's writhing, loosely draped female figure, the reader finds a nun in full habit, her hands clasped in prayer. The seraph with his phallic dart has become a heavenly dove blazing toward her on the upper left.[66] About the "Book" in Crashaw's title there is no question: it is the autobiography of St. Teresa of Avila (1515–1582), translated into English by Tobie Matthew as *The flaming hart, or, The life of the gloriovs S. Teresa,* published at Antwerp by Johannes Meursius in 1642 (an earlier printing at London in 1623 has disappeared entirely) and dedicated by Tobie to Queen Henrietta Maria.[67]

However strong the desire to make Bernini's sculpture the picture that speaks, the modest engraving actually suits Crashaw's *ekphrasis* much better, since he audaciously instructs the painter to transpose the two figures. In Crashaw's rearrangement of the scene it is the seraph who figures as the bashful nun: "Giue Him the veil, that he may couer / The Red cheeks of a riuall'd louer" (sig. o1). Teresa becomes the ravisher: "Giue her the DART for it is she / (Fair youth) shootes both thy shaft & THEE" (sig. o1). Teresa assumes that role through the power of her book to inflame the hearts of readers. The poem ends with the persona turning Teresa's dart on himself. Throughout the poem, the place of knowing is the heart—in the first instance Teresa's heart, then the persona's, then the reader's:

> O HEART! the aequall poise of lou'es [sic] both parts
> Bigge alike with wound & darts,
> Liue in these conquering leaues; liue all the same;
> And walk through all tongues one triumphant FLAME.
>
> (sig. o1v)

Throughout *Carmen Deo Nostro,* Crashaw celebrates the heart as the site of knowledge. The first poem in the collection is configured as an emblem. The engraved image shows a heart-shaped locket with a hinge on one side and a lock on the other. "*Non vi*" reads the Latin motto: "Not with force."[68] According to the poem's dedication, the heart in question belongs to one person in particular, Susan Villiers Feilding, 1st Countess of Denbigh, who served as lady of the bedchamber to Queen Henrietta Maria and remained her close friend. It is to "My Lady the Countsse of Denbigh" that the entire volume is dedicated on the title page.

Having undergone a conversion to the Catholic faith in 1645 (this, after having served for four years as Anglican rector of Little St. Mary's Church in Cambridge), Crashaw addresses the emblem "*Non Vi*" explicitly to Lady Denbigh. The ensemble of engraved heart, Latin motto, summary quatrain, and 68 lines of verse is presented as an act "Perswading her to Resolution in Religion, & to render her selfe without further delay into the Communion of the Catholick Church" (sig. a3v). The "selfe" here is to be distinguished from two other entities, "heart" and "soul." The key for opening the closed heart depicted in the engraving is possessed by "Allmighty LOVE" (sig. a4), who works his effects through wounding, through piercing the heart with shafts of light, which Crashaw's persona also imagines as a draft that can be drunk and, just 24 inches lower, as a penis that can be received into the vagina: "Meet his well-meaning Wounds, wise heart! / And hast to drink the wholsome dart" (sig. a4v). It is only when love has been received into the heart that soul comes into play. Near the beginning of the poem Crashaw's persona asks, "Say, lingring fair! why comes the birth / Of your braue soul so slowly forth"? (sig. a4). Images of pregnancy seem to inform such a question, as if the heart were the soul's womb. Later in the poem, the persona urges Lady Denbigh to meet the dart of love, the arrow of light, "with wide-spread armes: & see / It's seat your soul's iust center be" (sig. a4v).

In Crashaw, then, the entity-that-knows is not the mind but the soul, and the place where it does that knowing is not the brain or the pineal gland but the heart. *What* the soul knows is derived from its anatomical location. In Crashaw's epistemology, knowledge is not logo-centric: it does not consist in words. Quite the opposite. Crashaw's knowledge is logo-fugal: it *starts* with words—the words of St. Teresa's "Book," for instance—but it ends in the heart's flames. "The soul it selfe more feeles then heares" (sig. o3v), Crashaw declares to Lady Denbigh in a poem accompanying the gift of a prayer book. The nature of the soul's nonverbal knowledge is kinaesthetic, fusing vision, sound, smell, taste, and tactility. "Sweet," a word that can describe all five sensations, is Crashaw's favorite adjective. With respect to color, Crashaw's palette is surprisingly constricted, embracing only black, white, and red. The only colors in his verbal picture of St. Teresa are the white of her skin ("female FROST"), her blushes ("pale-fac't purple"), the seraphim's ardor ("The Red cheeks of a riuall'd louer"), and fire (the seraphim's "Rosy fingers, radiant hair, / Glowing cheek, & glistering wings") (sigs. N4v–o1). In the first of the St. Teresa poems, "The Hymne," Crashaw thrills to imagine the pale Teresa with her red wound among the black Moors whom she sought to convert (sigs. M4v–N1). In the ensuing "Apologie for the Fore-going Hymen [*sic*]," Crashaw's persona desires to drink the wine of love, "which can proue / Its Tincture from the rosy nectar" (sig. N3v). The conceit of"A Hymn. Svng as by the Three Kings," taking its cue perhaps from Melchior's proverbial blackness, focuses on the "Rosy MORN" of the Virgin Mother's blushes (sig. C2v) and the three kings' journey out of black Egypt, "A mutuall trade / 'Twixt sun & SHADE, / By confederat BLACK & WHITE" (sig. D2). This palette of black, white, and red seems to have been a conscious choice, to judge by a poem of "Covncel" to Lady Denbigh, in which Crashaw contrasts the multicolored "painted shapes, / Peacocks & Apes" of "this lower sphear" with the "fair sonnes of fire," the "golden throng," of heaven (sig. P1). Fire, indeed, is the essence of Crashaw's vision. It is not hue that colors his imagination but light value.

Perception in Crashaw's poems is not so much the "through-seizing" that the word "perception" literally means as the transumption or "across-taking" that the Catholic sacrament assumes to be happening when bread and wine are turned, by the words of the priest, into Christ's body and blood (*OED* "transume," *v.*, etymology).[69] Crashaw's "The Hymn. for the Bl. Sacrament" celebrates Christ's injunction to his followers:

Euer to doe what he once did.
And by a mindfull, mystick breath
That we may liue, reuiue his DEATH;

With a well-bles't bread & wine,
Transsum'd, & taught to turn diuine.
(sig. L4)

The specific words to be spoken by a mindful, mystic breath are those recorded in Matthew 26:26, Mark 14:22, and Luke 22:19: "Acipite et comedite, hoc est corpus meum" (Take and eat. This is my body).[70] What is "mindful" about these words? Hobbes, as we have noted in chapters one and three, takes the objects of the mind's knowing to be propositions, the result of "the proper use of *names* in Language."[71] Knowledge for Crashaw works the other way around: not from sensations to words but from words to sensations. Transumption begins with the ears' hearing the word "*corpus*" but ends with the mouth's eating and the soul's feeling. The *hoc* in the priest's mindful breath functions like Horace's *ut:* it brings together two logically unlike entities. As such, *hoc* provided the occasion for sustained debate among Catholic and Protestant apologists in the sixteenth and seventeenth centuries. The demonstrative *hoc,* as Catholic writers liked to point out, is neuter in gender and hence refers to *corpus,* the neuter word for "body," and not *panis,* the masculine word for "bread," which would take the masculine demonstrative *hic.*[72] Protestant polemicists, like Daniel Featley in *Transubstantion Exploded* (1638), will have none of this: "it seemes to be very absurd to say that the pronoune this doth not demonstrate something present. But our Lord tooke bread, and reaching it, said, Take eate this is my Body: he seemes therefore to have demonstrated bread."[73] More than that is hocus pocus.

Such an insistence on the correspondence of *this* word with *that* object or concept provides, as Hobbes rightly argues, the very basis for empirical science and logical reasoning. Sense experiences must be matched up with the words that name them. To judge from Britomart's rescue of Florimel from the House of Busyrane, that is Spenser's goal as well, even as he recognizes, indeed exults in the sensuous pleasure that the act of recognition inspires. When it comes to visual experience, Spenser is no prude. Along the spectrum of Renaissance thought (see figure 10) he belongs in the violet range, along with other self-reflective thinkers—More, Descartes, Reynolds, Davies, Cornwallis—who acknowledge the power of passions, even as they aspire to knowledge above, beyond, or apart from passions. Crashaw, surely, keeps company with Burton and Cavendish at the far black end of the spectrum. Usually Crashaw has been taken to be an example of what was new in the seventeenth century: Counter-

Reformation aesthetics (with its appeal to the senses) and Baroque style (with its dissolution of the solidities of the High Renaissance). It is just as possible to find in Crahsaw one last, rhetorically powerful instance of what was old in the seventeenth century: an assumption that knowing comes through feeling. In between these extremes, in the green part of the spectrum, stands Shakespeare, a mediator in the seventeenth-century crisis of consciousness.

CHAPTER FIVE

Listening for Green

The ship is at sea, and everybody on board is feasting, tippling, talking, and telling fabulous stories when Pantagruel starts hearing voices in the air—voices of people that no one can see. "The more we listen'd," says Rabelais' narrator, "the plainer we discern'd the Voices, so as to distinguish Articulate Sounds."[1] Sounds but no sources, voices but no faces: that's always disturbing. "We are all beshit," Panurge cries, "let's fly" (216). Pantagruel urges calm. Maybe the ship has sailed into the equilateral triangle mentioned in Plutarch, the space where unseen worlds converge. Or maybe what they're hearing are Homer's words. Didn't Aristotle say that Homer's words are always flying about? Or maybe the words are Plato's. "*Antiphanes* said, that *Plato*'s Philosophy was like words which being spoken in some Country during a hard Winter are immediately congeal'd, frozen up and not heard" (218; original emphasis): they're that hard to understand. Or maybe it's the singing of Orpheus's severed head, having floated here from the river Hebrus.

The frozen-word hypothesis turns out to be right. Pantagruel finds some words that haven't yet melted—and they turn out to be multicolored:

> He then throw'd us on the Deck whole handfulls of frozen Words, which seem'd to us like your rough Sugar-Plumbs, of many colours, like those us'd in Heraldry, some words *Gules,* [This means also Jests and merry sayings] some *Vert,* some *Azur,* some *Black,* some *Or,* [This means also fair words;] and when we had somewhat warm'd them between our Hands, they melted like Snow, and we really heard them, but could not understand them, for it was a Barbarous Gibberish. . . . (219–20)[2]

The captain remembers that near this spot, at the beginning of the winter that is now ending, a battle took place on the ice. What they are hearing are the sounds of that battle. In the meltdown, words dissolve into noise which the narrator delights to catalog: "hin, hin, hin, hin, his, tick, tock, taack, brededin, brededack, frr, frr, frr, bou, bou, bou, bou, bou, bou, bou, bou, track, track, trr, trr, trr, trrr, trrrrrr, on, on, on, on, on, on, ououououon, gog, magog, and I do not know what other barbarous words, which the Pilot said, were the noise made by the Charging Squadrons, the shock and neighing of Horses" (220–21).

Rabelais is not the only author to have heard colors. In William Shakespeare and John Fletcher's *The Two Noble Kinsmen,* there is a scene in which a character called the Doctor subjects a character called the Jailer's Daughter to a seventeenth-century equivalent of the psychoanalysis that Sigmund Freud performed on "Dora" and other hysterical women in early-twentieth-century Vienna. The Jailer's Daughter has fallen hopelessly in love with her father's prisoner Palamon and has gone mad. When the Doctor describes the cause of her madness as "a most thicke, and profound melancholy" (4.3.46–47), what he has in mind is not so much an emotion as the viscous, heavy qualities of black bile. "The intemperat surfeit of her eye," the Doctor surmises, "hath distemperd the / Other sences" (4.3.67–68).[3] The recommended cure is homeopathic. Since "it is a falsehood / She is in" (4.3.90), the Doctor prescribes a series of new falsehoods that will engage all the senses and "reduce what's / Now out of square in her, into their former law and / Regiment" (4.3.92–93). Put her in a dark place, he counsels the father, surround her with sweet smells, come to her in disguise as Palamon, invite her to eat and drink with you, "sing to her such greene / Songs of Love, as she says *Palamon* hath sung in / Prison" (4.3.78–79). An excess of blackness can be cured by hearing green.

Even Sir Isaac Newton was convinced that colors could be heard—or at least that color perception worked like hearing. In a letter to the Royal Society in 1675 Newton explains that colors, like sounds, result from vibrations. The medium for sound vibrations is air; for light rays the medium is ether, the substance that was believed to permeate planetary space beyond the layer of air—and even the spaces between particles of air and other matter here on earth (*OED,* "ether" 5.a). Just as bodies of lesser or greater volume and density produce lesser or greater sound waves in the air, so too surfaces of lesser or greater reflectance produce lesser or greater vibrations in the ether. And just as sound waves set up vibrations in the ear drum, so too light rays set up refractions in the optic nerve:

[T]he ends of the capillamenta of the optic nerve, which pave or face the retina, being such refracting superficies, when the rays impinge upon them, they must there excite these vibrations, which vibrations (like those of sound in a trunk or trumpet) will run upon the aqueous pores or crystalline pith of the capillamenta through the optic nerves into the sensorum (which light itself cannot do) and there, I suppose, affect the sense with various colours, according to their bigness and mixture."[4]

The biggest vibrations produce the strongest colors, the reds and the yellows; the lesser vibrations, the weaker colors, the blues and the violets. A chart that Newton included in his report to the Royal Society recognizes eight hues (in earlier writings he had recognized eleven), which are coordinated with the seven tones (plus a return to *do* in the octave) of the diatonic musical scale, purple corresponding to the low end of the scale, red to the high (see figure 16). Predictably from Aristotle, green is said to result from vibrations of middling strength—this, despite the fact that Newton's experiments had demonstrated violet and red to be the ends of the visible spectrum, not, as Aristotle thought, black and white.

An association of color with sound goes back to the very beginnings of Western culture. It is, in fact, Aristotle who is Newton's primary inspiration for the idea that sound and color both result from mathematically mappable ratios. As we noted in chapter two, mathematics is the first of three explanations of color that Aristotle considers in *De Sensu* and the one that he pushes. Numerical values have the advantage of explaining why some colors are more pleasing than others: "we may regard

1675.] ROYAL SOCIETY OF LONDON. 263

" Y the centres of thoſe ſemicircles, X Z the length of a muſical ſtring double to

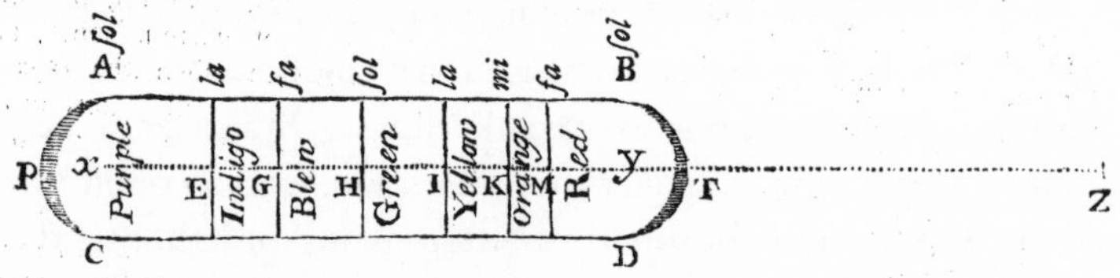

" X Y, and divided between X and Y, ſo as to ſound the tones expreſſed at the
" ſide (that is X H the half, X G and G I the third part, Y K the fifth part,
" Y M the eighth part, and G E the ninth part of X Y) and the intervals between
" theſe diviſions expreſs the ſpaces which the colours written there took up, every
" colour being moſt briſkly ſpecific in the middle of thoſe ſpaces.

Figure 16. Isaac Newton's chart coordinating seven hues with the seven tones of the diatonic musical scale, from his letter to the Royal Society (1675), in Thomas Birch, *The History of the Royal Society of London for the Improving of Natural Knowledge* (1757). (Reproduced by permission of the Folger Shakespeare Library.)

all these colours as analogous to concords, and suppose that those involving numerical ratios, like the concords in music, may be those generally regarded as most agreeable; as, for example, purple, crimson, and some few such colours, their fewness being due to the same causes that render the concords few."[5] With respect to sound, most people would agree with Aristotle: in music we don't *see* numbers or (most of us) even *think* numbers, we *hear* numbers. Color is more perplexing, but still Newton's hypothesis seems reasonable: in modern terms, what we're seeing in colors is nanometers. Numbers cannot, however, explain Rabelais' glee in imagining the different sounds that different colors make. Words, not numbers, are in play here: *gules,* the heraldic term for red, sounds like *jeux,* the French word for jests, while *or,* the heraldic term for gold, can easily be elided with *doré,* or gilded, which can apply to what English speakers would call "polished" speech.[6] Rabelais trades in synesthetic puns. Black and green for Shakespeare and Fletcher's Doctor are neither numbers nor words but physiological and psychological states. More is going on in these passages than meets the eye—or the ear. What would it mean to *hear* color? Or rather: what would it mean to *listen for* color? Sound theorists Barry Truax and Stephen Handel both insist on a crucial distinction between just hearing and the *directed* hearing that is listening.[7] What would it mean to listen for color? Pursuing that question with respect to a range of Renaissance texts will bring us, via phonetic linguistics, to questioning the Cartesian premises on which deconstruction is based. What would it mean, in particular, to listen for *green?*

To Listen with Passion

To listen for green would, for a start, mean to listen longingly. Etymologically at least, that should not take much effort. To *list* in the sense of "to listen" (*OED,* "list" *v.*[2]) is—or at least once was—to do the same thing as to *lust* (*OED,* "lust" *v.* †3). For me to say that a sound "me list" or "me listeth" is to say that I choose it, like it, desire it (*OED,* "list" *v.*[1] 1). Those songs of love that the Doctor recommended in *The Two Noble Kinsmen*—they invite both listing and lusting. But why should they be green? Why should songs of love be green and not red, the color of blood and lust—or blue, as so many love songs have been since the nineteen teens?[8] At least three reasons suggest themselves. Green was, and is, a color associated with youth and hence with rashness. Numerous popular proverbs—"You may be jogging while your boots are green," "Green wood makes a hot fire"[9]—explain the Nurse's recommendation of Paris to

Juliet: "An Eagle Madam / Hath not so greene, so quicke, so fair an eye / As Paris hath" (F 1623, 3.5.219–21). In medical terms, greenness of complexion was taken to be a symptom of the cool, moist anemia to which young women like the Jailer's Daughter were prone. In the heat of his passion, Romeo refuses to associate fiery-eyed Juliet with Diana, goddess of the moon, since "Her Vestal liuery is but sicke and greene" (2.1.50). Nonetheless, Juliet's father diagnoses his daughter's devotion to Romeo as the very illness that her lover has eschewed: "Out, you greene sicknesse carrion, out you baggage! / You tallow face!" (3.5.156–57). John Guillim, in his heraldry handbook, as we saw in chapter two, describes green as "a colour most wholesome and pleasant to the eie, except it be in a young Gentlewomans face."[10] In a more complementary context, it is a combination of green as the color of youth and green as love-longing that explains why green hues dominate Robert Peake's portrait of Princess Elizabeth (see plate 10).

There were, finally, physical reasons why love songs should be green. The occasion for Ficino's reasoning of green as the most pleasing color is a chapter in the second of his *De Vita Libri Tres* (1489) titled "The Conversation of the Old People Traversing the Green Fields under the Leadership of Venus." The subject at hand is not physics or chemistry or the aesthetics of color but physiology. Venus asks the old people to meditate on the thought that "the nature of green things [*rerum viridium naturam*], for so long as they stay green, is not only alive but even youthful and abounding with very salubrious humor and a lively spirit [*humoreque prorsus salubri et vivido quodam spiritu redundantem*]; and because of this a certain youthful spirit flows to us through the odor, sight, use, and frequent habitation of and in them."[11] To Ficino's way of seeing, green neither dilates the eye with too much light nor dulls the eye with too much darkness: rather, "the color green tempering most of all black with white, furnishes the one effect and the other, equally delighting and conserving the sight" (205). Be that as it may, green is also dangerous. Thomas Wright's association of green with the passion and passionate action with the putting of "greene spectacles before the eyes of our wit, to make it see nothing but greene" attracted our notice in chapter one.[12] Ficino's discussion of green in the context of old people who continue to act on passions more appropriate to younger, "greener" lovers registers a similar ambivalence.

The Doctor's diagnosis and Wright's description of perception suggest that "green" has significance beyond its proverbial, medical, and physical senses. In Wright's account, green is not something that one sees; it is something one sees *with*. It is not an external object but an internal state of being. The Jailer's Daughter will take notice of "green songs," because that is what her greensickness predisposes her to hear. In modern epistemology, green is regarded as a strictly optical phenomenon. Renaissance epistemology, as Rabelais, Shakespeare, Fletcher, Wright, and even Newton all suggest, was different. Green could be heard as well as seen. The charades proposed by the Doctor imply that it could also be smelled, tasted, and touched.

All told, listening for green calls into question at least three premises of modern epistemology: (1) that the senses function as five separate faculties, (2) that reason is a faculty that exists above and beyond the senses, and (3) that the knowing subject exists apart from the objects he or she perceives. The third challenge is the most fundamental of all. In the Doctor's analysis of the Jailer's Daughter's madness and in Wright's explanation of perception, external objects do not exist apart from the bodily ways in which the subject comes to know them. The thinking subject can try to subordinate sense perceptions to understanding, but Galenic medicine made thinking absolutely dependent on seeing, hearing, touching, tasting, and smelling.

In Middle English and in early modern Scots, as we learned in chapter one, "green" was recognized as a verb. *To green* was "to desire earnestly, to yearn, to long *after, for*" (*OED,* "green" v[2]). With respect to sound, the verb "to green" reverses the usual direction of sensation. Ordinarily sound comes to the listener from the outside. It penetrates the listener's body through the ears. Especially if one accepts the extramission theory of vision, in which light rays are projected outward from the crystalline sphere of the viewer's eyes to objects in the world around, hearing casts the subject in a more vulnerable position than seeing does. Take, for example, the visceral response to unpleasant sounds. In *Sylva Sylvarum,* Bacon explains why squeaking and shrieking, the sharpening of saws, and the grinding of stones set a listener's teeth on edge: "The *Cause* is, for that the *Obiects* of the *Eare,* doe affect the *Spirits* (immediately) most with *Pleasure* and Offence."[13] The emphasis here falls on "immediately." Colors in and of themselves do not, Bacon claims, much offend the eye. A painted representation of a horrible sight hardly carries the force of the thing itself. Smells, tastes, and touches involve bodily participation with the thing being experienced. "So it is *Sound* alone, that doth immediately, and incorporeally, affect most" (sig. Z4; original emphasis). Elsewhere in *Sylva Sylvarum,* Bacon catalogs "the passions of the mind"—fear, grief and pain, joy, anger, light displeasure or dislike, shame, wonder, laughing, and lust—and notes that "evermore the spirits, in all passions, resort most to the parts that labour most, or are most affected." Hence lust causes "a flagrancy in the eyes" (sig. BB1). And in listening, we may conclude, a flagrancy in the ears.

A direct physiological connection between hearing and genital desire is anatomized by John Donne in an undated Whitsuntide sermon on Acts 10:44, "While Peter yet spake these words, the Holy Ghost fell on all them which heard the word." "They say," Donne reports, "there is a way of castration, in cutting off the eares: There are certain veines behinde the eares, which, if they be cut, disable a man from generation."[14] For this curious intelligence Donne is ultimately indebted to Hippocrates' medical treatise "Airs, Waters, Places."[15] In Galen's anatomy of the human body, it would be *spiritus*—what Wright calls "purer spirits" (sig. D7)—that would carry sensation from the ears directly to the penis, just as, in the more conventional explanation, it is *spiritus* that carries sensation from the ears to the imagination and thence to the heart. According to Crooke, the coursing of *spiritus* in the veins can be compared to the moving of the wind: "it passeth & repasseth at his pleasure, vnseene, but not vnfelt; for the force and incursion thereof is not without a kinde of violence; so the seede although it be thicke and viscid, yet passeth thorough vessels which haue no manifest cauities; the reason is, because it is full & as it were houen with spirits."[16] To green for a particular sound would, in effect, change the direction of the energy: it would mean to listen from the inside out, from the penis to the ear.

In Book 2 of *The Faerie Queene,* the hapless swain who lies sleeping "in secret shade" (2.12.72.6) at the heart of Acrasia's Bower of Bliss is, the reader discovers, named Verdant, or "Green" (2.12.82.8). As usual in *The Faerie Queene,* the reader learns the personage's name only *after* he has been seen in action—or, in this case, in inaction, as Acrasia's victim has been situated among the bower's "shady Laurell trees," (2.12.43.2), "couert groues, and thickets close" (2.12.76.6) and its strangely *illegible* sounds. It is through sound, in fact, that Sir Guyon and the Palmer first come to know the bower:

> Eftsoones they heard a most melodious sound,
> Of all that mote delight a daintie eare,
> Such as attonce might not on liuing ground,
> Saue in this Paradise, be heard elsewhere:
> Right hard it was, for wight, which did it heare,
> To read, what manner musicke that mote bee:
> For all that pleasing is to liuing eare,

> Was there consorted in one harmonee,
> Birds, voyces, instruments, windes, waters, all agree.
> (2.12.70.1–9)

The passions that these sights and sounds engender in Verdant become Acrasia's physical possessions, as she bedews his lips with kisses, "And though his humid eyes did sucke his spright, / Quite molten into lust and pleasure lewd" (2.12.73.7–8). Greenness, in all its erotic appeal, is something that Andrew Marvell's garden shares with Spenser's Bower of Bliss.

The viewing and listening position that Sir Guyon and the Palmer assume in this episode—seeing but not seen, hearing but not being heard—was one in which Spenser's contemporaries loved to imagine themselves. One of the sights sought out by foreign visitors to England during Elizabeth's reign was an artificial grotto at Nonsuch Palace that featured statues of Diana and her nymphs spraying water on Actaeon. Thomas Platter locates "the grove" (*lucus*) quite precisely "at the entrance to the garden."[17] Just as Actaeon in *Metamorphoses*, Book 3, happened upon the sight of Diana and her nymphs bathing, so visitors to Nonsuch Palace and readers of *The Faerie Queene* might happen upon a green spectacle and its alluring sounds: splashing water, warbling birds, and greening love songs. Within the green matrix of birds, voices, instruments, winds, and waters, Sir Guyon and the Palmer hear a voice singing, "Gather the Rose of loue, whilest yet is time, / Whilest louing thou mayst loued be with equall crime" (2.12.75.8–9). The response of Spenser's "noble Elfe, and careful Palmer" (2.12.81.1) is suddenly to rush forth from their hiding place and throw "A subtile net" (2.12.81.4) over Acrasia and Verdant. Other spectator-listeners, in similar situations, were more apt to be taken than to take. The spectator-listener in "A Louers complaint," printed at the end of *Shake-speares Sonnets* in 1609, assumes an altogether sympathetic position vis-à-vis the voice he hears:

> From off a hill whose concaue wombe reworded,
> A plaintfull story from a sistring vale
> My spirrits t'attend this doble voyce accorded,
> And downe I laid to list the sad tun'd tale. . . .[18]

The "I" in these verses first hears and only *then* sees the "fickle maid full pale" (sig. K1v) whose tale he proceeds to rehearse in 38 of the poem's 47 stanzas. The maid's voice is "doble" not only because it echoes across the vale but because the spectator-listener makes *her* voice *his* voice. And he

The wofull complaint, and lamentable dea

To a pleaſant new tune.

Downe by a forreſt where as I did paſſe,
to ſee what ſport abroad there was,
Walking by a pleaſant ſpring,
the Birds in ſundry notes did ſing.
Long time wandring here and there,
to ſee what ſports in forreſts were,
At length I heard one make great mone,
ſaying, From me all ioyes are gone.

Thus to l
wiſhing
His torm
his hear

I ſlept in
becauſ
With foli
the tear
And carel
pitty he
Then dob
no eaſe

Thus he l
ſeuen l
Saying,
I find
For ſhe th
ſhe dot
And hath
that I

Ye gods a
ſith hea
For whilſt
ſhall ſhe
Euery tree
ſhall be
That they
Loue w

Nature di
ſcorning
And in as
as euer

Figure 17. Anonymous, "The wofull complaint, and lamentable death of a forsaken Louer" (London: Henry Gosson, 1625), detail. Woodcut shown actual size, 4 × 3 inches (10.5 × 7.8 cm). (Reproduced by permission of the Pepys Library, Magdalen College, Cambridge.)

listens passionately: it is his "spirrits," the coursing fluids in his sinews, that "attend" the double voice and dictate what he writes down for the reader's benefit.

In this posture of green listening, Shakespeare's persona replicates a subject position common in broadside ballads like "A Lover's Complaint, Being Forsaken of his Love" (1615, 1620, 1628–29, 1630, 1639, 1640), which puts into print passages from the "song of willow" that Desmonda sings in *Othello.*[19] It is not, in the first instance, her own passion that Desdemona voices but someone else's: "*The poore Soule sat singing, by a Sicamour tree*" (F 1623, 4.3.38). And not just the poor soul's passion but that of Barbary, the serving woman who taught Desdemona the song. The ballad's refrain locates the passion not in any one of these three people—Barbary, the poor soul, Desdemona—but in the listener. The refrain is a second-person command: "*Sing all a greene Willough*" (4.3.39). With respect to syntax, the "all" here hovers among several possibilities: the adjectival "nothing but" (*OED,* "all" A. *adj.* I.1), the adverbial "wholly, completely, altogether" (*OED,* "all" C. *adv.* 1), and the vocative "all of you." The green setting implicit in Desdemona's "song of willow" is graphically realized in "The wofull complaint, and lamentable death of a forsaken Louer," a broadside ballad printed in 1625 (see figure 17). The pose shown in the woodcut and described in the first stanza is precisely that of Edward Herbert in Isaac Oliver's miniature portrait (compare plate 11). It is not only the setting of woods and spring that links this production of popular culture with the high-culture trappings of Spenser's Bower of Bliss but the ambient sounds of birds. Unfortunately the "pleasant new tune" to which the ballad is to be sung cannot, from that scant information, be identified:

> Downe by a forrest where as I did passe,
> to see what sport abroad there was,
> Walking by a pleasant spring,
> the Birds in sundry notes did sing.
> Long time wandring here and there,
> to see what sports in forests were,
> At length I heard one make great mone,
> saying, From me all ioyes are gone.[20]

And so begins the ballad singer's recreation, in his or her own first personhood, of the forsaken lover's passion. What this ballad, Desdemona's willow song, and Shakespeare's "A Louers complaint" all invite is passionate listening, spirited listening, listening that dissolves distinctions among

"I," "he," "she," and "you." All green songs are species of *com* + *plaint*, of bewailing *with*, of beating one's head or, better yet, one's breast (*OED*, "complain" *v.*, etymology).

To Listen and Not Just Read

Overwhelmed by the consorted sounds of the Bower of Bliss, Spenser's narrator observes that it was hard "To *read*, what manner musicke that mote bee" (2.12.70.6, emphasis added). To listen for green would mean not only to listen longingly but to take in sound without regard to its legibility. Especially music. "*Tunes* and *Aires*, euen in their owne Nature, haue in themselues some Affinity with the *Affections*," Bacon observes in *Sylva Sylvarum*.

> As there be *Merry Tunes, Dolefull Tunes, Solemne Tunes; Tunes inclining Mens mindes to Pitty; Warlike Tunes; &c.* So as it is no Maruell, if they alter the *Spirits;* considering that *Tunes* haue a Predisposition to the *Motion* of the *Spirits* in themselues. But yet it hath been noted, that though this variety of *Tunes,* doth dispose the *Spirits* to variety of Passions, conforme vnto them; yet generally, *Musick* feedeth that disposition of the *Spirits* which it findeth. (sig. F2v)

To hear *green,* that is to say, one must first *hear* green. In the culture of Renaissance England, there is surely no more striking instance of hearing green, with the emphasis both ways, than the phenomenal popularity of the ballad "Greensleeves" and its progeny. An entry in the Stationers' Register on September 3, 1580, for "A newe northern Dittye of ye Ladye Greene Sleves" probably refers to a broadside that was handled, folded, pasted up, wadded, and worn to oblivion. The earliest surviving text dates from four years later, in the ballad anthology *A Handful of Pleasant Delights* (1584). Transcriptions of the tune began to appear in manuscripts of music for the lute about the same time. Within nine months of the first licensing, no fewer than seven spin-offs had been entered in the register or appeared in print.[21] In *Hero and Leander* (datable to the mid 1580s) Marlowe's blazon of the clothing that Leander so admires on Hero includes:

> wide sleeves greene, and bordered with a grove,
> Where *Venus* in her naked glory strove,
> To please the carelesse and disdainfull eies,
> Of proud *Adonis* that before her lies.[22]

The effect that Marlowe has in mind can be seen in the jacket shown in plate 18, where verdant antic work supplies the matrix within which neck, lips, and eyes are perceived. Marlowe's focus on sleeves can be explained in part by the relative expensiveness and ostentatiousness of these detachable garments. The focus on green may also stem from the northern origins specified on the original broadside. In Renaissance English imagination, the north is the preeminent land of balladry, of fierce fights like the Battle of Chevy Chase,[23] of dense oak forests that shelter Robin Hood as the lord of midsummer pageants,[24] and of the trickster lover Jocky, who figures in the repertory of the mid-sixteenth-century minstrel Richard Sheale as well as in numerous seventeenth-century broadside ballads.[25]

The ballad "Greensleeves" is more about green than it is about sleeves, as singing the ballad or hearing it sung readily reveals. The tune falls into four phrases, labeled A, B, C, and D. In the first stanza, phrases A and B are focused on the singer: they situate him as a spurned suitor. Virtually identical until the final cadence, both phrases reach a climaxes of pitch, volume, and passion on the words "loue" and "loued" before descending to the lowest pitches in the entire tune. Abruptly, phrases C and D turn the focus from the singer to the object of his love and sound out the highest pitches of the entire tune on the words "Greensleeues." The second stanza

Musical example 1. "Greensleeves." Adapted from Claude M. Simpson, *The British Broadside Ballad and Its Music* (1966).

sets in place the same structure of singer (phrases A and B) versus the object of the singer's love (phrases C and D). Succeeding stanzas then catalog in phrases A and B all the articles of clothing and other gifts that the singer has given the lady—kerchers, petticoats, jewels, gold-embroidered smock, red-gold girdle, purse, gay gilt knives, pincase, crimson stockings, white pumps, gown "of grossie green" (grassy green? green grosgrain?), satin sleeves, gold garters, silver aglets, a gelding to ride, green-clad men to serve as attendants, dainties to eat, "musicke still to play and sing"—before turning in each case to the same passionate climax on "Greensleeues" in phrases C and D. The effect of repetition after repetition of phrases C and D (eighteen in all according to the *Pleasant Delights* text) is to turn the words "Greensleeues" into a kind of mantra. By the end of the ballad, the high pitch on which those words are sung and the passion that the high pitch invites become something far more compelling than the article of clothing to which the words refer, far more compelling even than the lady whose pet name is derived from that article of clothing. One is struck by the name of one of the imitations licensed in 1580: "Countenaunce in Countenaunce is Greene Sleves."[26] "Greensleeues" becomes, in effect, the singer's passion. And the name of that passion is greensickness. In Bacon's terms, the tune of "Greensleeves" has, in itself, an affinity with melancholy that "feeds the disposition" of the spirits that the tune finds. To judge from the ballad's popularity, such spirits were rife in the 1580s.

Given its transformation of the singer's body—and the listener's—from hot and moist (the passion of lust) to cold and dry (the passion of melancholy), "Greensleeves" seems to offer a perfect example of the kind of music Philip Stubbes singles out for attack in *The Anatomy of Abuses in Ailgna,* first published three years after the original broadside of "Greensleeves" appeared. Music is a gift of God, Stubbes's spokesman Philoponus will concede, and is capable of delighting man and beast, reviving the spirits, comforting the heart, and making it readier to serve God, as David did in the Psalms, "but being vsed in publique assemblies and priuate conuenticles as directories to filthie dauncing, thorow the sweet harmonie & smoothe melodie therof, it estraungeth y[e] mind[,] stireth vp filthie lust, womannisheth y[e] minde[,] rauisheth the hart, enflameth concupisence, and bringeth in vncleannes."[27] Stubbes thinks first and foremost here of dance music not only because it sets bodies in lascivious motion but because it is wordless. Later in the same chapter, Stubbes contrasts the plenitude of pipers in every town, city, and country region with the deficit of divines. The written licenses granted to pipers, minstrels, and musicians will do them no good at the last judgment, Stubbes warns, "for the Worde of GOD is against your vngodly exercyses, and condemneth them to Hell" (sig. o5v). Pipers provide the sharpest possible contrast to expositors of the word of God because their music is wordless: they cannot pipe and sing at the same time. It was the passionate abandon of piped music, associated with Asia, that prompted Greek intellectuals to favor the lyre of Apollo, as Plutarch reports in his life of Alcibiades.[28] With his mouth a piper can do no more than blow air; a lyricist can imbue the air with words.

Trying to describe to Mistress Page the patent discrepancy between Sir John Falstaff's flattering words and his true intents, Mistress Ford declares in *The Merry Wives of Windsor,* "But they doe no more adhere and keep together, then the hundred Psalms to the tune of Greensleeues" (F 1623, 2.1.58–60). By the time *Merry Wives* was first performed in 1597–1598, "Greensleeves" had provided the tune for at least four moralizing ballads. But the Psalms—what could they have to do with ballads? More than one might think. Several psalms enjoin not just sung words but instrumental music and dancing. "Praise yee the LORD . . . ," begins the last of the 150 psalms in the King James Version. "Praise him with the sound of the trumpet: praise him with the psalterie and harpe. Praise him with the timbrell and dance: praise him with stringed instruments, and Organes." A marginal note in Robert Barker's 1616 printing notes that "trumpet" could be translated as "cornet" and that "dance" could mean "pipe."[29] How Philip Stubbes might have handled the second of these textual cruxes is not recorded. Ballads were originally dance songs, as the origins of the word in *ballare*—"to dance" (*OED,* "ballad" *n.,* etymology)—declare, and piping is good for dancing. The musical quality of the Psalms was realized in the worship practices of early modern England in three quite different modes: in the Gregorian chant of the Catholic rite, in the ballad stanzas of Thomas Sternhold and John Hopkins's *The Whole Booke of Psalmes,* and in the elegant compromise of Anglican chant.[30]

The Protestant right wing, with its commitment to the literal word of God recorded in the Bible, had good reason to be suspicious of Gregorian chant. For intoning the psalms the Latin rite used eight formulas, or "tones," that allowed singers to follow the rhythms and the rhetorical heft of the parallel lines in the original Hebrew texts, but during the offices these syllable-by-syllable formulas were framed by antiphons and responses that allowed the voice to float free of the text in sequences of abstract tones called melismas.[31] Take for example the psalm numbered 22 in the Vulgate ("Dominus regit me"), which has appeared as number 23 in English Bibles since the sixteenth century ("The Lord is my shep-

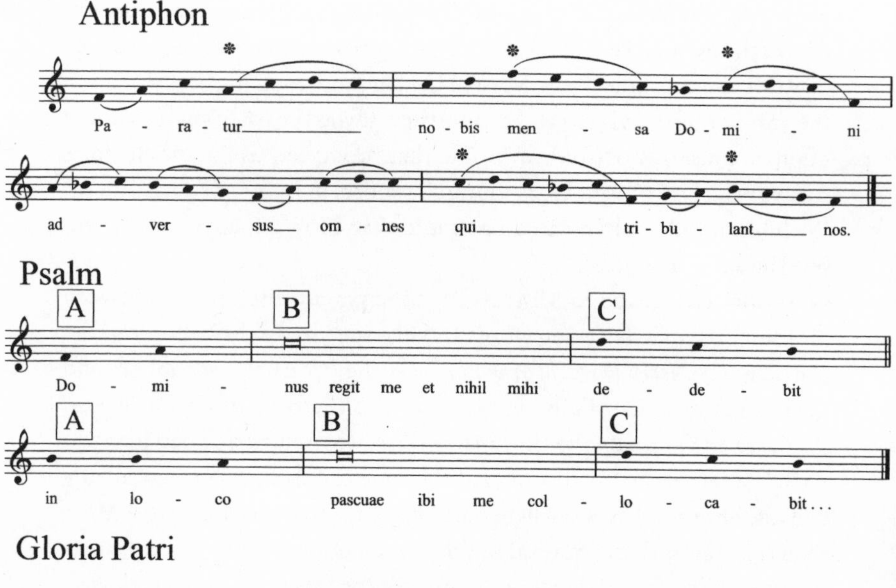

Musical example 2. Psalm 23, plainchant with antiphon before and Gloria Patri afterward. Adapted from Walter Howater Frere, *The Use of Sarum* (1898–1901).

herd"). According to the Use of Sarum, "Dominus regit me" was to be chanted daily as part of the Office of Prime, as well as at the Second Hour of Night during the Feast of Corpus Christi, which, as the eighth Thursday after Easter, generally fell during the green time of late May or early June.[32] In the Corpus Christi service, Psalm 22/23 was to be preceded by an antiphon, "Paratur nobis mensa Domini adversus omnes qui tribulant nos," anticipating one of the succeeding psalm's most famous lines ("Thou preparest a table before me in the presence of mine enemies") and was to be followed, as with all the psalms, by the *Gloria Patri* (Glory be to the Father, to the Son, and to the Holy Ghost . . .). The transcription of the entire sequence of Antiphon–Psalm–*Gloria Patri* in musical example 2 has been adapted from the most complete manuscript of music surviving from the pre-Reformation church in England.[33] The sequence is cast in the fifth tone. In the antiphon that precedes the psalm the melismas, the sequences during which the singing voices soar free of the text, are indicated by asterisks. For singing liturgists as well as their listening congregants, such moments represent moments for hearing green.

Plate 1. The Green Closet (1637–39) at Ham House, Surrey, as approached from the Long Gallery. (Photo by Andreas von Einsiedel. National Trust Photographic Library.)

Plate 2. Hans Holbein, *Portrait of Jean de Dinteville and Georges de Selve* (*The Ambassadors*) (1533), detail. Oil on oak panel. Original size of entire panel, 6 feet 9 inches × 6 feet 10 inches (207 × 209.5 cm); detail, 15 × 21 inches (38.5 × 55 cm). (© The National Gallery, London.)

Plate 3. Nicholas Hilliard, *Portrait of Elizabeth I* (1595–1600), as displayed in the Green Closet at Ham House, Surrey. Watercolor on vellum. 3¾ × 2¾ inches (9.5 × 7 cm). (Photo by Andreas von Einsiedel. National Trust Photographic Library.)

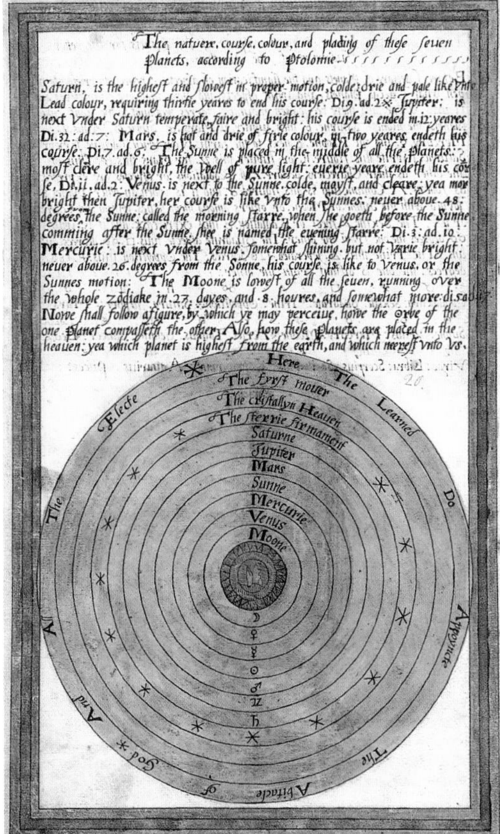

The nature, course, colour, and placing of these seuen planets, according to Ptolomie

Saturn, is the highest and slowest in proper motion, colde: drie and pale like vnto Lead colour, requiring thirtie yeares to end his course: Di.9. ad.2. Jupiter: is next vnder Saturn temperate, faire and bright: his course is ended in 12 yeares Di.32: ad.7: Mars, is hot and drie of firie colour, in two yeares endeth his course. Di.7. ad.6: The Sunne is placed in the middle of all the planets: most clere and bright, the well of pure light: euerie yeare endeth his course, Di.11. ad.2: Venus is next to the Sunne, colde, moyst, and cleare; yea more bright then Jupiter, her course is like vnto the Sunnes: neuer aboue 48 degrees from the Sunne: called the morning starre, when she goeth before the Sunne comming after the Sunne, shee is named the euening starre: Di.3: ad.10: Mercurie: is next vnder Venus, somewhat shining, but not verie bright: neuer aboue 26 degrees from the Sonne, his course is like to Venus, or the Sunnes motion: The Moone is lowest of all the seuen, running over the whole zodiake in 27 dayes, and 8 houres, and somewhat more: di.5. ad. Nowe shall follow a figure, by which ye may perceiue, howe the orbe of the one planet compasseth the other; Also, how these planets are placed in the heauen: yea which planet is highest from the earth, and which neerest vnto vs.

Plate 4. Verdure tapestry fragment (Flanders, early 16th century). Wool fibers. Cotehele House, Cornwall. 8 feet 4⅝ inches × 8 feet 6½ inches (258 × 263 cm). (Photo by Angelo Hornak. National Trust Photographic Library.)

Plate 5. Thomas Trevelyon, "The nature, course, color, and placing of these seven planets," from his pictorial and poetical commonplace book (1608), Watercolor on vellum. Size of leaf, 16⅜ × 9¾ inches (42 × 25 cm). (Reproduced by permission of Folger Shakespeare Library.)

Plate 6. Lukas de Heere, *Ancient Britons*, from "Beschrijving der Britsche Eilanden" (1590). Pen and ink on paper. Original image, 9⅜ × 6⅜ inches (24 × 16.5 cm). (© The British Library Board. All Rights Reserved [BL MS Add. 28,330, fol. 8v].)

Plate 7. Lukas de Heere, *Irish Men and Women*, from "Beschrijving der Britsche Eilanden" (1590). Pen and ink on paper. Original image, 10⅛ × 7⅞ inches (26 × 20.2 cm). (© The British Library Board. All Rights Reserved [BL MS Add. 28,330, fol. 34].)

Plate 8. *Green Lion Devouring the Sun*, from "The Rosary of the Philosophers" (1588). Watercolor, heightened with gold, on paper. Original image, 2¾ × 2⅞ inches (7.3 × 7.4 cm). (© The British Library Board. All Rights Reserved [BL MS Add. 29,895, fol. 119v].)

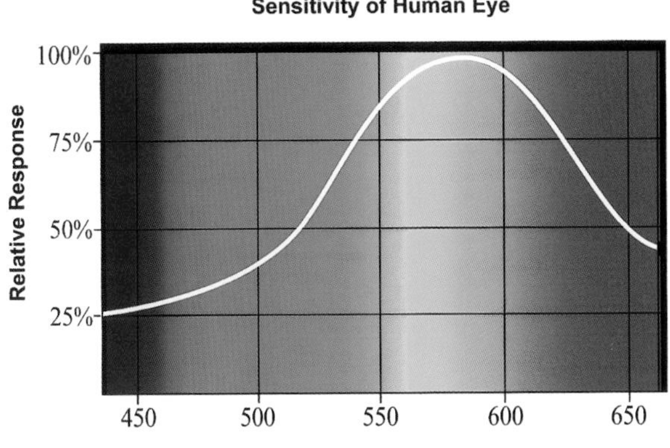

Plate 9. Sensitivity of the human eye to hues. The horizontal axis measures frequencies of light waves in nanometers; the vertical axis, strength of response by cones in percentages. (Reproduced by permission of Data Display Products, El Segundo, California.)

Plate 10. Robert Peake, *Portrait of Princess Elizabeth* (1603). Oil on canvas. Original image, 4 feet 10 inches × 1 foot 6 inches (134.6 × 95.3 cm). (© National Maritime Museum, London.)

Plate 11. Isaac Oliver, *Portrait of Edward Herbert, 1st Lord Herbert of Cherbury* (1613–14). Watercolor on vellum. Original image, 7 × 8⅞ inches (18.1 × 22.7 cm). (© Powis Castle. Photo by John Hammond. National Trust Photographic Library / The Bridgeman Art Library.)

Plate 12. Sheldon Workshops, *Spring*, detail, from a suite of four tapestries depicting the four seasons (one dated 1611), Hatfield House, Hertfordshire. Wool and silk fibers. Original size of entire panel, 10 feet 7 inches × 13 feet 9 inches (322.6 × 419.1 cm); detail, 5 feet 4 inches × 5 feet 9 inches (162.5 × 175.3 cm). (Reproduced by permission of the Marquess of Salisbury.)

Plate 13. Plate illustrating the first chapter of Genesis, from a 1616 edition of The Bible. Original image, 12½ × 7⅞ inches (32 × 20 cm). (Reproduced by permission of the Huntington Library, San Marino, California.)

Plate 14. Painted mirror (ca. 1700) hung atop a parkwork tapestry, Cotehele House, Cornwall. Size of mirror, 58½ × 53⅝ inches (150 × 137.5 cm). (Photo by Andreas von Einsiedel. National Trust Photographic Library.)

Plate 15. Paintings hung atop tapestries (inventoried 1601) in the Long Gallery, Hardwick Hall, Derbyshire. (Photo by Nadia MacKenzie. National Trust Photographic Library.)

Plate 16. High Great Chamber, with *Ulysses* tapestries and forest plasterwork (inventoried 1601), Hardwick Hall, Derbyshire. (Photo by Nadia MacKenzie. National Trust Photographic Library.)

Plate 17. Frenzied woman, border detail of the *Ulysses* tapestry (Flemish, 16th century, inventoried 1601), Hardwick Hall, Derbyshire. Wool fibers. Original size of this detail, approximately 33½ × 42 inches (86 × 108 cm). (Photo by John Hammond. National Trust Photographic Library.)

Plate 18. Embroidered jacket (English,1600–25), detail from back. Linen with silks. (Reproduced by permission of the Burrell Collection, Glasgow Museums, Glasgow.)

Plate 19. John Ballechouse (attr.), border detail of the *Conversion of Paul* (1600–1601), Hardwick Hall, Derbyshire. Painted cloth. Original size of this detail, approximately 35½ × 26 inches inches (91 × 67 cm). (Photo by John Hammond. National Trust Photographic Library.)

Plate 20. Queen Margaret's Chamber, Owlpen Manor, Gloucestershire, showing painted cloth of the story of Joseph (ca. 1680). (© Christopher Simon Sykes, The Interior Archive.)

Plate 21. Panel from painted closet (ca. 1610) from Hawstead Place, reassembled in Christchurch Mansion Museum, Ipswich, Suffolk. Size of each panel, approximately 15 inches square (38 cm). (By permission of Ipswich Borough Council Museum and Galleries.)

Plate 22. Sheldon Workshops, *The Judgment of Paris* (1595). Tapestry panel, wool fibers. Original size, 10 feet 5¾ inches × 11 feet 9 inches (321 × 360.5 cm). (V&A Images / Victoria and Albert Museum, London.)

Plate 23. Mortlake Workshops, *Hero and Leander*, after a cartoon by Franz Cleyn (designed 1625, woven late 17th century). Wool and silk fibers. Size of original, 9 feet 9 inches × 10 feet 5 inches (286 × 311 cm). (Reproduced by permission of the National Museums Liverpool.)

Plate 24. Sheldon Workshops (attr.), tapestry book cover (1614). Wool fibers. Original size, 6⅞ × 4⅞ inches (17.5 × 12.5 cm). (V&A Images / Victoria and Albert Museum, London.)

Plate 25. *Londinium*, detail of South Bank, from Georg Braun and Franz Hogenberg, *Civitates Orbis Terrarum,* 2nd Latin edition, vol. 1 (1617). Original size, 3⅛ × 2¼ inches (8 × 5.7 cm). (Reproduced by permission of the Huntington Library, San Marino, California.)

Plate 26. John Reynolds, *The Triumphs of God's Revenge* (1663). Hand coloring in watercolor or ink likely by Simon Bardon. Original image, 7¼ × 5⅜ inches (18.4 × 13.8 cm). (Reproduced by permission of the Folger Shakespeare Library.)

Plate 27. John Reynolds, *The Triumphs of God's Revenge* (1663). Hand coloring in watercolor or ink likely by Simon Bardon. Original page size, 7¾ × 12½ inches (19.6 × 31.7 cm). (Reproduced by permission of the Folger Shakespeare Library.)

Hiſt. V. *Alſemero and Beatrice-Joana.* 37

a fair houſe of his,ten leagues from *Alicant*, where he means to ſojourn,until he had concluded and ſolemnized the Match betwixt them : But he ſhall never be ſo happy, as to ſee it effected.

At the news of *Beatrice-Joana*'s departure, *Alſemero* is extreamly perplexed and ſorrowful, knowing not whether it proceeded from her ſelf,her father,or both;yea,this his grief it augmented,when he thinks on the ſuddenneſs thereof, which he fears may be performed for his reſpect and conſideration : the ſmall acquaintance and familiarity he hath had with her ; makes him that he cannot condemn her of unkindneſs; yet ſith he was not thought worthy to have notice of her departure, he again hath no reaſon to hope,much leſs to aſſure himſelf of her affection towards him. He knows not how to reſolve theſe doubts, nor what to think or do in a matter of this nature and importance; for thus he reaſoneth with himſelf, if he ride to *Briamata*, he may perchance offend the Father ; if he ſtay at *Alicant*, diſpleaſe the Daughter ; and although he be rather willing to run the hazard of his envy than of her affection, yet he holds it ſafer to be authorized by her pleaſure, and to ſteer his courſe by the compaſs of her commands : He therefore be-thinks himſelf of a means to avoid theſe extreams , and ſo findes out a Channel to paſs free betwixt that *Sylla* and this *Carybdis* ; which is , to viſit her by Letters : hee ſees more reaſon to embrace , than to reject this invention,and ſo providing himſelf of a confident Meſſenger, his heart commands his pen to ſignifie her theſe few lines.

ALSEMERO to BEATRICE-JOANA.

AS long as you were in Alicant, *I deemed it a heaven upon earth,and being bound for* Malta, *a thouſand times bleſſed that contrary wind which kept me from embarquing and ſailing from you ; yea, ſo ſweetly did I affect , and ſo dearly honour your beauty , as I entred into a reſolution with my ſelf , to end my voyage ere I began it , and to begin another, which I fear will end me. If you demand, or deſire to know what this ſecond voyage is, know, fair Miſtris, that my thoughts are ſo honourable , and my affection ſo religious , that it is the ſeeking of your favour , and the obtaining your ſelf to my Wife, whereon not only my fortunes, but my life depends. But how ſhall I hope for this honour, or flatter my ſelf with the obtaining of ſo great a felicity, when I ſee you have not only left me, but which is worſe, as I underſtand , the City for my ſake? Fair* Beatrice-Joana, *if your cruelty will make me thus miſerable, I have no other conſolation left me , to ſweeten the bitterneſs of my grief and misfortunes , but a confident hope , that death will as ſpeedily deprive me of my daies , as you have of my joyes.*

ALSEMERO.

I know not whether it more grieved *Beatrice-Joana* to leave *Alicant*, without taking her leave of *Alſemero*,than ſhe doth now rejoyce to receive this his Letter;for as that plunged her thoughts in the hell of diſcontent , ſo this raiſeth them to the heaven of joy ; and as then ſhe had cauſe to doubt of his affection, ſo now ſhe hath not only reaſon to flatter, but to aſſure her ſelf thereof : & therefore,though ſhe will not ſeem at firſt to grant him his deſire,yet ſhe is reſolved to return him an anſwer,that may give as well life to his hopes,as praiſe to her modeſty.Her letter is thus.

BEATRICE-JOANA to ALSEMERO.

AS I have many reaſons to be incredulous , and not one to induce me to beleeve , that ſo poor a beauty as mine ſhould have power to ſtop ſo brave a Cavalier (as your ſelf) from ending ſo honourable a Voyage, as your firſt, or to perſwade you to one ſo ſimple as your ſecond ; ſo I cannot but admire , that you in your Letter ſeek me for your Wife, when in your heart, I preſume, you leaſt deſire it : and where as you alledge your life and fortunes depend on my favour, I think you write it purpoſely,either to make tryal of your own wit , or of my indiſcretion , by endeavouring to ſee whether I beleeve that which exceeds all belief. Now as it is true , that I have left Alicant, *ſo it is as true, that I left it not any way to afflict you , but rather to obey my Father : for this I pray beleeve, that although I cannot be kinde, yet I will never be cruel to you. Live therefore your own friend, and I will never dye your enemy.*

BEATRICE-JOANA.

This Letter of *Beatrice-Joana* gives *Alſemero* much deſpair, and little hope;yet though he have reaſon to condemn her unkindneſs, he cannot but approve her modeſty and diſcretion , which doth as much comfort as that afflict him : ſo his thoughts are irreſolute,and withall ſo variable, as he knows not whether he ſhould advance his hand, or withdraw his pen again, to write to his Miſtreſs. But at laſt,knowing that the excellency of her Beauty, and the dignity of her Virtues deſerve a ſecond Letter ; he hoping it may obtain and effect that which his firſt could not,calls for Paper, and thereon traceth theſe few lines :

ALSEMERO to BEATRICE JOANA.

YOu have as much reaſon to aſſure your ſelf of my affection , as I to doubt of yours : and if Words and Letters, Tears and Vows, are not capable to make you beleeve the ſincerity of my zeal , and the honour of my affection ; what reſteth , but that I wiſh you could dive as deeply into my heart , as my heart hath into your beauty , to the end you might bee both Witneſs and Judge , if under Heaven I deſire any thing ſo much on Earth as to bee crowned with the felicity to ſee Beatrice-Joana *my Wife , and* Alſemero *her Husband ? But why ſhould I ſtrive to perſwade that , which you reſolve not to beleeve , or flatter my ſelf*

E *with*

Plate 28. Isaac Oliver, *A Party in the Open Air* or *Allegory on Conjugal Love* (disputed) (1590–95). Watercolor and gouache on vellum on card. Reproduced actual size, 4⅜ × 6⅝ inches (11.3 × 17 cm). (Photo by SMK. Reproduced by permission of Statens Museum for Kunst, Copenhagen.)

Plate 29. Isaac Oliver, *A Party in the Open Air* or *Allegory on Conjugal Love* (disputed) (1590–95), detail. Watercolor and gouache on vellum on card. Original size, ⅝ × 1⅛ inches (1.5 × 3 cm). (Photo by SMK. Reproduced by permission of Statens Museum for Kunst, Copenhagen.)

Plate 30. Wooden cabinet with drawers, English, early 17th century. Painted pine wood inlaid with mother of pearl. 24 × 19 × 10¾ inches (61 × 48.3 × 27.3 cm). (V&A Images / Victoria and Albert Museum, London.)

As for the psalm itself, the pattern for every line is the same: in the first measure (marked A in the example), an "intonation" that gets the line started (the first intonation on rising tones, all subsequent intonations on falling tones); in the second measure (B), a recitation of most of the line's syllables on a single tone; and in the third measure (C), a "mediation" on falling tones that forms bridge to the next line. Each line composes then a kind of arc that reaches its climax in the recitation. For chanting the psalm's last line (not shown in the example), the fifth tone provides an ending that goes through all the tones in a falling sequence and forms an aural bridge to the *Gloria Patri.*

The sharpest possible contrast to the antiphons in the Latin rite would seem to be offered by the plodding version of Psalm 23 in the collected settings of the psalms begun by Thomas Sternhold in 1547, augmented by John Hopkins in 1549, brought to completion with additions by other translators in 1562, and reprinted, according to the English Short Title Catalogue, more than seven hundred times—seven hundred!—before 1700.[34] Sternhold's translation of the 23rd Psalm in the 1562 edition is altogether typical in its syllable-by-syllable precision (see musical example 3). One syllable, one tone, no exceptions. The ubiquity of Sternhold and Hopkins's settings in early modern England (they were printed with many editions of the *Book of Common Prayer*) suggests that it is Sternhold's literal simplicity that Mistress Ford has in mind as a foil to Falstaff's duplicity. The second part of the title page to the 1562 edition and most subsequent editions declares that the word-by-word severity of the Sternhold and Hopkins psalter is intended as antidote not just to antiphony but to balladry (see figure 18). The verses as "collected into English metre" are lauded as "Very mete to be vsed of all sortes of people priuately for their solace & comfort: laying apart all vngodly Songes and Ballades, which tende only to the norishing of vyce, and corrupting of youth."[35] The title is correct in referring to English *meter,* not English *meters,* because most of

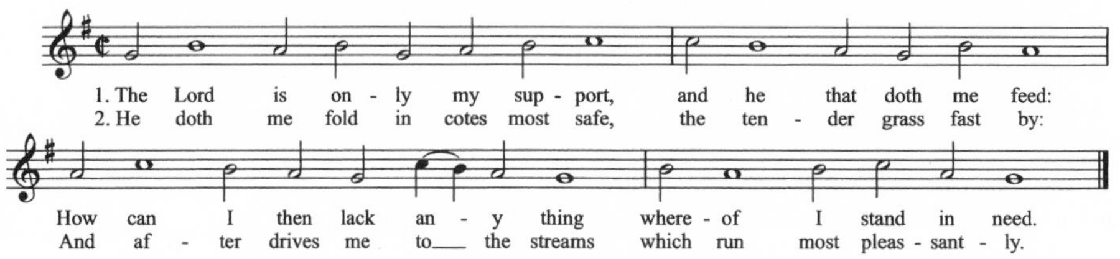

Musical example 3. Psalm 23, as arranged by Thomas Sternhold and John Hopkins. Adapted from *The Whole Booke of Psalmes* (1562).

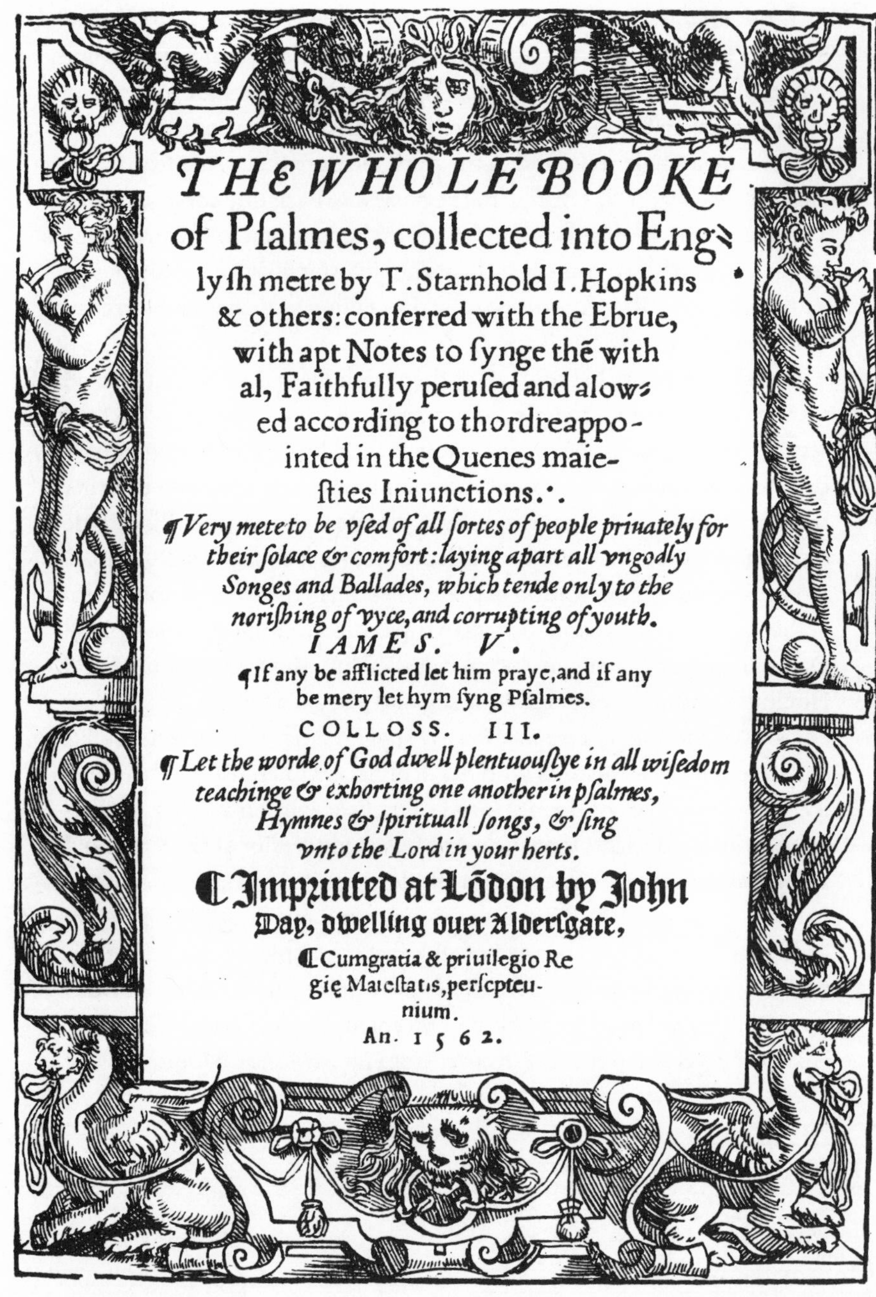

THE WHOLE BOOKE of Psalmes, collected into Englysh metre by T. Starnhold I. Hopkins & others: conferred with the Ebrue, with apt Notes to synge thē withal, Faithfully perused and alowed according to thordre appointed in the Quenes maiesties Iniunctions.

¶ Very mete to be vsed of all sortes of people priuately for their solace & comfort: laying apart all vngodly Songes and Ballades, which tende only to the norishing of vyce, and corrupting of youth.

IAMES. V.

¶ If any be afflicted let him praye, and if any be mery let hym syng Psalmes.

COLLOSS. III.

¶ Let the worde of God dwell plentuouslye in all wisedom teachinge & exhorting one another in psalmes, Hymnes & spirituall songs, & sing vnto the Lord in your herts.

¶ Imprinted at Lōdon by John Day, dwelling ouer Aldersgate,

¶ Cum gratia & priuilegio Regię Maiestatis, per septennium.

An. 1562.

Figure 18. Title page to Thomas Sternhold and John Hopkins, *The Whole Booke of Psalmes, collected into Englysh metre* (London: John Day, 1562). Shown actual size, 6⅝ × 4½ inches (17 × 11.75 cm). (© The British Library Board. All Rights Reserved [C.25.q.3].)

the 150 psalms have been turned into so-called common meter, quatrains of four feet/three feet/four feet/three feet—a sound pattern that is otherwise known as "ballad stanza."[36]

Aside from this dangerous commerce with ballads, Sternhold and Hopkins's *Whole Booke of Psalmes,* for all its logocentrism, is not altogether free of logofugality. In the 1562 edition, a crash course in how to read printed music is followed by "A Treatise made by Athanasius the great" that advises the reader-singer "in what manner ye may vse the Psalmes, according to the effect [that is, affect] of the minde" (sig. †7v). The fourth-century saint classifies the psalms according to the occasions for which they are appropriate—occasions that turn out to be not only dramatic situations but the passions that those situations enkindle. The 23rd Psalm, for example, is presented as a "feelin' good" song: "If thou seest thy selfe kept of the Lord and that thou prosperest, reioyce and syng the 23.Psalme" (sig. †8). (Contrast could hardly be sharper with the modern assumption that the time for "The Lord is my shepherd" is when the *Titanic* is sinking.) The book of psalms is presented by Athanasius as an instructional manual or mirror that turns affects into words:

> For as he whiche goeth to a kyng, composeth fyrst his behauiour, and setteth in order his wordes, least he should be counted rusticall and rude: so this deuine book, fyrst by choise of all motions, wherwith the soule is affected, warneth, then frameth and instructeth by diuers formes of speaking all suche as court vertue, and desyre to knowe the lyfe of the Sauiour. It is easy therefore for euery man to finde out in the Psalmes, the motion and state of his owne soule, and by that meanes, his own figure and proper condition. (sig. †7v)

"Motions," as we noted in chapter one, is a technical term: it specifies how passions were believed to work on the human body. Confronted with a pleasant or a disturbing sensation, a Renaissance subject was not just "moved"; he or she was physiologically *moved.* Athanasius's treatise was not always reprinted in subsequent editions of Sternhold and Hopkins (reprints in the 1598, 1602, 1605, and 1619 editions are cited by Hannibal Hammlin[37]), but the appropriateness of the volume for personal use, for solace and comfort, was maintained on many subsequent title pages. The grotesquerie that frames the title page to the 1562 edition (see figure 18) enhance Athanasius's verbal gestures toward passion. To later eyes, the tapestry-like design of strap work, female head with frantic hair, birds with outstretched wings, almost-nude musicians, gigantic leaf-forms, and griffins must have seemed distinctly odd. Jeremy Taylor's verbal framing of the texts in the plainly printed *Psalter of David: With Titles and Collects, according to the matter of each* Psalme (1646, 1647, 1650, 1655, 1661, 1668, 1672, 1679, 1683, 1691, 1696) takes no notice of affects. Psalm 23 is presented in the title as "A Prayer that God would guide, and feed, and support us as a shepheard doth his flock."[38] The collect or prayer that follows the psalms dutifully implores Christ to "guide," "feed," and "refresh" (sig. C8v). "Matter" is all: words in the title and words in the collect are designed to dictate how the reader experiences the words of the psalm itself. If any affect is implied, it is anxiety that prayerful reading of the psalm is supposed to allay.

Although the longer title to 1562 edition of Sternhold and Hopkins recommends the book's use by all sorts of people "priuately for their solace & comfort," it also alludes to "the Quenes maiesties Iniunctions" regarding public worship. The injunctions in question, set forth in 1559, required "that there be a modest distinct song, so used in all parts of the common prayers in the Church, but that the same may be plainly understood, as if it were read without singing."[39] And that is just what Sternhold and Hopkins deliver. By 1566, the title page was describing the metrical psalms as "allowed to be soong of the people together in churches."[40] Four-part harmonizations appeared in 1563 and were often reissued, making the volume even more appropriate for congregational worship. The 1559 *Book of Common Prayer,* in use with only minor changes until 1662, provides a "Table for the Ordre of the Psalmes to be sayde at Morning and Euening prayer," a plan that allows all 150 psalms are to be gone through in the course of a month.[41] Psalm 23 is appointed for evening prayer on the fourth day. Despite the word "sayde" in the table, a rubric in the order for morning prayer calls for Psalm 95 ("O Come let vs syng vnto the Lorde") to be "sayde or song" (sig. A2v)—a direction which presumably is meant to apply also to the two additional psalms appointed for morning prayer that day and the two appointed for evening prayer, including Psalm 23 on the fourth day of the month. The order for morning prayer even allows for the day's lessons from the Old Testament and New Testament to be sung. The rubric gives precedence to a reading of the texts by the minister "with a loude voice, that ye people may heare," but "in such places wher they do sing, there shal the lessons be song in a plain tune, after ye manner of distincte reading" (sig. A3). Singing that approximates reading: what these liturgical texts bespeak is an anxiety about any sort of music that is not grounded in language.

Tempting as it is to ascribe that logocentricism to Protestant dogma, it

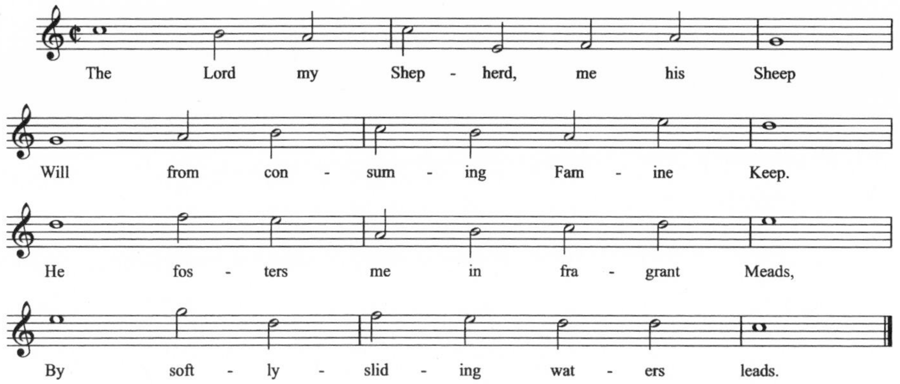

Musical example 4. Psalm 23, as translated by George Sandys and set by Henry Lawes. Transcribed from *A Paraphrase upon the Psalms of David . . . Set to New Tunes for Private Devotion* (1676).

is a fact that international style in setting words to music was turning away from strophic tunes to the word-for-word setting of words known in Italian as *stilo recitativo.* Claudio Monteverdi's operas *L'Orfeo* (1604), *Arianna* (1608), *Il Ritorno d'Ulisse in Patria* (1640), and *L'Incoronazione di Poppea* (1643) found their English counterparts in Henry Lawes's settings of John Milton's *Arcades* (1630–1634) and *Comus* (1634), his three books of *Ayres and Dialogues* (1653, 1655, 1658), and his settings of George Sandys's *A Paraphrase upon the Psalms of David* (1638).The serviceable rough-and-readiness of Sternhold's ballad stanzas becomes, in Sandys's paraphrases, the supple smoothness of rhyming tetrameter couplets. Lawes's musical setting of Sandys's Psalm 23 captures some of that suavity, even as it preserves some key features of Sternhold's setting (see musical example 4). Lawes's range of tones is greater (four tones above the key-note and six below, as compared with Sternhold's five tones above and two tones below), and his tonal arc of falling → rising → RISING → falling gives the melodic line an affective impetus that is missing from Sternhold's alternation of falling | rising | falling | rising. On the other hand, Lawes maintains Sternhold's penchant for beginning a line—in particular, the first line—with a held tone, even when the rhythm of the words does not call for it. Thus we get "*My* shepehard is the liuing Lorde" in Sternhold and the no less awkward "*The* Lord my Shepherd, me his Sheep" in Lawes (emphasis added in each case). The reason for these emphatic beginnings can perhaps be found in editions dated 1674 and later of John Playford's *An Introduction to the Skill of Musick* (1655, 1672, 1674, 1679, 1683, 1687, 1694, 1697, 1700, etc.), where a section on "RULES *and* DIRECTIONS For *SINGING the* PSALMS"

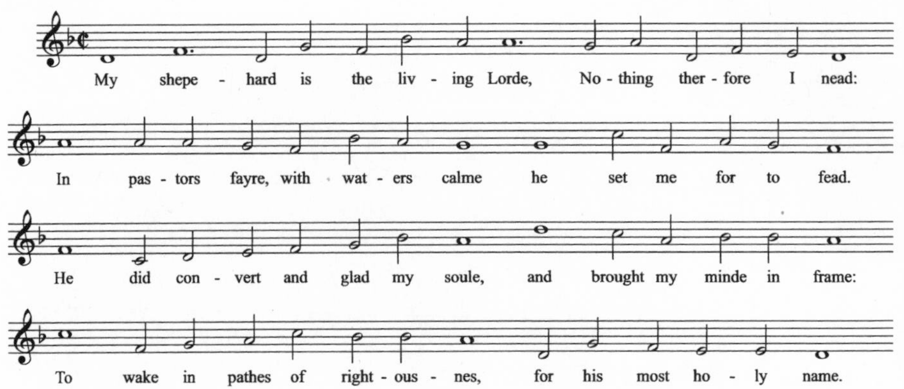

Musical example 5. Psalm 23, set to the "Low-Dutch Tune." Adapted from John Playford, *An Introduction to the Skill of Musick,* 7th edition (1674).

enjoins parish clerks to pay attention to the "Compass" of the tune (i.e., how many tones above and below the key-note it comprises) and establish the pitch so that everybody can sing the tune "without *squeaking* above, or *grumbling* below."[42] For the convenience of those parish clerks, Playford anthologizes 27 of "The most usual Common tunes Sung in Parish Churches" (sig. F5), including William Whittingham's translation of Psalm 23 from later editions of Sternhold and Hopkins, fitted in this case to the "Low-Dutch Tune" (see musical example 5). An emphatic beginning of the sort to be found in Sternhold and Hopkins and in Lawes (although not in Playford's "Low-Dutch Tune") ensures that all the singers start on the same pitch and hence are set to stay together from start to finish. One might imagine these four-square settings of the psalms—Sternhold's, Lawes's, and Playford's alike—as working in two dimensions: a horizontal dimension that hews to the line of words, syllable by syllable, and a vertical dimension that keeps the tune within a narrow seven- or eight-tone compass that avoids squeaks at the top and grumbles at the bottom. Dead center, line for line, is one tone = one syllable.

By Playford's time, a third mode of psalm singing was becoming established: Anglican chant. Or rather, it was becoming reestablished. During the Commonwealth, between 1645 and 1660, the only kind of church music allowed by law were metrical psalms. Within a few months of Charles II's restoration, however, musical establishments in the newly reopened cathedrals, in chapels at Oxford and Cambridge, and in the king's Chapel Royal were reviving chanting practices that had been prohibited by law in 1645.[43] Among those practices was the chanting of the psalms in four-part harmony. The 1674 and 1679 editions of Playford's *An Introduction to the Skill of Music* include a section on "THE ORDER OF PERFORMING THE DIVINE SERVICE IN *Cathedrals* and *Collegiate Chappels*" that notates several "tunes" for psalm singing—tunes that can be traced to the Catholic Rite of Sarum and that present compromises between Latin chant and metered hymns.[44] Musical example 6 shows the version of Psalm 23 from the 1662 *Book of Common Prayer* adapted to the "Canterbury Tune," one of two tunes that Playford recommends as "proper for Quires to Sing the *Psalms* . . . to the *Organ,* or sometime without it" (sig. M5).[45] Four voices in harmony of euphonious thirds and fifths chant most of the text (in the passages marked A and C), but they slow the pace and allow the harmony to bloom at the end of each phrase (B and D). The result is a surge of affect on each phrase that reaches a climax and finds momentary repose before the chant resumes. In the case of Psalm 23, sung to the "Canterbury Tune," those moments of climax and repose include the words "my shepherd" (passage B[1]) and "a green pasture" (passage B[2]). The earliest documentary evidence of such four-voice chanting is to be found in Thomas Morley's *A Plaine and Easie Introduction to Practical Musicke* (1597), where harmonizations of the eight tones of Latin plainchant are presented, suggesting that in certain places at least there was a continuous tradition of chanting in England right through the Reformation. The "Canterbury Tune" is in fact based on Psalm tone 4 in the Rite of Sarum.[46] Since its reestablishment in the 1660s, Anglican chant has remained the dominant mode of psalm singing in the Church of England and in Anglican communities

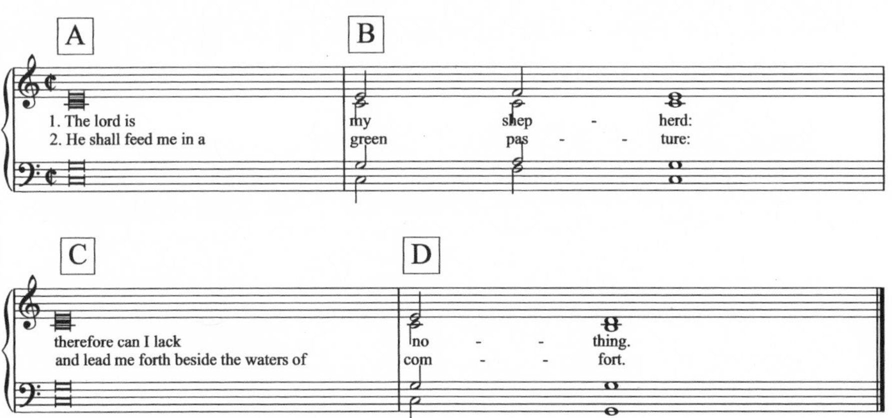

Musical example 6. Psalm 23, set to the "Canterbury Tune." Adapted from John Playford, *An Introduction to the Skill of Musick,* 8th edition (1679).

elsewhere, in parish churches as well as in the cathedrals and collegiate chapels that Playford mentions.[47] The reason for this staying power is not hard to seek: Anglican chant fosters efflorescence of green at the same time that it grounds the source of that efflorescence in words.

In producing his paraphrase on the psalms Sandys was, literally, producing a set of words "alongside" or "beyond" the words of the Hebrew original (*OED*, "para-" *prefix*, etymology). His version of Psalm 23 participates in what Hannibal Hamlin has called the pastoralization of that text in the sixteenth and seventeenth centuries, a series of attempts to merge Psalm 23's landscape and staffage with the *locus amoenus* of Virgil's eclogues and Theocritus's idylls.[48] Hamlin's survey of translations and paraphrases of Psalm 23 demonstrate the particular volatility of the phrase "green pastures." The Vulgate says only that the Lord as shepherd leads the psalmist "in locu pascuai"—"in place of pastures," as the Catholic Douai version (1580s, published 1609–1610) precisely translates it. The same phrase in the Bishops' Bible (1568) had been a "pasture full of grass." Having made its first appearance in the Coverdale Bible (1535), the phrase "a green pasture" persisted in the Great Bible (1539), the Geneva Bible (1560), and reprintings of the Coverdale psalms in connection with the Church of England liturgy (1559 and after), as well as in the "green pastures" of the King James Version (1611) and most modern translations. The pallidness of Sternhold's "pastors fayre" (see musical example 3) perhaps explains why William Whittington's more vivid "pastures green" supplanted Sternhold's original translation in most later editions of *The Whole Booke of Psalmes.* The ripeness of "in loco pascuai" for pastoral periphrasis is exemplified in Sandys's still more sensuous "fragrant Meads" (see musical example 4). Topping them all, however, is Richard Crashaw's dilation:

> Happy me! o happy sheepe!
> When my God vouchsafes to keepe;
> Even my God, Even he it is,
> That points me to these wayes of blisse;
> On whose pastures cheerefull spring,
> All the yeare doth sit and sing,
> And rejoycing smiles to see
> Their greene backs were his liverie. . . .[49]

Contentment for Crashaw is not to be found somewhere else, in a poetic conceit; it is right here, in *these* ways of bliss. Situating himself amid

Spring's green livery, Crashaw hears bliss as well as sees it. The cascading rhymes only eight syllables apart, the headlong trochees ("Happy . . . ," "Even . . . ," "All the . . . "), the assonance of /s/ ("bli*ss*," "*s*pring," "*s*it," "*s*ing," "rejoi*c*ing," "*s*miles," "*s*ee")—all of these sound effects swirl away from the literal simplicity of the Vulgate's "in loco pascuai." Instead, Crashaw delights in the musical potential of the words' very sounds, dissolving sense in sensation.

To Listen for It All

To listen for green would also mean to listen for the totality of sound, for all there is to hear. In the first instance that would mean learning to listen, really *listen,* to noise. The voices that Pantagruel hears in the anecdote that began this chapter emerge out of the sounds of wind and waves. That is the very matrix, according to Michel Serres, out of which all meaningful sounds emerge. Serres' version of *Genesis* starts at the seashore. "There, precisely, is the origin. *Noise* and nausea, *noise* and the nautical, *noise* and the navy belong to the same family. We musn't be surprised. We never hear what we call background noise so well as we do at the seaside."[50] Ναυτία → *nausia* → nausea → seasickness → disquiet → uproar → noise: knowing that genealogy can help us get our bearings amid the continuous sea of sound in which all hearing people are immersed.[51] To listen to noise, and not just hear it, we must listen in anticipation, in readiness for meaningful sounds like the voices that Pantagruel catches, isolates, and interprets. (Or do they catch, isolate, and interpret *him?*) There is an in-between time before Pantagruel and his fellows can make out what they are hearing: "The more we listen'd, the plainer we discern'd the Voices, so as to distinguish Articulate Sounds."[52] *Articulate:* that is to say, jointed, separated into segments (*OED,* "articulate" *a.,* etymology, A.I.1–2). It is ironic that what Pantagruel and his fellows ultimately hear as the multicolored pieces of ice melt are not voices but noises—albeit noises that become articulate when the narrator tries to transcribe them into letters: "hin, hin, hin, hin, his, tick, tock, taack, brededin, brededack, frr, frr, frr," and so forth (220). The color of this maritime matrix of sound, or so Aristotle reads it in his treatise *On Colors,* is green.[53] Green is more forward in the second of the environments in which Serres locates the emergence of meaning. Like the sea when seen and heard from the shore, a forest, when one is in it, lacks form, definition, limits. "How am I to tell," Serres wonders,

> any environment I've entered, become immersed in, that this wood I'm confronted with doesn't go on forever, that I'll get to the edge of the forest some day? I can't see the trees of this forest. A murmur, seizing me, I can't master its source, its increase is out of my control. The noise, the background noise, that incessant hubbub, our signals, our messages, our speech and our words are but a fleeting high surf, over its perpetual swell. (6)

A third environment of noise, a specifically *social* environment, is included in the list that sums up Serres' acoustic geopositioning: "sea, forest, rumor, noise, society, life, works and days" (6).

Rumor: it is the booming male voice of an actor with that name that drowns out the waiting audience's noises—their shuffling, fidgeting, coughs, and conversations—to begin Shakespeare's *2 Henry IV:* "Open your Eares," the voice commands: "For which of you still stop / The vent of Hearing, when loud *Rumour* speakes?" (Pro. 1–2). Like all plays mounted in London's public outdoor theaters, *2 Henry IV* emerges out of noise. As a commanding voice that can give a center to the theater's chaotic sounds, Rumor takes his place among the prologues to *Romeo and Juliet, Henry V* in the folio text, *Troilus and Cressida, All Is True,* and *The Two Noble Kinsmen* and male authority figures like Richard Gloucester in *Richard III,* Theseus in *A Midsummer Night's Dream,* and King Henry in *1 Henry IV.*[54] More often, however, Shakespeare directs several voices to speak as the play is beginning, and frequently those voices belong to minor characters: "Who's there?" (Bernardo to Francisco in *Hamlet* 1.1.1); "Tush, never tell me! I take it much unkindly / That thou, Iago, . . . should'st know of this" (Roderigo to Iago in *Othello,* 1.1.1–3); "I Thought the King had more affected the Duke of *Albany,* then *Cornwall*" (Kent to Gloucester in *The Tragedy of King Lear,* 1.1.1–2); "Nay, but this dotage of our General's / O'erflows the measure" (Philo to Demetrius in *Antony and Cleopatra,* 1.1.1–2). "Tush," "I thought," "Nay": these are markers of conversations already in progress, as if the voices have emerged out of the audience's own conversations. On occasion, Shakespeare's plays begin when scripted noise overwhelms the audience's noise: "*Thunder and lightening*" inaugurate *Macbeth* (SD before 1.1[55]); *Coriolanus* erupts onto the stage in "*a company of mutinous Citizens with staves, clubs, and other weapons*" who clamor all at once to speak (SD before 1.1); the opening stage direction to *The Tempest*—"*A tempestuous noise of thunder and lightening heard*" (SD before 1.1)—gives way to the cries of a sinking ship's master, boatswain, and passengers. On at least one occasion what the silenced audience is scripted to hear first is music. "If music be the food of love, play on," sighs Orsino in *Twelfth Night* (1.1.1).

All of these aural events—the "O" uttered by public voices of command, the "Tush" of private voices in conversation, rolls of thunder, staged hubbub, consorted music—belong to the same space as grotesquerie and antic work in tapestries. They offer the audience's ears a time for sense, common sense, imagination, fantasy, and passion to begin their play. Articulate speech in plays for the Renaissance theater happens between white and black. "White noise" is the modern term for neutral sound, produced when intensities are equal across all the frequencies that are present. You can hear it in the speakers when the CD player is turned on but no CD is being played. You can hear it, between the surges, as you stand on the seashore. You can hear it in the wind through the trees. You can hear it when you stand alone in an empty theater. "Black" is Thomas Dekker's descriptor for the random intensities and random frequencies you hear in the theater when other people—up to three thousand of them in the 1599 Globe—join you. It is the noise all of you make before the play begins—or after it is over. The cacophony that Dekker describes in *A Strange Horse Race* (1613) is described in more appreciative terms by the Swiss medical student Thomas Platter in his account of seeing *Julius Caesar* at the Globe in September 1599. "When the play was over," Platter writes, "they danced very marvelously and gracefully together as is their wont, two dressed as men and two as women."[56] It was likely the black stage hangings associated with the just-concluded tragedy that prompted Dekker's ironic choice of black to color the bumptious aural scene.[57] "I haue often seene, after the finishing of some worthy Tragedy or Catastrophe in the open Theaters," Dekker recalls, "that the Sceane after the Epilogue hath beene more blacke (about a nasty bawdy Iigge) then the most horrid Sceane in the Play was: The Stinkards speaking all things, yet no man vnderstanding any thing; a mutiny being among them, yet none in danger: no tumult, yet no quietnesse: no mischife begotten, and yet mischiefe borne: the swiftnesse of such a torrent, the more it ouerwhelmes, breeding the more pleasure."[58] Amid hand clapping, shouts, whistling, talking, and the bustle of three thousand people crowding the exit doors, plays in London's outdoor theaters dissolved into the noise out of which, three hours before, they emerged. White noise, black noise, and what comes in between: to listen for green in this dramatic soundscape would involve attending to the verges between noise and articulate speech.

With respect to speech itself, to listen for green is to listen not just for words or syllables but for the stream of sound that carries them along. Saussure's diagram of the undifferentiated "plane" of undifferentiated sounds beneath the "plane" of undifferentiated ideas (see figure 1) catches this flowing quality. The vertical lines indicating breaks in the stream are not only arbitrary but ultimately ineffectual. Even in the act of speaking, the sound flows on. When a person speaks, the vocal chords, the jaw, the tongue, and the palate are in constant motion. The result is a continuous stream of sound, not a chain of discrete sounds. Phonetic linguists recognize this situation even as they proceed to impose units of analysis on the continuous flow of sound. The smallest units are phonetic *features,* momentary configurations of sound frequencies produced when air is expelled while larynx, jaw, tongue, and palate are held in certain positions. One or more features can make up a phonetic *segment,* a sequence of frequencies that remains relatively unchanging long enough for speakers of a given language hear it as a *phoneme.* A sequence of phonemes, in turn, can be heard as an *utterance;* a sequence of utterances, as a *speaking turn.* In this sequence of sound formations complete breaks are few, occurring mainly between utterances and at the end of a speaking turn.[59] Note that *syllable* and *word* are absent from the sequence of sound formations. Strictly speaking, syllable and word are units of analysis appropriate to phonology (the study of sound structures), not phonetics (the study of sounds).[60] Precise measurements of how long it takes to make one alternating movement in the larynx or the mouth indicate an interval of 150–300 milliseconds. Normal conversation moves along at the pace of 10–20 segments per second, implying only 100 milliseconds in which to make the required adjustments in the vocal apparatus. The speaker has no choice, then, but to blend one segment into another by a process that phonetic linguists know as *coarticulation.*[61] Contractions stand as obvious orthographical signs of a phenomenon that is going on all the time, within words as well as between words, when a person speaks.

A visual representation of the whole process is made available by spectrographic analysis. Take, for example, Iago's warning to Othello, "Oh, beware my Lord, of iealousie, / It is the greene-ey'd Monster, which doth mocke / The meate it feeds on" (3.3.169–71). In figure 19, the horizontal axis measures time; the vertical axis measures frequencies of sound, heard as pitch. The only breaks in the continuous stream of sound that the actor speaking for Iago utters is the pause between "of iealousie" and "It is the greene-ey'd Monster," a pause between utterances. A closer approximation of Iago's speech in letters would look like this:

Obewaremylordofjealousy. Itisthegreeneyedmonsterwhichdothmockthemeatitfeedson.

That, indeed, is how each of the utterances would have been written down if Iago had been speaking in Latin and his words had been recorded

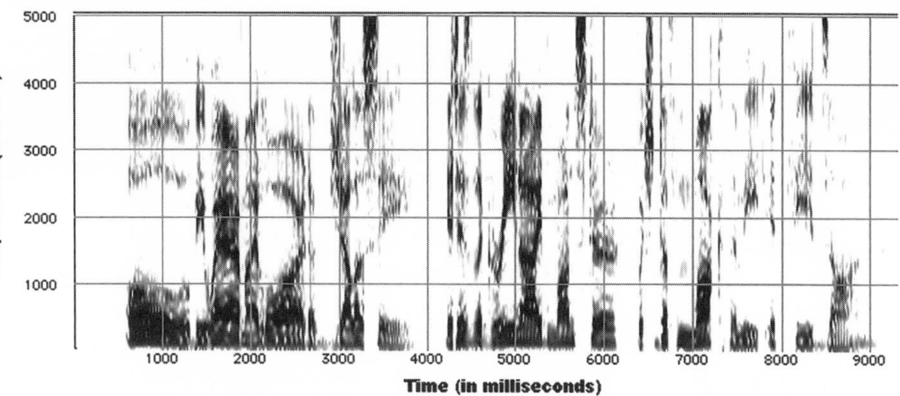

Figure 19. Spectrograph of William Shakespeare, *Othello*, 3.3.169–71. (Spectrograph by Dani Byrd.)

in the first century before the Common Era.[62] Really, though, there ought to be no letters at all. As Roy Harris observes in *Rethinking Writing:*

> The only kind of representation which is "faithful" to the phonetic facts would be one which did not divide the continuum into segments at all—as we see in a sound spectrogram. Alphabetic transcription inevitably misrepresents speech to the extent that it is obliged by its own conventions to mark a series of subdivisions that do not exist. For the semiologist, any belief that an optimally accurate alphabetic transcription mirrors the structure of the utterance is rather like supposing that the best kind of drawing of a jet of water must be one in which each droplet is separately shown.[63]

In the spectrograph of Iago's speech, many more sounds are present than the phonetic segments /o:/ b/i/w/a/r/m/ai/l/o/r/d/ and so forth. D. B. Fry estimates that modern subjects *listen to* only about half of the speech sounds they *hear.*[64] Why do most of us attend only to those particular sounds and not the others? Linguists have suggested several explanations, ranging from hardwired circuits in the brain to passive filtering to dependence on acoustic cues in the listening environment to the listener's own bodily knowledge of how meaningful sounds are produced by the vocal tract.[65] What happens to the other half of the sounds? They are there for the listening. Experiments carried out by the Haskins Laboratories at Yale University suggest that people choose between two distinct mind-sets when they listen to sound, one for speech and another for natural sounds and music. To these two modes of listening Reuven

Tsur has added a third—the "poetic mode"—that combines the other two.[66] Cultivating that third way of listening, he argues, should be possible for everyone, since it recapitulates the way children learn to speak, as they move from emotion-laden "expressive" sounds like /m/,/o:/,/ik/, and /ft/ to the strictly-business "referential" sounds of speech.[67] The in-between sounds in Iago's speech, the blurring of /o:/ into /b/i/w/a/r/, the elongation of /r/ in space and time all function, if only subliminally, as expressive sounds. As nonreferential sounds, their appeal is to the passions, not to reason. In terms of Renaissance epistemology, they belong to the spectrum of green. It is out of that green matrix that referential sounds—segments, phonemes, utterances—emerge.

In his attempt to establish scientific principles for the study of sound in *Sylva Sylvarum,* Bacon clearly wishes that all sounds were musical tones, definite in pitch, definite in duration. Speech sounds belong to the much larger category of "immusical sounds," a category that also includes "all *Whisperings,* all *voices of Beasts, and Birds,* (except they bee *Singing Birds;*), all *Percussions,* of *Stones, Wood, Parchment, Skins* (as in *Drummes;*) and infinite others" (sig. F1; emphasis original). It is the incommensurability of speech sounds that presents Bacon his greatest challenge: "It seemeth that Aire, (which is the Subiect of *Sounds*) in *Sounds* that are not *Tones,* (which are all *vnequall,* as hath beene said) admitteth much Varietie; As wee see in the *Voices* of *Liuing Creatures;* And likewise in the *Voices* of seuerall *Men;* (for we are capable to discerne seuerall *Men* by their *Voices;*) And in the *Coniugation of Letters,* whence *Articulate Sounds* proceed; Which of all others are most various." If musical tones are circles, squares, and triangles, speech sounds are "*Figures* . . . made of lines, Crooked and Straight, in infinite Varietie" (sig. F1v). Circles, squares, and triangles are susceptible to measurement and precise description; crooked and straight lines are not. Bacon is like most Renaissance writers in confidently referring to speech sounds as "letters." Other writers, like John Hart in his spelling-reform polemic *An Orthographie* (1569), follow Aristotle in referring to individual speech sounds as "voices." Even so, Hart believes that voices and letters ought to coincide: "euen as euery body is to be resolued into those Elements whereof it is composed, so euery word is to be undone into those voices only whereof it is made. Seeing then that letters are figures and colours wherewith the image of mans voice is painted, you are forced to graunt the writing should haue so many letters as the speach hath voyces, and no more nor lesse."[68] Hart and Bacon clearly want to be modern semantic linguists, but neither of them can ignore the embodiedness of spoken sound. That step in the history of linguistics required Descartes' decisive separation of outer phenomena from inner phenomena.

However much Renaissance writers wanted to describe speech as a sequence of discrete letters or voices, they nonetheless recognized that what gets *articulated* in articulate speech is continuous, undifferentiated sound. Spenser, in the House of Alma, hears it as the buzzing of bees (see chapter three.) In more scientific terms, the first English phonetician, Robert Robinson, recognizes that the articulation and projection of vowels and consonants require a third kind of sound, produced from the throat, which Robinson calls "vital sound." Out of it "all the sounds of different quantitie doe arise."[69] Modern commentators on Robinson have interpreted this "vital sound" as the equivalent of what we would call voiced sounds (as opposed to whispering), but there may be an indication here of the neutral /ə/, the schwa, that the vocal tract produces when no part of the apparatus is in motion.[70] The first, unstressed syllable of the English word *canoe* (/kənu/) is one instance of this neutral sound; so is the "uh . . . " made by many English speakers today as they try to gather their thoughts between utterances and hold onto their speaking turn.

To listen for all there is to hear would entail, finally, listening for the qualities of voice that make your reading of "O beware, my Lord, of ielousie" different from mine or the qualities of sound that make the playing of the "Greensleeves" tune on an alto recorder different from the playing of the same tune on a sackbut. What word can we put to those qualities? English really lacks one. The most common term is probably *timbre,* but that dates only from the mid-nineteenth century (the earliest citation in the *OED* is from Charlotte Brontë's *Shirley* [1849]) and, besides, it is French.[71] *Klang* (German for "tone") or *Klangfarbe* ("tone color") is another possibility, but its use in English also dates back no earlier than the mid-nineteenth century, and again its origins are foreign.[72] With respect to speech, John Hart, in *An Orthographie,* may be gesturing toward this phenomenon when he remarks that written letters function as "the figures and colours wherewith the image of mans voice is painted" (sig. 9-1). It is Thomas Morley, however, who comes closest to providing an indigenous term for tonal quality in *A Plaine and Easie Introduction to Practical Musicke* (1597)—although he derives that term from Italian. From Gioseffo Zerlino's *Le Institutione Harmoniche* (1558), Morley quotes with approval a comparison of harmony in music to color in painting: "euen as a picture painted with diuers cullours doth more delight the eie to beholde it then if it were done but with one cullour alone, so the eare is more delighted and taketh more pleasure of the consonants [consonances] by the diligent musicion placed in his compositions with varietie then of the simple concords put together without any varietie at all."[73]

In terms of practical music, just what does "color" mean? In chant of the fifteenth century, "color" was the term for embellishments that a singer might add to the vocal line—an intensification of affect like the "colors of rhetoric."[74] Elsewhere in *A Plaine and Easie Introduction,* Morley seems to equate "color" not with embellishments to a single vocal line but with harmony, with tones on multiple pitches (and often from multiple instruments and voices) sounded at the same time. Setting words to music, he explains, will sometimes compel a composer "to admit great absurdities in his musicke, altering both time, tune, cullour[,] ayre and what soeuer else" (sig. Y5v). "Air" in this passage and elsewhere seems to be the key or tonal mode of a piece. As for "color," what Morley has in mind are chords, groups of tones that are harmoniously related, but he is also anticipating the findings of modern acoustics: the timbre of a sound, even a single tone on one dominant frequency, results from the distinctive overtones, the parallel vibrations at other frequencies, that are set off in the air when the tone is produced by *this* particular voice or *that* particular instrument.

"If Musicke and sweet Poetrie agree, / As they must needs (the Sister and the brother) . . . ": the opening lines of a sonnet attributed to Shakespeare in *The Passionate Pilgrime* (1599) celebrates a Renaissance commonplace almost as ubiquitous as *ut pictura poesis.*[75] Morley's experience as a professional composer suggests a more complicated relationship between the siblings. For all his oft-quoted advice about "how to dispose your musicke according to the nature of the words which you are therein to expresse" (sig. AA2), Morley sometimes seems to place words and music in an oppositional relationship. For the words that a composer sets to music Morley's term is "dittie," literally something "dictated" (*dictatum*) to the composer, as if the words were given to him like a lecture, lesson, or academic exercise (*OED,* "ditty" *n.,* etymology). With respect to words, a musical composer takes dictation. "Dittie" versus harmony shapes up as yet another instance of the contest between *disegno* and *colore* that occupied us in chapters one, three, and four. Words in Morley's formulation act like a line or rule; harmonic color washes over that line. On occasion it can obliterate the line entirely. The musical form most free from the rule of words, Morley says, is "the fantasie, that is, when a musician taketh a point at his pleasure, and wresteth and turneth it as he list, making either much or little of it according as shall seeme best in his own conceit" (sig. AA4). Almost always, Morley observes, fantasies are designed for musical instruments, not for human voices.

To Listen for Sound's Own Syntax

Bacon with his "immusical sounds," Spenser with his buzzings, Hart with his sense that letters are "figures and colors" of the human voice, Robinson with his "vital sound": all of these Renaissance writers seem to be recognizing a prelinguistic matrix out of which articulate speech emerges. George Puttenham speaks for most of these writers in identifying this matrix with the irrational and hence with the passions. "There is no greater difference betwixt a ciuill and brutish vtteraunce," Puttenham observes in *The Arte of English Poesie,* "then cleare distinction of voices: and the most laudable languages are alwaies most plaine and distinct, and the barbarous most confuse [*sic*] and indistinct."[76] Hart brings the same criterion to his spelling reform scheme. "The letter ought to keepe the voyce, and not to be ydle, vsurped in sound or to be misplaced" (sig. C2v). Superfluous letters function, in Hart's hearing, like "vicious humors" that need to be purged (sig. C3v).

What constitutes the "plaine and distinct" speech that Puttenham uses as a criterion for distinguishing laudable languages from barbarous? For Hart it would be an exact correspondence of letters to voices. For Thomas Campion it would be verse that is free from rhyme. To Campion's ear, excessive rhyming is a kind of buzzing: "The facilitie and popularitie of Rime," Campion declares in *Observations in the Art of English Poesie,* "creates as many Poets as a hot sommer [creates] flies."[77] The Roman rhetoricians advised only sparing use of rhyme, Campion notes, "least it should offend the ear with tedious affectation" (sig. B6v). The term "affectation" is precisely chosen. Rhyme is a species of irrationality: "The eare is a rational sence and a chiefe iudge of proportion; but in our kind of riming what proportion is there kept when there remaines such a confusd inequalitie of sillables?" (sig. B7). Campion recognizes that repetition is basic to poetry's appeal. What he champions over the repetition of certain phonemes is the repetition of certain time values, as if English were like Latin in measuring how long vowels are held rather than how much stress they receive. One of the songs Campion contributed to Philip Rosseter's *A Book of Airs* (1601) illustrates the principle by exactly matching the time values of the musical notes with the time values of the sapphic meter that he has imposed on the conspicuously unrhymed English words (see musical example 7). In this precise alignment of note values and vowel val-

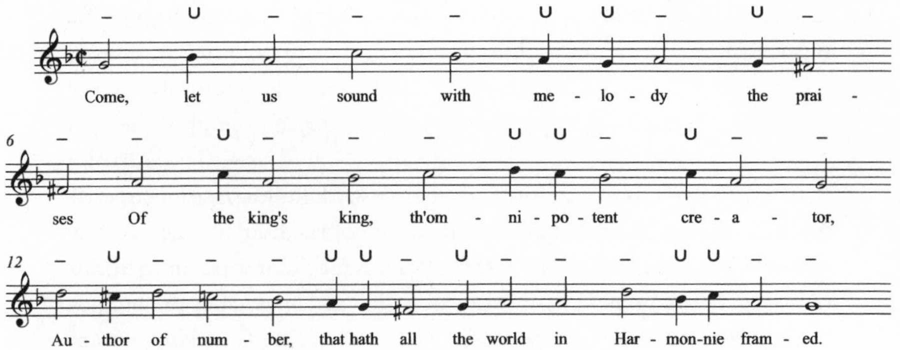

Musical example 7. Thomas Campion, "Come, Let Us Sound with Melody." Adapted from Philip Rosseter, *A Book of Airs* (1601).

ues, Campion provides a musical equivalent of Hart's orthography—and a radical example of logocentricism in music. The "childish titillation of riming" is to be abjured in large part because it works against rational clarity: "it inforceth a man oftentimes to abiure his matter and extend a short conceit beyond all bounds of arte" (sig. B7).

In *An Apologie for Ryme,* Samuel Daniel turns Campion's rationalist criteria against him. Rhythm and rhyme, Daniel feels, endow poetry with "the effect of motion."[78] Amid this motion, rhythmic patterns provide points of distinction, "being such as the Eare of it selfe doth marshal in their proper roomes, and they of themselues will not willingly be put out of their ranke" (sig. G4). Rhyme, for its part, provides "due staies for the minde, those incounters of touch as makes the motion certaine, though the varietie be infinite" (sig. G5). To Daniel's ear, both rhythm and rhyme thus serve to separate and to order sounds that would otherwise be experienced as continuous motion. By imposing form on this continuous motion, rhythm and rhyme recapitulate Genesis and, in so doing, shore up reason against engulfment by the passions: "For the body of our imagination, being as an vnformed *Chaos* without fashion, without day, if by the diuine power of the spirit it be wrought into an Orbe of order and forme, is it not more pleasing to Nature, that desires a certaintie, and comports not with that which is infinite, to haue these clozes, rather than, not to know where to end, or how farre to goe, especially seeing our passions are often without measure" (sig. G6). The quantitative verse that Campion proposes would, according to Daniel, work against right judgment, since it would divert the mind from the "matter" of the poem and call attention instead to sound *as sound:* "For seeing it is matter that satisfies the iudiciall, appeare it in what habite it will, all these pretended proportions of words, howsoeuer placed, can be but words, and peraduenture serue but to embroyle our vnderstanding, whilst seeking to please our eare, we inthrall our iudgement: to delight an exterior sense, wee smoothe vp a weake confused sense, affecting sound to be vnsound" (sig. G5v). All told, rhyme in Daniel's analysis serves as an antidote to endless motion, to confusion, to mere sensation, to the sway of the passions.

Ben Jonson, for one, would not be so sure. Jonson's poem "A Fit of Rhyme Against Rhyme" enacts, stanza by stanza, a tension between mindless sound and sound mind:

> Rime, the rack of finest wits,
> That expresseth but by fits,
> True Conceipt,
> Spoyling Senses of their Treasure,
> Cosening Judgement with a measure,
> But false weight.[79]

To give the reader's eye the same sharp contrast that the reader's ear can hear, Jonson not only offsets the lapidary *thereness* of "True Conceipt" but capitalizes it as if it were a Platonic Idea.[80] What exactly is the "Treasure" of which rhyme "spoils" the senses? The succeeding lines suggest that it is the true conceit, or right conception, that the understanding should be able to find in the imagination's transcript of sense experience. In the case of sound, that means an exact coincidence between sound and meaning:

> Wresting words, from their true calling;
> Propping Verse, for feare of falling
> To the ground.
> Joynting Syllabes, drowning Letters,
> Fastning Vowells, as with fetters
> They were bound!
> (29.7–12)

Three particular disruptions of the sound/meaning bond are cataloged in the latter three lines: contractions ("Joynting Syllabes" demonstrates the phenomenon by reducing the three syllables of *syl-la-ble* to two), obliterating distinctions between phonemes ("Letters" indicates Jonson's predisposition to see what he hears), and arranging vowels according to sound alone (the "fetters" privilege sound over sense). All three involve "drowning" discrete syllables and words in the stream of sound. Jonson's own *metier* as a verse maker is to be found in the chiseled, waterproof solidity of the short lines: "True Conceipt," "But false weight," "To the ground," "They were bound."

Better examples could not be found of Jonson's adherence to what he and his contemporaries understood as "the plain style." Traditionally associated with dialectic (the goal of which was simply to teach, not to move or delight), the plain style favored as close as possible an alignment between denotation and connotation.[81] In Jonson's case, the centripetal drive toward denotation is heightened by a preference not only for monosyllabic words but for monosyllabic words that begin and end with strong consonants: "*w*eigh*t*," "*g*roun*d*," "*b*oun*d*." In such words there is little possibility of "drowning Letters." In the stream of speech there are three types of landmarks that serve to divide the stream into discrete units: (1) vowels at syllable peaks, (2) abrupt consonants, and (3) low-frequency glides (the /j/ in *your*, the /w/ in *wore*) produced as the vocal apparatus moves from one position to another.[82] Generally speaking, vowels and glides enhance the stream effect of sound; consonants, especially the stops /p/, /b/, /t/, /d/, /k/, and /g/, contribute to an effect of distinctness.

The ratio of vowels to consonantal stops, particularly in how words begin and end gives us one way of comparing how Renaissance verse writers variously negotiate the stream of sound. Shakespeare's contemporary reputation for mellifluousness was something for which Jonson himself was partly responsible. In the catalog of Shakespeare's virtues that Jonson includes in *Timber, or Discoveries,* "true conceit" is conspicuously absent: Shakespeare, says Jonson, "had an excellent *Phantasie;* brave notions, and gentle expressions: wherein hee flow'd with that facility, that sometime it was necessary he should be stop'd."[83] Shakespeare's own complaint against an insubstantial rhymer in sonnet 85 ("My toung-tide muse in manners holds her still") can provide an example:

> I thinke good thoughts, whilst other write good wordes,
> And like vnlettered clarke still crie Amen,
> To euery Himne that able spirit affords,
> In polisht form of well refined pen.[84]

In the first line, made up entirely of monosyllabic words, the sharp distinction between "good thoughts" and "good words" is accentuated with terminal /d/ sounds and /t/ + /s/ sounds. That measured restraint quickly gives way, however, to an outpouring of resentment that gathers force in iambs that are almost anapests ("And like un*let*tered," "To every *hymn*") and in waves of initial vowels ("*A*nd," "*u*nlettered," "*A*men," "*e*very," "*a*ble," "*a*ffords") that spill over from line two to three and from line three to four before returning to a modicum of composure in the plosives of "*p*olished . . . *p*en." Need one point out that this twenty one–word, thrice-enjambed effusion is an indulgence in passion, in jealousy, in greensickness? Greenness here is something that can be heard as well as seen. Not for nothing did Jonson persistently associate Shakespeare with nature ("Sweet Swan of Avon!"), even as he acknowledged the durability of the "well torned, and true filed lines" that he himself aspired to write.

To listen for green would mean, then, allowing rhyme, alliteration, and assonance to divert the sense of hearing from its rational work. To listen for green would mean attending to sounds that spiral away from denotative meaning toward wordless sensation. Iago's warning enkindles Othello's jealousy precisely because of these green sound effects: "Oh, beware my Lord, of iealousie, / It is the greene-ey'd Monster which doth mocke / The meate it feeds on." The opening exclamation immediately wrests the imagination away from the regimen of words. As it happens, /o:/ is the most intense vowel sound in English: it strikes the ear more forcefully than other vowel sounds.[85] Joel Fineman has called attention to the pervasiveness of /o:/ in *Othello* and has interpreted its effect as an opening into the Lacanian Real and hence as a challenge to the fixity of language in the Symbolic Order.[86] The suggestiveness of Iago's /o:/ in Act Three, scene three, is at once audible. "But oh," Iago concludes the speech, "what damned minutes tells he ore, / Who dotes, yet doubts: Suspects, yet foundly loues?" Othello's responds in kind, like the singer of an antiphon: "O miserie" (3.3.174–75). The power of Iago's speech over Othello's passions is very much an effect of assonance and alliteration. Sounds of /o/ insinuate surprise or moaning in "l*o*rd," "jeal*ou*sy," "m*o*nster," "d*o*th," "m*o*ck," and "*o*n." Quick panting is invited by the /i/ sounds in "*i*t," "*i*s," "wh*i*ch," and again "*i*t." Stronger still is the keening intimated by the /i:/ sounds in "jealous*y*," "gr*ee*n," "m*ea*t," and "f*ee*ds." The ruminative /m/ in "*m*onster," "*m*ock," and "*m*eat" completes the job of aural seduction. The stops in "mo*ck*," "mea*t*," "i*t*," and "fee*d*s" give the completed utterance a deadly inevitability.

The passionate power of "willow" later in the play is unmistakable, especially as those sounds are sung again and again as a refrain in between the lines of a narrative: "*Sing Willough, Willough, Willough,*" "*Sing Willough, &c.,*" "*Sing Willough &c., / Willough Willough,*" "*Sing all a greene Willough must be my Garland*" (4.3.41, 43, 45–46, 49). The effect of these repeated utterances has as much to do with the passion of melancholy as it does with the visual image of a tree with drooping branches growing next to a flowing stream. The most familiar tune to Desdemona's song, a lute

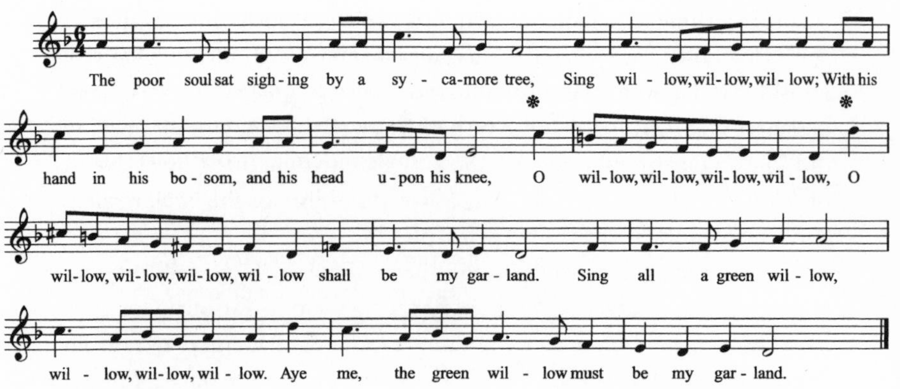

Musical example 8. "The Complaint of a Lover Forsaken." Adapted from British Library MS Add. 15117, a collection of English songs in treble voice, with tablature for lute (ca. 1630).

song dating from 1630, colors the ditty most intensely at just those moments when sound segments are not quite coalescing into phonemes. In musical example 8, the passion of melancholy rises to its climax in the two passages of (ironically) *falling* tones marked with asterisks—passages in which the ditty runs "O willow, willow, willow, willow." In the course of their descent, both phrases pass through tones that are unexpected in the scale of D minor. These tones are marked with a natural (♮) that raises the expected B-flat to a B-natural and two sharps (♯) that raise the expected C-natural to a C-sharp and the expected F-natural to an F-sharp. Morley sets up a gendered contrast between, on the one hand, "naturall motions" that stick to the expected scale—motions that he pronounces "more masculine"—and, on the other hand, "those accidentall cordes which are marked with these signes. ♯. ♭. which be in deede accidentall, and make the song as it were more effeminate & languishing" (sig. AA2). In o:/w/ /ɪ/ /o:/ Desdemona's passion devolves from words into deep green, just as the Jailer's Daughter's passion does when, in her first utterance, she tries to remember the refrain of a song she once knew: "I have forgot it quite; The burden on't was *downe / A downe a*'" (4.3.10–11). The Daughter's song, the ballad of "Greensleeves," Desdemona singing "Willow, willow, willow": all these complaints beckon the audience to listen for green.

The threat of words and syllables to devolve into non-semantic sound is always present in Renaissance verse, especially in the soft pastoral mode, where "Hey nonny nonny" threatens to break out at any time. On occasion we can see that devolution happen before our very eyes on the printed page, just as it happens within our very ears when we vocalize the text to ourselves. Take, for example, Nashe's spirited celebration of spring in *Summer's Last Will and Testament.* The /s/ sounds and anapestic rhythms of the first stanza, ringing out in sharp contrast to the stops of "*cold*" and "*sting*," fly free of words entirely in the stanza's final line. By the third stanza, bird songs have become pandemic throughout the human scene:

> Spring, the sweete spring, is the yeres pleasant King,
> Then bloomes eche thing, then maydes daunce in a ring,
> Cold doeth not sting, the pretty birds doe sing:
> Cuckow, iugge, iugge, pu we, to witta woo.
> The Palme and May make countrey houses gay,
> Lambs friske and play, the Shepherds pype all day,
> And we heare aye, birds tune this merry lay:
> Cuckow, iugge, iugge, pu we, to witta woo.
> The fields breathe sweete, the dayzies kisse our feete,
> Young louers meete, old wiues a sunning sit:
> In euery streete, these tunes our eares do greete,
> Cuckow, iugge, iugge, pu we, to witta woo.
> Spring the sweete spring.[87]

When the song's opening phrase, "Spring, the sweet spring," is repeated as a coda, the sound of /s/ has become far more suasive than the meanings denoted by "spring" and "sweet" the first time around. Especially in the original performance in 1592, when the lines were sung by Ver and his train,"*ouerlayd with suites of greene mosse, representing short grasse,*" Nashe's verses were calculated to appeal to the passions, not to the understanding alone. For readers with open ears, now as in 1592, Nashe's verses work a radical deconstruction on the English language.

This effect has not gone altogether unremarked by critics. Garrett Stewart has argued that an element of deconstruction is present in all written texts when they are vocalized, aloud or silently, in the act of reading: "Reading is the displacing without forgetting of one word by the next in the syntactic chain. When this displacement operates a shade too quickly or too slowly—one word shadowed in passing by its neighbor partly assimilated to it by recurring in it—the 'will' to morphophonemic structure is thus found exerting its full, indeed overflowing, pressure on the written sign."[88] The result is a "blurring at the borders" between phonemes that creates "the possibility of more paradigmatic choices than can simultaneously be made" (26). Stephen Booth delights in a similar plenitude of possibilities generated by the "physics" of metrical pairings, rhyme, alliteration, anaphora, and chiasmus: "All those literary phenomena are enabling acts, acts that enable their audiences to perceive two or more distinct identities at once and as one."[89] Booth's test case is Act Three, scenes nine and ten, of *Antony and Cleopatra.* What Stewart and Booth both listen for are new words, instances of "transegmental drift" (25) in Stewart's case and a "fusion and confusion of entities" (77) in Booth's.

The green potential in Renaissance verse is even more radical than that. It dissolves words, not into other words, but into non-semantic sound. It does not just break words down into phonemes that can be recombined with other phonemes in new and interesting ways; it *liquefies* words. That potential, present in all languages, whatever the time and place in which speakers and listeners find themselves, is positively encouraged by a physiology of knowing, current among speakers of English in the seventeenth century, in which the passions "hear" sensations before reason does. The sensations circulate throughout the body as an aerated fluid on which reason's imprint is always insubstantial. In *Syntactic Structures* (1957), Noam Chomsky gave first shape to the principle of deep structure that has undergirded all his subsequent work in linguistics. Beneath all the utterances possible in the English language Chomsky posits, not the arbitrary system of phonetic and semantic difference-marking that Saussure proposes, but a biologically innate set of mental capacities that determine the structures of *all* languages.[90] In effect, Chomsky takes the tentative vertical lines in de Saussure's diagram of thought and speech (see figure 1) and gives them physiological inevitability. If Saussure's *General Course in Linguistics* is the generative text for deconstruction, Chomsky's *Syntactic Structures* is the generative text for cognitive science. As an example of deep structure Chomsky sets up the following contrast:

> Sentences (1) and (2) are equally nonsensical, but any speaker of English will recognize that only the former is grammatical.
>
> (1) Colorless green ideas sleep furiously.
>
> (2) Furiously sleep ideas green colorless.[91]

That is to say, the syntax of English recognizes the structural logic of noun phrase + verb phrase (adjective + adjective + noun +verb + adverb) but not the illogic of adverb + verb (or is "sleep" a noun?) + noun + adjective (or is "green" a noun?) + adjective. And according to Chomsky and cognitive scientists, there are biological reasons why that should be so. Both sentences, however, are judged to be "nonsensical," because, in semantic terms, ideas cannot be both colorless and green at the same time, nor can ideas sleep, nor can sleep happen furiously. The very notion of "deep" structure implies a line, a vertical line, in which "levels" of language are "generated" from below:

sound (phonetics)
↑
semantics (lexicon and grammar)
↑
syntax: surface structure
↑
syntax: deep structure

Does listening merely reverse the direction of the arrows? Does the vertical line of space get turned into a horizontal line of time?

sound → semantics → syntax

Changing the orientation and the direction of the line frees up color. Depending on how greenly one listens, sounds can assume a syntax that does not lead straight to words. Why should not /g/r/iː/n/ in Chomsky's second sentence emerge into aural, even perhaps semantic presence out of the sibilants of "furiou*s*ly," "*s*leep," and "idea*s*" and then dissolve into the prolonged sibilant of "colorle*ss*"? The green potential is always present for critics who are willing to go deconstruction one better and listen to the totality of speech sounds beyond the 50 percent that are remarked as words. As Saussure realized, lines of difference are marks made on water.

The evidence that we have heard here—Donne's testimony that there is a direct connection between the ears and the genitals, the seductions of ballads like "Greensleeves," the melismas in pre-Reformation and High Church musical settings of the psalms, Verdant's swoon in the Bower of Bliss, the noises and enigmatic conversations that begin Shakespeare's scripts and the jigs that ended them in their original performances, the controversy between Campion and Daniel over rhyme—all suggest that Renaissance listeners were better attuned to this green potential than we are. In a word, they seem to have been adept at *ambient* listening. So calculated is our own listening that we have no need for a Philip Stubbes to set us wrong.

CHAPTER SIX

The Curtain between the Theatre and the Globe

In April of 1597 the Lord Chamberlain's Men lost their lease on the Theatre. Erected in 1576 in Shoreditch, north of the city walls of London, the Theatre enjoyed the distinction of being the first permanent, purpose-built playhouse in Britain since Roman times. Twenty-one years later, the lease on the land was up, and Shakespeare's troupe found themselves without a home. It was not until December 1598 that Richard Burbage, John Heminges, Shakespeare, and the other shareholders hired Peter Streete to dismantle the timbers of the Theatre (the 1576 lease covered the land, not the building), transport the posts and beams across the Thames to the South Bank, and reerect them there as the Globe. By mid-1599, the new Globe was up and running. There the company remained until all of London's public theaters were closed by parliamentary proclamation two generations later, in 1642.[1] For the twenty months between their eviction from the Theatre and their reestablishment at the Globe, the Lord Chamberlain's Men performed in an amphitheater that had been built in 1577 a few yards closer to Bishopsgate in the city walls. That interim space was named the Curtain. During their twenty months at the Curtain, Shakespeare's company scored some of their greatest successes: *The Merry Wives of Windsor*, *2 Henry IV*, *Much Ado About Nothing*, *Henry V*, and possibly *The Merchant of Venice*, as well as revivals of *The Comedy of Errors*, *Romeo and Juliet*, and likely *1 Henry IV*, not to mention first performances of Ben Jonson's comedy *Everyman in His Humor* and the anonymous domestic tragedy *A Warning for Faire Women*.[2] The building's site is remembered today in the name of Curtain Road, EC 2, a short street running through a district of disused cabinet works and upholsterers' shops that, at the time of this writing, were rapidly being converted into lofts, art galleries, coffee houses, and restaurants serving up style as well as food.[3]

The Curtain: the name seems an anomaly, since, as veterans of Shakespeare 101 know very well, there *was* no curtain at the Curtain—at least no curtain of the woven variety. In explaining the playhouse's name, Herbert Berry and other scholars have cited the curtain wall that surrounded the field, formerly part of Holywell Priory, in which the playhouse was erected.[4] Curtain, in the sense of drapery that parts in the middle or rises and falls from above, is reckoned by all theater historians to be a much later invention. Standard histories of the theater quite literally *depend on* the curtain that is supposed to have put actors and spectators into separate physical and conceptual spaces beginning in the early nineteenth century. In these histories, a curtain that can rise and fall or open and shut side to side *hangs down* between early modern theater on one side of the chronological divide and modern theater on the other. In *The Development of the English Playhouse,* for example, Richard Leacroft quotes at length Benjamin Wyatt's rationale for the proscenium arch that figured prominently in his 1812 design for the reconstructed Drury Lane Theatre. "The Proscenium must be considered as forming part of the Spectatory," Wyatt writes, "and *not* a part of the Scene; . . . it is a line of separation between the two, and is to the Scene what the frame of a Picture is to the Picture itself: namely, a boundary line to confine the eye of the Subject within that line, and prevent it from wandering to other objects."[5] By contrast, early modern stages are supposed to have resembled postmodern stages in their bareness—and in their demand that spectators collaborate with actors in filling that empty space with meaning. Peter Brook's vision of late-twentieth-century theater is an existential vision that responds to the same crisis of belief as Sartre, Lacan, and Beckett: "The curtain used to be the great symbol of a whole school of theatre—the red curtain, the footlights, the idea that we are all children again, the nostalgia and the magic were all of a piece. . . . But the day came when the same red curtain no longer hid surprises, when we no longer wanted—or needed—to be children again, when the rough magic yielded to a harsher common-sense; then the curtain was pulled down and the footlights removed." We may still expect the arts to reveal "the invisible currents that rule our lives," Brook concludes, "but our vision is now locked to the dark end of spectrum."[6]

It has pleased us, since the 1950s, to foist that ultraviolet darkness onto the Renaissance stage. Brook said let there be no more red, and there was no more red. In the late 1960s and early 1970s, the interior of the Royal

Shakespeare Theatre in Stratford-upon-Avon was stripped of its plush 1930s red decor and painted dark gray, turning the space into a large-scale version of the black box in which every university drama department in the English-speaking world mounts its productions.[7] Stages at the Theatre, the Curtain, and the Globe were like this, we tell ourselves: existential voids in which meanings were made out of next to nothing, out of words, costumes, and a few props. Reconstruction of Shakespeare's Globe near the original site from 1993 to 1997 forced a practical rethinking of these investments in blackness and emptiness. The stage was the last element of Shakespeare's Globe to be undertaken, not least because documented details about the back wall and its openings, about the canopy over the stage, about the columns that supported the canopy are so sketchy and oblique. A conference on "Finishing the Globe" in September 2002 brought together academic experts on theater history, architecture, timber construction, paintwork, emblem books, and Renaissance schemes of interior decoration. The convergence of their work can be witnessed in the elaborate painted effects that form the visual ground against which "original practices" performances take place at the Globe today. Andrew Gurr and Mariko Ichikawa's *Staging in Shakespeare's Theatres* is a notable exception among academic books in relieving modernist austerity with appreciation for the period painted finishes that make the reconstructed Globe anything but a neutral black box.[8] The very term "original practices" serves, however, to distance the aesthetic of 1599 from the aesthetic of 1999. Apart from Shakespeare's Globe in London, it is still Brook's dark end of the spectrum that defines the physical and conceptual space within which most contemporary productions of Shakespeare's scripts take place.

The bareness of the sixteenth- and early-seventeenth-century stage is an idea with a long history. Richard Flecknoe's *A Short Discourse of the English Stage,* appended to the script of *Love's Kingdom* (1664), sets in place a picture of the Renaissance stage that is by and large still being accepted today. "Now, for the difference betwixt our Theaters and those of former times," Flecknoe begins, "they were but plain and simple, with no other Scenes, nor Decorations of the Stage, but onely old Tapestry, and the Stage strew'd with Rushes, (with their Habits accordingly) whereas ours now for cost and ornament are arriv'd to the height of Magnificence."[9] ("Habits" in this context means habiliments, or costumes.) Flecknoe goes on to set up just the dichotomy between vision and sound, between spectacle and words, that still informs modern understandings of Shakespeare: "that which makes our Stage the better," Flecknoe tells his readers, "makes our Playes the worse perhaps, they striving now to make them more for sight, then hearing; whence that solid joy of the interior is lost, and that benefit which men formerly receiv'd from Playes, from which they seldom or never went away, but far better and wiser then they came" (sig. H3v). Here, in yet another guise, is the contest between *disegno* and *colore* that has drawn our attention before. The black-and-white simplicities of *disegno* are associated with hearing; the blandishments of color, with sight. Flecknoe's remarks had their effect on Edmund Malone, who probably is responsible for calling them to the attention of Thomas Percy, who quotes Flecknoe verbatim in the introduction to the theater section of *Reliques of Ancient English Poetry* (1765).[10] For his part, Malone surveys all the available evidence in his *Historical Account of the Rise and Progress of the English Stage* (1790; 2nd ed., 1800) and concludes, "The various circumstances which I have studied, and the accounts of the contemporary writers, furnish us, in my apprehension, with decisive and incontrovertible proofs, that the stage of Shakespeare was not furnished with *moveable painted scenes,* but merely decorated with curtains, and arras or tapestry hangings."[11]

"Merely"? The physical, visual, verbal, and aural evidence that has been collected in *The Key of Green* would call that qualifier into question. As it happens, all ten of the surviving scripts associated with the Lord Chamberlain's Men during their twenty months at the Curtain call, explicitly or implicitly, for the use of some sort of curtain, arras, or hanging cloth. Why have we paid so little critical attention to these artifacts? Partly because the one universally accepted piece of visual evidence about London's public theaters, Aernout van Buchel's copy of Johannes de Witt's sketch of the stage at the Swan Theatre in 1596, doesn't show them. Partly because we have been determined to see the Renaissance stage in existential, high-modernist terms as a bare platform full of intellectual possibilities but largely devoid of visual interest apart from costumes and a few strategic props.[12] But mostly because, with respect to stage performance like everything else, we want what we know to be clear and distinct. We have accepted Flecknoe's distinction between the black-and-white clarity and solidity of the verbal text, which we hear in performance and later can verify in the printed script, and the colored blur and ceaseless motion of the live visual experience, which eludes us as soon as it happens. Color and movement are not appropriate objects of knowledge. No wonder we have seized on the graspable, ownable, repeatable objects presented to hand, eye, ears, and brain by celluloid film, video tapes, and CDs. Delivering up *colore* as well as *disegno,* they seem to let us have it both ways.

The visual images in these media, projected by electrical energy onto a flat screen from in front or behind, and the soundtracks, processed electrically through two or more boxes, let us maintain the subject/object distance that has proved so reassuring since the late seventeenth century.

By contrast, those ten scripts for the Curtain suggest ways of watching and listening in which the relationship of subject and object is dynamic, not fixed. Flecknoe catches these differences in his choice of metaphors. "A good Play," he argues, "shu'd be like a good stuff, closely and evenly wrought, without any breakes, thrums, or loose ends in 'um." The play as tapestry unfolds in Flecknoe's two further metaphors: the play as "a good Picture well painted and designed; the Plot or Contrivement, the Design, the Writing, the Coloris, and Counterplot, the Shaddowings, with other Embellishments" and the play as "a well contriv'd Garden, cast into its Walks and Counterwalks, betwixt an Alley and a Wilderness, neither too plain, nor too confus'd" (sig. H1v). The latter two metaphors, as we know from park-work tapestries, are implicated in the first. Taking in a play, Flecknoe suggests, is like walking through a garden. It is an ambient experience in which wildness on the one hand is kept at bay by civility on the other—just the state of in-betweenness that we found in Renaissance garden designs in chapter two. In the case of Marvell's poem "The Garden," written a dozen or so years before Flecknoe's *Short Discourse* (or, if Nigel Smith's dating is right, four years later[13]), the experience of wildness impinging on civility is represented through words; in scripts for the Curtain, it happened to spectator-listeners' bodies, in a distinctive configuration of space, through a calculated rhythm of time. And it happened in color. If we want to understand the perceptual dynamics of Shakespeare's theater, we must turn our attention to the physical stuff against which, out of which, through which, between which the dramatized events took place. The ambient *listening* encouraged by the distinctive shape and timber construction of the Curtain was allied with ambient *looking.*[14] What wood and plaster were to sound, woven hangings were to vision. They provided the horizon for green thought in a version quite specific to theater. Giving due attention to this horizon offers an escape from the black box. Once outside the door, we arrive in the green shade amid which the Curtain and London's other suburban theaters were located, psychologically as well as geographically. The place of the stage in sixteenth-century London may have been the districts of unregulated commercial activity and pleasure seeking that Steven Mullaney has censused, but they were also, according to John Stow's *The Survey of London* (1598, 1599, 1603, 1618,

1633, 1657), open green spaces in which "the Youths of this Citie have in the Field exercised themselves, in leaping, dancing, shooting, wrestling, casting of the stone or ball, &c."[15] The two sports arenas that preceded the Globe on the South Bank (one is labeled "The beare bayting" and the other "The bowll baytyng") are set amid green fields in Georg Braun and Franz Hogenberg's 1572 view of London[16] (see plate 25).

Warp, Woof, and Words in the 1597–1599 Repertory

Of the ten surviving scripts that have been associated with the Lord Chamberlain's Men at the Curtain, six explicitly call for use of woven hangings in the course of the action. Evidence in the case of the four others is more indirect but nonetheless suggestive. The three revivals among the ten scripts suggest that scenic arrangements at the Curtain replicated what had been available at the Theatre and other places where the Lord Chamberlain's Men had been playing. Among the fools summoned forth for ridicule in Satyre 10, entitled "Humours," in John Marston's *The Scourge of Villanie* (1598) is the theater addict Luscus. "What ere he sayes," Marston jibes, "Is warranted by Curtaine *plaudeties.*"[17] Marston's sneer at Luscus's "pure *Iuliat* and *Romio*" (sig. H4) is plausibly taken by Roslyn Knutson as evidence that *Romeo and Juliet* was revived at the Curtain. Although the spokesman of Satire V in Everard Guilpin's *Skialetheia* (1598) boasts that he does not have to go to the Rose to enjoy *The Spanish Tragedy* or the Curtain to catch "one of *Plautus* Comedies" (why go out when you can read them at home?), he may be alluding to a recent revival of *The Comedy of Errors.*[18] The first documented performance of *Errors* had happened four years earlier as a feature of the Christmas revels at Gray's Inn.[19] The academic auspices of that performance have served to highlight the classical features of Shakespeare's comedy—the unities of time, place, and persons it takes over from Plautus and Terence—and have prompted a number of theater historians to wonder if the three houses mentioned in the script weren't realized as curtained booths or as curtained openings in the carved screen that still spans one end of Gray's Inn hall.[20] A woodcut from Johannes Trechsel's 1493 folio of Terence's comedies (see figure 20) suggests how Antipholus's house, "the Phoenix," the courtesan's house, "the Porcupine," and the Abbess's house, "the Priory" could have not only provided the players with openings for their entrances and exits but suggested the thematic geography of the comedy's action. Left and right doors flanking a central, curtained opening could have served the same purpose at the Curtain. With her unexpected appearance in

Figure 20. Terence, *Phormio* 1.2, in *Comoediae* (Lyon: Johannes Trechsel, 1493). (Library of Congress, Prints and Photographs Division [1493 J682].)

Act 5, the Abbess—none other than Egeon's long-lost wife, it turns out, and mother to the Antipholus twins—figures as a *dea-ex-machina.* It is she who sorts out "this simpathized one daies error."[21] If there were three openings, The Abbey would surely have been the middle one, a mythical space that reconciles the domestic securities of the Phoenix on the one hand with the imaginative vagaries of the Porcupine on the other. A curtain across that central space would have turned the Abbess's appearance into an epiphany appropriate for Christmas, a physical discovery that inaugurates all the ensuing discoveries of true identities.

Nothing in the text of *The Comedy of Errors* specifies curtains, but they are explicitly required for *Romeo and Juliet.* Like *The Comedy of Errors,* Shakespeare's tragedy of star-crossed lovers had been in the repertory for three or four years when the Lord Chamberlain's Men brought it to the Curtain. The 1597 quarto, published the same year the company decamped to the Curtain, says that Juliet drinks from the vial of sleeping potion that Friar Laurence has provided and "*fals vpon her bed within the Cur-*

taines" (Q1597, SD after 4.3.57). Whether the bed in question was situated behind curtains that separated the main stage from a space "within" or whether a curtained four-poster bed was "thrust out" onto the main stage has been much debated.[22] Despite the absence of a central opening in the Swan drawing, the existence of some sort of space "within"—curtained or not—is beyond question. Roughly eight hundred stage directions call for such a space, according to Alan Dessen and Leslie Thomson's *A Dictionary of Stage Directions in English Drama, 1580–1642*. Another ten stage directions require that a bed be thrust "out," "on," or "forth."[23] A detail of the title page to William Sampson's tragedy *The Vow Breaker* (acted 1625–1636, printed 1636) suggests what this stage-property bed might have looked like (see figure 21). Within or without, Juliet sleeping on her bed amid the curtains forces modern readers to get their bearings in a space that lacks rational perspective. The Oxford and the Norton editions imagine Juliet in a curtained bed and append to the quarto stage direction a qualifying phrase—"*pulling closed the curtains*" (SD after 4.3.57)—that keeps Juliet out of view while the Capulet household prepares for her wedding in the next scene. In another added stage direction, the Nurse "*draws back the curtains*" (SD after 4.4.38) a few minutes into that scene and discovers the seemingly dead Juliet. Malone is closer to Renaissance habits of viewing in being willing to entertain two spectacles, in two logically sep-

Figure 21. William Sampson, *The Vow Breaker. Or, The faire maide of Clifton* (London: John Norton for Roger Ball, 1636), title page detail. Original image, $2^{7}/_{2} \times 2$ inches (6.4 × 5 cm). (Reproduced by permission of the Huntington Library, San Marino, California.)

arate places, all at the same time: "As soon as Juliet has fallen on the bed, the curtains being still open, the nurse enters, then old Capulet and his lady, then the musicians; and all on the same spot. If they could have exhibited a bed chamber, and then could have substituted any other room for it, would they have suffered the musicians and the Nurse's servant to have carried on a ludicrous dialogue in one where Juliet was supposed to be lying dead?"[24] From chapter two, we have some sense of the imaginative space created by the bed curtains that unfold Juliet: a space in which sleeping, dreaming, pleasuring the body, dying, and moving within and between diverse shapes and forms are woven together in antic play.

If *1 Henry IV* was revived at the Curtain in connection with the premieres of *The Merry Wives of Windsor, 2 Henry IV,* and *Henry V,* spectators would have had two opportunities to enjoy comic business that crams Falstaff behind the arras. When the Sheriff arrives to search Mistress Quickley's tavern in *1 Henry IV,* Falstaff takes his cue from Prince Harry: "Go hide thee behind the Arras, the rest walke vp aboue" (Q1598, 2.5.506–7). Poins, Russell, and Gadshill disappear "above"; Falstaff disappears behind the woven cloth. When the Sheriff has departed, Peto calls out "Falstaffe" (or so the succeeding colon in the 1598 quarto suggests) and, not getting an answer, draws back the curtain to discover Falstaff "fast asleepe behind the Arras, and snorting like a horse" (Q1598, 2.5.534–35). There is a reprise in *Merry Wives* of stuffing Falstaff's ample bulk behind a thin cloth. When news comes that Mistress Page is about to break in on Falstaff's assignation with Mistress Ford—and discover that he is wooing two women at the same time—Falstaff plumps for the same strategy that worked so well in *1 Henry IV:* "I will ensconce mee behinde the Arras" (F 1623, 3.3.83–84)—an action confirmed by a stage direction in the 1602 quarto: "*Falstaffe stands behind the aras*" (SD after 3.2.85–86). What Mistress Page brings is warning that Master Ford is on his way, and Falstaff makes his exit from the scene in a basket of dirty laundry. The tavern scene in *2 Henry IV* (numbered 2.4 in modern editions) revisits in more somber circumstances the scene of hide-and-seek in *1 Henry IV,* perhaps with the same arras in view if the two parts were played on successive days. More likely is the possibility that Juliet's curtained bed makes a reappearance as Henry IV's sick bed in *2 Henry IV.* The king's commands, "I pray you take me vp, and heare me hence" (Q1600, 4.2.131) and "Set me the crowne vpon my pillow here" (Q1600, 4.2.137), suggest a litter if not a state bed. Once Harry has assumed the crown in *Henry V,* the curtain at the Curtain very likely became the gates of Harfleur. Act 3, scene 3 presents the following action on the stage: "*Enter the King and all his Traine before the Gates*" (F 1623, SD before 3.3.84). After the town's governor, speaking to Harry presumably from "above," has surrendered, the king commands, "Open your Gates" (F 1623, 3.3.134)—an action that almost certainly involved the central opening above which the governor has stood. The final stage direction reads, "*Flourish, and enter the Towne*" (F 1623, SD after 3.3.141). Possibly there were wooden doors that opened to admit the English army, but the segue from the third to the fourth scene in this act favors an arras, since the next scene, after the "gates" are closed, brings on Princess Catherine and her gentlewoman Alice for the lesson in anatomy that locates Catherine within the erotic space she occupies for the rest of the play. Despite the openness of the Renaissance stage, hangings could function to demarcate the shift from one fictional location to another.

Take, for example, the way Bobadilla first bounds into *Everyman in His Humor.* Customers at the Curtain in 1598 who had laughed at Falstaff's antics in *1 Henry IV* might have experienced déjà vu when Jonson's no less irrepressible gallant is first discovered in déclassé premises, lying on a bench, sleeping off a drunk. "Hostesse, hostesse," he calls out to the water carrier's wife Tib. "A cup of your small beere sweet hostesse" (1.3.85, 87).[25] Like Falstaff, he depends on his hostess for beverages, lodging, and credit. The route to this moment runs via a conversation between Matheo, the gullible man-about-town who comes seeking Bobadilla, and the water carrier Cob, who explains how Bobadilla ended up spending the night sleeping on a bench—a bench that Cob locates fictionally "above": "What *Tib,* shew this gentleman vp to Signior *Bobadilla*" (1.3.55–56). In the event, Bobadilla is discovered "within": "*Bobadilla discouers himselfe: on a bench; to him Tib*" (SD before 1.3.85). Any possibility that Bobadilla "discovers himself" simply by unwrapping the cloak in which he has been sleeping is put to rest by the stage direction in the revised text printed in the 1616 folio of Jonson's self-collected works: "*Bobad. is discouered lying on his bench*" (SD at 1.5.1).[26] The curtain or arras that is pulled back to discover Bobadilla also serves to suggest a shift in fictional location from somewhere "below" in Cob's house to a sleeping space "above." The fluidity of the Renaissance stage is not compromised by observing the way curtains can facilitate movement from city gates to castle chamber in *Henry V,* from "below" to "above" in *Everyman in His Humor,* from "within" to "without" in *Much Ado About Nothing.* Shakespeare's script for *Much Ado* makes no explicit reference to arras, hangings, or curtain, but a tapestry of park work or verdure would make a convenient place for Beatrice to hide when Hero and Ursula plant the seed that Benedick loves her. Beatrice, according to Ursula, "euen now/Is couched in the wood bine couerture" (Q1600, 3.1.29–30).

The changes wrought by the curtain in *The Merchant of Venice* and *A Warning for Faire Women* involve shifts—not in places of being, but in ways of hearing and seeing. While it is likely that Portia's chamber at Belmont might be hung with tapestries, the curtain that is drawn back during the casket-choosing scenes in *The Merchant of Venice* has less to do with the fictional location of those scenes than with epistemology. Morocco is the first to choose among the three caskets—gold, silver, and lead—that contain Portia's marital fate. "Goe, draw aside the curtaines," Portia commands, "and discouer/the seuerall caskets to the noble Prince" (Q1600, 2.7.1–2). After Morocco has chosen the golden casket and made his exit, Portia gleefully commands, "draw the curtaines, go,/Let all of his complexion choose me so" (Q1600, 2.7.78–79). Aragon's turn comes in Act 2, scene 9. This time it is Nerissa who speaks the command to a "Seruiture": "Quick, quick/pray thee, draw the curtain strait" (Q1600, 2.9.1). Once Aragon has made his foolish choice of silver, Portia draws the scene to a close by commanding, "Come, draw the curtaine, *Nerissa*" (2.9.83). The routine is presumably repeated, even though the curtain is not specifically mentioned, when Bassanio correctly chooses the lead casket in the second scene of Act 3. At issue in all three scenes is a receding sequence of questions that involve "within." Especially in the first scene, the spectators must wonder, "What is within, behind that curtain?" A feeling of anticipation, even urgency is communicated by the repetition of "go" (or "goe") in connection with Morocco's choice and "quick, quick," "strait," and "come" in connection with Aragon's. All three suitors try to guess what is contained within the three caskets. By metonymy the content of the leaden casket is Portia herself: "Away then," she tells Bassanio. "I am locked in one of them./If you do love me, you will find me out" (3.2.40–41). Ultimately, "that within which passeth show" is a lesson in ethical judgment: "*You that choose one by the view,*" reads the scroll in the leaden casket, "*Chaunce as faire, and choose as true*" (Q1600, 3.2.131–32).[27]

"This true and home-borne Tragedie" is how the presenter, a figure named Tragedy, sums up the bloody events of *A Warning for Faire Women. Containing,* The most tragicall and lamentable mur-*ther of Master George Sanders of London Marchant, nigh Shooters hill. Consented vnto By his owne wife.*[28] The play begins with a debate among Comedy, History, and Tragedy that ends with female-gendered Tragedy "*turning to the people,*" according to the stage direction, and gesturing toward "all this faire circuite" and "this round" (sig. A3) in just the way the Chorus to *Henry V* gestures toward "this wooden O." The story that Tragedy presents happens in two registers: a dramatized narrative in the homely manner of *Arden of Faversham* and a series of gruesome "shews" or "masks" that anticipate Jacobean revenge tragedies like *Women Beware Women.* The space between those two dramatic registers is guarded by curtains. After George Sanders, Master Browne, Mistress Drury, and Trusty Roger have set on its way a plot that might well turn out to be a comedy of adultery, Tragedy appears with a blood-filled bowl in hand to announce the first masque. Until now, Tragedy tells the spectators, "you haue but sitten to behold, / The fatal entrance to our bloudie sceane." Now you will get what you've been waiting for:

> Al we haue done, hath only beene in words,
> But now we come vnto the dismall act.
> And in these sable Curtains shut we vp
> The Comicke entrance to our direful play.
> (sig. C4v)

That "these sable Curtains" were no less physically present than "this fair circuit" is indicated by History's exclamation to Comedy in the play's prologue, "Looke, *Comoedie,* I markt it not til now, / The stage is hung with blacke: and I perceiue / The Auditors preparde for Tragedie" (sig. A3). Forty years later, Richard Brathwait in *The Two Lancashire lovers* (1640) could describe "a Tragick Theatre hung about with Arras presenting a numerous confluence of feares and cares," and twenty years later still stage directions in scripts by John Dryden and others indicate that black hangings persisted as special effects on the Restoration stage.[29] At the Curtain in 1597–1599, the demonstrative "these" suggests practicable stage properties in the form of black hangings—or perhaps tapestries or cloths depicting tragic histories—that could supply the entrance point for the Furies whom Tragedy immediately summons ("Come forth," he commands [sig. D1]) and for the dumb-show protagonists who appear at "this fatall doore" (sig. D1) and are ushered on stage by the Furies to a wine-charged banquet that emboldens the adulterous lovers to murder the inconvenient George Sanders. Two other "shows," both presided over by Tragedy, anticipate later turns in the dramatic narrative in quite the same way. In Tragedy's formulation, the sable curtains separate comedy from tragedy, words from sights, things anticipated ("you haue but sitten") from things enjoyed ("now we come to the dismall act"). Getting behind those curtains, Tragedy implies, is what the spectator/listeners most desire.

A Warning for Fair Women, like *The Merchant of Venice*, displays a professional sophistication about the dramatic power of speeches that turn into spectacles. "The dismal act" that Tragedy announces to the spectator-listeners, like the three casket tests in *The Merchant of Venice*, invites altered states of looking and listening. These scenes unfold in space and time, and they engage the spectator-listeners' bodies in quite specific ways. The spectators—standing in the Curtain's yard, sitting in its galleries, even disposing themselves about its platform stage just a few feet from the actors—are situated within a space that promises them, but does not yet let them see, depths beyond, behind, within. Words pique their desire, even as staged events keep deferring that pleasure until one or more carefully timed moments of discovery, usually well into the two hours' traffic of the stage and often toward the end. The experience of both *A Warning for Fair Women* and *The Merchant of Venice* becomes, in imagination at least, an act of perambulation like Edward Herbert following the Earl of Dorset into his gallery and discovering behind a curtain of green taffeta his own portrait, like Prince Arthur and Sir Guyon's move from fantasies to "picturals" to rolls of written memories in Alma's tower in Book 2 of *The Faerie Queene*, like Poliphilus's penetrating the three tapestry veils in *The Strife of Love in a Dream*, like Marvell's progression toward a green thought in "The Garden."

From the green spectacles surveyed in chapter four, we might expect a further shift in looking and listening when, after words have turned into vision, vision turns back into words. *A Warning for Fair Women* and *The Merchant of Venice*, like most other scripts for the Renaissance stage, satisfy that expectation. The judgment scene in *Warning* anticipates a certain later play in the Lord Chamberlain's Men's repertory, just as it echoes the Chorus to *Henry V* during the same season. The "fetching forth" of George Sanders's body in the play's third masque leads to the offenders' being "Discouerd where they thought to be vnseene" and being called to judgment: "Then triall now remaines as shall conclude,/ Measure for measure, and lost bloud for bloud" (sig. o3). As Tragedy's summation suggests, the words accompanying the recognition in *A Warning for Fair Women* come saturated with passion. The scroll that Bassanio finds in the leaden casket in *The Merchant of Venice* supplies the expected caption to the portrait of Portia that the casket also contains, but Bassanio's response conjoins portrait and caption in words no less bloody, no less replete with passion, than Tragedy's words:

Maddam, you haue bereft me of all words,
Onely my bloud speakes to you in my vaines,
And there is such confusion in my powers,
As after some oration fairely spoke
By a beloued Prince, there doth appeare
Among the buzzing pleased multitude,
Where euery something being blent together,
Turnes to a wilde of nothing, saue of ioy
Exprest, and not exprest . . . [30]

In those words-that-refuse, Bassanio speaks not only for himself but for the buzzing pleased multitude, whose viewing of the portrait and hearing of the scroll pulses in their veins and verges on a "wild" of nothing.

Until the moments in these scripts when the curtain is pulled aside, words and spectacle might seem to work in tension, if not in opposition. The drawing open and drawing closed of "these sable Curtains" in *Warning* and of the curtain hiding the caskets in *Merchant* would seem to illustrate one of the commonplaces that Nicholas Ling collects in *Politeuphuia. Wits Commonwealth* (1598): "Eloquence is like a cloath of Arras, figured and set forth with stories, because both in the one and the other the thinges fashioned, are then seene when they are opened, & are not subiect to sight, neither bring delight when they are folded vp and hidden."[31] The classical authority for this observation is specified in Francis Bacon's *Apothogems New and Old* (1625): "Themistocles said of Speech; *That it was like Arras, that spred abroad shewes faire Images, but contracted, is but like packs.*"[32] As *A Warning for Fair Women* and *The Merchant of Venice* both demonstrate, the situation at the Curtain was not a matter of either/or. In moments of revelation, when the arras was pulled aside, spectator-listeners could experience eloquence in both forms, a coming together of words and vision, within a suddenly unified perceptual space, at a keenly anticipated moment in time.

A Motley to the View

If the ten scripts associated with the Lord Chamberlain's Men at the Curtain are any indication, we need to imagine woven hangings of some sort—arras, tapestry, curtain, traverse—as a frequent if not constant visual feature of stages in early modern London's outdoor theaters. The absence of such an artifact in de Witt's drawing of the Swan Theatre may be the result of any number of considerations, including de Witt's preoccupation with the physical structure of the building.[33] De Witt, or perhaps the copyist van Buchel, supplies Latin labels for each of the theater's architectural elements: *mimbrum aedes* for the tiring house, *proscaenium* for the playing platform, *planities siue arena* for the pit, and so forth. By contrast, the illustrator's interest in dramatic action seems minimal, and his interest in the attending spectators, absolutely nil. If, despite the Swan drawing, woven hangings were always or usually present, then the potentiality they possessed must have been almost as great as the potentiality of the stage doors that loom so large in de Witt's drawing. Who or what was going to emerge? What places in the fiction would the hangings assume? What surprise might be waiting behind them? How would that surprise alter the viewers' perceptions?

Just such a sense of expectation is witnessed in the prologue that John Tatham supplied for the removal of the Revels Company from the Fortune Theatre to the Red Bull in 1640. Enjoy the new space, the prologue says,

> Only wee would request you to forbeare
> Your wonted custome, banding *Tyle,* or Peare,
> Against our *curtaines,* to allure us forth.
> I pray take notice *these* are of more Worth,
> Pure Naples Silk, not *Worstead. . . .*[34]

Those tiles and pears are projectiles of eager visual imaginations, fixated on a stage property that modern scholars have barely let themselves notice. In another poem, Tatham reminds his friend Master W. B. of their last meeting "with the Globe," perhaps just a figure of speech for getting out and about but more likely a reference to the King's Men's outdoor theater: "When last we did encounter with the GLOBE, / The Heavn's was pleas'd to grace us with his robe / Of settled motions" (sig. C1v). On *this* occasion, the waters of Aquarius dictate otherwise, sending Tatham off on a circle through the Zodiac that eventually lands Tatham and W. B. in Taurus, at the Bull Head tavern.

What did the arras, tapestry, curtain, or traverse look like? The pride Tatham takes in the Red Bull's "pure Naples silk" as opposed to the Fortune's "worsted" fabric (a combination of wool and other fibers) recalls Flecknoe's disdainful reference to "old Tapestry." The same class distinction between silk and wool seems to be registered in the induction to Jonson's *Cynthia's Revels,* acted by the Chapel boys' company at the indoor Blackfriars Theatre in 1601. In the induction, the third gentleman refuses the suggestion that he sit "in state on the stage": "Away, wagge;

what, would'st thou make an implementation of me? Slid the boy takes me for a piece of *perspectiue* (I hold my life) or some silke cortaine, come to hang the stage here! sir cracke, I am none of your fresh pictures, that vse to beautifie the decaied dead arras, in a publike theatre."[35] Jonson's editors, Herford and Simpson, offer no explanation for this image of a fresh picture amid a decayed tapestry.[36] The hanging arrangements at Cotehele House and Hardwick Hall, where mirrors and paintings are hung on top of tapestries, supply that missing reference (see chapter four and plates 14 and 15). The rich silk that Jonson's indignant gentleman contrasts with decayed arras is the fabric of his own clothing. A reference in *Epicoene* suggests that the indoor Blackfriars Theatre, like the outdoor theaters, was hung with woolen tapestry, not silk cloth. Truewit plots with his friends to gull Daw and La Foole. "Doe you obserue this gallerie? or rather lobby, indeed?" Truewit asks his conspirators. "Here will I act such a *tragicomoedy* betweene the *Guelphes,* and the *Ghibellines,* DAW and LA-FOOLE—which of 'hem comes out first, will I seize on: (you two shall be the *chorus* behind the arras, and whip out beweene the *acts,* and speake)."[37] And so they do. Tapestry on the Blackfriars *scenae frons* is referred to again in Jonson's self-justifying dedication of *The New Inn* "To The Reader." In its Blackfriars premiere in 1629, Jonson complains, his play was damned by the gentlemen who sat on stage and were more interested in displaying themselves than attending to the play: "Arm'd, with this praeiudice, as the *Stage*-furniture, or *Arras*-clothes, they were there, as Spectators, away. For the faces in the hangings, and they beheld alike."[38]

Andrew Gurr and Mariko Ichikawa, thanks to their involvement with restoration of Shakespeare's Globe, are virtually alone among modern theater historians in directing students' attention to stage hangings and speculating about their design: "The central opening was concealed behind a hanging or elaborate cloth woven in panels with pictures of scenes from classical myths. This cloth of 'arras' which concealed the central opening, through which Hamlet stabs Polonius, was a heavy tapestry weave."[39] The central hangings, they go on to explain, were only used for special entrances or "discoveries," like the caskets in *The Merchant of Venice,* the gold treasure that Volpone worships, the Duchess of Malfi's murdered children, and Faustus's study. Gurr and Ichikawa's description matches, and perhaps was inspired by, a detail from the engraved title page that Thomas Rawlins supplied for the 1640 printing of Nathaniel Richards's *The Tragedy of Messallina The Roman Emperesse. As it hath beene Acted With generall Applause divers times, by the Company of his Majesties Revells* (see figure 22).

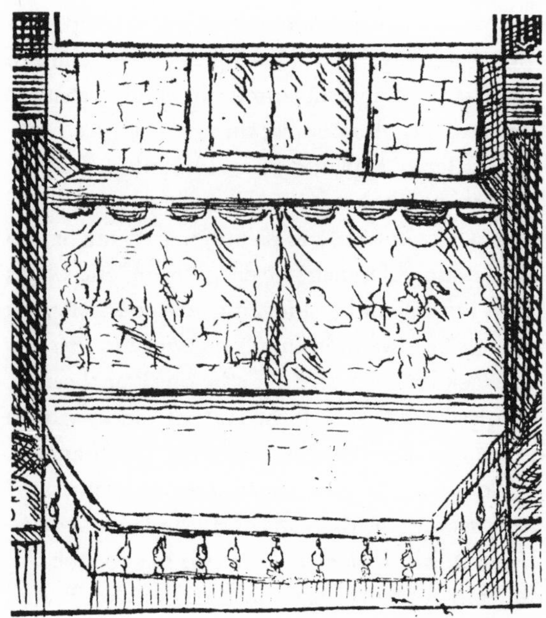

Figure 22. Thomas Rawlins (engraver), title page of Nathaniel Richard, *The Tragedy of Messallina The Roman Emperesse* (London: Thomas Cotes for Daniel Frere, 1640), detail. Original image, 1⅞ × 1 inches (4.7 × 2.5 cm). (Reproduced by permission of the Folger Shakespeare Library.)

Figure 23. John Payne (engraver), title page of William Alabaster, *Roxana Tragaedia* (London: William Jones, 1632), detail. Original image, 1⅞ × 1¼ inches (4.8 × 3.2 cm). (Reproduced by permission of the Folger Shakespeare Library.)

For this image, Rawlins may have been indebted to the representation of a stage that had figured in the frontispiece to William Alabaster's Latin tragedy *Roxana,* acted at Trinity College, Cambridge, in 1592, but not printed until 1632, eight years before Rawlins came up with his own picture (see figure 23). As John Astington has pointed out, Rawlins himself was the author of a play, *The Rebellion,* that had been acted in the same indoor theater as *Messalina,* the Salisbury Court, by the same company, the King's Revels, during the same decade, the 1630s.[40] What's more, Rawlins seems to have had a personal stake in the printed text of *Messalina,* as witness the commendatory verses he contributed, praising Richards for turning a story of lust triumphant into a latter-day morality play: "*Romes* mightie Whore by thee adornes the Stage: / For to convert not to corrupt this *Age.*"[41] Among the commendatory verses that Richards's friends contributed to the printed text, Rawlins's comes last, just before the cast list. There may be some credibility, therefore, to the details that Rawlins supplies in his engraved frontispiece.

The curtained space "above," very different from the spectators' gallery shown in the *Roxana* image, is in fact called for several times in Richards's script, when the empress Messalina watches her three lovers fight each other with swords (sig. D4v), when she contemplates the prospect of taking a new lover Montanus (sig. D5v), when she and her main lover Silvius are "*gloriously crown'd in an Arch-glitering Cloud aloft*" (sig. F1v), when an emissary of the absent emperor Claudius appears in the same space and turns the plot toward its tragic end, and possibly when Messalina mounts the scaffold for her execution (sig. F7). Although the script never explicitly calls for use of the hangings that Rawlins shows spanning the entire rear of the stage, *Messalina* is supplied with "Two severall Antimasques of Spirits and Bachinalls" (sig. B1) that could have made good use of the curtained opening. In the first of these shows three Furies enter and "*dance an Anticke*" that stirs "a Plurisie of lust" in the empress's veins (sig. C3v). The second show presents "*the Antique Maske consisting of eight Bachinalians*" (sig. F1v) whose dancing frames the crowning aloft of Messalina and Silvius. Two other spectacular moments might likewise have capitalized on the curtains: the scene in which Silvius's chaste wife is "*drawne out upon a Bed as sleeping*" and succeeds in persuading Silvius not to murder her (sig. C7v) and the prelude to Messalina's execution when "*Two Spirits dreadfully enter and (to the Treble Violin and Lute) sing a song of despaire*" (sig. F6). Perhaps, indeed, all the play's entries and exits were made through the curtains. Rawlins's engraving shows no other entry onto the stage. With or without additional entry points, the woven or painted design that Rawlins sketches would have provided an appropriate imaginative frame for the play's representations of lust triumphant. Amid suggestions of trees and land contours, a Cupid figure on the right prepares to shoot an arrow toward a figure holding a staff or branch on the left. Whether or not the images in Rawlins's curtain are woven or painted is not certain, but the implied visual aesthetic is clear enough.

The allusions in Jonson's plays *Cynthia's Revels* and *The New Inn,* taken together with Rawlins's image of the stage for *Messalina,* suggest that narrative events on the stage platform were played in front of—and often enough *out of*—woven or painted hangings. The effect for spectators in the house would not have been dissimilar to the effect of a Sheldon tapestry, with its invitation for the free play of common sense, fantasy and imagination before the main event is fixed for contemplation and provided with words (see chapter four and plate 22). At the Globe, the antic effect was enhanced by carvings in the tiring-house wall. The contract for the Fortune Theatre specifies that the columns of the theater's "fframe and Stadge forward" shall be made like that of the Globe, "palasterwise, wth carved proporcōn̄s Called Satiers to be placed & sett on the Topp of every of the same postes."[42] The carved satyrs of the Globe's and the Fortune's *scenae frontes* shape up as grotesque figures of the sort we have seen in tapestries. Did these figures extend antic work that was to be seen in the woven hangings themselves? The Sheldon tapestries suggest as much.

What about human figures? Jonson's reference to "faces in the hangings" and the bow-and-arrow-armed figure in Rawlins's engraving imply that human forms, too, could have been present in cloths and curtains (something of the effect can be seen in plate 15). With or without those figures in the hangings, however, the actors themselves would have presented themselves to the spectators as part of a figure/ground ensemble. Against—and in one case amid—the arabesque ground of the curtain shown in the frontispiece to Francis Kirkman's *The Wits, or, Sport upon Sport* it is the actors who provide the figures. (This particular fabric design, by the way, has been copied for the stage arras in the reconstructed Blackfriars Playhouse in Staunton, Virginia. Theirs is dark blue.) Kirkman's nostalgic celebration of great moments from the pre–Civil War stage was published two years into the Restoration, in 1662, and was reissued in expanded form in 1672 and 1673. In the frontispiece, famous characters from the Elizabethan, Jacobean, and Caroline stage cavort on a stage platform that features a curtain at the back (see detail in figure 24). The striped canopy atop this curtain may help to explain the "canopy"

Figure 24. Francis Kirkman, *The Wits, Or, Sport upon Sport* (London: Henry Marsh, 1662), title page detail. Original image, $3\frac{1}{8} \times 3\frac{3}{4}$ inches (8.9×9.5 cm). (Reproduced by permission of the Folger Shakespeare Library.)

mentioned in some stage directions—a device that could be used in conjunction with or perhaps instead of hangings.[43] The figure who pokes his body out amid the arras's curvilinear forms on the title page to *The Wits* identifies himself in a banderole as Bubble, the clown who goes around spouting the all-purpose phrase "Tu Quoque" in John Cooke's comedy *Greene's Tu Quoque*, acted by Queen Anne's Men at the Red Bull in 1611 and printed three years later. "Tu quoque" means "and you," as when a person responds to the greeting "God save you" by saying "And you," but Bubble puts the phrase to all sorts of malaprop uses.

What hue or hues might purchasers of *The Wits* put to the curtain in the frontispiece? What hue or hues dominated the decayed arras that Jonson associates with public theaters or the hangings with inert faces that he locates in the Blackfriars Theatre? Evidence from a number of quarters suggests green: the silk damask that shows off the pictures in the Green Closet at Ham House (see plate 1), the damask silk curtain that hangs behind Holbein's *The Ambassadors* (plate 2), the verdure tapestry from Cotehele House (plate 4), the *millefleurs* landscape of the Sheldon *Spring* (plate 12), the park-work tapestry behind the painted mirror at Cotehele House (plate 14), the pictures hung atop tapestries in the Long Gallery at Hardwick Hall (plate 15), the continuous landscape in the painted cloths at Owlpen Manor (plate 20), the outsized plant forms in the Sheldon *Judgment of Paris* (plate 22), and the border work in the Mortlake *Hero and Leander* (plate 23). The combination of landscape features and human figures in Rawlins's illustration for *Messalina,* sketchy as those elements are, fits with this general picture, in which the ground for human figures is supplied by plant forms and green arabesques.

Against the green ground provided by woven and painted hangings certain other hues came to prominence when costumed actors made their appearance. Donne suggests the general effect in one of his *Juvenalia* (1633). What should you do when you come to court and see "a *gay* man leaning at the wall, so *glistering,* and so *painted* in many *colours* that he is hardly discerned from one of the *pictures* in the *Arras*"?[44] Not envy him, as fools would, but laugh at him. To envy him would be to act like dullards "at the hearing of *Comedies* or other witty reports" (sig. D2) who laugh even though they don't get the joke. Tapestry viewing and comedy hearing are, in this anecdote, presented as similar experiences. "Glistering," which seems to refer to the "*broad gold laces*" (sig. D2) worn by Donne's gay man, is precisely the description applied to the garments that divert Stephano and Trinculo from their murderous plot in *The Tempest* ("*Enter* Ariell, *laden with glistering apparell, &c.,*" F 1623, SD before 4.1.193). To brightness of "glistering," Donne's reference adds a variety of painted hues.[45] If the visual matrices at the Curtain and other theaters were green, what were the dominant colors worn by stage figures like Bubble? Clues are contained in the inventory of costumes that Phillip Henslowe had drawn up for the Lord Admiral's Men in 1598. For more than 40 percent of the 233 costumes in the inventory, colors are specified. By far the largest number are various hues of red (21 instances), followed by black (19 instances), white (17 instances), various hues of "tawny" or "peach" (14 instances), and green (10 instances). If this list is any indication, color design in London's theaters replicated the evolution of color sensitivity in human vision (in which red sensitivity is postulated to have developed first) as well as systems of color naming among the world's cultures (in which red is generally the first color to be distinguished from black and white). (These matters are discussed in chapters one and two.) More significant, however, are the passions with which these hues enkindled. Those passions were situated in two different groups of bodies: first the actors', then the spectators'.

Lomazzo's *Tratatto dell'Arte de la Pittura* (English translation, 1598) consolidates earlier books like Antonio Telesio's *Libellus de coloribus* (1528), Fulvio Morato's *Del significate de colori de mazzolli* (1535), and Ludovico Dolce's *Dialogo, nel quale si ragiona della qualità, diversità e proprietà de i colori* (1565) in giving hues quite precise significations. Red, because of its associations with blood and fire, is identified by Lomazzo with revenge, valor, "ardent affections," "courage and stomacke."[46] Black, as might be expected, is associated with mourning, sorrow, and evil but also, Lomazzo adds, with constancy and with obstinacy. Context is all: "blacke and all other colours signifie either good or euill, as they are rightly applied" (sig. KK3v). White signifies "simplicity, puritie, and elation of the minde" (sig. KK3v), to which some authors in Lomazzo's survey would add blame and joy. About tawny, Lomazzo, at least in Haydock's truncated translation, has little to say, associating it seasonally with March. Lomazzo follows Telesio and Dolce in identifying green rather singlemindedly with hope. What one saw in the theater against the green matrix of the hangings was thus not just certain persons but certain passions. And those passions were communicated to the spectators. Colors with their diverse qualities, Lomazzo says, citing Aristotle, produce diverse effects in beholders. Thus hues in the red range "cause courage, prouidence, fiercenesse and boldnesse by stirring vp the minde like fire" (sig. KK2v). Black breeds "tardity, musing, melancholie, &c" (sig. KK2v); white, "a kind of simple attentio[n] more melancholy then otherwise" (sig. KK2v). Tawny and green belong to a range of hues that "yeelde a pleasurable sweetnesse" (sig. KK2v). In a summary statement, Lomazzo locates precisely the faculty of perception in which these effects are produced: "In a word all mixt colours, differing each from other, procure earnest desire, variety, and *Phantasticalnesse*" (sig. KK2v, original emphasis).

Included in Henslowe's costume list are seven "anteckes cootes," presumably intended for performers playing clowns, mountebanks, and other ludicrous characters.[47] One wonders if these seven antics' garments were not versions of fools' "motley," that is to say, fabrics woven from two or more colors (*OED*, "motley" *n.* and *a.* A.1.a). The seven antics' coats occur in an entry just after "Will. Sommers sewtte" (the historical Will Sommers was Henry VIII's professional fool) and just before a "fooles coate, cape, and babell" (318). Babell: nice. The spelling of Henslowe's clerk catches the synaesthesia of what a fool looks like as he carries about his bauble, or, head-on-a-stick ("This driueling loue," Mercutio exclaims, "is like a great naturall, that runs vp and downe to hide his bable in a hole" [*Romeo and Juliet* Q1597, 2.3.84–85]) and what a fool sounds like as he babbles on ("leaue thy vaine bibble babble," the Fool advises Malvolio, in a turnabout of roles [*Twelfth Night* F 1623, 4.2.98–99]). Could there be a relation between *motley* (the *OED* suggests links with *motes,* particles of dust) and *mots* (words)? Hamlet's decision "to put an Anticke disposition on" (Q1604, 1.5.173) may involve, not just words, but a change of costume from a melancholic's black to a fool's motley.

The Rat behind the Arras

Folded in a trunk, the colors in Henslowe's inventory would have been inert, like a dyer's pigments or a limner's inks. Put onto a human body, they would have become colors in motion. Two elements present in performance are missing in the printed images from *Roxana, Messalina,* and *The Wits.* Color is one; motion is the other. The curtains in each of these illustrations are not just hanging limply: they are shown as moving, as alive. In John Payne's engraving for *Roxana* (figure 23) the curtain is being whisked back, possibly by action of the figure on the left. Even without actors present, Rawlins's depiction of the stage for *Messalina* (figure 22) shows the curtain on the right pulled back suggestively, as if to indicate someone about to enter or something about to be discovered. The printer of *The Wits,* Henry Marsh, finds four metaphors in his preface for the scenes collected in the volume and shown in the frontispiece: "humors," "fancies," "experiments," and "drolleries"[48] (see figure 24). The common denominator is movement. Dramatization of characters' humors, Marsh points out, "have no such *fixedness* and indissoluble *connexion* to the Design, but that without *injury* or *foricible revulsion* they may be *removed* to an *advantage*" (sig. A3v; original emphasis). Fancy, as we know from Edward Reynolds, owes its "quicknesse and volubilitie" to "those springings and glances of the heart, grounded on the sudden representation of sundry different objects."[49] The experiments Marsh has in mind involve "the making of a *fluid* a *solid* Body" (sig. A3v). And "*Rump Drolls*" move laughter (sig. A4).

What purchasers of *The Wits* could see in the frontispiece is Bubble popping out from behind the curtain, putting his best leg forward. The vignette recalls testimonials to Richard Tarlton's ability to move laughter just by showing his face. Whether he did so using a curtain or a door the witness does not state, but something had to make the sudden discovery of that face possible.[50] In his jest book *A Nest of Ninnies,* Robert Armin, the clown who joined Shakespeare's company about 1599 and played Feste in *Twelfth Night* and The Fool in *King Lear,* tells how Henry VIII's fool, Will Sommers, used a curtain to good effect in curing the king's melancholy. The king's foul mood, Will tells Harry, "must haue a good showre to clense it, & with that goes behind the Arras. *Harry* (saies he) ile go behind the Arras and study three questions, and come againe, see therefore you lay aside this melancholy muse, & study to answere me. I (quoth the King) they will be wise ones no doubt. At last out comes *William* with his wit, as the foole of the play doth with an anticke looke, to please the beholders."[51] Will's third question does the trick. "What it is that being borne without life, head, lippe or eye, yet doth runne roaring through the World till it dye?" (sig. F3). A fart. In Armin's anecdote, as on the stages of early modern London, dramatic antics, verbal as well as visual, emerge out of the woven antics of curtain, arras, tapestry, and traverse.

Like swords, like crowns, like thrones, like beds, hangings in the Renaissance theater constituted a stage property, an object that could function in performance as an extension of actors' moving bodies. Surely the most famous instance occurs in *Hamlet,* in the bedroom scene. Hearing Hamlet's approach, Polonius tells Gertrude, "Ile silence me euen here" (Q1604, 3.4.4)—"here" being almost certainly the same arras behind which Polonius and Claudius hid to overhear Ophelia's conversation with Hamlet inthe first scene of Act 3. The first quarto has the Polonius figure say to Gertrude, "I'le shrowde my selfe behinde the Arras" (Q1603). Enter Hamlet. Just at the moment when Hamlet commands Gertrude to sit down and proposes to "set you vp a glasse / Where you may see the most part of you" (Q1604, 3.4.19–20), Gertrude calls for help, and Polonius behind the arras cries out, too, "What how helpe" (Q1604, 3.4.23). "How now, a Rat," Hamlet exclaims—and stabs Polonius, presumably through the arras. (The 1604 quarto contains no stage direction at this point, and the folio says simply, "*Killes Polonius*" [F 1623, SD at 3.4.23]). Hamlet's placement of Gertrude's mirror somewhere in front of the arras might have recalled, to the eyes of certain spectators at least, the arrangements for hanging mirrors and portraits exemplified at Cotehele House and Hardwick Hall (see plates 14 and 15) and the refusal of Jonson's gentleman in *Cynthia's Revels* to sit on the stage and blend in with the tapestry work.

"Rat behind the arras" is not an entry you will find in either of the standard modern compilations of early modern English proverbs, but writers and playwrights other than Shakespeare were demonstrably fascinated by the image.[52] Seneca's *Moralia* may be the ultimate source for these references. In chapter 15, Seneca recalls a simpler time in which men and women could see their surroundings clearly and therefore trust them: "There were as yet no Beds of State, no Ornaments of Pearl, or Embrodery, nor any of those Remorses that attend them; but the Heavens were their Canopy, and the Glories of them their Spectacle. The Motions of the Orbs; the Courses of the Stars, and the wonderful order of Providence was their Contemplation: There was no fear of the House falling; or the Russling of a Rat behind the *Arras*"[53] The circumstances of Polonius's death in the lost *Hamlet* that Shakespeare rewrote must remain speculative, but two later productions by the King's Men offer reprises of *Hamlet,* Act 3, scene 4. John Fletcher's tragicomedy *Women Pleased,* acted by the King's Men in 1620, includes a scene in which a character named Bartello hides himself up the chimney (in physical fact, the acting space "above"), comments on the stage action from that vantage point, then is searched out by two boys, one of whom ascends the gallery while the other looks behind the arras. According to the stage direction, "First Boy *goes in behinde the Arras*" (4.3.175) and says, "Madam here be de Rat, de Rat Madam" (4.3.178).[54] In William Heminge's *The Jew's Tragedy,* acted by the King's Men six years later, several scenes involve characters using the arras as a hiding place. In the last of these scenes, Eleazer withdraws "*behinde the arras,*" while Zarek promises to deal on his behalf with a troublesome character. An Attendant catches onto the ruse and comments, apparently aside, "A ratt behinde the hangings."[55] For Thomas Wright in *The Passions of the Mind in Generall* (1601, 1604, 1621, 1630), the rat behind the arras figures as an image for passions coursing through the human body: "as a Rat running behinde a painted cloth, betrayeth her selfe; euen so, a passion lurking in the heart, by thoughts and speech discouereth it selfe."[56]

Between

The general use of hangings to organize theatrical space and time and to arouse and satisfy passions can be sorted into more specific occasions, all of which can be coordinated with uses of tapestries, curtains, and painted cloths in Renaissance households. According to Dessen and Thomson's census, no fewer than 115 stage directions in surviving scripts from 1580 to 1642 call for use of arras, curtains, hangings, tapestries, or traverses.[57] Having tracked down every single one of them, I can report that all but a few are coordinated with six kinds of dramatic events. In order of frequency those events comprise:

- hiding
- discovering
- sleeping, dying (rising to sexual climax), dreaming, dying (falling into oblivion), or being murdered
- reading, writing, or dozing
- eating and drinking
- changing fictional locations

Boundaries between categories are not fixed: a given episode may involve hiding *and* discovering, discovering *and* dreaming, dreaming *and* reading, and so on. Limiting the examples to plays acted by Shakespeare's company at the Theatre, the Curtain, the Globe, and the Blackfriars Theatre does not, according to my own count, distort the overall picture for all companies active in the period, taking into account not only kinds of scenes but how often those scenes figure in scripts.

Falstaff absenting himself behind the arras in Mistress Quickly's tavern and Mistress Ford's house, Polonius using the arras to overhear Hamlet's colloquy with Gertrude, the First Boy finding a rat behind the arras—figuratively, at least—in Fletcher's *Women Pleased,* the attendant's aside about "A rat behind the hangings" in Heminge's *The Jew's Tragedy:* hiding scenes like these account for 28 instances out of Dessen and Thomson's 115, about 25 percent of the total. The common use of tapestries and painted cloths to define and to seal off domestic spaces surely explains why such scenes are so frequent in scripts for the stage; the unpleasant things those tapestries and cloths helped to shut out and conceal—the coldness of stone walls, drafts of wind, vermin, prying eyes, listening ears—perhaps explains the feelings of suspicion that often attend these scenes. Cozy or fearful: it all depends on where the spectators' attention is focused. *Behind* and *before* seem to be the controlling prepositions. A speech and a stage direction in Jonson's *Volpone,* acted by the King's Men in 1606, suggest, however, that *above* and *below* might also figure. In Act 5, scene 3, Mosca convenes all the suitors and lets them know they are not in the will. In previous scene, before the suitors come on, Volpone says, "I'll get vp / Behind the cortine, on a stoole, and hearken; / Sometime, peepe ouer; see, how they doe looke."[58] And so he does: in the third scene comes the stage direction "*Volpone peepes from behinde a trauerse*" (5.3.9). But how, editors have wondered. One possibility is that the stool provides all the height

Volpone needs to peep "over": he merely parts the curtain near the top. Also possible is that Volpone watches from a curtained space *above* like the one shown in Rawlins's *Messalina* illustration (see figure 22). Twenty-five years after *Volpone*'s premiere, the King's Men acted Philip Massinger's *The Emperor of the East,* in which eavesdroppers are revealed to have been listening and watching *above.* "*The curtaines drawne aboue,*" reads the stage direction at 1.2.288, "THEODOSIUS, *and his* EUNUCHES *discover'd,*" along with a third character, Philanax.[59] Theodosius, the emperor of the play's title, has heard about the beauties of the virgin Athenais and has asked to be brought "Some place where I may looke on her demeaner" (sig. C1v). That space turns out to be *above.* Theodosius is captivated by Athenais's allure and later marries her.[60]

Twenty-seven stage directions in Dessen and Thomson's census (about 24 percent of the total) have to with something or someone suddenly being revealed. To *dis*cover someone or something is to find *out* that someone or something, to bring it from *behind* to *before.* The effect, depending on the circumstances, can be confirmation of someone or something already known, or it can be surprise. In the cases of Falstaff, Bobadilla, Polonius, Volpone, and Theodosius, spectators know in advance what is hidden behind the arras. In a way, the spectators are *there* themselves. An altogether different dynamic occurs when spectators do *not* know what to expect when the curtain is pulled aside, as when Portia commands for the first time, "Goe, draw aside the curtaines, and discouer / The seuerall Caskets" (*Merchant of Venice,* F 1623, 2.7.1–2). The later discoveries of the same three caskets figure as confirmations of what the spectators already know to be there. On occasion, confirmation can be confounded with surprise, as when Falstaff and Bobadilla are discovered to be drunk and snoring or when Polonius is discovered to be dead.

Although the King's Men used the device at the Curtain in 1597–1599, it was in their later repertory (1609–1642) that they exploited such discovery scenes to the full. Some sort of curtain is implied by Paulina's speeches in the last scene of *The Winter's Tale,* acted at the Globe, likely in 1609. The statue of Hermione that Paulina shows Leontes in Act 5, scene 3 must be hidden by a curtain at the beginning of the scene, since Leontes begs her later, "Doe not draw the Curtaine" (F 1623, 5.3.61), and Paulina twice threatens, "Ile draw the Curtaine" (5.3.68) and "Shall I draw the Curtaine" (5.3.83). Leontes's reference to the fictional location as "Your Gallerie" (5.3.10), a place that contains "many singularities" (5.3.12), and Paulina's own reference to the space as "the Chapell" (5.3.86) suggest that the ritual being enacted here is like the Earl of Dorset's taking Edward

Herbert into his gallery, showing him many curiosities, and then drawing back a curtain of green taffeta to reveal to his astonished friend the portrait Dorset secretly had arranged to be copied (see chapter one and figure 2) or the religious custom of shrouding the crucifix during Lent with a curtain (often green in the south of England) and opening it on Easter (see chapter one and plate 2). A religious aura likewise invests the curtain in Beaumont and Fletcher's *The Mad Lover,* acted by the King's Men nine years later, when the protagonist Calis uses the space behind the arras as a chapel not unlike Lady Drury's oratory at Hawstead[61] (see plate 21). Earlier in the play, a masque of Orpheus has taken place in front of the arras. Another masque of Orpheus, this one in Massinger's *The City Madam* (1632), shows how the arras could function as the visual focus for visual spectacles. Stage directions in *The City Madam* at the end of Act 4 and the beginning of Act 5 seem to have nothing to do with the present action: "*Whil'st the Act plays, the Footstep, little Table, and Arras hung up for the Musicians*" (4.4.160) and "*Musicians come down to make ready for the song at Aras*" (5.1.7). Suddenly, however, these stage directions make sense in Act 5, scene 3, when a pageant of Orpheus and Eurydice takes shape as the play's visual, aural, and narrative climax. Massinger's script enacts the coming-to-be recounted in Spenser's *Castle of Alma* (see chapter four), as visual elements and illegible sounds coalesce into an emblematic event, complete with verbal text. Reference in the stage directions to music between the acts ("Whil'st the Act plays") locates the printed text of *The City Madam* at the Blackfriars.[62]

What happens when the curtain falls, rises, or is pulled aside? An epiphany is one possibility; a spectacle of horror is another. The masques that Tragedy summons forth, possibly from behind the Curtain's sable curtains, in *A Warning for Fair Women* present particularly visceral examples. Those members of Shakespeare's troupe who had worked with Lord Strange's Men in the early 1590s already had experience of such scenes in a revival of Thomas Kyd's *The Spanish Tragedy.* In Act 5, Hieronimo uses a play-within-the-play to kill his son's murderers. The cue for that episode in the script's 1592 printing comes in this stage direction: "Enter H*eronimo:* he knocks vp the curtaine."[63] What does it mean to "knock up" the curtain? To lift it up with a stick or rod? To pull it aside with the same device? However that action is managed, the play-within-the-play is located in a space that is physically, fictionally, and psychologically quite separate from the main action. Heronimo's use of a framed illusion to secure his real-world revenge is a devise that was repeated again and again in the revenge tragedies of the early seventeenth century.[64] Hamlet's failed attempt with "The Murder of Gonzalo" in Shakespeare's tragedy contrasts with Hamlet's success in the play's sources and quite possibly in the earlier *Hamlet* on which Shakespeare based his rewrite. In the story's ultimate source, Saxo Grammaticus's *Historiae Danicae* (first printed in 1514), Amleth traps the Claudius figure and all his courtiers in a banquet room, gets them drunk, cuts down "the hanging which his mother had knitted, which covered the inner as well as the outer walls of the hall," and sets the entrapped courtiers on fire.[65] It is likely that Kyd's Hieronimo uses the curtain again at the conclusion of the play-within-the-play to reveal his son's body. "Beholde the reason vrging me to this," Hieronimo tells the king and, according to the stage direction, "Shewes his dead sonne." He continues: "See heere my shew, look on this spectacle" (sig. K4).

John Webster, in *The Duchess of Malfi* (1614), is drawing on the same iconic tradition when he dictates in Act 4: "*Here is discouer'd, (behind a Trauers;) the artificiall figures of Antonio, and his children; appearing as if they were dead.*"[66] So, too, is William Davenant in *The Unfortunate Lovers* (1638) when Altophil first "Drawes the hangings" and then "*Drawes the hangings further*" to reveal the bodies of people he has murdered.[67] A painting of a murdered brother is what the curtain is opened to reveal in William Heminge's *The Fatal Contract* (1639).[68] The Queen shows the picture to the Eunuch and explains that she keeps it to whet her appetite for revenge. Later in the play the Eunuch "*drawes the Canopie*" to discover the Queen and her favorite Landrey asleep (sig. H3), then tricks them into drinking poison, ties them to chairs, and "*draws the Curtain again*" (sig. I1), being careful to leave "a peeping hole" (sig. I1) for them to witness the murders he proceeds to carry out on their faction at court. He then opens the curtain to reveal to the audience the nearly dead Queen and Landrey.

Epiphany and horror did not limit what sweeping aside hangings might bring to light. Ridiculous spectacles were likewise possible. Jasper Mayne's comedy *The City-Match* (1637) includes a scene in which a sharpster named Quartfield displays his accomplice Timothy in the guise of a freak-for-show: "*Drawes a Curtain behind it Timothy a sleepe like a strange fish.*"[69] A sign nearby proclaims just what Londoners might pay a penny to see at a fair or on the city streets or, again for a penny, read about in a broadside ballad: "*Within this place is to be seene / A wondrous Fish. God save the Queene*" (sig. H1v). The exhibition is even accompanied by a song. At end of the scene comes the stage direction "*They drawe the Curtain before him*" (sig. I1v). The comedy's climax in Act 5, scene 7 plays out a madcap version of what Dorset does with Herbert and Paulina with Leontes. "*Enter to them two Footmen, bearing the Frame of a great Picture,*" goes the stage direction, "*Curtains drawne*" (sig. R1). Warehouse, Mistress Holland, and Mistress Scruple (a Puritan schoolmistress) wonder what subject the curtained picture might show: Mars and Venus, Aretine's erotic postures, nymph and satyr (Warehouse's choice), the rape of Lucrece (Mistress Holland's), the fall of Babylon or a fat monk spewing forth churches (Mistress Scruple's). After these possible matches of words and images comes the stage direction "*Draws the Curtaine within are discovered Bright & Newcut*" (sig. R1)—two characters that have been carrying on amorous intrigues with Mistress Warehouse. But, disappointed Mistress Holland complains, the figures in the "*Night-peeces*" (sig. R1) are in their *clothes!*

Juliet's falling on her bed within the curtains typifies a third type of discovery, this one having to do with sleeping, sexual play, dreaming, dying, or being killed. Dessen and Thomson's list includes 25 stage directions of this type, about 23 percent of the whole. Ambiguity as to whether Juliet falls within curtains hung across one of the entrances to the stage or within the curtains of a stage prop bed points up the overdetermination of stage hangings in these situations. They can be bed curtains, tapestries lining the walls of a bedchamber, a visualization of dreams, fancy work enfolding a scene of epiphany or horror: one of these, some of these, all of these, as the script provides cues and spectators' fantasies respond. In a jocular speech designed to wake the drugged Juliet, the Nurse goes from sleep ("fie you sluggabed" [Q1599, 4.4.29]) to anticipation of wedding-night bliss ("the next night I warrant / The Countie *Paris* hath set vp his rest, / That you shall rest but little" [4.4.32–34]) to erotic fantasy ("I, let the Countie take you in your bed, / Heele fright you vp yfaith" [4.4.37–38]) before she realizes the terrible truth: "Lady, Lady, Lady? / Alas, alas, helpe, helpe, my Ladyes dead" (4.4.40–41).

Numerous plays confirm Juliet's Nurse's association of curtains with lascivious goings-on. The Jailer's Daughter in *The Two Noble Kinsmen,* driven to frenzy by her unrequited love for Palamon, is overwatched by the Doctor and her father the Jailer (hiding behind an arras?) as she imagines the torments of lovers in the afterlife: "One cries, o, that ever I did it behind the arras, and then howles; th'other curses a suing fellow and her garden house" (Q1634, 4.3.51–53). Marston's satiric spokesman Mendoza in *The Malcontent,* acted by the King's Men at the Globe, probably in 1604, sets the scene for wanton sex: "sweete sheetes, waxe lightes, antique bed postes, cambricke smocks, villanous curtaines, arras pictures, oylde hinges, and all the tongue-tide lasciuious witnesses of great creatures wantonnesse."[70] It is perhaps theatrical practice, as well as bed furnishings, that explain the curtains that are pulled back to reveal Lucrece's suicide in Jan Muller's engraving (see figure 14). A companion piece by Muller shows, within the same curtained space, the rape that occasions her self-murder. The association of bed curtains with death to be seen in Muller's image as well as in *Romeo and Juliet* continues a well-established theatrical tradition. In *2 Henry VI,* acted by Lord Strange's Men in 1590, stage directions for three scenes use stage hangings as if they were bed curtains. In the first of these scenes, "the Curtaines being drawne, Duke *Humphrey* is discouered in his bed, and two men lying on his brest and smothering him in his bed" (Q1594, SD at 3.2.1). Later in the scene, "*Warwicke* drawes the curtaines and showes Duke *Humphrey* in his bed" (SD at 3.2.146). The next scene uses bed curtains to stage a second murder: "Enter King and *Salsbury,* and then the Curtaines be drawne, and the Cardinall is discouered in his bed, rauing and staring as if he were madde" (SD at 3.3.1, sig. F1v). The Cardinal dies shortly thereafter. *Thomas of Woodstock* (also known as *1 Richard II*), possibly revived by the King's Men after its original performances in 1592, presents the conspirator Lapoole directing two murderers to kill Woodstock in his bed. "*He draws the curtains*" and discovers Woodstock in bed.[71] "*Thunder and lightning*" accompany the murder (5.1.55).

Associations of bed curtains with erotic pleasure on the one hand and with death on the other are not surprising, but a confluence of the two seems quite specific to Renaissance imagination. The fusing of dying with *dying,* as witnessed in *Romeo and Juliet,* is continued in *Othello.* Possibly a curtained stage prop bed is present when Desdemona follows Othello's orders in Act 4, scene 3 and undresses for bed, singing the "song of willow" that expresses her erotic melancholy (see chapter five). It is certainly present when Othello returns to murder her in Act 5. (Perhaps, indeed, the bed with its shut curtains has remained on stage during the fight scene between Cassio and Roderigo in the first scene of Act 5, a scene that finds its location with respect to "this Bulke" (Q1622, 5.1.1; F 1623 reads "this Barke")—likely one of the columns supporting the stage canopy—behind which Roderigo hides in wait. In the following scene, after he has smothered Desdemona, Othello says to himself, "let me the Curtaines draw" (Q1622, 5.2.113) and then admits Emilia, who has been clamoring at the door. It is presumably Emilia who hears Desdemona within the bed cry, "O falsly, falsly murdered" (5.2.126) and flings open the curtains. Once Emilia, slain by Iago, and Othello, slain by his own hand, have joined Desdemona on the bed, the curtains are closed. "The obiect poysons sight," Lodovico commands, "Let it be hid" (5.2.374–75). In Davenant's *The Cruel Brother,* acted by the King's Men in 1627, "*A Chayre at the Arras*" sets the scene (5.1) for Corsica's death at the hands of her brother, punishment for her adultery with the Duke of Siena.[72] Later "*The Duke (on his Bed) is drawne forth,*" presumably through the same arras, for a scene of confrontation with own guilt (sig. K1). The discovery scene in Hemming's *The Fatal Contract* (1639) shows a similar confluence of adultery and death when the Queen and Landrey are discovered asleep in bed and then are murdered.

Equally specific to Renaissance imagination are the 15 stage directions (about 14 percent) that associate hangings with reading and writing. A chair and table in Queen Margaret's Chamber at Owlpen Manor (see plate 20) suggest the ambient green in which Renaissance readers might sit down with a book. The interplay of visual images and written texts in such settings, as we observed in chapters one and four, might produce a "semiotic virtuosity" in which images and texts were mutually enhanced.[73] A similar virtuosity is to be found in curtain scenes that represent "the study"—scenes that seem calculated to heighten, for a moment, the interplay of the visual and the verbal that goes on in drama all the time. A scene in Thomas Dekker's comedy *Satiro-Mastix,* mounted by the Lord Chamberlain's Men in 1601, shows "Horrace *sitting in a study behinde a Curtaine, a candle by him burning, bookes lying confusedly.*"[74] First Horace speaks in soliloquy, as he scribbles away at an epithalamium for Sir Walter Terrel's wedding, then he joins in banter with his boon companion Asinius Babo. At least seven other scripts acted by the company in later years deploy hangings to define the space behind the curtain as a closet, cell, library, studio, or study: Peter Fabel's in *The Merry Devil of Edmonton* (1602), Pope Alexander's in Barnabe Barnes's *The Devil's Charter* (1606), Henry VIII's in *All Is True* (1613), Caliste's in Fletcher's *The Lovers' Progress* (1623), Trifle's in Davenant's *The News from Plymouth* (1635), Eurithea's in Davenant's *The Platonic Lovers* (1635), Claramente's in Davenant's *The Distresses* (1639), and possibly, as we shall consider, Prospero's in *The Tempest* (1611).

As with bed curtains and bedchambers, an association seems to be made in such scenes with the tapestries, painted cloths, damask hangings, and painted panels that actually adorned small private spaces like the Green Closet at Ham House (plate 1), Queen Margaret's Chamber (plate 20), and Lady Ann Drury's Oratory (plate 21). A curtain—indeed, what looks to be the same *green* curtain—defines the book-filled studies shown in Holbein's portraits of Sir Thomas More and Erasmus.[75] Like the surrounds of his sometime chancellor in Holbein's portrait, the king's study in Shakespeare's *Henry VIII* is a place for privacy, reading, and contemplation. The last time the spectators of the play have seen the king (1.4), he was full of high spirits, having crashed Cardinal Wolsey's banquet as a masker. Now, the Lord Chamberlain tells Norfolk and Suffolk (2.2), the king is struggling with a bad conscience for having married his brother's wife: "I left him priuate, / Full of sad thoughts and troubles" (F 1623 2.2.14–15, sig. v1). That is the state in which Norfolk and Suffolk now find him. "*The King drawes the Curtaine and sits reading pensiuely,*" according to the stage direction (SD after 2.2.62). Norfolk and Suffolk's visit comes as an unwelcome intrusion. Similar physical arrangements characterize Trifle's study in Davenant's *News from Plymouth* (1635). The clerk Dash draws the curtain, "Trifle *discover'd in his Study, Papers, Seale and Wax before him.*"[76] In several plays acted by the King's Men, studies behind the curtain are associated with forbidden books, black arts, and commerce with the devil.[77] No less remarkable is an association of the curtain with dozing while reading—and thus with liminal states of consciousness. In Davenant's *The Distresses* (1639), Leonte "*steps to the Arras softly, draws it. Claramante is discovered sleeping on her Book, her Glass by.*"[78] The tapestry book cover produced by the Sheldon Workshops (see plate 24) suggests how design motifs from arrases might appear on the very verge of printed pages. Four years earlier, in Davenant's *The Platonic Lovers,* it was music, not reading, that had put the reclusive figure into a doze. Amadine has just said of Eurithea, "I left her with Lute, whose Musick I believe, has woo'd her to a gentle sleep," when Theander "*Draws a Canopy;* Eurithea *is found sleeping on a Couch, a Veil on, with her Lute.*"[79]

"*Here Prospero discouers Ferdinand and Miranda, playing at Chesse*" (F 1623, SD at 5.1.174): no curtain is explicitly called for in this stage direction for *The Tempest,* but Alonso's response casts the moment as a scene of discovery like the 27 instances in Dessen and Thomson's compilation of stage directions having to do with "arras," "curtain," "draw," "hangings," and "traverse." What might have been a scene of horror, the drowned body of Ferdinand, turns out to be an epiphany, a revelation of Ferdinand, very much alive, playing chess with his future wife. Alonso first wonders if what he is seeing is "a vision of the Island" (5.1.179). Not so, Sebastian says: "A most high miracle" (5.1.180). In leading Alonso and the others to the *moment* of revelation, Prospero has pointedly defined the *place* of revelation: "This Cell's my Court" (5.1.168). Our survey of scripts acted by the King's Men until 1642 invites us to consider Prospero's cell as one instance among many of the curtain-as-study. All of the features associated with such scenes are present here: privacy, books, pen and papers, contemplation, magic—even sleeping and dreaming. It is remarkable how many times in *The Tempest* characters fall asleep: Miranda (1.2), Gonzalo, Adrian, Francisco, and Alonso (2.1), and, by report at least, Prospero himself (3.2). "'Tis a custom with him," Caliban tells Stephano and Trinculo, "I'th afternoone to sleepe: there thou maist braine him, / Having first seiz'd his bookes" (3.2.88–89). Whether Prospero's custom was to fall asleep *over* his books is not said, but Prospero takes his place among other stage figures in the King's Men's repertory who fall asleep in a study or closet. Most suggestive of all is the quality Prospero's cell shares with similar spaces in other plays, a quality of liminal consciousness, of dozing, of dreaming that finds its visual focus in a curtain or arras.

Massinger's comedy *The Guardian* (1633) is one of four plays in Dessen and Thomson's list (about 5 percent of the total) that call for hangings to be used in connection with eating and drinking.[80] Tapestries, painted cloths, or rich fabrics might adorn the walls of a dining room, of course, but in all four scripts the curtain combines functions from other curtain scenes: hiding, discovering, taking erotic pleasure. In Massinger's script, for example, Jolante is pretending to be in mourning for her banished husband Severino but is actually awaiting her lover Monteclaro when the stage direction occurs "Enter *Jolante (with a rich banquet, and tapers) (in a chaire, behind a curtain).*"[81] As chance would have it, Monteclaro is intercepted on the dark street by Severino, who has returned from exile in disguise and sends Monteclaro home before he himself bursts in on Jolante and finds her, not plunged in mourning, but ready for a lovers' banquet. The curtain perhaps half hides Jolante, since she speaks a guilty soliloquy before her husband discovers her.

The dramatic character of the hangings in Massinger's script are thus precisely those suggested in the printed illustrations for *Roxana, Messalina,* and *The Wits:* multiple, layered, fluid. The fluidity resides in the way the hangings separate the banqueting space "within" from the city street "without." In the action that precedes Severino's discovery of his wife the main stage is established as a city street. "That is the house, / And there's the key," Jolante's maid tells Monteclaro; "You'll find my Lady / Ready to entertain you" (sigs. K5v–K6). Most of the remaining scenes in Dessen and Thomson's census involve drawing aside or drawing close a curtain to indicate a change in fictional location. In the unlicensed script of *Sir Thomas More,* perhaps intended for the Lord Chamberlain's Men early in their tenure at the Theatre, the transition from scene 1, an unspecified public place, to scene 2, a court session presided over by the Lord Mayor, is indicated by this stage direction: "*An arras is drawn, and behind it, as in sessions, sit the Lord Mayor, Justice Suresby, and other Justices, Sheriff More and the other Sheriff sitting by.*"[82] As in all the other instances, an arras is plausible in a courtroom, but its presence here has less to do with the fictional scene than with stage dynamics.

In moments like this one, entrances and exits made through curtains function as the Renaissance equivalent of "tracking shots" in motion pictures—calculated moves by the camera to take the spectator into different fictional locales. Modern investment in the bareness of the early modern stage makes E. K. Chambers's attempt to classify scenic locations seem quaint and misguided. All but a few scenes in Elizabethan plays, Chambers claims, can be divided into "open country," "some public spot in a city," "threshold scenes," and "chamber scenes."[83] The next-to-last category, Chambers calculates, may be the largest: "I do not think it has been fully realized how large a proportion of the action of Elizabethan plays passes at the doors of houses" (3:59–50). The category also includes porches, lobbies, courtyards, the gates of palaces and castles, and the spaces before a church or temple, a friar's cell, an inn, a stable, or a shop. Logically, tapestries, arrases, and painted cloths do not belong to any of these threshold spaces; logistically, they belong to all of them. They enfold them. If spectators' experience of stage hangings was fundamentally an ambient affair—the curtained space invited spectators to project their imaginations, even if they could not move their bodies, toward an unseen *behind* or *within*—then one can appreciate the frequency and the importance of liminal scenes or "tracking shots" in arousing the spectators' passions.

The term "hangings" is too inert. Far from just *being* there, stage fabrics in Shakespeare's theater were involved in actions, in doing things. Beds were thrust forth between them, swords were thrust through them, they were drawn back, they were closed, through them on certain occasions actors went out and in, they moved the spectators' imaginations from one place to another. For actors on the stage, the curtain could be implicated in all sorts of activities: hiding, discovering, sexual pleasuring, sleeping, dying, reading, writing, dreaming, eating, moving from one place to another. For spectators in the house, they were sites of expectation, enticements for looking, invitations to the play of fantasy, preparations for the focused seeing and listening that define dramatic scenes. In Renaissance theaters the curtain functioned exactly opposite to the way Themistocles says it does in speech. Speech may be like an arras that, spread abroad, shows fair images but, contracted, looks like a pack; in the theater, regardless of how fair the images in an arras may be, the eloquence is in the contraction. The governing preposition for the dynamics of stage curtains is not *within* or *without, above* or *below, into* or *out of*—as frequent as these dynamics may be—but *between.*

The Green Room

The passion inspired by the curtain, I have been suggesting, is a desire not just to hear the words and see the spectacle but to *go there.* On occasion, spectators were physically able to do just that, and we can follow them. To make such a move, one has to stop thinking of the curtain as a barrier and consider it as a medium. It has been hard since the late eighteenth century to think of stage curtains in terms other than Wyatt's: they separate the "scene" from the "spectatory." Now, we tell ourselves, we can do without that separation. Even Malone, for all his historical research, cannot imagine Shakespeare's theater without a curtain hanging from the proscenium arch. The stage itself may lack painted scenery, displaying nothing more to the spectators' eyes than curtains or hanging arrases and tapestries, but in his remarks on Henry VIII's study in *All Is True,* Malone is careful to distinguish the "traverse" that the king pulls aside from "the principal curtains that hung in the front of the stage."[84] F. G. Fleay, whose *Introduction to Shakespearian Study* (1877) instructed several generations of school children and university students, likewise imagines a curtain separating the actors from the spectators—even though he delights to imagine himself and his readers as among the select few who might sit on the stage, behind the curtain. We can spend six pence to stand in the pit, Fleay tells his young charges, go up into the boxes for one or two shillings, or hire a stool for a shilling more and sit right on the stage. It's the last option, of course, that we will choose, smug bourgeois that we are. "Let us then enter the actors' door," Fleay suggests, "pass through the tiring-room, lift the traverse curtain, and take our places. We see that in honour of the new piece mats are spread on the stage, instead of the usual rushes. But the pit on the other side the green curtain are impatient, and are throwing missiles at us. Just lift it up, and return one or two at the ringleader of the understanders."[85] Thank goodness we, on *this* side of the green curtain, are well behaved. The "locality of the scene," Fleay goes on to explain, "is placarded on the tapestry that is hung round the stage" (73). Burbage, dressed in tragic black, enters to speak the prologue.

By now it should be clear that there *was* a curtain at the Curtain; it just wasn't where Malone and Fleay thought it was. Rather than separating the spectatory from the scene, it separated the spectatory *and* the scene from . . . what? Montaigne, like most Europeans of his time, assumed that a curtain will hang at the *back* of the stage, not at the front. His essay "Of the Inequality amongst Us" likens an emperor in his public appearances to actors in the theater: "For, as enterlude-plaiers, you shall now see them on the stage, play a King, an Emperor, or a Duke, but they are no sooner of[f] the stage, but they are base rascals, vagabond abjects, and porterly-hirelings, which is their natural and originall condition."[86] (John Florio, in his 1603 translation, rather overdoes Montaigne's "valets et crocheteurs misérables."[87]) The emperor's pomp, Montaigne continues, quoting Lucretius, is like great emeralds with "their grasse-greene-light" set off in gold, or a Thalassian vest (translated by Charles Cotton in 1685–1686 as "Sea-Green vest"[88]) worn out by too much lovemaking: "view him behinde the curtaine, and you see but an ordinarie man, and peradventure more vile, and more seelie, then the least of his subjects" (sig. N4v). *Before* the curtain one finds spectacle in all its sumptuousness; *behind* the curtain one discovers reality in all its untidiness. And so it would have been at the Curtain. The tiring house was likely a crowded and chaotic place, crammed with props and trunks of costumes. At the same time, what might be discovered behind the curtain, as we have seen from our survey of stage directions, was quite the opposite: a dazzling spectacle, a beguiling mystery, a thrilling horror. London's playhouses as fitted out in the 1660s and 1670s, after theater became legitimate once again, preserved this earlier arrangement. Most staged action in Restoration plays took place in front of a curtain, now hung within an elaborate frame. The curtain was customarily raised after the prologue, to reveal, behind the frame, illusionistic scenery that could be changed by means of wings and shutters, all within view of the audience. The curtain did not fall again until the epilogue. In the meantime, staged action might occasionally move into the frame, but for the most part, the painted scenes remained just that: painted scenes.[89] In these arrangements, one can see a continuation of the custom of displaying gallery paintings by pulling aside a curtain and its equivalent in pre-Commonwealth theaters, the dropping or whisking aside an arras or traverse to discover scenes in the space "within."

In the 1670s and afterwards what one might discover behind the curtain, though not necessarily in a direct line of vision, was the green room. The space behind the scene was still being called a "tiring room" in the 1660s and 70s, as witness Samuel Pepys, John Dryden, and William Wycherley—and a 1662 order by the Lord Chamberlain for 110 yards of "green bayes" to reline the walls of the upper tiring room at the Cockpit-in-Court.[90] A coarse woolen cloth, baize had long been used for linings, coverings, and curtains.[91] Samuel Pepys, in a 1667 diary entry, refers to the backstage space at the Dorset Garden Theater as the "scene room," a term that also occurs in scripts by Nathaniel Lee and William Mountfort.[92] Was it those 110 yards of green baize at the Cockpit that turned the tiring room and the scene room into the green room? The earliest printed occurrence of the term "green room" comes in Thomas Shadwell's comedy *A True Widow,* acted at the Dorset Garden Theater in 1678 and published the next year. Act 4 is set in a theater, perhaps the Dorset Garden itself, and in the course of the action there the London sophisticate Stanmore successfully fends off Lady Busy's matchmaking attempts by exposing the prospective bride, Gertrude, as the "very foolish and whorish" country girl described in the dramatis personae.[93] Gertrude has prostituted herself, Stanmore announces, with the coxcomb Selfish, who told Stanmore so himself: "*Selfish,* this Evening, in a green Room, behind the Scenes, was before-hand with me, she ne'r tells of that" (sig. I3v). An association of the green room with amorous intrigue is continued in Mr. W. M.'s play *The Female Wits* (Drury Lane, 1697), where Praiseall flirts with the company's actresses and then effuses, "I'll treat you all in the Green Room with Chocolate," and in Colley Cibber's comedy *Love Makes a Man* (Drury Lane, 1700), where Clodio, "a pert Coxcomb" played by Cibber himself, boasts to his nephew, "Yes, Sir, I do know *London* pretty well, and the Side-box, Sir, and behind the Scenes, ay, and the Green Room too, and all the Girls, and Women-Acresses there, Sir."[94]

Why green? Did the walls in the actors' quarters of a certain seventeenth-century theater just happen to be painted that color? Did the green baize ordered for the Cockpit's tiring room start a fashion? The association of baize fabric specifically with the color green, as with billiards tables, card tables, desktops, and "the green baize" of the House of Commons, seems to be a nineteenth-century phenomenon.[95] Was green chosen for the tiring room because the color was considered restful for actors' eyes? Did green figure in the coat of arms of one of the aristocratic sponsors of dramatic companies in the sixteenth or seventeenth century and hence determine the color of the livery worn by that aristocrat's servants? (George Bryan has made that suggestion in his investigation of the origins of the term "green room," but vert does not figure in the coats of arms of Ferdinando Stanley, Lord Strange, or of Henry and George Carey, Lords Chamberlain.[96]) Any one of these possibilities, or several of them together, might account for the green in the green room, but one thing remains certain: *A True Widow, The Female Wits,* and *Love Makes a Man* all associate the green room with passion—and passion of a very precise kind.

Whatever the term's origins, whenever it came into common usage, "the *green* room" captures perfectly the liminality of the space behind-the-curtain. It can be a space for spectacle-beyond-the-spectacle, as with Hermione's effigy, the chess game in Prospero's cell, and the wax works designed to terrify the Duchess of Malfi. It is also a space where sweaty bodies get that spectacle together and put it across to the spectators. In the eyes of theater addicts like Marston's Luscus—and, I confess, myself—it is both things at once. The green room shapes up as both metatheatrical and infra dig. The position of spectators vis-à-vis that liminal space might seem to have undergone a sea-change when London's theaters reopened in the 1660s and French ways of managing dramatic illusion dictated the architecture of theaters like the Dorset Garden. To appreciate the magnificence that Flecknoe imagines as distinguishing plays of his own day from Shakespeare's—magnificence designed, according to Flecknoe, "more for sight than hearing"—would seem to require a calculated distance between spectators and scene. What were green room haunters like Pepys but the Restoration equivalents of Jonson's stage-sitting gentlemen? To be sure, Pepys and his peers, unlike Jonson's dull-witted gentlemen, had to get up from their chairs, take to their feet, and walk to the green room. They would not necessarily have had to cross the stage to get there. The green room in the 1673 Drury Lane Theater seems to have been accessible from outside the building.[97] The effect would have been the same, however, as for Jonson's gentlemen: passionate proximity. In both cases, the green room marks the spot where spectators join the spectacle.

The green room in London's late-seventeenth-century theaters put behind the curtain what could be found *at* the curtain in earlier-seventeenth-century theaters. Jonson's complaints in *Cynthia's Revels* and *The New Inn* insinuate stage-sitters into weave of the tapestries and hangings that lined the stage. What Jonson's Third Gentleman in *Cynthia's Revels* could have seen and heard from that position was not so different from what Pepys could have seen and heard in the green room at Dorset Garden and Drury Lane. Present in both cases is the exquisite irony of joining the dramatic illusion and yet being able to see the flesh and hear the breathing that make that illusion possible. And the result, in both cases, seems to have been a rush of passion. What is to be found behind the curtain in Renaissance theaters? Perhaps, as in Beaumont and Fletcher's *The Mad Lover* or Massinger's *The City Madam*, Orpheus descending. Perhaps Will Slye taking off Orpheus's attire and retiring himself in the clothes of a vagabond abject. Perhaps—no, certainly—both. What we discover at the back of Peter Brook's theater is more solidly *there:* a brick wall, painted black.

Let us think outside the black box. The curtain at the Curtain invites us to imagine a visual matrix alive with motion out of which figures emerge with quickness and volubility, before they are fixed for contemplation by the understanding. Hangings in the Renaissance theater provided a constantly present focal point for curiosity, expectation, desire, passion. The curtain with its graphic design might be regarded by Derrida as a weaving, web, or infolding. By Lacan, as an opening into the hyper-verbal Real. By Bakhtin, as visual polyphony, a babble of many possible stories out of which some are called to dramatic life during the play. By Merleau-Ponty and other phenomenologists, as a chaos of sensations within which meaning is framed in a culturally structured act of *epoche.* In all these senses, the curtain is a medium. *Theatron,* the Greek word from which our word *theater* derives, means "viewing place." The theater gives us a point of view. What we see from that position is, according to Jaques in *As You Like It,* nothing less than all the world. In Prospero's words, it is the great globe itself. The Theatre and the Globe: between those two entities a medium was required in 1597–1599 and is still required today. That medium was and is the Curtain.

AFTERWORD

Coloring Books

Here—color this, but do try to stay within the lines. More often than not, that is what children are told when an adult hands them a coloring book. Most of us never forget the lesson. Not that most of us ever have occasion to color a book except when we highlight what we want to remember with a felt-tip "reference marker," as the device is called in office supply catalogs. Yellow dominates the field, but pink, blue, and green are also available. Most word-processing programs offer a digital equivalent under the "highlight" function. A definitive history of coloring books is, apparently, still to be written. The earliest examples I have been able to find are do-it-yourself botanical books from the later eighteenth century—bound collections of engraved black-and-white plates of flowers "to which is added an accurate description of their colours with instructions for drawing and painting."[1] The market for *The Florist,* published about 1760, is specified as "gentlemen and ladies delighting in that art," but by the 1780s, books with the same title and format were being addressed to "the little Misses and Masters of Great Britain"[2]—establishing an association between coloring and childhood that was confirmed in the nineteenth century and continues to this day.

Although specimens survive from the 1850s, '60s, and '70s, coloring books really came into their own in the 1880s.[3] One might have expected as much. These late-nineteenth-century books combine a Romantic embrace of childhood imagination on the one hand with the steady grip of Victorian discipline on the other. In *The Young Artist's Coloring Guide* (1850) and *The Little Painter* (1860), each plate was reproduced twice, a hand-colored exemplar on the left-hand page (color lithography did not come in until the 1870s), giving the young user a precise guide for how to color the plate on the right-hand page.[4] In *The "Little Folks" Painting Book* (1879), published in conjunction with *Little Folks* magazine (1871–1933), the hand-colored exemplar was limited to the frontispiece, but the disciplinary intent remains the same. "It is, of course, apparent," says the preface, "that in a book of this description, the talents of young artists must be chiefly directed to the fitting choice of colours, and their harmonious arrangement."[5] The intricacy of Kate Greenaway's drawings for *The "Little Folks" Painting Book* (other than having the color removed, they are no different from the lithographs she supplied for scores of children's books in the later nineteenth century) must have made staying within the lines a cruel challenge. Lines more suited to a child's free hand became available only in the twentieth century. In the meantime, the educational impulse behind the original coloring books remained—and has remained—strong. At the time of this writing, it is possible to order the following titles: *Shakespeare / Coloring Book* (1983), a *Shakespeare Coloring Book* (1990), and *Shakespeare's Coloring Book* (1993). In all these specimens, those from the nineteenth century and those published more recently, we encounter a modern version of the centuries-old contest between *disegno* and *colore* that we noticed in chapter one and elsewhere in this book. The black lines are presented as rules of discipline, as lesson plans, as limits to imaginative play, while the spaces within those lines—and outside those lines—are open to the scandal of color.

It may be only since the 1850s that we have had *coloring* books, but coloring *books* has been going on since the invention of printing. An illumination from a professionally limned copy of the Bible appears as plate 13. Searches of the catalogs of the Folger Shakespeare Library, the Huntington Library, the British Library, the Bodleian Library, and other archives turn up scores of atlases and books on heraldry in which hand coloring has provided information that black ink on white paper could never convey. To judge from surviving copies, these two kinds of books in particular seem to have been designed with the idea that somebody would fill in the lines of the illustrations with water color. In the case of maps, coloring enhances legibility; in the case of heraldry, coloring is as essential to the books' subject as lions rampant and ermines couchant. Randle Holme, in *The Academy of Armory* (1688, 1693, 1701), notes that it was customary for black-and-white engravings to indicate different colors with different hatchings (see figure 8). Green, for example, was "Hetched or Expressed by Lines bendways to the *Dexter Side*."[6] More often, however, printers of heraldry books left blank spaces that could be filled in by professional limners or even by the purchaser. Emblem books were also candidates for hand coloring, as several examples in the Sterling Maxwell Collection at Glasgow University attest.[7]

For readers since the nineteenth century, it has been natural to regard such books as examples of a manual technology made obsolete by color lithography and, more recently, by digitalized color printing. The touch of a professional hand was prized by collectors of rare books in the eighteenth, nineteenth, and twentieth centuries, but, unless the original owner was famous, the penned corrections, marginal comments, pointing index fingers, and running quotation marks added by early owners were looked upon as defacements. The "new bibliography" has reversed this judgment. Annotations now shape up as all too rare evidence of how readers read, how they took the printed text and made it *theirs*.[8] Except for pen-drawn index fingers that hold the place for long-rotted fingers that once took the book in hand and quotation marks that isolate parts of the text as something the reader might later have said aloud in his or her own voice, the graphic evidence of reading practices is largely verbal: this word underscored, that passage paraphrased in the margin, preferably in Latin. Simon Bardon shows us that not every Renaissance person read printed texts this way.

Who Simon Bardon may have been remains unknown, but how he felt about what he read in the fourth edition of John Reynolds's *The Triumphs of Gods Revenge against the Crying and Execrable Sinne of (Wilful and Premeditated) Murther* (1663) remains patently clear. Bardon's signature in what looks to be a seventeenth-century italic hand is the first of two signatures on the title page of the Folger Library's copy (the second signature, that of Hubert J. Norman, looks to be nineteenth or early twentieth century.) Bookplates and the Folger's catalog notes establish four other owners, all of them in the nineteenth and early twentieth centuries, by which time the folio volume had become a valuable commodity.[9] Almost certainly, then, it was Bardon or someone in his family, and not one of the later owners, who took a hint from the title page's red and black ink ("Triumphs," "Murther," "Tragical Histories," and "Never Published or imprinted in any other Language" all scream out in red) and decided to hand color not only some of the engravings that John Payne made for the volume but parts of the printed text as well. Plate 26 shows how Bardon has selectively colored the engraving that illustrates the major events in Book 1, History 4, the story of Beatrice-Joana's use of a servant, De Flores, to murder her suitor Piracquo so that she can marry her lover Alsemero.

The story is best known today as the main plot in Thomas Middleton and William Rowley's tragedy *The Changeling*, acted by Lady Elizabeth's Company at the Phoenix Theatre in May 1622 and at court a few months later. The first edition of Reynolds's *The Triumph of Gods Revenge* (1621; first published without illustrations) was one of Middleton and Rowley's main sources.[10]

The hues that Bardon uses for the eight scenes seem to have been chosen as much for their affective values as their naturalistic appropriateness. Thus in the upper left a small vaulted chamber hides Beatrice and Alsemero, as she, dressed in green, kneels before her lover and presents him with a letter or a book. Bardon has covered over the whole scene with a red wash, so that the green color first applied to Beatrice's gown shows through only in a small area outside the red wash at the lower left. Green as the color of amorous passion probably dictated Bardon's original choice. Beatrice wears a high-intensity green skirt in the fourth scene (middle rank, center) as she takes De Flores as a second lover. Piracquo, Beatrice-Joana's inconvenient suitor, wears hose and jerkin of a less intense green as he is murdered by De Flores in the next scene (middle rank, right). When Alsemero discovers Beatrice and De Flores in bed together (bottom rank, left), the bed curtains are the same intense green that Beatrice was wearing earlier. The final scene (bottom rank, right), in which Alsemero is beheaded for his jealous murders, has been washed with green (a bluer green than before) in exactly the way the first scene was washed with red. Two additional hues complete Bardon's palate: pink (the cloak of Beatrice's father in the second scene, top rank, right, and Piracquo's hose in the scene where he is murdered by Alsemero, bottom rank, center) and orange (Beatrice's skirt in the third scene, middle rank, left).

That Bardon chose these hues for their associations with the passions of lust and jealousy is indicated by the way he has color-coordinated the red wash of the first scene with red washes over the texts of the letters that Beatrice and Alsemero exchange (see plate 27). In Reynolds's version of the story, Beatrice and Alsemero have met in the city of Alicante, where Alsemero lingers before voyaging to Malta to take up a soldier's career. When Beatrice's father gets wind of Alsemero's courtship, he removes his daughter, already affianced to Piracquo, to a country estate. Alsemero sends letters in pursuit. "As long as you were in *Alicant,*" Alsemero writes to Beatrice, "I deemed it a heaven upon earth. . . . yea, so sweetly did I affect, and so dearly honour your beauty, as I entred into a resolution with myself, to end my voyage ere I began it, and to begin another, which I fear will end me."[11] Beatrice's reply is calculatedly coy: "As I have many reasons to be incredulous, and not one to induce me beleeve, that so poor a beauty as mine should have power to stop so brave a Cavalier (as your self) from ending so honourable a Voyage, as your first, or to perswade you to one so simple as your second; so I cannot but admire, that you in your Letter seek me for your Wife, when in your heart, I presume, you least desire it" (sig. E1). Red words, indeed. Simon Bardon's copy of *The Triumphs of Gods Revenge* provides vibrant testimony that seventeenth-century readers' responses were not limited to the markings of difference made by black ink on white paper. Color keys the words to the images.

Pointing index fingers, quotation marks, underscoring, displays of learning in the margins: these marks characterize scholarly reading practices in the early twenty-first century no less than in the early seventeenth century. Imagination, fancy, and passion are confined within the lines. In Rei Terada's formulation, only texts feel.[12] What would it mean to read in Simon Bardon's mode, color brush in hand? Or *not* to select what the publisher of *The "Little Folks" Painting Book* calls "the fitting choice of colours"? Or willfully to color outside the lines? Or to try to obliterate the tyranny of the line altogether in what Derrida calls the gush, the flood, the wash of color? Green in its materiality, its bodily physicality, its psychological apprehension, its resistance to the fixed points and lines of geometry presents an extreme case of the challenges confronted by historical phenomenology as a critical method.

Plate 28 reproduces in actual size ($4\frac{1}{2} \times 6\frac{3}{4}$ inches) a watercolor and gouache painting on vellum that modern scholars have attributed to Isaac Oliver. Given its handy size, the piece of vellum asks not only to be seen but touched. Framed, it might hang on the wall in a space like the Green Closet at Ham House, perhaps with a green or red curtain covering it, but more likely its original owner would have kept it in a drawer inside a cabinet designed specifically for storing treasures and important papers—perhaps a cabinet like the one shown in plate 30, painted black and gold and inlaid with mother of pearl. To view the painting, you would (if you were the owner) have to open the doors, pull out the drawer, remove the piece of vellum, and hold it in your hand, probably in both hands, or possibly place it on a table in front of you. In either case, you would be looking down at the drawing, probably keeping your eyes 18 inches or so away. If it were a friend who was showing you the drawing (as the Earl of Dorset showed Edward Herbert the likeness shown in figure 2), you might not ever touch the object yourself, but you still would be viewing it in intimate circumstances, your eyes above, not opposite, the painted surface.

Just what would you see in Oliver's miniature? What would the object in front of you look like? Feel like? Most viewers, then and now, would probably see through the colored pigments affixed to the vellum with gum and honey to the human figures, the animals, the land, the shrubs, the trees, the rocks, the lake, the sky that seem to exist beneath the colored surface. If you paused long enough to consider the surface, you might also detect the presence of another hand, the artist's hand. Although a high degree of finish seems to have been expected in Renaissance English painting—Roy Strong and other scholars have called attention to the static jewellike quality of English miniature portraits[13]—Oliver's design communicates a strong sense of left-to-right movement. The three black-clad ladies and their orange-clad escort are positioned closest to the viewer's own space and hence provide the likeliest entry point into the painted fiction, particularly for literate viewers who were used to reading from left to right. The orange-clad gentleman gestures emphatically to the viewer's right, the group of yellow-clad figures toward whom he gestures are themselves all inclined to the right, the large dog in the foreground, the leaping dog in the middle ground, and the galloping horse in the background are all moving from left to right, even the trees twist and turn toward the right. The leaves register a left-to-right movement that can be detected, if one looks close enough, in the brush strokes with which the pigments (originally dissolved in that most fugitive of media, water) have been applied to the vellum's surface. The orange-clad gentleman's extended left hand emerges as the picture's most eloquent gesture, as it directs the viewer's eyes into and across the painted scene, as it bridges the spatial gap between the two main groups of human figures, as it suggests the touch of the artist's own hand (see plate 29). There is a tactile quality to Oliver's painting—traces of the hand in several forms—that is every bit as strong as in Jan Muller's engraved lines depicting Lucrece's suicide (see figure 5). Add to the linear rhythms of Oliver's design the hues, the saturated intensity, and bright values of the right-hand lady's yellow gown, the right-hand gentleman's yellow hose, the flautist's yellow-orange doublet, the blond wood of the lady's lute, and the yellow-orange of the adjacent gentleman's hat, and an imaginative plunge into those green woods seems all but irresistible. A male figure in bright blue breeches with a yellow hat invites the viewer into the perspective depths—from light green to emerald green to blue green—where hunting is in progress. In retrospect the black- and orange-clad figures that provided our entry into the painting seem distinctly odd—and distinctly dull.

So what is Oliver's little painting *about?* The Statens Museum for Kunst in Copenhagen, which bought the painting in 1976, has cataloged it with two titles: *Selskab i det frie* (*A Party in the Open Air*) and *Allegori på den aegteskabelige kaerlighed* (*Allegory on Conjugal Love*). According to these titles, the painting is about two things: what it *depicts* and what it *means.* The "allegory" title derives from a 1995 Tate Gallery exhibition *Dynasties: Painting in Tudor and Jacobean England 1530–1630.* The catalog entry summarizes late-twentieth-century scholarship: "This miniature is probably an allegory on conjugal love. The scene of strolling and merry-making figures can be read as a moralizing comment on different types of love, particularly the married and unmarried states, represented by two distinct groups on either side of the picture."[14] Plausible enough. But what to make of the pull to the right? What to make of those yellow and yellow-orange hues, those intense saturations, those bright values, those green and blue depths? Oliver's painting may be *about* conjugal love, but it is also *about* color and rhythm. Two congeries of hues/saturations/values compete for attention: black/white/red/orange on the left versus white/yellow/green/blue on the right. What is more, the predominantly black/white hues on the left assume static vertical forms, while the predominantly yellow/green hues on the right lean, curve, incline, beckon.

If the Tate Gallery catalog is right, a viewer is supposed to forget these sensations in an act of verbal distancing: "Ah! An allegory on conjugal love!" So much for rhythm, so much for color, so much for perspective depth. To end in words is to end in an act of *judgment.* That may have been the case as well for viewers in 1599. But where, for a modern viewer, is the *affection* in what Hilliard regards as a complete response, "an *affectionate* good judgment"? Affect, for an Renaissance viewer, was part and parcel of knowing Oliver's picture. Historicist criticism of the sort printed in the Tate Gallery catalog asks us to write off sensation and affect. The insidious outcome is that, when we see another painting by Oliver, or indeed a painting by any other artist working in England in the 1590s, we are apt to *begin* with judgment, with a verbal formulation that guides and restricts our looking at the painting. We begin, in a word, with *prejudice,* with prejudging. The result: all judgment, no passion. "An allegory on conjugal love": one could hardly find a starker reaction to the status of color as "an unthinkable scandal." The Tate catalog's attempt to contain Oliver's painted image within black-inked words on white paper turns color into a surplus, an excess, an insolence that is most conveniently overlooked. A correct reading of the painting demands that we ignore hue, saturation, and intensity and give our verbal allegiance to the black-and-white-clad figures to the left, where probably we began our exploration of the painting. Otherwise, the moral of the painting—"Married love is best"—makes no sense. Must that verbal act of judgment entail a refusal of sensual pleasure? Why end where we began?

All acts of knowing, as we observed in chapter one, happen within three coordinates: space, time, and body. Color presents an extreme case of that basic situation. It resists verbalization, in particular verbalization through naming. The syntactical unit that best captures the situation of the knowing subject, Michel Serres claims in *Angels* and in *The Troubadour of Knowledge,* is not nouns, not adjectives, not even verbs, but prepositions. What Serres describes in these texts is a *relational* way of knowing. Prepositions, literally, *pre-pose* the body. They *position* it *before,* both temporally and spatially and implicate the body in ways of knowing the world that are far more complicated than the subject/object binary implicit in nouns, in the act of naming: "weaving space, constructing time, they are the precursors of every presence."[15] We might think of the Cartesian model in terms of prepositions: the knower is positioned *opposite* or *against* the thing known. *About* collapses that objective distance. The root sense of the word, derived from Anglo-Saxon *be* (by) + *utan* (outside), is a movement *around the outside* (*OED,* "about" etymology).

In Aristotle's physics of color, "about" defines the surfaces of objects, which reflect light rays in varying degrees according to the porosity of those surfaces. In Galen's physiology, "about" describes the coursing, throughout the perceiver's body, of the aerated fluid that communicates sense experience from the brain to the heart and passions from the heart to the brain. In tapestry designs from the Sheldon Workshops, "about" locates the antic work that engages imagination and fancy before understanding fixes the narrative subject for visual contemplation and verbal interpretation. In Horace's famous dictum about picture and poetry, "about" functions as the *ut* that conjoins *poesis* with *pictura.* In poststructuralist linguistics, "about" marks the space—the empty space—between the name and the thing being named. In historical phenomenology, "about" serves as a reminder of a simple truth: all knowledge comes about within a particular configuration of space, time, and body. To read aboutwise requires movement: the reader must follow the speaker around the garden, walk through a series of chambers, view the portrait atop the tapestry now closer and now farther away, project imagination beyond the

IIE QVEENE. 141

9

For, elſe my feeble veſſell craz'd, and crackt
Through thy ſtrong buffets and outrageous blowes,
Cannot endure, but needs it muſt be wrackt
On the rough rocks, or on the ſandy ſhallowes,
The whiles that loue it ſteres, and fortune rowes;
Loue my lewd Pilot hath a reſtleſſe mind
And fortune Boat-ſwaine no aſſurance knowes,
But ſaile withouten ſtarres, gainſt tide and wind:
How can they other do, ſith both are bold and blind?

10

Thou God of winds, that reigneſt in the ſeas,
That reigneſt alſo in the Continent,
At laſt blowe vp ſome gentle gale of eaſe,
The which may bring my Ship, ere it be rent,
Vnto the gladſome port of her intent:
Then when I ſhall my ſelfe in ſafety ſee,
A table for eternall moniment
Of thy great grace, and my great ieopardee,
Great *Neptune*, I avow to hallow vnto thee.

11

Then ſighing ſoftly ſore, and inly deepe,
Shee ſhut vp all her plaint in priuie griefe;
For, her great courage would not let her weepe,
Till that old *Glaucé* gan with ſharpe repriefe
Her to reſtraine, and giue her good reliefe,
Through hope of thoſe, which *Merlin* had her told
Should of her name and nation be chiefe,
And fetch their being from the ſacred mould
Of her immortall wombe, to be in heauen enrol'd.

12

Thus as ſhe her recomforted, ſhe ſpyde,
Where farre away one all in armour bright,
With haſtie gallop towards her did ride;
Her dolour ſoone ſhe ceaſt, and on her dight
Her helmet, to her Courſer mounting light:
Her former ſorrowe into ſuddaine wrath,
Both cooſen paſſions of diſtroubled ſpright,
Conuerting, forth ſhe beates the duſty path;
Loue and deſpight attonce her courage kindled hath.

13

As when a foggy miſt hath ouercaſt
The face of heauen, and the cleare aire engroſt,
The world in darkneſſe dwels, till that at laſt
The watry South-winde from the ſea-bord coſt
Vpblowing, doth diſperſe the vapour loſt,
And poures it ſelfe forth in a ſtormy ſhowr;
So the faire *Britomart* hauing diſclo'ſt
Her clowdy care into a wrathfull ſtowre,
The miſt of griefe diſſolv'd, did into vengeance powre.

Figure 25. Sir Brook Bridges, annotations to Book 3, canto 4, of Edmund Spenser, *The Faerie Queene* (London: Humphrey Lownes for Matthew Lownes, 1609). Original page size, 9 × 5½ inches (22.8 × 14 cm). (Reproduced by permission of the Folger Shakespeare Library.)

arras, open the doors of the cabinet and take out the painted vellum, penetrate the painted vellum's wooded depths. Each of these actions exemplifies ambient reading. "About" invites us to think in terms of prepositions, not propositions.

In its concern with bodies in space and time and their relationship to the ambient world, historical phenomenology can lay claims to being a form of "green" criticism in a sense that embraces more than pigments and light rays.[16] Historical phenomenology recognizes that a text is situated within a series of "horizons" that includes the visceral effects of varying light rays, the acoustic properties of language, and historically specific conceptions of the human body, as well as the regimes of power that we are more used to studying.[17] Phenomenology, in Husserl's practice, may involve "bracketing" the world in order to attend to the thinker's own consciousness of the world, but historical phenomenology remains acutely attentive to the environment in which knowledge is formed. The gesturing hand in Oliver's miniature suggests that openness. The index finger is prominent, but the hand is an *open* one. In that respect it seems quite different from the closed hand and pointing index finger that many Renaissance readers used when they wanted to remember a certain word, phrase, or passage.[18] The hand shown in figure 25 is one of many that Sir Brook Bridges (d. 1728) left in his copy of *The Faerie Queene* (1609 edition), now in the Folger Library. It insistently points toward words, albeit towards words that conjoin poetry and picture. When Bridges wants to remember words alone, he typically writes a Latin tag in the margin, as he does next to Book 3, canto 4, stanza 9, about the dangers to one's "feeble vessell" when Love is the "lewd Pilot": "*Apta Allegoria,*" Bridges writes in the margin.[19] The hand further down the page points toward one of the passages in which Bridges takes special delight, passages in which a striking visual simile ends in a revelation, illumination, or discovery. What is revealed, illuminated, or discovered is not necessarily a moralization (the Latin tags take care of that) but a passion. In this case it is the mist-clearing storm of Britomart's wrath when she espies Marinell along the seacoast and forthwith attacks him. Bridges points insistently toward words, even though those words open out into picture and passion. Almost all of the 107 fists that Bridges has supplied for *The Faerie Queene* point toward a striking instance of *ut pictura poesis.* The open hand in Oliver's miniature gestures less certainly toward an assemblage of space (a forested landscape), time (the viewer's journey through the painting), and body (his own and thirty others)—an assemblage that produces, when the viewer is added to the picture, an experience of color. In this case, as so often in the culture of Renaissance England, the generative hue is green. If we want to read *toward* color, we must refuse Hobbes's logic (it points in the opposite direction) and follow instead the sequence of gestures suggested by Bridges and Oliver, *from* words *to* "picture" *to* sensations. To do so, we must first of all unlock the black-and-white doors that for too long have kept us out.

Notes

INTRODUCTION

1. The notion of cultural keywords comes from Raymond Williams, *Keywords: A Vocabulary of Culture and Society,* rev. ed. (New York: Oxford University Press, 1983). I make the claim for "green" as a current keyword despite its failure to make Tony Bennett, Lawrence Grossberg, and Meaghan Morris, eds., *New Keywords: A Revised Vocabulary of Culture and Society,* (Oxford: Blackwell, 2005), where the g's are limited to "Gay and Lesbian," "Gender," "Gene/Genetic," "Generation," "Globalization," and "Government."

2. Scott Slovic, "Ecocriticism: Embracing Multitudes, Practising Doctrine," in *The Green Studies Reader: From Romanticism to Ecocriticism,* ed. Laurence Coupe (London: Routledge, 2000), 160.

3. John Partridge, *The Widowes treasure, plentifully furnished with sundry precious and approoued secretes in Physicke and Chirurgey* (London: Edward Alde for Edward White, 1588), sig. B6; Richard Johnson, *The most famous history of the seauen champions of Christendome* (London: J. Danter for Cuthbert Burbie, 1596), sig. Z3; *Oxford English Dictionary Online* (Oxford: Oxford University Press, 2007 and earlier), http://dictionary.oed.com, accessed March 18, 2008, "green baise," "green cloth"; Francis Bacon, *New Atlantis* (London: [unspecified], [1658?]), sig. C1v; William Shakespeare, *The Tragedie of Othello, the Moore of Venice* in *Mr. William Shakespeares Comedies, Histories, and Tragedies* (London: Isaac Jaggard and Edward Blount, 1623), sig. tt4v; Donne, *Poems, by J.D.* (London: John Marriot, 1633), sig. FF3v. Unless otherwise noted, definitions, etymologies, and pronunciations throughout this book are taken from *Oxford English Dictionary Online* (http://dictionary.oed.com, accessed at various times between 2000 and 2008). Further references to the *OED* are cited in the text. It was Chris Kyle who pointed me in the direction of the Commons' green baise. I am grateful to Alan Sinfield for calling the Donne passage to my attention. Further references to Donne's poem are cited in the text.

4. See Claude Lévi-Strauss, *Le Cru et le Cuit* (Paris: Plon, 1964), trans. John and Doreen Weightman as *The Raw and the Cooked* (New York: Harper and Row, 1969), where the natural versus the man made becomes the structural principle that explains Amerindian culture, including social organization as well as religion, story telling, and visual arts.

5. Michel Pastoureau, *Blue: The History of a Color,* trans. Markus I. Cruse (Princeton: Princeton University Press, 2001); Amy Butler Greenfield, *A Perfect Red: Empire, Espionage, and the Quest for the Color of Desire* (New York: HarperCollins, 2005).

6. Herman Pleij, *Colors Demonic and Divine: Shades of Meaning in the Middle Ages and After,* trans. Diane Webb (New York: Columbia University Press, 2004).

7. Linda Woodbridge, *The Scythe of Saturn: Shakespeare and Magical Thinking* (Urbana: University of Illinois Press, 1994), 152–205.

8. John Gage, *Color and Culture: Practice and Meaning from Antiquity to Abstraction* (Berkeley: University of California Press, 1993); Gage, *Color and Meaning: Art, Science, and Symbolism* (Berkeley: University of California Press, 1999); Philip Ball, *Bright Earth: Art and the Invention of Color* (Chicago: University of Chicago Press, 2001).

9. Katharine Park, "The Organic Soul," in *The Cambridge History of Renaissance Philosophy,* ed. Charles B. Schmitt (Cambridge: Cambridge University Press, 1988), 470–71.

10. Thomas Wright, *The Passions of the Mind in Generall* (London: Valentine Simmes for Walter Burre, 1604), sig. E1.

11. Antonio R. Damasio, *Descartes' Error: Emotion, Reason, and the Human Brain* (New York: Putnam, 1994) and Damasio, *The Feeling of What Happens: Body and Emotion in the Making of Consciousness* (New York: Harcourt Brace, 1999).

12. I follow Randolph Starn, "A Postmodern Renaissance?" *Renaissance Quarterly* 60.1 (2007): 1–24, in taking the term "Renaissance" always to have been a problematic point of intersection between past and present, in which the modern present has used the past to construct its own identity in the very act of using the classical past to construct a Renaissance present.

13. Alex Byrne and David R. Hilbert isolate these questions as the fundamental concerns of the all essays collected in *Readings on Color: I. The Philosophy of Color* (Cambridge, MA: MIT Press, 1997), xi–xii.

14. Patricia Ticineto Clough, "Introduction," in *The Affective Turn: Theorizing the Social,* ed. Patricia Ticineto Clough with Jean Halley (Durham, NC: Duke University Press, 2007), 1–33.

15. Nancy G. Siraisi, *Medieval and Early Renaissance Medicine* (Chicago: University of Chicago Press, 1990); Gail Kern Paster, *The Body Embarrassed* (Ithaca, NY: Cornell University Press, 1993); Jonathan Sawday, *The Body Emblazoned* (London: Routledge, 1995); David Hillman and Carla Mazzio, eds., *The Body in Parts* (London: Routledge, 1997), and Andrea Carlino, *Books of the Body: Anatomical Ritual and Renaissance Learning,* trans. John Tedeschi and Anne C. Tedeschi (Chicago: University of Chicago Press, 1999).

16. Michael C. Schoenfeldt, *Bodies and Selves in Early Modern England: Physiology and Inwardness in Spenser, Shakespeare, Herbert, and Milton* (Cambridge: Cambridge University Press, 1999) and Gail Kern Paster, *Humoring the Body: Emotions and the Shakespearean Stage* (Chicago: University of Chicago Press, 2004).

17. Mary Thomas Crane, *Shakespeare's Brain: Reading with Cognitive Theory* (Princeton, NJ: Princeton University Press, 2001), draws on cognitive linguistics to study concept- and word-formation in Shakespeare's writings. Ellen Spolsky, *Word vs. Image: Cognitive Hunger in Shakespeare's England* (Basingstoke, UK: Palgrave, 2007), extends arguments made in *Satisfying Skepticism: Embodied Knowledge in the Early Modern World* (Basingstoke, UK: Ashgate, 2001)—arguments that connect early modern anxieties about im-

ages, for example, with such modern concepts as fuzzy categorization, habituation, and homeostasis.

18. "The brain is often compared to a computer—but what kind of computer? Computers come in two very different kinds: analogue and digital. . . . Digital computing requires many switches which must work fast and with high reliability. The brain does not look like this. It looks much more like a collection of analogue *neural nets*" (Richard L. Gregory, *Eye and Brain: The Psychology of Seeing,* 5th ed. [Princeton, NJ: Princeton University Press, 1997], 82).

19. Angus Fletcher, *The Colors of the Mind: Conjectures on Thinking in Literature* (Cambridge, MA: Harvard University Press, 1991); James Elkins, *The Object Stares Back: On the Nature of Seeing* (New York: Simon & Schuster, 1996); Barbara Maria Stafford, *Visual Analogy: Consciousness as the Art of Connecting* (Cambridge, MA: MIT Press, 2001); Charles Altieri, *The Particularities of Rapture: An Aesthetics of the Affects* (Ithaca, NY: Cornell University Press, 2003); Teresa Brennan, *The Transmission of Affect* (Ithaca, NY: Cornell University Press, 2004).

20. David Howes, *Sensual Relations: Engaging the Senses in Culture and Social Theory* (Ann Arbor: University of Michigan Press, 2003).

21. Robert N. Watson, *Back to Nature: The Green and the Real in the Late Renaissance* (Philadelphia: University of Pennsylvania Press, 2006), 5.

22. Timothy Morton, *Ecology without Nature: Rethinking Environmental Aesthetics* (Cambridge, MA: Harvard University Press, 2007), 33–34. My own relationship to "nature" in the pages that follow can be positioned somewhere in between Morton's wary distance and the embrace of the essayists collected in *Green Shakespeare: From Ecopolitics to Ecocriticism,* ed. Gabriel Egan (London: Routledge, 2006).

23. Ferdinand de Saussure, *Course in General Linguistics,* ed. Charles Bally and Albert Sechehaye, trans. Wade Baskin (New York: Philosophical Library, 1959), 122.

24. The changes, Aristotle says, are due to different effects of sunlight: "all water in process of time first turns yellow-green on blending with the rays of the sun; it then gradually turns black, and this further mixture of black and yellow-green produces herb-green" ("On Colors" 794.b.25–29, in *The Complete Works of Aristotle,* ed. Jonathan Barnes [Princeton, NJ: Princeton University Press, 1984], 1:1223). Unless otherwise noted, all references in Aristotle are to this edition.

25. Michel Serres, *Genesis,* trans. Geneviève James and James Nielson (Ann Arbor: University of Michigan Press, 1995), 1. I am grateful to Julian Yates for first pointing me in Serres' direction.

26. A judicious and succinct account of phenomenology as a school of nineteenth- and twentieth-century philosophy is provided by Dermot Moran, *Introduction to Phenomenology* (London: Routledge, 2000), esp. 60–191 (Husserl), 192–247 (Heidegger), and 391–434 (Merleau-Ponty).

27. Jean-François Lyotard, *Phenomenology,* trans. Brian Beakley (Albany: State University of New York Press, 1991). According to Lyotard, all objects of historical inquiry are never really objects. The analyst is connected with what she analyzes along a continuum of time: the past is both "now" and "no longer" as the future is both "now" and "not yet" (115–16). Never truly objective, the analyst is always implicated in the past, just as history is always implicated in the future: "we can grasp history neither through

objectivism nor subjectivism, and even less through a problematic union of the two, but only through a deepening of both which leads us to the very existence of historical subjects in their 'world,' on the basis of which objectivism and subjectivism appear as two equally inadequate options through which these subjects can understand themselves in history" (131).

CHAPTER ONE

1. Andrew Marvell, *Miscellaneous Poems* (London: Robert Boulter, 1681), sigs. I1–I1v, incorporating "pleasures" from Bodleian MS Eng. poet. d.49, as suggested in *The Poems of Andrew Marvell,* ed. Nigel Smith, rev. ed. (London: Pearson Longman, 2007), 157–58. Future quotations from the 1681 printing of "The Garden" are cited in the text by stanza number. I am grateful to Joseph Summers, who in a graduate seminar at the University of Rochester first made me pause over Marvell's phrase "green thought."

2. Christina Georgina Rossetti, "What Is Pink? A Rose Is Pink" in *Sing-Song: A Nursery Rhyme Book* (1872), in *The Complete Poems,* ed. R. W. Crump (Baton Rouge: Louisiana State University Press, 1979), 2:31. Just what is green seems to vary from version to version of Rossetti's poem. Leaves are specified in a version found on an early literacy Web site (http://www.earlyliterature.ecsd.net/colors.htm [accessed January 17, 2005]), and a leaping frog at a story book site for toddlers (http://www.lil-fingers.com/colors/green1.html [accessed January 17, 2005]).

3. Gregory, *Eye and Brain,* 20–22 (see intro., n. 18); R. W. G. Hunt, *Measuring Colour* (Chichester, UK: Ellis Horwood, 1987), 17–19; Leo M. Hurvich, *Color Vision* (Sunderland, MA: Sinauer, 1981), 26–39.

4. Ball, *Bright Earth,* 47–48 (see intro., n. 8); Hunt, *Measuring Colour,* 25; Marcia B. Hall, *Color and Meaning: Practice and Theory in Renaissance Painting* (Cambridge: Cambridge University Press, 1982), 2, 237, 238, 240.

5. Louis Hjelmslev, *Prolegomena to a Theory of Language* (1969), cited in Catherine Belsey, *Critical Practice* (London: Routledge, 1980), 39. The vagaries of Welsh in comparison with English were brought to a wide readership in "How Grue is Your Valley?" *The Economist* 18 January 2007. I am grateful to Elizabeth Harvey for this reference.

6. The hypothesis being tested in the World Color Survey was first advanced in Brent Berlin and Paul Kay, *Basic Color Terms: Their Universality and Evolution* (Berkeley: University of California Press, 1969). Accounts of the anthropological testing of the hypothesis and subsequent changes to the model are provided in Paul Kay and Chad K. McDaniel, "The Linguistic Significance of the Meanings of Basic Color Terms," in *Readings on Color,* ed. Alex Byrne and David R. Hilbert (Cambridge, MA: MIT Press, 1997), 2:399–441, and John Lucy, "The Linguistics of 'Color,'" in *Color Categories in Thought and Language,* ed. C. L. Hardin and Luisa Maffi (Cambridge: Cambridge University Press, 1997), 320–46. An archive of data and interpretations are available on the World Color Survey's Web site (http://www.icsi.berkeley.edu/wcs/).

7. Gage, *Color and Culture,* 79 (see intro., n. 8).

8. Stephen Greenblatt and M. H. Abrams, eds., *The Norton Anthology of English Literature,* 8th ed. (New York: Norton, 2006), 1:1696. The seventh edition misquoted the line in question and turned it into a much more manageable simile: "*Like* a green thought

in a green shade" (Abrams and Greenblatt, eds. [New York: Norton, 2001], 1:679, emphasis added).

9. *Andrew Marvell*, ed. Frank Kermode and Keith Walker (Oxford: Oxford University Press, 1990), 299. The *meta* in metaphysical is even more emphatic in this gloss than in Kermode's earlier paraphrase in *The Oxford Anthology of English Literature* (1973): "making the visible world seem as nothing compared with what can be imagined by the contemplative" (1155). Concerning "green" itself, Kermode and Walker observe in their headnote, "The poet makes the green of the garden stand for solitude against crowds, retirement against action, sensual delight free of sexual pursuit, the satisfaction of the sense against that of the mind; it is not the green of hope, the *benedicta viriditas* of alchemy, the green of the hermetic emblem, but the poet's green" (297).

10. Kermode and Walker's Platonist gloss, and others like it, ultimately derive from H. M. Margoliouth's scholarly edition of Marvell's poems and letters, first published by Oxford University Press in 1927 and updated in subsequent editions with additional commentary by Pierre Legouis and E. E. Duncan-Jones. Margoliouth's distinction between two possible interpretations has divided commentators ever since: "*Annihilating . . . Thought* may be taken as meaning either 'reducing the whole material world to nothing material, i.e. to a green thought' or 'considering the whole material world as of no value compared to a green thought'" (*The Poems and Letters of Andrew Marvell*, ed. H. M. Margoliouth, 3rd ed., rev. Pierre Legouis and E. E. Duncan-Jones [Oxford: Clarendon Press, 1971], 1:168). Platonizing readers have of course preferred the first alternative. Either way, however, we are left with a matter/mind polarity—and not a clue about what Marvell might have meant by green.

11. David Norbrook and H. R. Woudhuysen, eds., *The Penguin Book of Renaissance Verse* (London: Penguin, 1992), 475. See also Andrew Marvell, *The Complete Poems*, ed. Elizabeth Story Donno (Harmondsworth, UK: Penguin, 1972), 257.

12. Smith, *The Poems of Andrew Marvell*, 158.

13. Nigel Smith dates the poem as late as 1668 (*The Poems of Andrew Marvell*, 156).

14. *The Works of Andrew Marvell, Esq.* (London: E. Curll, 1726), 2:8–11; *The Works of Andrew Marvell, Esq.* (London: T. Davies, 1756), 2:167–173; Edward Thompson, ed., *The Works of Andrew Marvell, Esq. Poetical, Controversial, and Political* (London: Henry Baldwin for the editor, 1776), vol. 3, sigs. GGG2v–GGG3v.

15. *The Works of Andrew Marvell* (1726), 1:18 (original emphasis).

16. *The Works of Andrew Marvell* (1776), vol. 3, sig. 0001v. Further quotations are cited in the text by volume and signature.

17. Quoted in Margoliouth, *The Poems and Letters of Andrew Marvell*, 1:227.

18. Andrew Marvell, *Complete Poems*, ed. Alexander B. Grosart ([London]: [Robson], 1872), 1: lxvi.

19. An argument to this effect is made by Diane Kelsey McColley, "Perceiving Habitats: Marvell and the Language of Sensuous Reciprocity," in *Poetry and Ecology in the Age of Milton and Marvell*, ed. McColley (Aldershot, UK: Ashgate, 2007), 13–41.

20. Jacques Derrida, *The Truth in Painting*, trans. Geoff Bennington and Ian McLeod (Chicago: University of Chicago press, 1987), 169, 172. Further quotations are cited in the text.

21. Gage, *Color and Culture*, 117–39.

22. Stephen Melville, "'Color has not yet been named': Objectivity in Deconstruction," in *Deconstruction and the Visual Arts: Art Media, Architecture,* ed. Peter Brunette and David Wills (Cambridge: Cambridge University Press, 1994), 45.

23. This situation is explored with commonsense groundedness and philosophical elegance by Kathleen Akins and Martin Hahn, "The Peculiarity of Color," in *Color Perception: Philosophical, Psychological, Artistic, and Computational Perspectives,* ed. Steven Davis (New York: Oxford University Press, 2000), 215–47.

24. Francis Bacon, *The Advancement of Learning,* ed. Michael Kiernan (Oxford: Clarendon Press, 2000), 93, cited in the *OED,* "phenomenon"1.b.

25. The term *noumena* is Kant's coinage. The distinction between *phenomena* and *noumena* is sharpest in the first edition of *Critique of Pure Reason* (1781): "Appearances, so far they are thought as objects according to the unity of the categories, are called *phenomena.* But if I postulate things which are mere objects of understanding, and which, nevertheless, can be given as such to an intuition, although not to one that is sensible... such things would be entitled *noumena* (*intelligibilis*).... For if the senses represent to us something merely *as it appears,* this something must also in itself be a thing, and an object of a non-sensible intuition, that is, of the understanding. In other words, a [kind of] knowledge must be possible, in which there is no sensibility, and which alone has reality that is absolutely objective" (A 249), in Immanuel Kant, *Critique of Pure Reason,* trans. Norman Kemp Smith [Basingstoke, UK: Palgrave Macmillan, 2003], 265–67, original emphasis). By "categories," Kant refers to quantity, quality, relation, and modality, which he takes to be the conditions of all forms of human experience—conditions that exist transcendentally, beyond human experience.

26. Barry Stroud, *The Quest for Reality: Subjectivism and the Metaphysics of Colour* (Oxford: Oxford University Press, 2000), 69–95, 118–44, uses color to critique our "metaphysical urge" (209) to posit an objective reality based on what we sense subjectively. I am grateful to Michael Colson for pointing me to Stroud's book.

27. The English term "the Enlightenment" seems to derive from a German term, *Aufklärung,* for French philosophy in the eighteenth century. According to the *OED,* the earliest usage of the term in English dates from the 1860s—more than a hundred years *after* the phenomenon being designated (*OED,* "enlightenment" 2). Associations among (1) Newton's experiments with light, (2) rational inquiry, and (3) the democratic public spheres of England and Holland are pursued in the chapter "All Was Light" in Mordechai Feingold, *The Newtonian Moment: Isaac Newton and the Making of Modern Culture* (New York: New York Public Library, 2004), 143–67. The ways in which Locke's ideas about language dictated the nature of writings about optical experiments is Geoffrey Cantor's subject in "Light and Enlightenment: An Exploration of Mid-Eighteenth-Century Modes of Discourse," in *The Discourse of Light from the Middle Ages to the Enlightenment,* ed. David C. Lindberg (Los Angeles: Clark Library, 1985), 69–106.The social parameters of experimental discourse are set in place by Andrew Barnaby and Lisa J. Schnell, *Literate Experience: the Work of Knowing in Seventeenth-Century English Writing* (New York: Palgrave Macmillan, 2002), 11–54.

28. Donne, "The Extasie," in *Poems, by J.D.,* sig. NN3v (see intro., n. 3).

29. On the extramission theory of vision see David C. Lindberg, *Theories of Vision from Al-Kindi to Kepler* (Chicago: University of Chicago Press, 1976), 3–6, and Willem

van Hoorn, *As Images Unwind: Ancient and Modern Theories of Visual Perception* (Amsterdam: Amsterdam University Press, 1972), 42–71.

30. James Elkins, *The Object Stares Back: On The Nature of Seeing* (New York: Simon and Shuster, 1996), 46–85.

31. "Perceive" is derived from (via Anglo-Norman *perceivre*) the classical Latin *percipere,* meaning to take possession of, seize, get, obtain, receive, gather, collect, to apprehend with the mind or senses, to understand, perceive, from *per* + *capere,* to take, seize, lay hold of (*OED,* "perceive" etymology).

32. Christopher Rowell, "A Seventeenth-Century 'Cabinet' Restored: The Green Closet at Ham House," *Apollo* 143 (April 1996): 18–24. Further references to Rowell's article are cited in the text. Additional details in my description of the Green Closet are taken from the National Trust guidebook to Ham House: Christopher Rowell, Cathal Moore, and Nino Strachey, *Ham House,* rev. ed. (London: National Trust, 1999). I am grateful to Victoria Bradley, House and Collections manager at Ham House, for help in securing a photograph of the Hilliard miniature; and to Nigel Byrne, assistant curator, for precisely measuring the room for me. On Charles's display spaces as models for Murray's closet, see Linda Levy Peck, *Consuming Splendor: Society and Culture in Seventeenth-Century England* (Cambridge: Cambridge University Press, 2005), 180.

33. *The Life of Edward, First Lord Herbert of Cherbury,* written by himself, ed. J. M. Shuttleworth (London: Oxford University Press, 1976), 60.

34. Rowell, "A Seventeenth-Century 'Cabinet' Restored," 21.

35. William Shakespeare, *Twelfth Night, or What You Will,* in *Mr. William Shakespeares Comedies, Histories, & Tragedies,* sig. Y4 (see intro., n. 3), numbered 1.5.223–25 in William Shakespeare, *The Complete Works,* ed. Stanley Wells and Gary Taylor, 2nd ed. (Oxford: Clarendon Press, 2005). Unless otherwise indicated, further quotations from Shakespeare's plays are taken from the 1623 first folio (hereafter, F 1623) but are cited in the text using act, scene, and line numbers from the Oxford edition.

36. John North, *The Ambassadors' Secret: Holbein and the World of the Renaissance* (London: Hambledon and London, 2002), 247–48, 318.

37. The portrait of Erasmus (on loan to the National Gallery, London) is reproduced as plate 78 and the portrait of More (now in the Frick Collection, New York) is shown as plate 90 in Susan Foister, Ashok Roy, and Martin Wyld, *Holbein's "Ambassadors": Making and Meaning* (London: National Gallery, 1997). The green curtain in the Erasmus picture hangs on rings from a rod and has partly been pulled back to show a shelf of books and a glass beaker beyond.

38. Rowell, "A Seventeenth-Century 'Cabinet' Restored," 20–21.

39. Vitruvius's recommendations are promulgated in Sir Henry Wotton, *The Elements of Architecture . . . from the Best Authors and Examples* (London: John Bill, 1624): a northern exposure is to be preferred for all rooms "that are appointed for gentle Motion, as *Galleries,* especially in warme Climes, or that otherwise require a steadie and vnuariable light, as *Pinacothecia* (saith *Vitruuius*) by which he intendeth, (if I may guesse at his Greeke, as wee must doe often euen at his Latine) certaine *Repositories* for workes of rarity in Picture or other Arts, by the Italians called *Studioli,* which at any other Quarter, where the course of the *Sunne* doth diuersifie the *Shadowes,* would loose much of their grace" (sig. A4v). Murray had accompanied Prince Charles, the Duke of Bucking-

ham, and Watton on the 1623 diplomatic mission to woo the Spanish Infanta as a wife for Charles. The example of Felipe II as a collector of Italian painting inspired all four Englishmen.

40. Rowell, "A Seventeenth-Century 'Cabinet' Restored," 22.

41. Stephen J. Campbell, "The Study, the Collection, and the Renaissance Self," in *The Cabinet of Eros: Renaissance Mythological Painting and the Studiolo of Isabella d'Este* (New Haven, CT: Yale University Press, 2004), 29–57 (further quotations are cited in the text). Barbara Stafford studies the visual regimes of Renaissance wonder cabinets—the cues they provided for thought and feeling—in "Artificial Intensity: The Optical Technologies of Personal Reality Enhancement," in *Center or Margin: Revisions of the English Renaissance in Honor of Leeds Barroll,* ed. Lena Cowen Orlin (Selinsgrove, PA: Susquehanna University Press, 2006), 291–305. More mundane uses of closets—and further down the social scale—are studied in Lena Cowen Orlin, *Locating Privacy in Tudor London* (Oxford: Oxford University Press, 2007), 296–396.

42. Derrida, *The Truth in Painting,* 169.

43. Jacques Derrida, *Of Grammatology,* trans. Gayatri Charavorty Spivak, corrected ed. (Baltimore, MD: The Johns Hopkins University Press, 1998), 158. The context for Derrida's aperçu is nostalgia in Rousseau's writings, in particular, Rousseau's verbal evocations of his mother and his mistress Thérèse Levasseur: "*There is nothing outside of the text* [there is no outside-text; *il n'y a pas de hors-texte*]. . . . What we have tried to show by following the guiding line of the 'dangerous supplement,' is that in what one calls the real life of these existences 'of flesh and bone,' beyond and behind what one believes can be circumscribed in Rousseau's text, there has never been anything but writing; there have never been anything but supplements, substitutive significations which could only come forth in a chain of differential references" (158–59).

44. Ludwig Wittgenstein, *Remarks on Color,* ed. G. E. M. Anscombe, trans. Linda L. McAlister and Margarete Schättle (Berkeley: University of California Press, 1978), part 3, sec. 61. Unfortunately, the remarks on color have been separated by Wittgenstein's editors from his remarks on other matters, which have been published separately (see note 46). Further quotations from *Remarks on Color* are cited in the text by part and section number. Critical analysis of Wittgenstein's reflections are provided by Jonathan Westphal, *Colour: Some Philosophical Problems from Wittgenstein* (Oxford: Blackwell, 1987).

45. Elsewhere in *Remarks on Color,* Wittgenstein draws a distinction between the statements "I feel X" ("Ich empfinde X") and "I observe X" ("Ich beobachte X") (1.57), echoed later as a distinction between "I see (hear, feel, etc.) X" ("Ich sehe [höre, fühle etc] X") and "I am observing X" ("Ich beobachte X") (3.261).

46. Ludwig Wittgenstein, *Culture and Value,* ed. G. H. Von Wright and Heikki Nyman, trans. Peter Winch (Chicago: University of Chicago Press, 1980), 84e. Further quotations from *Culture and Value* are cited in the text by fascicle number. In other passages, Wittgenstein allies Shakespeare's plays with dreams: "if Shakespeare is great, as he is said to be, then it must be possible to say of him: it's all wrong, things *aren't like that*—and yet at the same time it's quite right according to a law of its own" (83c; original emphasis).

47. Wittgenstein, *Remarks on Color,* 3.43 (original emphasis).

48. In Derrida, *Of Grammatology,* "supplement" is defined in these terms: "the concept of the supplement . . . harbors within itself two significations whose cohabitation

is as strange as it is necessary. The supplement adds itself, it is a surplus, a plentitude enriching another plenitude, the *fullest measure* of presence. . . . But the supplement supplements. It adds only to replace. It intervenes or insinuates itself *in-the-place-of;* if it fills, it is as if one fills a void. If it represents and makes an image, it is by the anterior default of a presence. . . . The sign is always the supplement of the thing itself" (144–45; original emphasis).

49. Derek Jarman, *Chroma: A Book of Color* (Woodstock, NY: Overlook Press, 1994), 63.

50. Gage, *Color and Culture,* 29–38.

51. Friedrich Nietzsche, *Morgenröthe,* trans. by R. J. Hollingdale as *Daybreak: Thoughts on the Prejudices of Morality* (Cambridge: Cambridge University Press, 1997), 182, with German text from Nietzsche, *Werke,* ed. Giorgio Colli and Mazzino Montinari (Berlin: De Gruyter, 1967–), series 5, 1:266. Further quotations in English are taken from Hollingdale's translation and are cited in the text by page number; quotations in German are taken from Colli and Montinari's edition and are cited by volume and page number.

52. Ball, *Bright Earth,* 17–18, surveys current scholarly opinion on the Greeks' color sense and concludes that the Greeks were much more interested in value than in hue.

53. J. D. Mollon, "Uses and Evolutionary Origins of Primate Colour Vision," in *Evolution of the Eye and Visual System,* ed. John R. Cronly-Dillon and Richard L. Gregory (Boca Raton, FL: CRC Press, 1991), 306–19. Mollon's hypothesis is tested against experiments and tissue analysis by scores of other biologists and is largely confirmed in a massive review article by B. C. Regan and others, "Fruits, Foliage and the Evolution of Primate Colour Vision," *Philosophical Transactions of the Royal Society: Biological Sciences* 356 (2001): 229–83.

54. R. Kuschel and T. Monberg, "'We don't talk much about colour here': A Study of Colour Semantics on Bellona Island," *Man* 9 (1974): 213–42, cited in Gage, *Color and Meaning,* 30 (see intro., n. 8), in a section entitled "Disdain for Color."

55. Gage, *Color and Culture;* Gage, *Culture and Meaning,* n. 20, n. 49; Lindberg, *Theories of Vision from Al-Kindi to Kepler;* Nicholas Pastore, *A Selective History of Theories of Visual Perception 1650–1950* (New York: Oxford University Press, 1971); Alex Byrne and David R. Hilbert, eds., *Readings on Color,* 2 vols. (Cambridge, MA: MIT Press, 1997).

56. Plato *Timaeus* 67c–68d, in *Plato: Complete Works,* ed. John M. Cooper (Indianapolis: Hackett, 1997), with Greek text from *Plato,* vol. 7, ed. R. G. Bury. Loeb Classical Library (Cambridge, MA: Harvard University Press, 1947). Further quotations, taken from Cooper's English edition, are cited in the text.

57. Plato *Timaeus* 68a. I am grateful to Daniel Richter for help in construing this passage (from the Bury edition). According to Richter, λαμπός (*lampros,* "bright") is a common word, often applied to the sun and the stars, while στίλβος (*stilbos,* "glittering," "glistening") is a rarer word, often applied to polished metal surfaces like shields and weapons.

58. According to Gage, "Greek and Roman Antiquity passed down to its posterity a set of assumptions about colour which were modified only slowly and which gave far more prominence to the value of light and shade than they gave to hue" (*Color and Culture,* 27)—a set of assumptions that were still operative in Descartes' speculations and

Newton's experiments with light in the seventeenth century. On Plotinus, see Eyjólfur Kjaler Emilsson, *Plotinus on Sense-Perception: A Philosophical Study* (Cambridge: Cambridge University Press, 1988), 36–62; on Ficino, see Michael J. B. Allen, "The Soul as Rhapsode: Marsilio Ficino's Interpretation of Plato's *Ion*," in *Studies in Marsilio Ficino's Plato's Third Eye* (Aldershot, UK: Variorum, 1994), XV:125–48; on Kepler see Lindberg, *Theories of Vision from Al-Kindi to Kepler,* 188, and Lindberg, "Laying the Foundations of Geometrical Optics: Maurolico, Kepler, and the Medieval Tradition," in *The Discourse of Light,* 3–65; on Newton, see Willem van Hoorn, *As Images Unwind: Ancient and Modern Theories of Visual Perception* (Amsterdam: Amsterdam University Press, 1972), 213–20, and A. Rupert Hall, *All Was Light: An Introduction to Newton's* Opticks (Oxford: Clarendon Press, 1993), 127–63. Descartes' insistence in *Principles of Philosophy* that proper objects of knowledge as "clear and distinct" is taken up in chapter three.

59. Aristotle *De Sensu* 439.a.23–25. From διαφάνεια comes the English word "diaphanous," which, according to the *OED,* entered the language in the early seventeenth century with specific reference to Aristotle ("diaphanous" *a.*), as well as the less familiar "diaphaneity," imported as a scientific term in the 1660s. Aristotle's theory will occupy us in more detail in chapter two.

60. Pliny *Natural History* 35.7, trans. Philemon Holland as *The historie of the vvorld: common called, The naturall historie of C. Plinius Secundus* (London: Adam Islip, 1634), sig. ZZ2v. See also Gage, *Color and Culture,* 29.

61. Gage, *Color and Culture,* 29–30.

62. Thomas Browne, *Pseudodoxia Epidemica, or Enquiries into very many perceived tenents and commonly presumed truths* (London: Edward Dod, 1646), sig. SS1v. The whole passage on the coloration of plants begs the question: "Thus although a man understood the generall nature of coloures, yet were it no easie probleme to resolve, Why grasse is green? Why Garlick, Molyes, and Porrets have white roots, deep green leaves, and blacke seeds? Why severall docks, and sorts of Rhubarb with yellow roots, send forth purple flowers? Why also from Lactary or milky plants which have a white and lacteous juice dispersed through every part, there arise flowers blue and yellow? Moreover beside the specificall and first digressions ordained from the Creation, which might bee urged to salve the variety in every species; why shall the marvaile of Peru produce its flowers of different colours, and that not once, or constantly, but every day and variously? Why Tulips of one colour produce some of another, and running through almost all, should still escape a blew? And lastly, why some men, yea and they a mighty and considerable part of mankinde, should first acquire and still retaine the glosse and tincture of blacknesse? which who ever strictly enquires, shall finde no lesse of darknesse in the cause, then blacknesse in the effect it selfe" (sigs. SS1v–SS2). Compare Aristotle (attr.) *On Plants* 827.b.19–33.

63. Rembert Dodoens, *A Niewe Herball, or Historie of plants* (Antwerp: Henry Loë for Gerard Dewes, 1578); John Gerard, *The Herball or General Historie of Plantes* (London: John Norton, 1597); William Lawson, *A New Orchard and Garden* (London: Roger Jackson, 1623); Hugh Plat, *The Garden of Eden* (London: William Leake, 1652).

64. Zirka Z. Filipczak, *Hot Dry Men, Cold Wet Women: The Theory of Humors in Western European Art 1575–1700* (New York: American Federation of Arts, 1997), 14–23, 68–77.

65. Pliny, *Natural History*, trans. Holland, sig. GG5v.

66. According to Michael Wheeler, *Reconstructing the Cognitive World: The Next Step* (Cambridge, MA: MIT Press, 2005), Descartes' distinction between a sensing entity and a perceiving entity continues to haunt cognitive science. A move beyond that distinction is "the next step" that Wheeler advocates.

67. Katharine Park and Richard Kessler, "The Concept of Psychology," in *The Cambridge History of Renaissance Philosophy*, ed. Charles B. Schmitt (Cambridge: Cambridge University Press, 1988), 455–63.

68. Thomas S. Kuhn, *The Structure of Scientific Revolutions*, 3rd ed. (Chicago: University of Chicago Press, 1996).

69. Gage, *Color and Culture*, 153.

70. Aristotle *On the Soul* 3.8, ref. 432.a.6–9. Aristotle's position was reduced to a standard formula, "There is nothing in the intellect that was not first in the senses," cited in Katherine Park, "The Organic Soul," in *The Cambridge History of Renaissance Philosophy*, 470. Park's accounts of Renaissance ideas about both the embodied soul (464–84) and the intellective soul (485–534) remain indispensable. See also her unpublished thesis "The Imagination in Renaissance Psychology" (master's thesis, University of London, 1974). A thorough and discerning analysis of accounts of perception by Plato, Aristotle, Plotinus, Proclus, Porphyry, St. Augustine, and other ancient authorities—and Descartes' adaptation of their positions—is offered by Richard Sorabji, *Self: Ancient and Modern Insights about Individuality, Life, and Death* (Chicago: University of Chicago Press, 2006), 212–61. Arthur F. Kinney, *Shakespeare and Cognition: Aristotle's Legacy and Shakespearean Drama* (London: Routledge, 2006) explores what Aristotle's epistemology implies with respect to subject-object relations, particularly stage props like crowns, rings, bells, and wills.

71. Luigi Galvani's theory that muscles were moved by "animal electricity," proposed in the late eighteenth century, was confirmed, measured, and explained in experiments carried out by Emil du Bois-Reymond in the 1840s and was elaborated on and publicized by Hermann von Helmholtz in experiments and theoretical writings that continued into the 1870s. See Kathryn M. Olesko and Frederic L. Holmes, "Experiment, Quantification, and Discovery: Helmholtz's Early Physiological Researches, 1843–50," and Walter Kaiser, "Helmholtz's Instrumental Role in the Formation of Classical Electrodynamics," in *Hermann von Helmholtz and the Foundations of Nineteenth-Century Science*, ed. David Cahan (Berkeley: University of California Press, 1993), 50–108, 374–402.

72. Wright, *The Passions of the Mind in Generall*, sig. E2 (see intro., n. 10). Further quotations are taken from this edition and are cited in the text.

73. In genre these thirty books range from the medical (John Archer's *Every Man his own Doctor . . . Shewing How every one may know his own Constitution and Complection . . . Treating also of Air, Passions of Mind, Exercises of Body, Sleep, Venery & Tobacco, &c.* [1671, 1673, 1678]) to the philosophical (Nicholas Mosley's *Psychosophia: or, Natural and divine contemplations of the passions & faculties of the soul of man* [1653]) to the religious (Nicolas Coeffeteau's *A table of humane passions. With their causes and effects* [1621]) to the ethical (Wright's *The Passions of the Mind in Generall* [1604] and Edward Reynolds, *A Treatise of the Passions and Faculties of the Soul of Man* [1640]) to the political (Jean-François Senault's *The use of passions* [1649, 1671]) to the satirical (Thomas Jordan's *Pictures of the Passions,*

fancies, & affections. Poetically deciphered in variety of characters [1641]). For a context to all this discourse about the passions—much of it French-inspired—see Richard Scholar, *The* Je-Ne-Sais-Quoi *in Early Modern Europe* (Oxford: Oxford University Press, 2005), esp. "The Stroke of Passion: Pascal and the Poets," 125–81.

74. Marin Cureau de la Chambre, *The Characters of the Passions,* trans. R. W. (London: Thomas Newcomb for John Holden, 1650), sig. S6. Further quotations are cited in the text.

75. Lilli Alanen, *Descartes's Concept of Mind* (Cambridge, MA: Harvard University Press, 2003), 44–77. Alanen frames her argument as a corrective of, in particular, Gilbert Ryle's *The Concept of Mind* (1949). Damasio's *Descartes' Error* (see intro., n. 11) is a more recent, no less influential, instance of the same hyperrational view of Descartes.

76. René Descartes, *The Passions Of the Soule,* trans. anon. (London: A.C. for J. Martin and J. Ridley, 1650), sig. B5, coordinated with René Descartes, *Oevres philosophiques* (Paris: Garnier, 1973). Further quotations from the English translation are cited in the text by signature number; quotations from the French text, by volume and page number.

77. The word *emotion* in this and other passages in the English translation of Descartes' treatise carries the literal sense of an "out-moving" (Latin *ex* + *movere*). Understood as an agitation or disturbance of mind, Descartes' use of the word *emotion* predates the earliest citation in the *OED* by ten years (*OED,* "emotion" 4.a).

78. Thomas Hobbes, *Humane Nature: Or, The fundamental Elements of Policie* (London: T. Newcomb for Francis Bowman, 1650), sig. D6. Future quotations are cited in the text by signature number.

79. Alan Sinfield, *Faultlines: Cultural Materialism and the Politics of Dissident Reading* (Berkeley: University of California Press, 1992).

80. Edward Herbert, *De Veritate, prout Distinguitur a Revelatione, a Verisimili, a Possibili, et a Falsi,* 3rd ed. (London, 1645), trans. by Meyrick H. Carré as *On Truth in Distinction from Revelation, Probability, Possibility, and Error,* in *De Veritate* (Bristol: University of Bristol, 1937), 189, with interpolations in square brackets from the Latin text, sig. N4v. Further quotations are cited in the text.

81. In Antonio Damasio's formulation, "consciousness begins as the feeling of what happens when we see or hear or touch . . . it is a feeling that accompanies the making of any kind of image—visual, auditory, tactile, visceral—within our living organisms. Placed in the appropriate context, the feeling marks those images as ours and allows us to say, in the proper sense of the terms, that we see or hear or touch" (*The Feeling of What Happens,* 26 [see intro., n. 11]).

82. Philip Massinger, *The Maid of Honour* (London: John Beale for Robert Allot, 1632), sig. C4.

83. John Locke, *An Essay concerning Humane Understanding* (London: Elizabeth Holt for Thomas Basset, 1690), sig. G2, cited in the *OED* as an example of "consciousness," definition 4.a: "the state or faculty of being conscious, as a condition and concomitant of all thought, feeling, and volition." Further quotation from Locke's treatise is cited in the text by signature number.

84. Smith, *The Poems of Andrew Marvell,* 156.

85. Kermode and Walker, *Andrew Marvell,* 299.

86. Pliny, *Natural History,* trans. Holland, sig. ZZ4.

87. *The Raigne of K. Edward the Third* 2.1.1–2, in *The Shakespeare Apocrypha,* ed. C. F. Tucker Brooke (Oxford: Clarendon Press, 1908), 73. Further quotations are cited in the text by act, scene, and line numbers.

88. Marvell, *Miscellaneous Poems,* sig. H3.

89. *Middle English Dictionary* (Ann Arbor: University of Michigan Press, 1952–2001), *grenen,* v.2 (http://ets.umdl.umich.edu/m/med/ [September 12, 2006]). I am grateful to Sarah McNamer for this reference.

90. *The Poems of James VI of Scotland,* ed. James Craigie (Edinburgh: Blackwood, 1955), 1:80. Further quotations are cited in the text by page number.

91. Gage, *Color and Culture,* 155–56, discusses the larger phenomenon of black in seventeenth-century fashion and painting.

92. Phillip Stubbes, *The Anatomie of Abuses* (London: Richard Jones, 1583), sig. M2.

93. The phrase is Maria's in *Twelfth Night* 2.3.141.

94. Phillip Stubbes, *The Second part of the Anatomie of Abuses* (London: William Wright, 1583), sig. o7v.

95. Pliny's original Latin diction is cited from Pliny, *Naturalis Historiae,* ed. Karl Mayhoff, (Leipzig: Teubner, 1887), 5:239; Pliny, *Natural History,* trans. Holland, 35.6, sig. YY6v ("all colors").

96. On the distinction been colors *austeri* and colors *floridi* see Gage, *Color and Culture,* 15, and Ball, *Bright Earth,* 13–16.

97. John Lyly, *Campaspe,* sig. D1v (3.4.99–100 in Lyly, *Campaspe,* ed. G. K. Hunter, and Lyly, *Sappho and Phao,* in *The Revels Plays,* ed. David Bevington [Manchester: Manchester University Press, 1991], 98). Further quotations are taken from the original printing and cited in the text by act, scene, and line from Hunter's edition as well as by signature.

98. Hunter's footnote to this passage in his edition of *Campaspe* (97–98) traces the history of this topos and identifies "grace" with Pliny's term *charis.*

99. Ṣeneca, *Controversiae,* trans. M. Winterbottom. Loeb Classical Library. (Cambridge, MA: Harvard University Press, 1974), 1:xviii. Subsequent quotations from Seneca's *Controversiae* are taken from this translation and are cited in the text. See also Gage, *Color and Culture,* 15, 30.

100. Andrew Cowell, "The Dye of Desire: The Colors of Rhetoric in the Middle Ages," *Exemplaria* 11.1 (1999): 115–39.

101. Raymond Williams, *Marxism and Literature* (Oxford: Oxford University Press, 1977), 128.

102. Rei Terada, *Feeling in Theory: Emotion after the "Death of the Subject"* (Cambridge, MA: Harvard University Press, 2001), 156.

103. Eve Kosofsky Sedgwick and Adam Frank, *Touching Feeling: Affect, Pedagogy, Performativities* (Durham, NC: Duke University Press, 2003), 114.

104. Robert Cockcroft, *Rhetorical Affect in Early Modern Writing: Renaissance Passions Reconsidered* (Basingstoke, UK: Palgrave, 2003), 36. Further references to Cockcroft are cited in the text.

105. In *The Secret History of Emotion from Aristotle's* Rhetoric *to Modern Brain Science* (Chicago: University of Chicago Press, 2007), Daniel M. Gross states that "subjective experiences such as emotion have an essential social component and are best treated with *social analysis* of the sort developed in the rhetorical tradition, not scientific analy-

sis that must reduce social phenomena in certain critical ways so as to function properly as science" (33–34; original emphasis). Gross takes pains to distinguish his rhetorical/social approach to emotions from Damasio's scientific/anatomical approach. Like me, Gross locates a paradigm shift in the seventeenth century, when "a fascination with corporeal dynamics on the Aristotelian, and not the Cartesian, model" still held sway (40; see also 39–50).

106. Williams, *Marxism and Literature,* 125. Philippa Berry, Margaret Tudeau-Clayton, and their collaborators depart from similar premises in *Textures of Renaissance Knowledge* (Manchester: Manchester University Press, 2003): "the knowledge systems of Renaissance or early modern culture are multiple, unstable, complex and overlapping, sometimes contradictory and frequently strange. In consequence, we need to develop new interpretative skills, most importantly perhaps new practices of reading, in order to elucidate the subtle imbrication of different knowledges within this richly textured cultural context" (2).

107. *Norton Anthology of English Literature,* 683; Kermode and Walker, *Andrew Marvell,* 1157; Smith, *The Poems of Andrew Marvell,* 159; Andrew Marvell, *Poems,* ed. James Reeves and Martin Seymour-Smith (New York: Barnes and Noble, 1969), 174.

108. Plato *Ion* 534.b.

CHAPTER TWO

1. BL MS Lansdowne 30, no. 83, quoted in John Martin Robinson, *Arundel Castle: A Seat of The Duke of Norfolk E.M.: A Short History and Guide* (Chichester: Phillimore, 1994), 16.

2. On Larkin's sumptuous large-scale portraits, see Roy C. Strong, *William Larkin: Icons of Splendour* (Milan: Franco Maria Ricci, 1995). The largest collection of Larkin's work, begun by Thomas Howard, 1st Earl of Suffolk (1561–1626), hangs today in the Ranger's House, Blackheath, near London. An illustrated catalog is provided in John Jacob and Jacob Simon, *The Suffolk Collection: Catalogue of Paintings* (London: Greater London Council, 1975). See also Karen Hearn, ed., *Dynasties: Painting in Tudor and Jacobean England 1530–1630* (London: Tate Publishing, 1995), catalog nos. 135–36. On the social cachet of red, an expensive hue to obtain, see Jane Schneider, "Fantastical Colors in Foggy London: The New Fashion Potential of the Late Sixteenth Century," in *Material London, ca. 1600,* ed. Lena Cowen Orlin (Philadelphia: University of Pennsylvania Press, 2000), 107–27.

3. Catherine Richardson, personal communication, January 5, 2006. I am grateful to Vanessa Harding for alerting me to Richardson's research and putting me into contact with her. Richardson's *Domestic Life and Domestic Tragedy in Early Modern England: The Material Life of the Household* (Manchester, UK: Manchester University Press, 2007), provides tables summarizing the data base of inventories (210–26), as well as a masterly survey of "Objects and Spaces in the Early Modern House" (64–103).

4. William Harrison, "The Description of England," in Raphael Holinshed, *The First and Second Volumes of Chronicles* (London: Henry Denham, 1587), vol. 1, sig. R3. Further quotations are cited in the text by volume and signature numbers.

5. Paul Hentzner, *Itinerarium Germaniae, Galliae, Angliae, Italiae* (1612), trans. by Richard Bentley, ed. by Horace Walpole, as *Paul Hentzner's Travels in England, During*

the Reign of Queen Elizabeth (London: Edward Jeffrey, 1797), 64. Further quotations are cited in the text by page number and refer to the translated edition.

6. A. Reid Barbour similarly treats "stuff" as a conceptual category in "Nashe and the Stuff of Prose," *Deciphering Eliabethan Fiction* (Newark: University of Delaware Press, 1993), 64–81.

7. Patricia Fumerton, *Cultural Aesthetics: Renaissance Literature and the Practice of Social Ornament* (Chicago: University of Chicago Press, 1991); Margreta de Grazia, Maureen Quilligan, and Peter Stallybrass, eds., *Subject and Object in Renaissance Culture* (Cambridge: Cambridge University Press, 1996); Anne Rosalind Jones and Peter Stallybrass, *Renaissance Clothing and the Materials of Memory* (Cambridge: Cambridge University Press, 2000); Jonathan Gil Harris and Natsha Korda, eds. *Staged Properties in Early Modern English Drama* (Cambridge: Cambridge University Press, 2000); and Peck, *Consuming Splendor* (see chap. 1, n. 32).

8. William Shakespeare, *Henry V,* in *Mr. William Shakespeares Comedies, Histories, & Tragedies,* sig. H6v (see intro., n. 3); and Shakespeare, *The Complete Works,* 3.5.16 (see chap. 1, n. 35).

9. James Thaxter Williams, *The History of Weather* (Commack, NY: Nova Science Publishers, 1998). Brian Fagan, in *The Little Ice Age: How Climate Made History 1300–1850* (New York: Basic Books, 2000), warns, "A modern European transported to the height of the Little Ice Age would not find the climate very different, even if winters were sometimes colder than today and summers very warm on occasion, too. There was never a monolithic deep freeze, rather a climatic seesaw that swung constantly backwards and forwards, in volatile and sometimes disastrous shifts" (48; see also xi–xviii, 47–59). Elaine Barrow and Mike Hulme stress the equitability of the British climate due to the land's maritime position, its location in the path of mid-latitude westerly winds, and its proximity to the mild waters of the northeast Atlantic Ocean ("Describing the Surface Climate of the British Isles," in *Climates of the British Isles, Past and Future* [London: Routledge, 1997], 33; see also 33–62).

10. H. H. Lamb, "The Climate Problem," in *Climate, History, and the Modern World,* 2nd ed. (London: Routledge, 1995), 8–20, and "How We Can Reconstruct the Past Record," 74–105.

11. Data available at http://www.met-office.gov.uk/climate/uk/averages/19712000/area/england.html (accessed May 5, 2005).

12. Lamb, "The Climate Problem," figures 30 and 31 (pages 84–85).

13. "The soil is fruitful, and abounds with cattle, which inclines the inhabitants rather to feeding than ploughing, so that near a third part of the land is left uncultivated for grazing" (Walpole, *Paul Hentzner's Travels in England,* 62).

14. Thomas Platter, *Beschreibung der Reisen durch Frankreich, Spanien, England und die Niederlande 1595–1600,* trans. by Clare Williams as *Thomas Platter's Travels in England 1599* (London: Jonathan Cape, 1937), 185. Further references to this book are given in the text and refer to the translated edition.

15. Joan Thirsk, *The Rural Economy of England* (London: Hambledon, 1984), 67; Robin A. Butlin, "The Enclosure of Open Fields and the Extinction of Common Rights in England *circa* 1600–1750: A Review," in *Change in the Countryside: Essays on Rural England, 1500–1900,* ed. H. S. A. Fox and R. A. Butlin (London: Institute of British Geographers,

1979), 65–82; B. K. Roberts, "Field Systems of the West Midlands," in *Studies of Field Systems in the British Isles,* ed. Alan R. H. Baker and Robin A. Butlin (Cambridge: Cambridge University Press, 1973), 188–231.

16. John Norden, *The Surueyors Dialogue* (London: Hugh Astley, 1607), sig. Q7v (original emphasis). Further quotations are cited in the text by signature number.

17. Folger MS V.b.232 has been reproduced as *The Trevelyon Miscellany of 1608* (Seattle: University of Washington Press, 2007). The Wormsley manuscript has been reproduced, with elaborate commentary and cross-references to the Folger manuscript, in Nicolas Barker, ed., *The Great Book of Thomas Trevilian: A facsimile of the manuscript in the Wormsley Library,* 2 vols. (London: Roxburghe Club, 2000). Further references to the Wormsley manuscript are to this edition and are cited by volume and page numbers.

18. This type of inlay using ancient stones was known as Cosmati work, after the Cosmatus family of Rome, who specialized in such work in the fourteenth century. A full account of the materials and techniques of this craft tradition, as well as the history and iconography of the Westminster installation, is offered by Richard Foster, *Patterns of Thought: The Hidden Meaning of the Great Pavement of Westminster Abbey* (London: Cape, 1991). Specimens of the green porphyry and other stones are illustrated in figures 23–38 (on pages 36–37), and the pavement itself in figure 13, as well as in figures showing details. See also figure 41 in Foister et al., *Holbein's "Ambassadors"* (see chap. 1, n. 35), where the Great Pavement as Westminster is offered as an analogue for the mosaic floor in Holbein's group portrait if not its actual source.

19. Henry S, Turner, *The English Renaissance Stage: Geometry, Poetics, and the Practical Spatial Arts 1580–1630* (Oxford: Oxford University Press, 2006), calls attention to the superimpositions in early modern English (and in early modern English culture) among "plat," "plot," and "platform," with reference to surveying, garden design, script writing, and performance spaces. On "landscape" as a critical term, see Garrett A. Sullivan, Jr., *The Drama of Landscape: Land, Property, and Social Relations on the Early Modern Stage* (Palo Alto, CA: Stanford University Press, 1998), 1–6, who highlights the complicated relations between typographical features and dramatic representations of those features.

20. Clive Hicks, *The Green Man: A Field Guide* (Helboughton, Norfolk: Compassbooks, 2000), 34–63.

21. [Julia Hamilton Somerset,] Lady Raglan, "The Green Man in Church Architecture," *Folklore* 50.1 (1939): 45–57. Hicks, *The Green Man,* provides the most balanced account of this complicated phenomenon (1–12). Skepticism about mythic interpretations is also registered by Fran and Goeff Doel, *The Green Man in Britain* (Stroud, Gloucestershire: Tempus, 2001), who likewise note that the very name "the green man" is a modern coinage that did not exist in the sixteenth and seventeenth centuries, except as the name for Robin Hood or another forester on alehouse signs (13–24).

22. Hicks, *The Green Man,* 85–86.

23. Kathleen Basford, *The Green Man* (1978; repr. Cambridge: D. S. Brewer, 1996), 9–14.

24. Fran and Geoff Doel's warning against romanticizing the leaf masks in medieval churches rings true: "although nature is seen by the environmentalists as entirely on the side of enlightened man against the forces of industrialisation, commercialisation and politics which threaten the habitat of the planet, early man had a more ambivalent atti-

tude towards the forces of nature which could destroy him" (*The Green Man in Britain,* 117). Jeanne Addison Roberts, in *The Shakespearean Wild: Geography, Genus, and Gender* (Lincoln: University of Nebraska Press, 1991), identifies linkages in Shakespeare's plays, especially the comedies set in forests, between the wildness males perceived in nature and the wildness they perceived in women.

25. It was during the period of his exile that Heere probably painted the huge allegorical portrait of Henry VIII and his heirs that hangs today at Studeley Castle, Gloucestershire, and possibly the often-reproduced panel from the British Royal Collection showing Queen Elizabeth enacting the judgment of Paris—by keeping the golden apple for herself. See Hearn, *Dynasties,* catalog nos. 29 (*Elizabeth I and the Three Goddesses*) and 35 (*The Family of Henry VIII: An Allegory of the Tudor Succession*).

26. According to Clare Williams's introduction to *Thomas Platter's Travels in England,* (136–40), fully half of Hentzner's *Itinerarium,* is copied straight out of the Latin texts in Camden's *Britannia* (see note 29, below) and in Georg Braun and Franz Hogenberg's giant atlas *Civitates Orbis Terrarum* (1572). Platter, for his part, draws on Hentzner and other travelers who preceded him.

27. William Camden, *Britannia,* trans. by Philemon Holland as *Britain, or A chorographicall description of the most flourishing kingdomes, England, Scotland, and Ireland, and the ilands adjoyning* (London: F. Kingston, R. Young, and I. Leggatt for George Latham, 1637), sig. K2v.

28. Hearn, *Dynasties,* catalog no. 120, also reproduced and discussed in Jones and Stallybrass, *Renaissance Clothing and the Materials of Memory,* 50–52. The colors of the clothing worn by the figures in Heere's drawing confirm Dolly MacKinnon's conclusions from studies of charitable bequests in the seventeenth century: "Women were well versed in the colours and cloth-types (dyed and undyed) that denoted social status, as well as spirituality. Grey, green, brown, sorrel (red/brown), and red rough spun cloth were considered sober colours and were deemed appropriate for those below the middling sort such as husbandmen or the deserving poor," in contrast to the richly colored silks and satins deemed appropriate for those above the middling sort ("'Charity is worth it when it looks that good': Rural Women and Bequests of Clothing in Early Modern England," in *Women, Identities and Political Cultures in Early Modern Europe,* ed. Stephanie Tarbin and Susan Broomhall (Aldershot, UK: Ashgate, 2008). I am grateful to Dolly MacKinnon for sharing her findings with me.

29. Randle Holme, *The academy of armory, or, A storehouse of armory and blazon* (Chester: printed for the author, 1688), sig. HH4v. Further quotations are cited in the text by signature number.

30. In choosing the word "read," I follow the distinction Jones and Stallybrass draw between "fashion" and "livery" in *Renaissance Clothing and the Materials of Memory,* (17–21). For us, choice of clothing functions as a form of self-expression, even if the range of choice is dictated by what everyone else (or at least everyone else of our gender, age group, and financial means) is wearing. In traditional societies, by contrast, clothing functions as "livery," as garments and accessories that are not chosen by the wearer but de-*livered* to him. Livery functions as a readily readable indication of the wearer's social identity. Is there a deep-seated connection between *livery* and *livre,* between *liberata* and *liber*?

31. Edmund Campion and Meredith Hanmer, *Two Histories of Ireland* (Dublin: Society of Stationers, 1633), sigs. A6–A6v.

32. Edmund Spenser, "A View of the State of Ireland" (1596), in Campion and Hanmer, *Two Histories,* sig. D1. Further quotations are taken from this printing and are cited in the text.

33. It was perhaps Pliny the Elder who set the example in *A Natural History,* Book 19, chapter 4. In Pliny's account, the liminal character of gardens can be witnessed even in windows. Beds of flowers and sweet-smelling herbs were once held in such high esteem, Pliny reports, that "a man could not heretofore come by a Commoners house within the city, but he should see the windowes beautified with green quishins, wrought and tapissed with floures of all colours, resembling daily to their view the gardens indeed which were in out villages: insomuch, as being in the very heart of the city, they might think themselues in the country" (sig. B6v). Thieves have changed all that, Pliny regrets, necessitating bars and shutters. The green window-cloths and flower-embroidered cushions at Arundel Castle came, then, with a long pedigree.

34. Francis Bacon, *The Essayes or Counsels, Civill and Morall,* ed. Michael Kiernan (Cambridge, MA: Harvard University Press, 1985), 141 (original emphasis). Further quotations are cited in the text.

35. Bruce R. Smith, "Landscape with Figures: The Three Realms of Queen Elizabeth's Countryhouse Revels," *Renaissance Drama* n.s. 8 (1978): 52–115. On the design of sixteenth- and seventeenth-century gardens in England, see also Paula Henderson, *The Tudor House and Garden: Architecture and Landscape in the Sixteenth and Seventeenth Centuries* (New Haven, CT: Yale University Press, 2005), esp. 179–211; John Dixon Hunt, *Garden and Grove: The Italian Renaissance Garden in the English Imagination, 1600–1750* (Princeton, NJ: Princeton University Press, 1986); and Roy C. Strong, *The Renaissance Garden in England* (London: Thames and Hudson, 1979). Sixteenth- and seventeenth-century writings on gardens by the likes of Bacon, Marvell, Milton, Evelyn, and others are usefully collected in John Dixon Hunt and Peter Willis, eds., *The Genius of the Place: The English Landscape Garden, 1620–1820* (New York: Harper & Rowe, 1975), 48–136. The close relations between interior galleries and external gardens are traced in Orlin, *Locating Privacy in Tudor London,* 234–38 (see chap. 1, n. 41).

36. The designs are reproduced in Rowell et al., *Ham House* (see chap. 1, n. 30), 53 (Smythson) and 54–55 (Slezer and Wyck).

37. John Maplet, *A Greene Forest, or a Naturall Historie* (London: Henry Denham, 1567), sig. A6. Further quotations are cited in the text by signature number.

38. Francis Bacon, *Sylva Sylvarum, or A Naturall History in Ten Centuries* (London: W. Lee, 1627), sig. A1. Further quotations are cited in the text by signature number.

39. Compare Aristotle: "All water in process of time first turns yellow-green on blending with the rays of the sun; it then gradually turns black, and this further mixture of black and yellow-green produces herb-green" (*On Colors* 794.b.25–29).

40. A succinct account of Aristotle's formulations about color vis-à-vis other ancient theorists is provided by Jonas Gavel, *Colour: A Study of its Position in the Art Theory of the Quattro- and Cinquecento* (Stockholm: Almqvist & Wiksell, 1979), 13–43. The rest of Gavel's book witnesses the dominant influence of Aristotle's ideas in the fifteenth and sixteenth centuries. See also Gage, *Color and Culture,* 11–27 (see intro., n. 8).

41. Helkiah Crooke, *ΜΙΚΡΟΚΟΣΜΟΓΡΑΦΙΑ; A Description of the Body of Man* (London: William Jaggard, 1615.), sig. NNN1. Further quotations from Crooke are cited in the main text by signature number.

42. Gage's chapter "Colour under Control: The Reign of Newton" (*Color and Culture,* 153–76) includes a full account of seventeenth-century experiments with color by Newton, Huyghens, and others. See also Hall, *All Was Light,* esp. 5–32 (see chap. 1, n. 56). A succinct scientific account of Newton's discoveries is provided by Gregory, *Eye and Brain,* 14–23 (see intro., n. 18).

43. This precise ordering is proposed by Gage, *Color and Culture,* 12–13, who compares and synthesizes Aristotle's remarks on hue in several treatises. In all these schemes, Gage concludes, "Green appears . . . to be the central intermediate colour between (black) earth and (white) water" (13). In his edition of *De Sensu* in Aristotle's *Parva Naturalia* (Oxford: Clarendon Press, 1955), 206, David Ross interprets the passage at 442. a.18–25 as implying that blue and violet are at the center of the spectrum. Most medieval and Renaissance commentators, however, put green in that position. I am grateful to Daniel Richter for his help in construing the Greek text.

44. On Fludd, see Gage, *Color and Culture,* figures 1 (page 9) and 133 (page 171).

45. In *Bright Earth,* Philip Ball states the situation concisely: "While barely a dozen natural dyestuffs proved stable enough to be useful in the ancient and medieval world, more than four thousand synthetic dyes now bring color to our industrialized societies" (33). Despite the changes in production, some Renaissance names survive today in catalogs of high-end artists' pigments, among them "sap green" (diarylide yellow + hydrated synthetic iron oxide + chlorinated phthalocyanine) and "terra verte" (natural iron oxide), as specified in the 2006 catalog of Williamsburg Art Materials.

46. The standard history of dyeing is Franco Brunello, *The Art of Dyeing in the History of Mankind,* trans. Bernard Hickey (Vicenza: Neri Pozza Editore, 1973), who offers an account of medieval and early modern practices (117–20). See also his chapter, "The Revolution of Synthetic Dyestuffs" in the nineteenth century (275–321). Carole Frick, *Dressing Renaissance Florence: Families, Fortunes, and Fine Clothing* (Baltimore, MD: The Johns Hopkins University Press, 2002), 101–3, 170–76, provides a catalog of sixteenth-century dyestuffs and their relative expensiveness. The epoch-marking shift in the nineteenth century is detailed by Esther Leslie, *Synthetic Worlds: Nature, Art, and the Chemical Industry* (London: Reaktion, 2005). See also Stuart Robinson, *A History of Dyed Textiles* (Cambridge, MA: MIT Press, 1969), 28–38, and François Delamare and Bernard Guineau, *Colors: The Story of Dyes and Pigments,* trans. Sophie Hawkes (New York: Abrams, 2000).

47. Nicholas Hilliard, *A Treatise Concerning the Arte of Limning,* ed. R. K. R. Thornton and T. G. S. Cain (Manchester: Carcanet, 1981), 62. Further quotations are cited in the text.

48. Henry Peacham, *The Arte of Dravving with the Pen, and Limming in Water Colours* (London: Richard Braddock for William Jones, 1606), sig. H3v. (Parts of this text were incorporated into *The Compleat Gentleman* in 1622, 1627, 1634, and 1661.)Further quotations are cited in the text.

49. Robert Herrick, "To the Virgins, to make much of Time," in *Hesperides: Or The Works Both Humane and Divine* (London: John Williams and Francis Eglesfield, 1648), sig. G7.

50. I can attest this by having examined numerous examples in the Victoria and Albert Museum, London, and the Burrell Collection, Glasgow, in October 2005.

51. Cited in Gage, *Color and Culture,* 154.

52. Ball, *Bright Earth,* 114–15 (see intro., n. 8).

53. For Alciati's original image, see Arthur Henkel, *Emblemata: Handbuch zur Sinnbildkunst des XVI. und XVII. Jahrhunderts* (Stuttgart: J. B. Metzler, 1967), col. 1292. The later version is reprinted, and the verses translated, in Andrea Alciati, *A Book of Emblems: The Emblematum Liber in Latin and English,* ed. and trans. John F. Moffitt (Jefferson, NC: McFarland, 2004), 139–40. Whitney's text is quoted from Geffrey Whitney, *A Choice of Emblemes* (Leiden: Plantyn, 1586), sigs. R3v-R4. Further quotations are taken from this edition and are cited in the text.

54. William Shakespeare, "A woman's face with Nature's own hand painted," in *Shake-speares Sonnets. Neuer before Imprinted* (London: Thomas Thorpe, 1609), sig. C1.

55. Paolo Lomazzo, *Trattato dell'Arte de la Pittura* (1584), trans. by Richard Haydocke as *A Tracte Containing th'Artes of Curious Paintinge Caruinge, & Buildinge* (Oxford: Joseph Barnes, 1598), sig. ¶5. Further quotations are cited in the text by signature number. On Lomazzo's substituted text and its connection with stage plays, see Tanya Pollard, *Drugs and Theater in Early Modern England* (Oxford: Oxford University Press, 2005), 81–100.

56. John Gage's account of "The colours of heraldry" in *Color and Culture,* 80–82, is indespensible.

57. Ball, *Bright Earth,* 15.

58. Gerard Legh, *The Accedence of Armorie* (London: Henrie Ballard, 1597), sig. B4v. Further quotations are cited in the text by signature number.

59. Lomazzo, sigs. LL1–LL1v, adapting Ludovico Dolce, *Dialogo . . . nell quale ragiona delle qualità, diuersità, e proprietà de I colori* (Venice: Giovanni Battista, Marchio Sessa, 1565), sigs. C4v–C5v. Dolce's treatise in turn incorporates and expands Antonio Telesio, *Libellus de Coloribus* (Venice, 1528), which has been republished as Antonius Thylesius, *On Colour 1528,* ed. Roy Osborne, trans. Don Pavey (London: Color Academy, Micro Academy, 2002). The section on sadness versus hope is one of Dolce's additions.

60. Bacon, *Sylva Sylvarum,* sigs. M6v–M7v (original emphasis). Further quotations are cited in the text. "Disgest" is a variant of "digest" in the sense of "To mature, or bring to a state of perfection, especially by the action of heat" (*OED,* "digest *v.,*" 8, *obs.*).

61. Alchemy's combination of technological and spiritual concerns as two intersecting discourses is made by Gage, "The Peacock's Tail," in *Color and Culture,* 139–52. According to Bette Jo Teeter Dobbs, *The Foundations of Newton's Alchemy, or "The Hunting of the Greene Lyon"* (Cambridge: Cambridge University Press, 1975), the seventeenth century witnessed a cleavage between these once allied concerns. Alchemy continued to provide the vocabulary for chemical experiments, and the basic premise of alchemy, the transmutability of metals, was accepted by Newton and Boyle (48–92).

62. Gareth Roberts, *The Languages of Alchemy* (London: British Library, 1997), 8.

63. Among Newton's manuscripts preserved at King's College, Cambridge, is one containing texts entitled "The hunting of ye green lyon," "The standing of ye glass for ye time of putrefaction & congelation of ye medecine," and "Notes upon ye hunting of ye green lyon" (Keynes MS 20, cited in Dobbs).

64. "The Rosary of the Philosophers" (1550; BL MS Add. 29,895, dated 1588), fol. 119v. Further quotations are cited in the text.

65. Adam McLean, ed., *The Rosary of the Philosophers* (Edinburgh: Magnum Opus Hermetic Sourceworks, 1980), provides detailed commentary on BL MS Add. 29,895. The first of the manuscript's 20 illustrations shows a fountain with three streams illustrating the compound state of humanity: mineral, vegetable, and spiritual. The last of the images, 127 leaves later, shows the resurrected Christ. The meditating reader's route from the Alpha of the creation of man to the Omega of Christ's resurrection comes via images depicting the marriage of the red male sun and the silver female moon. In a sequence repeated twice over, the sun and the moon marry, copulate, merge into a single hermaphroditic body, die, produce a golden soul that ascends toward heaven, and are resurrected by a golden rain. The green lion devouring the sun follows the second of these resurrections. Immediately after comes a representation of the Holy Trinity, followed by the final image of the resurrected Christ.

66. Roger Bacon (attr.), *The Mirror of Alchimy Composed by the Thrice-Famous and Learned Fryer, Roger Bachon* (1597), ed. Stanton J. Linden (New York and London: Garland, 1992), 13.

67. Maplet, *A Greene Forest, or a Naturall Historie,* sig. A7v.

68. George Ripley, *The Compound of Alchymy, Ed., Ralph Rabbards. (1591),* ed. Stanton J. Linden (Aldershot, UK: Ashgate, 2001), 63.

69. Michel Foucault,defines *èpistême* as "the total set of relations that unite, at a given period, the discursive practices that give rise in epistemological figures, sciences, and possibly formalized systems" (*The Archeology of Knowledge,* trans. A. M. Sheridan Smith [New York: Pantheon, 1972], 191). On analogy as the *èpistême* specific to the sixteenth and early seventeenth centuries, see Foucault, *The Order of Things: An Archeology of the Human Sciences,* (New York: Pantheon, 1970), 17–44.

70. "The Table of Hermes," the ur-text of the whole alchemical tradition, is printed in Bacon, *The Mirror of Alchimy,* 16.

71. The Wormsley editor entertains the possibility of an alchemical connection but cites a reference in Pierre Erondelle's *The French Garden* (1605), implying that "The Green Dragon" was the name of a shop where anything could be had (Barker, *The Great Book of Thomas Trevilian,* 1:12, 49–53).

72. Numerous instances in poems by Donne, Marvell, and Milton, among others, have been pointed out by Roberts, *The Languages of Alchemy,* and by Lyndy Abraham, *Marvell and Alchemy* (Aldershot, UK: Scolar, 1990).

73. Abraham, *Marvell and Alchemy,* 22–23.

74. Marvell, *Miscellaneous Poems,* sig. I1 (see ch. 1, n. 1); Abraham, *Marvell and Alchemy,* 92.

75. My summary account of the operations of cones and rods is informed by Richard A. Normann, Ido Perlman, and Peter E. Hallett, "Cone Photoreceptor Physiology and Cone Contributions to Color Vision," in *The Perception of Color,* ed. Peter Gouras (Boca Raton, FL: CRC Press, 1991), 146–62. On the interactions between two sets of signals to produce the sensation of a third hue, see Bevil R. Conway, *Neural Mechanisms of Color Vision: Double-Oppoent Cells in the Visual Cortex* (Boston: Kluwer, 2002), 10–14. The reception of signals from the retina in the cerebral cortex is mapped by A. David Mil-

ner and Melvyn A. Goodale, *The Visual Brain in Action,* 2nd ed. (Oxford: Oxford University Press, 2006), 25–66. Milner and Goodale cite anatomical, electrophysical, and psychological research that confirms two distinct neural "channels" from the retina to the cerebral cortex, one that transmits color signals and one that transmits "broad-band" signals excluding color (28, 38). The two sets of signals are intermingled in the cerebral cortex (38).

76. A fifty-page review article by B. C. Regan, C. Julliot, B. Simmen, F. Viénot, P. Charles-Dominique, and J. D. Mollon, "Fruits, Foliage and the Evolution of Primate Colour Vision," *Philosophical Transactions of the Royal Society: Biological Sciences* 356 (2001): 229–83, by and large confirms a hypothesis current since the nineteenth century that a dichromatic system of green/red vision preceded the trichromatic system of green/red/blue that human beings and most higher primates possess today. It was, so runs the argument, an adaptive need to distinguish ripe fruit from green foliage that produced the older dichromatic system. The argument has received its most sustained treatment in a series of articles by J. D. Mollon, "Uses and Evolutionary Origins of Primate Colour Vision," in *Evolution of the Eye and Visual System,* ed. John R. Cronly-Dillon and Richard L. Gregory (Boca Raton, FL: CRC Press, 1991), 306–19. See also Miller and Goodale, *The Visual Brain in Action,* and Michael H. Rowe, "Trichromatic Color Vision in Primates," *News in Physiological Sciences* 17 (2002): 93–98.

77. Cited in Mellon, "'Tho' She Kneel'd,'" 21–23, and "Uses and Evolutionary Origins," 306–7, from Robert Boyle, *A Disquisition about the Final Causes of Natural Things . . . To which are Subjoyn'd . . . Some Uncommon Observations about Vitiated Sight* (London: John Taylor, 1688), sig. S6. Further reference to this text is taken from the original source and is cited by signature number.

78. Lindberg, *Theories of Vision from Al-Kindi to Kepler,* 178–208 (see chap. 1, n. 27), Ball, *Bright Earth,* 42–45, 195, 314; R. Steven Turner, *In the Eye's Mind: Vision and the Helmholz-Hering Controversy* (Princeton, NJ: Princeton University Press, 1994), 265–71; Gregory, *Eye and Brain,* 1997), 121–28; and Hurvich, *Color Vision* (see chap. 1, n. 3).

79. Plato *Timaeus* 45b. I am grateful to Daniel Richter for help in construing Plato's Greek text.

80. Aristotle "On the Generation of Animals" 744.a.6.

81. Aristotle "History of Animals" 492.a.1–4.

82. Aristotle (attr.) "Problems" 959.a.24–26.

83. Aristotle (attr.), *The Problemes of Aristotle, with other Philosophers and Physitians* (London: Godfrey Emondson, 1634), sig. B3.

84. Gavel, provides a convenient table in which the meanings and affects of 19 hues are tabulated according to 15 writers about color, including Lomazzo. "Hope" dominates the tabulation for green (*Colour,* 138–43).

85. Hearn, *Dynasties,* 185–86. The portrait of Elizabeth hangs today in the National Maritime Museum, Greenwich; the companion portrait of Henry, Prince of Wales, is in the collection of the Metropolitan Museum of Art, New York.

86. For illustrations of these possible exemplars see Hearn, *Dynasties,* catalog no. 74 (Clifford) and no. 120 (Lee).

87. Roy C. Strong, *The English Renaissance Miniature* (London: Thames and Hudson, 1983), 43.

88. Gavel, *Colour*,119–32. See also James Elkins, *The Poetics of Perspective* (Ithaca, NY: Cornell University Press, 1994), who demonstrates that the modern metaphor of "putting things in perspective" as an act of rationalizing has been imposed upon fifteenth- and sixteenth-century art rather than being derived from it.

89. Donne, *Poems, by J.D.*, sig. R1 (see intro., n. 3). Further reference to this work is cited in the text.

90. On the fusion of the erotic and the political in tournaments see Louis Adrian Montrose, *The Subject of Elizabeth: Authority, Gender, and Representation* (Chicago: University of Chicago Press, 2006); Roy C. Strong, *Splendor at Court: Renaissance Spectacle and the Theatre of Power* (Boston: Houghton Mifflin, 1973); and Frances Yates, "Elizabethan Chivalry: The Romance of the Accession Day Tilts," *Journal of the Warburg and Courtauld Institutes* 20 (1957): 4–25.

91. The classic study, albeit focused on an earlier period, is Mary Frances Wack, *Lovesickness in the Middle Ages: the Viaticum and Its Commentaries* (Philadelphia: University of Pennsylvania Press, 1990). On the early modern period, see Gail Kern Paster, *Humoring the Body: Emotions and the Shakespearean Stage* (Chicago: University of Chicago Press, 2004), 88–118, an account that is especially attentive to the etiology of green sickness in Galenic physiology; Carol Thomas Neely, *Distracted Subjects: Madness and Gender in Shakespeare and Early Modern Culture* (Ithaca, NY: Cornell University Press, 2004), 69–98; and Ursula Potter, "Greensickness in *Romeo and Juliet:* Considerations on a Sixteenth-Century Disease of Virgins," in *The Premodern Teenager: Youth in Society 1150–1850*, ed. Konrad Eisenbichler (Toronto: Centre for Reformation and Renaissance Studies, 2002), 271–91.

92. John Fletcher and William Shakespeare, *The Two Noble Kinsmen* (London: Thomas Cotes, 1634), sig. C4; and Shakespeare, *The Complete Works*, 1.3.90–91,.

93. Edward Herbert, *Occasional Verses* (London: Thomas Dring, 1665), sig. F2.

94. Hearn, *Dynasties*, 139.

95. Shuttleworth, *The Life of Edward, First Lord Herbert of Cherbury*, 38 (see chap. 1, n. 31). Further quotations are cited in the text by page number.

96. Strong, *The English Renaissance Miniature*, 184. Strong mistranscribes the motto as "*Magia Sympathia.*"

97. This parallel is noticed by Mary Edmond, *Hilliard and Oliver: The Lives and Works of Two Great Miniaturists* (London: R. Hale, 1983), 112.

98. Robert Burton, *The Anatomy of Melancholy* (Oxford: John Lichfield, 1632), title page.

99. Wright, *The Passions of the Mind in Generall*, sig. E2 (see intro., n. 10).

100. The result is *conditional* knowledge: "Now I hold neither that we can know everything, nor that we can know nothing; but I think there are some things which can be known. And they are those which are testified to by the presence of a faculty, though the faculty and the object are not necessarily in conformity with each other even when they are both present. For unless the intermediate conditions are favourable, each factor is confined to its own sphere. Accordingly, I hold that truth, being a matter of conformity between objects and faculties, is highly conditional. I conclude from the analysis of the laws and reciprocal relationship between truths that every faculty can be brought to conform with its appropriate object under certain conditions" (Edward

Herbert, *De Veritate, prout Distinguitur a Revelatione, a Verisimili, a Possibili, et a Falsi,* 3rd ed. [London, 1645], trans. by Meyrick H. Carré as *On Truth in Distinction from Revelation, Probability, Possibility, and Error,* in *De Veritate* [Bristol: University of Bristol Press, 1937], 78). Further quotations are taken from this translation and are cited in the text by page number.

101. Strong, *The English Renaissance Miniature,* 180.

CHAPTER THREE

1. Michel Foucault, considers "contrast" to be the dominant *èpistême* of the seventeenth and eighteenth centuries, succeeding "resemblance" (*The Order of Things,* 52–53 [see chap. 2, n. 69]).

2. Alexander Pope, *An essay on Man. In Epistles to a Friend.* Epistle 2 (London: J. Wilford, 1734), sig. D1v (original emphasis). Further quotations are cited in the text by signature number.

3. Frantz Fanon, *Black Skin, White Masks,* trans. Charles Lam Markmann (1952; New York: Grove Press, 1967) is probably the most famous in a series of books critiquing black/white thinking with respect to skin color. For the early modern period, see Kim F. Hall, *Things of Darkness: The Economies of Race and Gender in Early Modern England* (Ithaca, NY: Cornell University Press, 1995).

4. Although Aristotle and his successors had regarded black and white as colors in their own right–indeed as ur-colors from whose admixture all other colors are produced—debate about whether black and white were really colors began as early as the early fifteenth century, when Alberti in his treatise *On Painting* argued that, for a painter at least, "black and white are not true colours, but, one might say, moderators of colours" (quoted in Gage, *Color and Culture,* 118 [see intro., n. 8]). The modern status of black and white is summed up in the Wikipedia entry on "black": "Black can be defined as the visual impression experienced in directions from which no visible light reaches the eye. (This makes a contrast with whiteness, the impression of any combination of colors of light that equally stimulates all three types of color-sensitive visual receptors.)" (http://en.wikipedia.org/wiki/Black [accessed May 25, 2007])

5. On the *paragone* of *disegno* versus *colore,* see Gage, *Color and Culture,* 117–38.

6. See Ferdinand de Saussure, *Course in General Linguistics,* ed. Charles Bally and Albert Sechehaye, trans. Wade Baskin (New York: Philosophical Library, 1959), part 2, chap. 4, sec. 4: "A linguistic system is a series of differences of sound combined with a series of differences of ideas; but the pairing of a certain number of acoustical signs with as many cuts made from the mass of thought engenders a system of values; and this system serves as the effective link between the phonic and psychological elements within each sign" (120). With respect to the bar: "The *Nacht* : *Nächte* relation can be expressed by an algebraic formula *a* / *b* in which *a* and *b* are not simple terms but result from a set of relations. Language, in a manner of speaking, is a type of algebra consisting solely of complex terms" (122). Further quotations are taken from this edition and are cited in the text by part, chapter, and section number.

7. Jaques Derrida, "Différance" (1968), in *Margins of Philosophy,* trans. Alan Bass (Chicago: University of Chicago Press, 1982), 1–27. The images of *assemblage,* interlacing,

weaving, and web are insinuated near the beginning of the essay: "the assemblage to be proposed has the complex structure of a weaving, an interlacing which permits the different threads and different lines of meaning—or of force—to go off again in different directions, just as it is always ready to tie itself up with others" (3).

8. Jacques Derrida, "The Double Session" (1970), in *Dissemination,* trans. Barbara Johnson (Chicago: University of Chicago Press, 1981), 213. I am grateful to Shao-Ling Ma for drawing my attention to this essay.

9. Hilliard, *A Treatise Concerning the Arte of Limning,* 84 (see chap. 2, n. 47). Further quotations are taken from this edition and are cited in the text by page number.

10. Zuccarro's line drawing of Elizabeth is reproduced as catalog item 100 in Hearn, *Dynasties,* 153 (see chap. 2, n. 2). On Lomazzo's analysis of Titian's shadow effects, see chapter two.

11. Quoted in Gage, *Color and Culture,* 153.

12. Jane Schneider, "Fantastical Colors" (see chap. 2, n. 2).

13. Philip Sidney, *Syr P.S. His Astrophel and Stella Wherein the excellence of sweete poesie is concluded* (London: John Charlewood for Thomas Newman, 1591), sigs. B1, I1; Edmund Spenser, *Amoretti and Epithalamiom* (London: William Ponsonby, 1593), sig. A5v; and Samuel Daniel, *Delia and Rosamond Augmented. Cleopatra* (London: Simon Waterson, 1594), sig. C2v. The precisely chosen palette of colors in Shakespeare's sonnets—precisely chosen for their physiological significance—has been studied by Elizabeth D. Harvey, "Flesh Colors and Shakespeare's Sonnets," in *A Companion to Shakespeare's Sonnets,* ed. Michael Schoenfeldt (Oxford: Blackwell, 2007), 314–28.

14. Shakespeare, *Shake-speares Sonnets. Neuer before Imprinted,* sig. I2v (see chap. 2, n. 54).

15. Paul Kay, Brent Berlin, Luisa Muffi, and William Merrifield, "Color Naming Across Languages," in Hardin and Maffi, ed., *Color Categories in Thought and Language,* 21–56 (see chap. 1, n. 6).

16. On Pliny's specification of the four colors in Apelles' palate, see chapter one above, and Gage, *Culture and Culture,* 29–38.

17. The staging of Apelles' conversation with his beautiful sitter in John Lyly's comedy *Campaspe,* acted before Queen Elizabeth in the early 1580s, is discussed in chapter one.

18. Katharine Park and Eckhard Kessler credit Joannes Thomas Freigius with the invention of the word *psychologia* in 1575. See their succinct account of "The Concept of Psychology," in *The Cambridge History of Renaissance Philosophy,* ed. Charles B. Schmitt and Quentin Skinner (Cambridge: Cambridge University Press, 1988), 455–63.

19. The ways in which Western philosophers have answered these quesitons are explored in Paul J. J. M. Bakker and Johannes M. M. H. Thijssen, eds., *Mind, Cognition, and Representalism: The Tradition of Commentaries on Aristotle's* De Anima (Aldershot, UK: Ashgate, 2007). See especially Robert Pasnau, "The Mind-Soul Problem," 3–19, and Cees Leijenhorst, "Attention Please! Theories of Selective Attention in Late Aristotelian and Early Modern Philosophy," 205–30.

20. Plato *Timaeus* 35.a–b. Further quotations from Plato are cited in the text.

21. Aristotle *On the Soul* 413.b. Further quotations from Aristotle are cited in the text.

22. Richard Sorabji lays out the differences between Aristotle and Plato in terms of how each explains the felt unity in a person's perceptions: "Plato answers [in *Theaetetus* 184B–186E] that the senses must converge (*sunteinein*) on something unitary (*mia*), the soul (184D), and at 186A–187A he stresses the soul's reasoning activities as needed for these discriminations. Aristotle substitutes for soul one particular capacity of the soul, the common sense, and he repeatedly stresses that its role of comparing different types of sensible[s] requires it to be unitary" (*Self: Ancient and Modern Insights about Individuality, Life, and Death* [Chicago: University of Chicago Press, 2006], 246–47).

23. Even so subtle and sympathetic an editor as Thomas P. Roche, Jr., cannot resist providing an endnote to stanza xviii, when Alma the castle's lady makes her first appearance—an endnote that states baldly, and in advance of the tour, "Her castle is an allegory of the body, the mortal part of man" (Edmund Spenser, *The Faerie Queene,* ed. Thomas P. Roche, Jr. [London: Penguin, 1978], 1126). No mystery, no discovery, no leap from sense experience to rational thought.

24. Spenser, *The Faerie Queene,* 2.9.50.1–7. Further quotations from *The Faerie Queene* are cited in the text by book, canto, stanza, and line numbers.

25. Qutoed in Edmund Spenser, *The Faerie Queene,* Book 2, ed. Edwin Greenlaw (Baltimore, MD: The Johns Hopkins University Press, 1933), 278.

26. Quoted in ibid., 284. In his comment on 2.12.8, Upton seems to register a certain displeasure at Spenser's coyness: "See the 1st stanza, where the poet opens the allegory: nor has the reader any occasion to be put in mind, that this castle is the human body, and Alma the mind; and that this miscreated troop of besiegers are vain conceits, idle imaginations, foul desires, &c" (284).

27. Spenser, *The Faerie Queene,* ed. Roche, 1126.

28. Robinson, *Arundel Castle,* 18–19 (see chap. 2, n. 1).

29. Robinson, *Arundel Castle,* 43–60.

30. Sigmund Freud, *New Introductory Lectures on Psycho-Analysis,* vol. 23 in *The Complete Psychological Works,* ed. and trans. James Strachey (London: Hogarth Press, 1964), 73. Further quotations are cited in the text by page number.

31. Sigmund Freud, *The Interpretation of Dreams* (1900), vol. 4 in *The Complete Psychological Works,* ed. and trans. James Strachey (London: Hogarth Press, 1953), 227: "In the case of dreams in which the field of vision is full of movement and bright colors, in contrast to the drabness of other dreams, it is scarcely possible not to interpret them as 'dreams with a visual stimulus'; nor can one dispute the part played by illusions in the case of dreams characterized by noise and a confusion of voices."

32. Carl Jung, *Aion: Researches into the Phenomenology of the Self,* trans. R. F. C. Hull (New York: Pantheon, 1953), 8. Further quotations are cited in the text by page number. Jung's shadow also carries a racial coloring. In an account of his travels in Africa, Jung describes a series of dreams registering his conviction that Africans, to a much greater degree than Europeans, live in the shadow. In one of these dreams, Jung first wrestles with "a handsome, dark Arab of aristocratic, almost royal bearing" and later, having conquered him, compels his dark adversary, now seated in a perfectly white room, to read from "an open book with black letters written in magnificent calligraphy on milky-white parchment"—a book that Jung himself has written (Jung, *Memo-*

ries, Dreams, Reflections, ed. Aniela Jaffé, trans. Richard and Clara Winston [New York: Pantheon, 1965], 243).

33. Carl Jung, "A Study in the Process of Individuation" (1950), in *Archetypes and the Collective Unconscious,* trans. R. F. C. Hull, 2nd ed. (Princeton, NJ: Princeton University Press, 1968), 294. Further quotations are cited in the text by page number.

34. Jacques Lacan, "The Mirror Stage as Formative of the *I* Function" (1949), in *Ècrits,* trans. Bruce Fink (New York: Norton, 2006), 76. Further quotations are cited in the text by page number.

35. Jacques Lacan, "The Instance of the Letter in the Unconscious" (1957), in *Ècrits,* 414. In fine: "language, with its structure, exists prior to each subject's entry into it at a certain moment in his mental development" (413).

36. Marvell, *Miscellaneous Poems,* sig. I1v (see chap. 1, n. 1).

37. John Twigg, *The University of Cambridge and the English Revolution 1625–1688* (Cambridge: Cambridge University Press, 1990), 11–41.

38. On philosophical syncretism at Cambridge—and more generally in England—in the first half of the seventeenth century see Angelica Duran, *The Age of Milton and the Scientific Revolution* (Pittsburgh: Dusquesne University Press, 2007), 38–40; Barbara J. Shapiro, *A Culture of Fact: England 1550–1720* (Ithaca, NY: Cornell University Press, 2000), 182; Nicholas Murray, *World Enough and Time: The Life of Andrew Marvell* (New York: St. Martins Press, 2000), 15–22; John Dixon Hunt, *Andrew Marvell: His Life and Writings* (Ithaca, NY: Cornell University Press, 1978), 21–26; Aharon Lichtenstein, *Henry More: The Rational Thought of a Cambridge Platonist* (Cambridge, MA: Harvard University Press, 1962); and Rosalie Colie, *Light and Enlightenment: A Study of the Cambridge Platonists and Dutch Arminians* (Cambridge: Cambridge University Press, 1957). C. A. Patrides's anthology *The Cambridge Platonists* (Cambridge, MA: Harvard University Press, 1970) provides a representative range of writings by the thinkers in question.

39. Rosalie Colie, *"My Echoing Song": Andrew Marvell's Poetry of Criticism* (Princeton, NJ: Princeton University Press, 1970), 298.

40. Henry More, *A Platonick Song of the Soul,* ed. Alexander Jacob (Lewisburg, PA: Bucknell University Press, 1998), 151, 255. Quotations from More's poems are cited in the text by book, canto, stanza, and line numbers.

41. Christopher Tilmouth, *Passion's Triumph over Reason: A History of Moral Imagination from Spenser to Rochester* (Oxford: Oxford University Press, 2007) maps the same territory as a chronological three-part story in which neo-Stoic hostility to passion gives way to a neo-Aristotelian revaluation, followed by bifurcation into scientific reason versus libertine indulgence.

42. Raymond Williams, *Marxism and Literature* (Oxford: Oxford University Press, 1977), 121–27.

43. Richard Crashaw, "A Hymn to the Name and Honour of the Admirable Saint TERESA," in *Steps to the Temple; The Delights of the Muses; and, Carmen Deo Nostro* (London: Henry Herringman, 1670), sig. E8v. This poem was first printed in the 1646 edition of Crashaw's collected poems.

44. The publishing history of these three writers, at least in England, suggests how uneven this progression was. Descartes' *The Passions Of the Soule* was not reprinted during Marvell's lifetime, even though multiple editions of Descartes' *Discourse on Method,*

Meditations on First Philosophy, and *Principles of Philosophy* were published in England between 1649 and 1680, many of them in Latin. During the same period, La Chambre's residual ideas about spirits leaving the body had hardly been forgotten. No fewer than eight English versions of La Chambre's works on the passions appeared in the second half of the seventeenth century, the last of them, volume 2 of *The Characters of the Passions*, as late as 1693. Demand for Hobbes's *Humane Nature* was strong enough for three editions to be printed in 1650–1651, a swell of interest that the publication of *Leviathan* in 1651 helped to sustain. Three separate printings of *Leviathan* in 1651 were followed by further editions in 1676, 1678, 1680, and (in Latin) 1681.

45. Robert Burton, *The Anatomy of Melancholy*, ed. Thomas C. Faulkner, Nicolas K. Kiessling, and Rhonda L. Blair (Oxford: Clarendon Press, 1989), 1:152.

46. Edward Phillips, *The new world of English words, or, A general dictionary containing the interpretations of such hard words as are derived from other languages . . . together with all those terms that relate to the arts and sciences . . .* (London: E. Tyler for Nathaniel Brook, 1658), sig. C2 (original emphasis).

47. For a lively, sympathetic appreciation, see Angus Fletcher, "The Irregular Aesthetic of *The Blazing World*," *Studies in English Literature* 47.1 (2007): 123–41.

48. At the time of this writing, the two texts are most readily available in two different volumes, with two different editors and from two different publishers: Margaret Cavendish, *The Blazing World and Other Writings*, ed. Kate Lilley (London: Penguin, 1994); and Cavendish, *Observations upon Experimental Philosophy*, ed. Eileen O'Neill (Cambridge: Cambridge University Press, 2001). The first book listed does not include *Observations*.

49. Margaret Cavendish, *Observations upon Experimental Philosophy. To which is added, The Description of a New Blazing World* (London: A. Maxwell, 1666), sig. b*1v (emphasis to "both" added).

50. Anne Conway, *The Principles of the Most Ancient and Modern Philosophy*, trans. Allison P. Coudert and Taylor Corse (Cambridge: Cambridge University Press, 1996), 39. Further references to this work are cited by page number in the text.

51. "Now, some people are pregnant in body, and for this reason turn more to women and pursue love in that way, providing themselves through childbirth with immortality and remembrance and happiness, as they think, for all time to come, while others are pregnant in soul. . . . In my view, you see, when he makes contact with someone beautiful and keeps company with him, he conceives and gives birth to what he has been carrying inside him for ages" (Plato *Symposium* 209.a–c). Jeffrey Masten, in *Textual Intercourse: Collaboration, Authorship, and Sexualities in Renaissance Drama* (Cambridge: Cambridge University Press, 1997), pursues the homoerotic implications in this topos for collaborating playwrights like Beaumont and Fletcher.

52. Walter Raleigh (attr.), *Sir Walter Raleigh's Sceptick, or Speculations and observations of the magnificency and opulency of cities. His Seat of government. And letters to the Kings Majestie, and others of qualitie. Also, his demeanor before his execution* (London: William Bentley, 1651), sigs. B2–B3 (original emphasis). I am grateful to Gail Kern Paster for bringing this book to my attention.

53. On Barrow's attempts to reconcile spirit and matter see Betty Jo Teeter Dobbs, *The Foundations of Newton's Alchemy*, 99–102 (see chap. 2, n. 61); and Percy H. Osmond, *Isaac Barrow, His Life and Times* (Society for Promoting Christian Knowledge, 1944), 27–33.

54. A. Rupert Hall, *All Was Light*, 22–23 (see chap. 1, n. 58).

55. Francis Glisson, *De natura substantiae energetica, seu, De vita naturae* (London: E. Flesher, 1672), esp. sigs. B2–B2v.

56. Bacon, *The Advancement of Learning*, 93–94 (see chap. 1, n. 24).

57. Crooke, *ΜΙΚΡΟΚΟΣΜΟΓΡΑΦΙΑ*, sig. YY5v (see chap. 2, n. 41). Further quotations from Crooke are cited in the main text by signature number.

58. These particular sensations Crooke doesn't choose randomly but takes from Aristotle: "Each sense then is relative to its particular group of sensible qualities: it is found in a sense-organ as such and discriminates the differences which exist within that group; e.g. sight discriminates white and black, taste sweet and bitter, and so in all cases. Since we also discriminate white from sweet, and indeed each sensible quality from every other, with what do we perceive that they are different? It must be by sense; for what is before us is sensible objects. . . . Therefore discrimination between white and sweet cannot be effected by two agencies which remain separate; both the qualities discriminated must be present to something that is one and single" (*De Anima* 426.b.9–20).

59. Hall, *All Was Light*, 13–17.

60. Robert Boyle, *Experiments and Considerations Touching Colours* (London: Henry Herringhman, 1664), sigs. B7, B7v, C1v. Further quotations are cited in the text by signature number.

61. Michel de Montaigne, *Essais*, trans. by Charles Cotton as *Essays of Michael, seigneur de Montaigne in three books* (London: T. Basset, M. Gilliflower, and W. Hensman, 1685–1686), sig. PP6v. Further quotations are cited in the text by signature number.

62. An English translation had to wait until the twentieth century, when Meyrick H. Carré translated the 3rd Latin edition as *On Truth in Distinction from Revelation, Probability, Possibility, and Error* in *De Veritate* (Bristol, UK: University of Bristol Press, 1937). Carré's translation is the text used in this analysis, with occasional reference in parenthesis to the Latin text printed in the 3rd London edition. R. D. Bedford stresses the Neoplatonic and hermetic elements in Herbert's writing (*The Defence of Truth: Herbert of Cherbury and the Seventeenth Century* [Manchester, UK: Manchester University Press, 1979]). Eugene D. Hill is more interested in Herbert's anticipations of eighteenth-century deism (*Edward, Lord Herbert of Cherbury* [Boston: Twayne, 1987], 18–35).

63. Herbert, *On Truth in Distinction from Revelation, Probability, Possibility, and Error* in *De Veritate*, trans. Carré, 103–4.

64. More dedicates *A Platonick Song of the Soul* to his father, Alexander More, a graduate of Emanuel College, Cambridge: "You having from my childhood tuned mine ears to Spencers rhymes, entertaining us on winter nights, with that incomparable Peice of his, *The Fairy Queen*, a Poem as richly fraught with divine Morality as Phansy" (139).

65. 1 Corinthians 13:12 (*The Holy Bible containing the Old Testament, and the New; newly translated out of the original tongues . . .* [London: Robert Barker, 1616]). Unless otherwise noted, all quotations from the Bible are taken from this edition.

66. René Descartes, *The Correspondence*, vol. 3 of *The Philosophical Writings of Descartes*, ed. John Cottingham, Robert Stoothoff, Dugald Murdoch, and Anthony Kenny (Cambridge: Cambridge University Press, 1991), 361. Further quotations from Descartes' correspondence are cited in the text by volume and page number.

67. Textbooks for introductory philosophy courses have cast Descartes as the only begetter of empiricism and its discontents–a misperception that Antonio R. Domasio's otherwise salutary counterargument in *Descartes' Error: Emotion, Reason, and the Human Brain* has helped to maintain. My appreciation for the nuances, qualifications, and inconsistencies in Descartes' thought is indebted to Alanen, *Descartes's Concept of Mind* (see chap. 1, n. 72); Timothy Reiss, *Mirages of the Selfe: Patterns of Personhood in Ancient and Early Modern Europe* (Palo Alto, CA: Stanford University Press, 2004), 469–87; David E. Johnson, "Descartes's *Corps,*" *Arizona Quarterly* 57.1 (2001): 113–52; and John Sutton, *Philosophy and Memory Traces: Descartes to Connectionism* (Cambridge: Cambridge University Press, 1998).

68. René Descartes, "Principles of Philosophy," in vol. 1 of *The Philosophical Writings of Descartes,* trans. Cottingham, Soothoff, and Murdoch, 174–75.

69. René Descartes, *The Passions of the Soule,* (London: J. Martin and J. Ridley, 1650), sig. B11v. Further quotations are cited in the text by signature number.

70. Edward Reynolds, *A Treatise of the Passions and Faculties of the Soule of Man* (London: R. H. For Robert Bostock, 1640), sig. G3. Further quotations are cited in the text by signature number. In the dedicatory epistle, Reynolds remarks that it had been at the princess's insistence that he overcame his misgivings about his youthful work: "For so farre hath your Highnesse vouchsafed (having hapned on the sight of this Tractate) to expresse favour thereunto, as not onely to spend houres in it, and require a Transcript of it, but further to recommend it by your Gracious judgement unto publike view" (sig. A4).

71. John Davies, *Nosce Teipsum,* in *The Poems of Sir John Davies,* ed. Robert Krueger (Oxford: Clarendon Press, 1975), 20–23. Further quotations are are cited in the text by "elegy" and line numbers. Krueger's commentary includes a thorough account of Davies' borrowings from Cicero, La Primaudaye, Montaigne, and Mornay (325–28).

72. William Cornwallis, *A Second part of Essayes* (London: Edmund Mattes, 1601), sig. MM6v. Further quotations are cited in the text.

73. Thomas Browne, *Nature's Cabinet Unlock'd. Wherein is Discovered The Natural Causes of Metals, Stones, Precious Earths, Juyces, Humors, and Spirits . . .* (London: Edward Farnham, 1657), sig. o5v. Further quotations are cited in the text by signature number.

74. William Harvey, *Exercitatio Anatomica de Motu Cordis et Sanguinis in Animalibus* (Frankfurt: Fitzer, 1628; London, 1649), trans. as *The Anatomical Exercises of Dr. William Harvey . . . Concerning the Motion of the* Heart *and the* Blood (London: Francis Leach, 1653), sig. **6v (original emphasis).

75. Thomas Willis, *Cerebri Anatome* (1664), with anatomical illustrations by Christopher Wren, as discussed by Carl Zimmer, *Soul Made Flesh: The Discovery of the Brain—and How It Changed the World* (New York: Free Press, 2004).

76. Isaac Newton, "A Letter of Mr. *Isaac Newton* . . . containing his New Theory about *Light* and *Colours,*" in *Philosophical Transactions,* 19 February 1671/72, sig. HHHH2. On Newton's working hypotheses, see Hall, *All Was Light,* 127–63.

77. Pierre de La Primaudaye, *The French Academie, Fully Discoursed and finished in foure Bookes,* trans. Thomas Bowes, Richard Dolman, and W. P. (London: Thomas Adams, 1618), sig. MM6v.

78. Kenelm Digby, *Two Treatises, in the one of which, the nature of bodies; in the other, the nature of mans soule; is looked into: in way of discovery, of the immortality of reasonable soules* (Paris: Gilles Blaizot, 1644), sig. MM2. Further quotations are cited in the text by signature number.

79. Amid this range, green occupies a special place: white is cold and dry, but "blacke, as also greene, (which is neere of kinne to blacke) are growing colours, and are the dye of heate incorporated in aboundance of wett: as we see in smoake, in pitte-coale, in garden ground, and in chymicall putrefactions: all which are blacke; as also in yong herbes; which are generally greene as long as they are yong and growing" (Digby, *Two Treatises,* sig. KK3v).

80. Fulke Greville, "A Treatise of Humane Learning," in *Certaine Learned and Elegant Workes of the Right Honorable Fulke Lord Brooke, Written in his Youth, and familiar Exercise with Sir Philip Sidney* (London: E. P. for Henry Seyle, 1633), stanza 6, lines 1, 5–6, sig. D1v. Further quotations are cited in the text by stanza and line numbers.

81. Thomas Hobbes, *Humane Nature: Or, The fundamental Elements of Policie. Being a Discoverie Of the* Faculties, Acts, *and* Passions *of* The Soul of Man, *from their original causes; According to such Philosophical Principles as are not commonly known or affected* (London: T. Newcomb, 1650), sig. B9v (original emphasis). Further quotations are cited in the text by signature number.

82. Ralph Cudworth, *The True Intellectual System of the Universe: The First Part; Wherein, All the Reason and Philosophy of Atheism is Confuted; and Its Impossibility Demonstrated* (London: Richard Royston, 1678), Book 1, chap. 2, sec. 5, sigs. B3, B4v (original emphasis). Further quotations from Cudworth are taken from this edition and are cited in the text by book, chapter, and section numbers as well as signature numbers. An abridgement was published in 1732; a full reissue, in 1743.

83. Phillip Stubbes, *The Anatomie of Abuses Contayning a Discouerie, or Briefe Summarie of Such Notable Vices and Imperfections, as Now Raigne in Many Christian Countreyes of the Worlde: But (Especiallie) in a Verie Famous Iland Called Ailgna* (London: Richard Jones, 1583), title page. Further quotes are cited in the text by signature number.

84. John Locke, *An Essay concerning Humane Understanding,* sig. F3 (see chap. 1, n. 83). Further quotations are cited in the text by signature numbers.

85. Donna Haraway, "Situated Knowledges: The Science Question in Feminism and the Privilege of Partial Perspective," *Feminist Studies* 14.3 (1988): 582–83.

CHAPTER FOUR

1. Lucy Gent, *Picture and Poetry 1560–1620: Relations between literature and the visual arts in the English Renaissance* (Leamington Spa: James Hall, 1981), 6. In connection with "pictures" in poetry, Gent cites Abraham Fraunce, *The Third Part of the Countess of Pembroke's Yvychurch* (1592), ed. Gerald Snare (Berkeley: University of California Press, 1975), 9, 13, 14, 20.

2. *Horace, His Art of Poetrie Made English by Ben Iohnson,* in Ben Jonson, *Works* (1640), volume 2, repr. in *Ben Jonson,* vol. 8, ed. C. H. Herford, Percy Simpson, and Evelyn Simpson (Oxford: Clarendon Press, 1947), line 539, page 329, translating *Horatius de Arte Poetica,* line 378, printed on the facing page. Further quotations from Horace's Latin text

and from Jonson's translation are taken from this edition and are cited in the text by line numbers.

3. Lawrence I. Lipking, *The Ordering of the Arts in Eighteenth-Century England* (Princeton, NJ: Princeton University Press, 1970), provides a full account of this sorting-out process. Although as early as 1712, Anthony, Earl of Shaftesbury, had pronounced "comparisons and parallel[s] . . . between painting and poetry . . . almost ever absurd and at best constrained, lame and defective," it was G. F. Lessing in *Laokoön* (1766) who distinguished the synchronic, spatial character of painting from the diachronic, temporal character of poetry in terms that later painters, poets, and philosophers have been able to deny only in self-conscious acts of rebellion.

4. Plutarch's paraphrase of Simonides appears in *De Gloria Atheniensium* 3.347a. Sidney, in *The Defence of Poesy,* is altogether typical in making Horace's observation part of the very definition of poesy, but is quite unusual in realizing that the observation is, after all, a metaphor: "Poesie therefore is an arte of imitation, for so *Aristotle* termeth it in this word *Mimesis,* that is to say, a representing, counterfetting, or figuring foorth: to speake metaphorically a speaking picture, with this end: to teach and delight" (Philip Sidney, *The Defence of Poesie* [London: Printed for William Ponsonby, 1595], sig. C2v). Further quotations from the *Defence* are taken from Ponsonby's 1595 printing and are cited in the text by signature number.

5. *Timber, or Discoveries,* in Herford, Percy, and Simpson, eds., *Ben Jonson,* 8:609. Further quotations from *Timber* are taken from this edition and are cited in the text by page number.

6. Compare the Gospel of John 1.1: "In the beginning was the Word, and the Word was with God, and the Word was God."

7. Lucien Febvre and Henri-Jean Martin, *The Coming of the Book: The Impact of Printing 1450–1800,* trans. David Gerard (1976; repr., London: Verso, 1997); Elizabeth Eisenstein, *The Printing Revolution in Early Modern Europe* (1983; Cambridge: Cambridge University Press, 2005); Adrian Johns, *The Nature of the Book: Print and Knowledge in the Making* (Chicago: University of Chicago Press, 1998); John Barnard and D. F. McKenzie, eds., *The Cambridge History of the Book in Britain,* vol. 4, 1557–1695 (Cambridge: Cambridge University Press, 2002); Roger Chartier, *Inscription and Erasure: Literature and Written Culture from the Eleventh to the Eighteenth Century,* trans. Arthur Goldhammer (Philadelphia: University of Pennsylvania Press, 2007).

8. Stephen J. Campbell, *The Cabinet of Eros,* 46 (see chap. 1, n. 41), appropriating the term "semiotic virtuosity" from Arjun Appadurai, *The Social Life of Things: Commodities in Cultural Perspective* (Cambridge: Cambridge University Press, 1986).

9. Scholarship on fabrics, tapestries, needlework, and other woven furnishings in sixteenth- and seventeenth-century England is dispersed but choice. In David Jenkins, ed., *The Cambridge History of Western Textiles,* 2 vols. (Cambridge: Cambridge University Press, 2003), see Edith Standen and Jennifer Wearden, "Early Modern Tapestries and Carpets, c. 1500–1780," 1:597–630; Natalie Rothstein and Santina M. Levey, "Furnishings c. 1500–1780," 1:631–58; and Aileen Ribeiro, "Dress in the Early Modern Period c. 1500–1780)," 1:659–89. See also Geoffrey Beard, *Upholsterers and Interior Furnishing in England 1530–1840* (New Haven, CT: Yale University Press, 1997), Liz Arthur, *Embroidery 1600–1700 at the Burrell Collection* (London: Trafalgar Books, 1995); Jenny Gibbs, *Curtains and*

Draperies: History, Design, Inspiration (Woodstock, NY: Overlook, 1994); Donald King and Santina Levey, *The Victoria & Albert Museum's Textile Collection: Embroidery in Britain from 1200 to 1750* (London: V&A Publications, 1993); Pamela Clabburn, *The National Trust Book of Furnishing Textiles* (London: Viking for the National Trust, 1988); and Eileen Harris, *Going to Bed: The Arts and Living* (London: HMSO for V&A Publications, 1981).

10. The most expansive account of ekphrasis as a trope is to be found in James A. W. Heffernan, *Museum of Words: The Poetics of Ekphrasis from Homer to Ashbery* (Chicago: University of Chicago Press, 1993).

11. On recognition as the principle of knowledge, see *Phaedo* 72–76 and *Phaedrus* 250. d–e, where Plato gives the affect attached to this act of recognition his most extended attention. He begins by distinguishing the direct knowledge enjoyed by the psyche before it joined the perceiver's body: "Now beauty, as I said, was radiant among the other objects; and now that we have come down here we grasp it sparkling through the clearest of our senses. Vision, of course, is the sharpest of our bodily senses, although it does not see wisdom. It would awaken a terribly powerful love if an image of wisdom came through our sight as clearly as beauty does, and the same goes for the other objects of inspired love" (*Phaedrus* 250.d–e).

12. Aristotle *Poetics* 1450.a.35. Further quotations from the *Poetics* are cited in the text References to the Greek text are taken from Aristotle, *The Poetics,* ed. T. E. Page. Loeb Classical Library (London: Heinemann, 1946).

13. "Here, then, we may say that light is a nature inhering in the transparent when the latter is without determinate boundary. But it is manifest that, when the transparent is in determinate bodies, its bounding extreme must be something real; and that colour is just this something we are plainly taught by facts—colour being actually either at the limit or being itself that limit, in bodies. (Hence it was that the Pythagoreans named the superficies of a body its hue.) For it is at the limit of the body, but it is not the limit of the body; but the same natural substance which is coloured *outside* must be thought to be so inside too" (Aristotle *De Sensu* 439.a.27).

14. Sophocles, *Oedipus Tyrannos,* trans. by Robert Fagles as *Oedipus the King,* ll. 1306–7, in *Three Theban Plays* (Harmondsworth, UK: Penguin, 1984), 232.

15. P. Ovidius Naso, *Metamorphoses,* trans. by George Sandys as *Ouid's Metamorphosis Englished, mythologiz'd, and represented in figures* (Oxford: John Lichfield, 1632), 1.1–2, sig. A1, translating "*In nova fert animus mutatas dicere formas / corpora.*" Unless otherwise noted, all further quotations from the *Metamorphoses* are taken from the 1632 edition of Sandys's translation and are cited in the text by book and line numbers geared to Ovid, *Metamorphoses,* ed. and trans. Frank Justus Miller, 2 vols. Loeb Classical Library (London: Heinemann, 1925), but signature numbers of the 1632 English printing as well. "Ovidian physics" is Kristen Poole's inspired coinage for Ovid's representations of instable bodies within unstable spaces. See "The Devil's in the Archive: *Doctor Faustus* and Ovidian Physics," *Renaissance Drama* n.s. 35 (2006): 191–219.

16. Lynn Enterline, *The Rhetoric of the Body from Ovid to Shakespeare* (Cambridge: Cambridge University Press, 2000), 30–35. I am grateful also to Heather James for drawing my attention to the contest of Arachne and Pallas in an unpublished essay, "Spenser and the Gods," to be included in her forthcoming book *Taking Liberties: Ovid in Renaissance Poetry and Political Thought.* On Spenser's treatment of the contest in *Muiopotmos,* see

Craig Rustici, "*Muipotmos:* Spenser's 'Complaint' against Aesthetics," *Spenser Studies* 13 (1999): 165–77; and Robert A. Brinkley, "Spenser's *Muiopotmos* and the Politics of Metamorphosis," *English Literary History* 48.4 (1981): 668–76.

17. Compare Arthur Golding's translation in *The.xv.Bookes of P. Ouidius Naso, entytuled Metamorphosis* (London: William Seres, 1567), sig. K4v: "To hir that for desire of praise so stoutly helde hir owne, / What guerdon she shoulde hope to haue for hir attempt so madde, / Foure like contentions in the foure last corners she did adde." Further quotations from Golding's translation are cited in the text by signature number.

18. Another example can be seen in the epic suite of ten tapestries, the *Triumphs of Scipio,* for which Giulio Romano provided cartoons. Realizations of those designs by the Brussels workshops of Cornelius and Heinrich Mattens are set within borders made up of arches, each of which contains an allegorical personage. Eight of the original ten tapestries from the suite are in collections in Europe and North America. The two I have seen are on display at Hurst Castle, San Simeon, California. To my eyes, the seemingly random character of the allegorical figures and the offhand way in which they are duplicated and repeated attests to a need for verbal grounding, even when the picture-space itself is vast, even when the relationship of words of visual images is cryptic and oblique. In the Hurst Castle examples, Resurrectio (Christ emerging from the tomb), Senectus (an old man), Tempus (Father Time), Raptus (a woman being carried away by force) seem to have little, if anything, to do with the story of Scipio. The vestigial quality of these figures is especially apparent in the way Tempus ("time . . . ") and Fugit (" . . . flies") have been relegated to separate compartments.

19. Compare Golding's translation (1567): "Round about the utmost Veridge was set / A narrow Traile of pretie floures with leaues of Iuie fret" (sig. K5).

20. Enterline, *The Rhetoric of the Body from Ovid to Shakespeare,* 34.

21. Charles Paul Segal, *Landscape in Ovid's* Metamorphoses*: A Study in the Transformations of a Literary Symbol* (Wiesbaden: F. Steiner Verlag, 1969), 1–19.

22. John Milton, *Paradise Lost a Poem Written in Ten Books* (London: Peter Parker, Robert Boulter, Matthias Walker, 1667), 4.125–26, sig. M1. Further quotations from *Paradise Lost* are cited in the text by book and line numbers.

23. Rayna Kalas focuses on just such effects in *Frame, Glass, Verse: The Technology of Poetic Invention in the English Renaissance* (Ithaca, NY: Cornell University Press, 2007).

24. On Hardwick Hall, its architecture, its furnishings, and the course of its building, the primary source is Mark Girouard, *Robert Smythson and the Elizabethan Country House* (New Haven, CT: Yale University Press, 1983), 143–62. See also Girouard, *Life in the English Country House: A Social and Architectural History* (New Haven, CT: Yale University Press, 1978), 116–18; Peter Thornton, *Seventeenth Century Interior Decoration in England, France, and Holland* (New Haven, CT: Yale University Press, 1983), 172, 221–22 (seating), 180 (cushions), 106, 123–24, 135–43 (hangings); Anthony Wells-Cole, *Art and Decoration in Elizabethan and Jacobean England: The Influence of Continental Prints 1558–1625* (New Haven, CT: Yale University Press, 1997), 247–95; Santina M. Levey, *An Elizabethan Inheritance: The Hardwick Hall Textiles* (London: National Trust, 1998); and Santina M. Levey and Peter Thornton, *Of Houshold Stuff: The 1601 Inventories of Bess of Hardwick* (London: National Trust, 2001).

25. Levey and Thornton, *Of Household Stuff,* 2001, 47, 48.

26. *The Loves of Hero and Leander a mock poem: with marginall notes, and other choice pieces of drollery* (London, 1653), sigs. D2–D2v.

27. Levey and Thornton, *Of Houshold Stuff,* 48.

28. Rothstein and Levey, "Furnishings c. 1500–1780," 634.

29. The room also includes a 15 × 15-foot bay window opening out onto the actual Derbyshire landscape beyond. These measurements are specified in Girouard, *Robert Smythson and the Elizabethan Country House,* 143–62.

30. Levey, *An Elizabethan Inheritance,* 77–78.

31. Levey and Thornton, *Of Houshold Stuff,* 47–48. Further details from this inventory are cited in the text by page number.

32. Wells-Cole, *Art and Decoration in Elizabethan and Jacobean England,* 272–73.

33. Ovid, *Metamorphoses,* trans. Golding, sig. E8v.

34. Nicholas Mander and Karin Mander, *Owlpen Manor: A Short History and Guide* (Dursley, Gloucestershire: Owlpen Manor, 2000), 5–7, 29–42. I am grateful to Lena Orlin for first telling me about Owlpen Manor and its painted cloths.

35. Catherine Richardson, *Domestic Life and Domestic Tragedy in Early Modern England,* 210 (see chap. 2, n. 3).

36. On the attribution to Ballechouse and the sources of the narrative design see Wells-Cole, *Art and Decoration in Elizabethan and Jacobean England,* 275–89.

37. Shakespeare, *2 Henry IV,* sig. G3v; 2.1.157–63; and *1 Henry IV,* sig. F3; 4.2.27–28 (signature numbers are from *Mr. William Shakespeares Comedies, Histories, & Tragedies,* [see intro., n. 3]; and act, line, and scene numbers are from Shakespeare, *The Complete Works* [see chap. 1, n. 35]). References to painted cloths in *1* and *2 Henry IV,* along with other references, are catalogued in the standard essay on these little-studied objects, Nicholas Mander, "Painted Cloths: History, Craftsmen and Techniques," *Textile History* 28.2 (1997): 119–48. Apart from the suites still hung in their original settings at Owlpen Manor and Hardwick Hall, other publicly accessible examples are housed in the Luton Museum and Art Gallery, Luton, Bedfordshire; the Anne of Cleves House, Lewes, Sussex; Gainsborough Old Hall Museum, Gainsborough, Lincolnshire; Christchurch Mansion Museum, Ipswich, Suffolk; and the Shakespeare Birthplace Trust, Stratford-upon-Avon, Warwickshire (in storage in 2007, awaiting restoration of Hall's Croft).

38. Mander, "Painted Cloths," 129.

39. John Cullum, *The History and Antiquities of Hawsted in the County of Suffolk* (London: John Nichols, 1784), sig. S3v: "Contiguous with one of the bedchambers was a wainscoted closet, about seven feet square; the pannels painted with various sentences, emblems, and mottos. It was called *the painted closet;* at first probably designed for an *oratory,* and, from one of the sentences, for the use of a lady. The dresses of the figures are of the age of James I. This closet was therefore fitted up for the first lady Drury, and perhaps under her direction. The paintings are well executed; and now put up in a small apartment at Hawstead House" (original emphasis). Cullum's dimensions of "about seven feet square" are to be contrasted with the room's current dimensions of nine feet square; one of the four walls in the current configuration does not contain panels.

40. Norman K. Farmer, Jr., *Poets and the Visual Arts in Renaissance England* (Austin: University of Texas Press, 1984), 77–117, provides a full description of the room's iconography and numerous black-and-white illustrations.

41. Campbell, "Myth and the Articulation of Gender and Space," in *The Cabinet of Eros,* 59–86.

42. Campbell, *The Cabinet of Eros,* 46.

43. Nicholas Hilliard, *A Treatise Concerning the Arte of Limning,* 76 (see chap. 2, n. 47).

44. On the history and surviving output of the Sheldon workshops see Anthony Wells-Cole, "Tapestry," in *Art and Decoration in Elizabethan and Jacobean England,* 220–34; Wells-Cole, "Elizabethan Sheldon Tapestry Maps," *Burlington Magazine* 132 (1990): 392–40; E. A. B. Bardnard and Alan J.B. Wace, "The Sheldon Tapestry Weavers and their Work," *Archaeologia* 78 (1928): 255–314; and John Humphreys, *Elizabethan Sheldon Tapestries* (Oxford: Oxford University Press, 1928).

45. Edward Phillips, *The new world of English words,* sig. C2 (see chap. 3, n. 46). Further quotations are cited in the text by signature number.

46. Patrick Hume, *Annotations on Milton's Paradise Lost wherein the texts of sacred writ, relating to the poem, are quoted, the parallel places and imitations of the most excellent Homer and Virgil, cited and compared, all the obscure parts render'd in phrases more familiar, the old and obsolete words, with their originals, explain'd and made easie to the English reader* (London: Jacob Tonson, 1695), sig. MM1.

47. Henry Wotton, *The Elements of Architecture . . . from the Best Authors and Examples* (London: John Bill, 1624), sig. N1. Further quotations are cited in the text by signature number.

48. Vitruvius Pollio, *De Architectura,* ed. and trans. Frank Granger. Loeb Classical Library (Cambridge, MA: Harvard University Press, 1962), 2:104–5.

49. Michel de Montaigne, *Essais* 1.28, trans. by John Florio as *The Essayes or Morall, Politike and Millitarie Discourses of Lo: Michaell de Montaigne* (London: Valentine Sims for Edward Blount, 1603), sig. I3. Compare Montaigne's original: "Considérant la conduite de la besogne d'un peintre que j'ai, il m'a pris envie de l'ensuivre. Il choisit le plus bel endroit et milieu de chaque paroi, pour y loger un tableau élaboré de toute sa suffisance. Et le vide tout autour, il le remplit de crotesques, qui sont peintures fantasques, n'ayant grâce qu'en la variété et étrangeté" (*Essais de Michel de Montaigne, Livre I,* ed. André Tournon [Paris: Imprimerie Nationale, 1998], 310). I am grateful to David LaGuardia for this reference.

50. Ellen Spolsky argues that grotesquerie in the sixteenth and seventeenth centuries performed a particular kind of cognitive work: "the grotesque celebrated category mixes and syncretism" (*Word vs. Image,* xiii). As such, it preserved visual, analogical modes of thought that Spolsky identifies with the Catholic Church and contrasts with Protestantism's insistence on words and with Descartes' insistence on clear and distinct ideas as proper objects of thought: "The grotesque represents the co-existence of previously unmixable categories, without any claim that they can be merged. Both parts of the mix are still visible, neither occluded" (141). I share with Spolsky an identification of grotesque work with desire (Spolsky's "hunger"). Spolsky's attention is trained specifically on visual images in *Iconotropism: Turning toward Pictures* (Lewisburg, PA: Bucknell University Press, 2004).

51. Edmund Spenser, *The Faerie Queene,* 2.9.50.8–9 (see chap. 3, n. 23). Further quotations from *The Faerie Queene* are cited by book, canto, stanza, and line numbers.

52. It is not just the mythological subject matter that has encouraged an indulgence of fancy in the Sheldon *The Judgment of Paris.* Most surviving tapestries from the Sheldon workshops, like most surviving painted cloths, depict episodes from the Bible. A suite of four panels showing the story of Joseph's half brother Judah, from Genesis 38–49, are designed along similar lines. One of the panels, on display at Aston Hall, Birmingham, is illustrated in Wells-Cole, *Art and Decoration in Elizabethan and Jacobean England,* 230, fig. 384.

53. Most of the surviving productions of the Sheldon Workshops are cushion covers, not tapestries, but these woven designs put into play, albeit on a smaller scale, the same dynamic between antic volatility and narrative solidity that can be observed in *The Judgement of Paris.* Examples are on display in the Victoria and Albert Museum in London, the Burrell Collection in Glasgow, the Metropolitan Museum of Art in New York, and elsewhere.

54. Jacques Derrida, "The Animal That Therefore I Am (More to Follow)," trans. David Wills, *Critical Inquiry* 28.2 (2002):399. "These relations," Derrida observes, "are at once close and abysal, and they can never be totally objectified."

55. On this transmutation in style see F. P. Wilson, *Elizabethan and Jacobean* (Oxford: Clarendon Press, 1946) and John Buxton, *Elizabethan Taste* (London: Macmillan, 1963). Van Dyck's place in the shift is explored in two exhibition catalogues: Arthur K. Wheelock, Jr., *Anthony Van Dyck* (Washington: National Gallery of Art, 1990), and Oliver Millar, *Van Dyck in England* (London: National Portrait Gallery, 1982).

56. "Tapestry," in *Encyclopædia Britannica Online,* (http://search.eb.com/eb/article-73794 [accessed December 28, 2006]).

57. According to Rowell, Moore, and Strachey, Cleyn was a principal member of William Murray's design team when Ham House, including the Green Closet, was remodeled in the 1630s (*Ham House,* 61 [see chap. 1, n. 32]).

58. Hentzner, *Itinerarium Germaniae, Galliae, Angliae, Italiae,* Bentley, ed., 21–23 (see chap. 2, n. 5). Further quotations are cited in the text by page number.

59. Francesco Colonna, *Hypnerotomachia Poliphili* (1499), trans. by Robert Dallington (?) as *Hypnerotomachia. The strife of loue in a dreame* (London: Simon Vvaterson, 1592), sig. o1. Further quotations are cited in the text by signature number. Two other editions of the translation, signed by "R.D.," were printed in 1592, with different publishers' names on the title page.

60. My description of the type sizes and styles in *Lucrece* is based on measurements that Stephen Tabor, Curator of Rare Books at the Huntington Library, and I carried out, using protocols in Philip Gaskell, *A New Introduction to Bibliography* (Oxford: Oxford University Press, 1972), 12–17. I am grateful to Stephen for so generously sharing his expertise. The printer's ornament on sig. B1 figures as number 8 in the inventory of ornaments and alphabets included in A. E. M. Kirwood, "Richard Field, Printer, 1589–1624," *The Library,* 4th ser. 12.1 (1931): 1–39. I am grateful to Adam Hooks for bringing this article to my attention.

61. William Shakespeare, *Lucrece* (London: Richard Field for John Harrison, 1594), sig. F1. Further quotations are cited in the text by signature number.

62. Hentzner, *Itinerarium Germaniae, Galliae, Angliae, Italiae,* Bentley, ed., 22.

63. Jan Muller, *Cleopatra,* H.44, B.9, c. 1590, as cataloged in F. W. H. Hollstein, *Dutch and Flemish Engravings, Etchings, and Woodcuts, ca. 1450–1700* (Amsterdam: M. Hertzberger, 1949–2007), 14:107.

64. *Hamlet* 2.2.561–62, in F1623. Joseph Roach uses this speech as the occasion for investigating just what actors thought they were doing when they assumed a passion (*The Player's Passion: Studies in the Science of Acting* [Newark: University of Delaware Press, 1985], 23–57).

65. Abrams and Greenblatt, eds., *The Norton Anthology of English Literature,* 8th ed., (see chap. 1, n. 8), 1:1650. The 8th edition drops a concluding sentence from the 7th: " Such use of the sensory and sensual to render the spiritual is a cornerstone of Counter-Reformation aesthetics and of baroque art" (Abrams and Greenblatt, eds. [New York: Norton, 2000], 1:640–41).

66. It was apparently Crashaw himself who imagined the poem's protagonists in these guises, and in these dispositions. "An Epigramme Vpon the pictures in the following Poemes" by Thomas Car, prefaced to *Carmen Deo Nostro,* describes all the pictures in the book—or at least the originals in the manuscript from which the book was printed—as Crashaw's own designs, "first made with his owne hand, admirably Well" (Richard Crashaw, *Carmen Deo Nostro, Te Decet Hymnus*[:] *Sacred Poems* (Paris: Peter Targa, 1652), sig. a3. Further quotations from *Carmen Deo Nostro* are cited in the text by signature number.

67. For bibliographical information on *Carmen Deo Nostro* and for numerous shrewd and helpful annotations I am indebted to George Walton Williams, ed., *The Complete Poetry of Richard Crashaw* (New York: New York University Press, 1968).

68. Biblical inspiration for the English verses that follow may come from Song of Songs 5:2: "I sleepe, but my heart waketh: *it is* the voyce of my beloued that knocketh, *saying,* Open to mee, my sister, my loue, my doue, my undefiled: for my head is filled with deaw, *and* my lockes with the drops of the night." Or perhaps Revelation 3:20: "Behold, I stand at the doore, and knocke: if any man heare my voice, and open the doore, I will come in to him, and will sup with him, and he with me."

69. "Transume" itself is defined (†3) as to transmute, change, convert (*into* something else), with citation of this passage from Crashaw.

70. Matthew 26:26, Latin Vulgate and King James versions, as transcribed at http://www.latinvulgate.com (accessed December 30, 2006).

71. Hobbes, *Humane Nature,* sig. D6 (see chap. 1, n. 78).

72. Nicholas Sander in *The Supper of Our Lord Set Foorth According to the Truth of the Gospell and Catholike Faith* (Louvain, 1566) gives this interpretation a classic statement. Christ's "dede of taking bread, and of blessing," Sander argues, "shewed his words to be directed unto y[t] which was in his hand, or lay before him (which was bread before) it must nedes be, that the pronoun (*this*) so showed to his Apostles y[e] thing already subiect vnto their eyes, that much more it serued to teache their understanding verily, this, which appeared to them bread, to be in substance, at the ending of the words, his own body" (sig. YY1v).

73. Daniel Featley, *Transubstantiation Exploded* (London: G. Miller for Nicholas Bourne, 1638), sig. I5v.

CHAPTER FIVE

1. François Rabelais, *Gargantua et Pantagruel,* Books 4 and 5, trans. by Peter Motteux as *Pantagruel's Voyage to the Oracle of the Bottle. Being the Fourth and Fifth Books of the Works of Francis Rabelais, M.D.,* (London: Richard Baldwin, 1694), 216. Further quotations are taken from Motteux's translation and are cited in the text by page number. I am grateful to Anston Bosman for this reference. English translation of Rabelais began with Sir Thomas Urquhart's *The First Book of the Works of Mr. Francis Rabelais* (1653).

2. The explanations in square brackets are Motteux's additions.

3. William Shakespeare and John Fletcher, *The Two Noble Kinsmen,* 1634 quarto text, in *Shakespeare's Plays in Quarto,* ed. Michael J. B. Allen and Kenneth Muir (Berkeley: University of California Press, 1981), 67. The line is numbered 4.3.3 in Shakespeare, *Complete Works,* 1249 (see chap. 1, n. 35). Quotations in this chapter from Shakespeare are from quarto or folio texts, as noted, with act, scene, and line references supplied from the Oxford edition. Further quotations are cited in the main text by act, scene, and line numbers.

4. Newton's letter to the Royal Society, not published at the time, is transcribed in Thomas Birch, *The History of the Royal Society of London for the Improving of Natural Knowledge,* vol. 3 (London: A Millar, 1757), 262. Further quotations are cited by volume and page number. On Newton's attempts to calibrate color and coordinate it with sound, and the context of those attempts in European culture of the sixteenth and seventeenth centuries, see Gage, *Color and Culture,* 153–76, 227–46; and Gage, *Color and Meaning,* 134–43 (see intro., n. 8). Gage's chapter titled "The Sound of Color" in *Color and Culture,* (227–46) provides an historical survey that ranges from the Greek "chromatic" musical scales to medieval and Renaissance notions of harmony as "color" to Romantic sonority to Scriabin's synesthesia.

5. Aristotle *De Sensu* 440.a.1. Further quotations are cited in the text by reference number.

6. I make these connections with full acknowledgment that Donald M. Frame's more general pronouncement is true: "Much of the wordplay in this chapter hinges on the polysemism of the French word *mot.* Normally meaning simply 'word,' it can also mean a jest or a joke, as in the expression *bon mot.* The word *paroles* in the title also means 'word,' but usually the spoken word, where as a *mot* may be either spoken or written. Since *gueule* may mean either 'throat' or 'mug' or the heralid color red (gules), that will lead, a little later, into the listing of colors of words" (*The Complete Works of François Rabelais,* trans. Donald M. Frame [Berkeley: University of California Press, 1991], 899).

7. Barry Truax, *Acoustic Communication* (Norwood, NJ: Ablex, 1984), 19–24; Stephen Handel, *Listening: An Introduction to the Perception of Auditory Events* (Cambridge, MA: MIT Press, 1989), 134–62, 185–217.

8. Samuel Charters claims that the term "blues" can be traced back to "Elizabethan English" ("Workin' on the Building: Roots and Influences," in *Nothing But the Blues,* ed. Lawrence Cohn [New York: Abbeville Press, 1993], 17–18). But the *OED,* cites the first use of the term in print as W. C. Handy's song "The Memphis Blues" (1912). Charters likewise recognizes Handy's song as having put "the blues" into public circulation.

9. "You may be jogging while your boots are green," derived from Shakespeare, *The Taming of the Shrew* (see 3.2.213); F. P. Wilson, ed., *The Oxford Dictionary of English Proverbs,* 3rd ed. (Oxford: Clarendon Press, 1970), 412, 337.

10. John Guillim, *A Display of Heraldrie,* 2nd ed. (London: Richard Badger for Ralph Mab, 1632), sig. D2v.

11. Marsilio Ficino, *Three Books on Life,* trans. Carol V. Kaske and John R. Clark (Binghampton, NY: Medieval and Renaissance Texts and Studies, 1989), 204–5. Further references are cited in the main text.

12. Wright, *The Passions of the Mind in Generall,* sig. E2 (see intro., n. 10). Further quotations are cited in the text by signature number.

13. Bacon, *Sylva Sylvarum,* sig. Z4 (original emphasis) (see chap. 2, n. 38). Further quotations are cited in the text.

14. John Donne, *Collected Sermons,*.ed. George R. Potter and Evelyn M. Simpson (Berkeley: University of California Press, 1959), 5:55.

15. Hippocrates, "Airs, Waters, Places," in *Hippocratic Writings,* ed. G. E. R. Lloyd (Harmondsworth, UK: Penguin, 1978), 165–66. For this reference, I am indebted to Kathy Rowe.

16. Crooke, *ΜΙΚΡΟΚΟΣΜΟΓΡΑΦΙΑ,* sig. Q3v (see chap. 2, n. 41). Further quotations are cited in the main text by signature number.

17. Platter, *Beschreibung der Reisen durch Frankreich, Spanien, England und die Niederlande 1595–1600,* trans. Williams, 195 (see chap. 2, n. 14). A full account of this grotto, located in an area of the park that other observers called "the wilderness," is provided by John Dent, *The Quest for Nonsuch* (London: Hutchinson, 1962), 119–20.

18. Shakespeare, "A Louers complaint," *Shake-speares Sonnets,* sig. K1v (see chap. 2, n. 54).

19. On this particular broadside ballad, its connections with the "Song of Willow" in *Othello,* and the multiple genders of subject positions in ballads more generally see Bruce R. Smith, "Female Impersonation in Early Modern Ballads," in *Women Players in England, 1500–1660: Beyond the All-Male Stage,* ed. Pamela Brown and Peter A. Parolin (Aldershot, UK: Ashgate, 2005), 284–301.

20. "The wofull complaint, and lamentable death of a forsaken Louer" (London: Henry Gosson, [1625]), Pepys collection 1:354–55, accessible at the University of California Santa Barbara, Early Modern Center, English Ballad Archive (http://emc.english.ucsb.edu/ballad_project/citation.asp?id=20165).

21. Claude M. Simpson, *The British Broadside Ballad and Its Music* (New Brunswick, NJ: Rutgers University Press, 1966), 268–78.

22. "Hero and Leander,"1.11–14, in *The Complete Works of Christopher Marlowe,* ed. Fredson Bowers, 2nd ed. (Cambridge: Cambridge University Press, 1981), 2:431.

23. Woodbridge, *The Scythe of Saturn,* 152–205 (see intro., n. 7).

24. David Wiles, *The Early Plays of Robin Hood* (Cambridge: D. S. Brewer, 1981), 7–30.

25. Thomas Wright, ed., *Songs and Ballads with Other Short Poems, Chiefly of the Reign of Philip and Mary* (London: J. B. Nichols, 1860), 119–24.

26. Simpson, *The British Broadside Ballad and Its Music,* 269.

27. Philip Stubbes, *The Anatomy of Abuses* (London: Richard Jones, 1583), sig. o4v. Further quotations are cited in the text.

28. Plutarch, *Lives of the Noble Grecians and Romans Compared Together,* trans. Sir Thomas North (London: Thomas Vautroullier and John Wright, 1579), 211–12.

29. Psalm 150:1, 3–4.

30. Hannibal Hamlin's emphasis in *Psalm Culture and Early Modern English Literature* (Cambridge: Cambridge University Press, 2004) is primarily on translations and adaptations, although music figures prominently in the two full chapters he devotes to Sternhold and Hopkins and their seventeenth-century imitators (19–110). Also useful to the account I offer here is Maurice Frost, *English and Scottish Psalm and Hymn Tunes c. 1543–1677* (Oxford: Oxford University Press, 1953).

31. Willi Apel, *Gregorian Chant* (Bloomington: Indiana University Press, 1958), 208–26.

32. Francis Proctor and Christopher Wordsworth, *Breviarum ad Usum Insignis Ecclesiae Sarum* (Cambridge: Cambridge University Press, 1879–86), 1:mlxvii; 2:39.

33. Walter Howard Frere, *The Use of Sarum,* vol. 2 (Cambridge: Cambridge University Press, 1901), xxxii–xxxvi, lxix, See also Terence Bailey, "Latin monophonic psalmody," Grove Music Online (Oxford: Oxford University Press, 2007) (http://www.grovemusic.com [accessed January 19, 2007])

34. Hamlin, *Psalm Culture and Early Modern English Literature* 19–50; Frost, *English and Scottish Psalm and Hymn Tunes,* 3–15; "Sternhold, Thomas," English Short Title Catalogue (http://eureka.rlg.org [accessed January 13, 2007]),

35. Thomas Sternhold and John Hopkins, *The Whole Booke of Psalmes, collected into Englysh metre* (London: John Day, 1562), title page. Further quotations from Sternhold and Hopkins, unless otherwise noted, are taken from this edition and are cited in the text by signature number.

36. It was also known, in its day, as "Sternhold's meter." Hamlin notes that, since very few ballad texts date from earlier than Sternhold's publication, it may actually have been his psalms that dictated the sound-shape of ballads, and not the other way around (*Psalm Culture and Early Modern English Literature,* 24).

37. Hamlin, *Psalm Culture and Early Modern English Literature,* 29–30.

38. Jeremy Taylor (attr.), *The Psalter of David: With Titles and Collects according to the matter of each* Psalme (London: R. Royston, 1646), sig. C8v. Further quotations are cited in the text by signature number.

39. Quoted in Hamlin, *Psalm Culture and Early Modern English Literature,* 28.

40. Sternhold and Hopkins, *The Whole Booke of Psalmes,* title page.

41. Church of England, *The booke of common prayer, and administration of the Sacramentes, and other rites and ceremonies in the Churche of Englande* (London: Richard Jugge and John Cawode, 1559), sig. A8v. Further quotations are cited in the text by signature number.

42. John Playford, *An Introduction to the Skill of Musick* (London: W. Godbid for J. Playford, 1674), sig. F4 (original emphasis). Playford's own edition of *The Whole Book of Psalms* went through 21 editions between 1695 and 1757. The fourteen editions of his anthology *The Dancing Master* published between 1652 and 1709 remain one of the major sources for earlier ballad tunes like "Greensleeves."

43. Ruth M. Wilson, *Anglican Chant and Chanting in England, Scotland, and America 1660 to 1820* (Oxford: Clarendon Press, 1996), 21–58.

44. Ruth Wilson identifies Playford's source as Edward Lowe's *A Short Direction for the Performance of Cathedral Service* (1661) (ibid., 28). Books like Lowe's *Short Direction* and James Clifford's *The Divine Service and Anthems usually sung in His Majesties Chappel and in all Cathedrals and Collegiate Choires in England and Ireland,* (1664) were necessary to reestablish musical practices that had once been passed down in person from musician to musician until the chain was broken from 1645 to 1660. As a result of this oral transmission, documentary sources for chanting practices in the sixteenth century are few, a notable exception being Thomas Morley's harmonizations of the eight tones of Latin plainsong in *A Plain and Easy Introduction to Practical Musicke* (1597).

45. Text taken from Church of England, *The Book of Common Prayer,* sig. BB6v.

46. Wilson, *Anglican Chant and Chanting in England, Scotland, and America,* 41.

47. Peter Le Huray and John Harper, "Anglican Chant," Grove Music Online (http://www.grovemusic.com [accessed January 18, 2007]).

48. Hannibal Hamlin, "Another Version of Pastoral: Enlgish Renaissance Translations of Psalm 23," *Spenser Studies* 16 (2002): 167–96, and *Psalm Culture and Early Modern English Literature* (2004), 147–72. Further citations in the text of Hamlin's survey refer to the *Spenser Studies* article.

49. Williams, ed., *The Complete Poetry of Richard Crashaw,* 5 (see chap. 4, n. 67). As Williams notes, *were* = *wear.*

50. Serres, *Genesis,* 13 (original emphasis) (see intro., n. 25). Further quotations are cited in the text by page number.

51. For the missing links in this chain via Occitan, Old French, Middle French, and Anglo-Norman French, see both *OED,* "noise" *n.,* etymology (where the connection between *noise* and *nausea* is specified as "probable") and *OED,* "nausea" *n.,* etymology.

52. Rabelais, *Gargantua et Pantagruel,* 216.

53. See chap. 2, n. 32.

54. On ambient noise as the aural matrix out of which Shakespeare's emerged in their original performances and on the function of male voices in focusing the audience's aural attention see Bruce R. Smith, "Within the Wooden O," in *The Acoustic World of Early Modern England: Attending to the O-Factor* (Chicago: University of Chicago Press, 1999), 206–45, and "What Means This Noise?" in *"Noyses, Sounds, and Sweet Aires: Music in Early Modern England,"* ed. Jesse Ann Owens (Washington: Folger Shakespeare Library, 2006), 20–31.

55. All stage directions (SDs) are quoted in original orthography.

56. Platter, *Beschreibung der Reisen durch Frankreich, Spanien, England und die Niederlande 1595–1600,* Williams, trans.,166.

57. The script of *A Warning for Faire Women,* acted by Shakespeare's company in 1599, gestures toward black stage hangings that remained on display throughout the performance and sable curtains through which spectacular entrances could be made. This particular stage practice evidently copied the custom of draping the interiors of houses with black during wakes and periods of mourning.

58. Thomas Dekker, *A Strange Horse Race* (London: Nicholas Okes for Joseph Hunt, 1613), sig. C4v.

59. Noam Chomsky and Morris Halle, *The Sound Pattern of English* (New York: Harper and Row, 1968), 1–55; Handel, *Listening,* 147–160; John Laver, *Principles of Pho-*

netics (Cambridge: Cambridge University Press, 1994), 95–118: Ian R. A. MacKay, *Phonetics: The Science of Speech Production* (Boston: Allyn and Bacon, 1987), 125–52; John Laver, "Linguistic Phonetics," in *The Handbook of Linguistics,* ed. Mark Aronoff and Janie Rees-Miller (Oxford: Blackwell, 2001), 150–79.

60. Abigail Cohn, "Phonology," in Aronoff and Rees-Miller, *The Handbook of Linguistics,* 180–212.

61. MacKay, *Phonetics,* 129–30; Kenneth N. Stevens, *Acoustic Phonetics* (Cambridge, MA: MIT Press, 1998), 48.

62. M. B. Parkes, *Pause and Effect: An Introduction to the History of Punctuation in the West* (Berkeley: University of California Press, 1993), 9–19.

63. Roy Harris, *Rethinking Writing* (Bloomington: Indiana University Press, 2000), 136–37.

64. D. B. Fry, *Homo Loquens: Man as a Talking Animal* (Cambridge: Cambridge University Press, 1977), 83.

65. MacKay, *Phonetics,* 290–91.

66. Reuven Tsur, *What Makes Sound Patterns Expressive?* (Durham, NC: Duke University Press, 1992), 1–51.

67. Tsur, *What Makes Sound Patterns Expressive?* 52–88, draws on an argument first advanced by Roman Jakobson in *Child Language, Aphasia, and Phonological Universals* (Berlin: Walter de Gruyter, 1968).

68. John Hart, *An Orthographie* (London: William Seres, 1569), sigs. 9–9v. Further quotations are cited in the text by signature number.

69. Robert Robinson, *The Art of Pronuntiation* (London: Nicholas Oakes, 1617), sig. B2.

70. E. J. Dobson, *English Pronunciation 1500–1700,* 2nd ed. (Oxford: Clarendon Press, 1968), 1:200–14; Laver, "Linguistic Phonetics," 166.

71. *OED* defines "timbre" as "the character or quality of a musical or vocal sound (distinct from its pitch and intensity) depending upon the particular voice or instrument producing it, and distinguishing it from sounds proceeding from other sources." In French, the term originally referred to the sound of a small bell (*OED* "timbre," etymology). Murray Campbell, "Timbre (1)," Grove Music Online (http://www.grovemusic.com [accessed January 26, 2007]), explains the factors that produce this effect: "The frequency spectrum of a sound, and in particular the ways in which different partials grow in amplitude during the starting transient, are of great importance in determining the timbre."

72. *OED* "clang," 3. The earliest citation of this word is from 1867. A more precise definition is provided by Kevin Mooney, "Klang (1)," at Grove Music Online (http://www.grovemusic.com [accessed January 26, 2007]): "A composite musical sound consisting of a fundamental pitch (*Grundton*) and its upper partials (*Obertöne*), as opposed to noise (*Geräusch*) and to the phenomenon of sound itself (usually *Schall*); it is sometimes used as a synonym for *Klangfarbe* ('timbre' or 'tone-colour')."

73. Thomas Morley, *A Plaine and Easie Introduction to Practicall Musicke* (London: Peter Short, 1597), sig. X1. Further quotations are cited in the text by signature number.

74. Ernest H. Sanders, "Color (1)," Grove Music Online (http://www.grovemusic.com [accessed January 26, 2007]).

75. William Shakespeare (attr.), *The Passionate Pilgrime* (London: William Jaggard, 1599), sig. B2.

76. George Puttenham, *The Arte of English Poesie,* ed. Gladys Doidge Willcock and Alice Parker. (Cambridge: Cambridge University Press, 1936), 73.

77. Thomas Campion, *Observations in the Art of English Poesie* (London: Richard Field for Andrew Wise, 1602), sig. B6v. Further quotations are cited in the text.

78. Samuel Daniel, *An Apologie for Ryme,* in *A Panegyrike Congratulatory* (London: Edward Blount, 1603), sig. G4. Further quotations are cited in the text.

79. *The Vnder-wood* 29.1–6 in Herford, Simpson, and Simpson, *Ben Jonson,* 8:183 (see chap. 4, n. 2).

80. For an appreciation of Jonson's sense of the thing-ness of a single words and his connections with the making of dictionaries in the seventeenth century see Judith H. Anderson, "Stones Well Squared," in *Words That Matter: Linguistic Perception in Renaissance English* (Palo Alto, CA: Stanford University Press, 1996), 101–36.

81. Wesley Trimpi, *Ben Jonson's Poems: A Study of the Plain Style* (Palo Alto, CA: Stanford University Press, 1962), ix, 6.

82. Stevens, *Acoustic Phonetics,* 248–49.

83. *Timber,* in Herford, Simpson, and Simpson, *Ben Jonson,* 8:584

84. Sonnet 85.5–8 in William Shakespeare, *Shakespeare's Sonnets,* ed. Stephen Booth (New Haven, CT: Yale University Press, 1977), 74.

85. D. B. Fry, *The Physics of Speech* (Cambridge: Cambridge University Press, 1979), 126–27.

86. Joel Fineman, "The Sound of O in *Othello:* The Real of the Tragedy of Desire," in *The Subjectivity Effect in Western Literary Tradition: Essays toward the Release of Shakespeare's Will* (Cambridge, MA: MIT Press, 1991), 143–64.

87. Thomas Nashe, *A Pleasant Comedy, Called Summer's Last Will and Testament* (London: Simon Stafford for Walter Burre, 1600), sigs. B3–B3v. In this printing, the song appears in italics.

88. Garrett Stewart, *Reading Voices: Literature and the Phonotext* (Berkeley: University of California Press, 1990), 7–8. Further quotations are cited in the text by page number.

89. Stephen Booth, "Poetic Richness: A Preliminary Audit," *Pacific Coast Philology* 19.1–2 (1984): 76.

90. My understanding of Chomsky's linguistics is informed by V. J. Cook, *Chomsky's Universal Grammar: An Introduction,* 2nd ed. (Oxford: Blackwell, 1996); Howard Lasnik, "Grammar, Levels, and Biology," in *The Cambridge Companion to Chomsky,* ed. James McGilvray (Cambridge: Cambridge University Press, 2005), 60–83; Laura-Ann Pettito, "How the Brain Begets Language," in McGilvray, *The Cambridge Companion to Chomsky,* 84–101; and Judith Greene, *Psycholinguistics: Chomsky and Psychology* (Harmondsworth, UK: Penguin, 1972).

91. Noam Chomsky, *Syntactic Structures,* 2nd ed. (New York: Mouton de Gruyter, 2002), 15. I am grateful to David Jenness for bringing this passage to my attention.

CHAPTER SIX

1. Andrew Gurr, *The Shakespearean Stage 1574–1642,* 3rd ed. (Cambridge: Cambridge University Press, 1992), 31, 45–48, 79; and Gurr, *The Shakespearean Company, 1594–1642* (Cambridge: Cambridge University Press, 2004), 10, 31.

2. This total of ten represents an amalgamation of lists drawn up by Roslyn Lander Knutson, *The Repertory of Shakespeare's Company 1594–1613* (Fayetteville: University of Arkansas Press, 1991), 179–209; Gurr, *The Shakespearean Company,* 10; Roslyn Lander Knutson, "Playing Companies and Repertory," in *A Companion to Renaissance Drama,* ed. Arthur F. Kinney (Oxford: Blackwell, 2002), 187; and Andrew Gurr and Mairko Ichikawa, *Staging in Shakespeare's Theatres* (Oxford: Oxford University Press, 2000), 26–27.

3. By the end of the nineteenth century, Curtain Road had become a center of furniture making and upholstering—an identity that the district maintained until the 1990s. See William Page, ed., *The Victoria History of the County of Middlesex* (London: Constable, 1911), 2:141. It is a nice irony that the thoroughfare is now returning to its sixteenth-century identity as a place for diversion and pleasure vis-à-vis the nearby City.

4. Herbert Berry, "Playhouses," in Kinney, *A Companion to Renaissance Drama,* 151. The *OED* includes under "curtain" a fortification-specific meaning of "the plain wall of a fortified place; the part of the wall which connects two bastions, towers, gates, or similar structures" (4.a) but cites no instances earlier than 1569, eight years before the Curtain was built, and makes no allowance for a wall not anchored by towers or other fortified structures. The sense of "curtain" as "a piece of cloth or similar material suspended by the top so as to admit of being withdrawn sideways" (1.a) is much older, with citations going back to 1186. A map of 1746, reproduced in James Bird and Philip Norman, eds., *Survey of London* (London: Batsford, 1922), identifies Curtain Road as "The Curtain" and shows a wall still running, at that date, along its western side (8:182).

5. Benjamin Wyatt, *Observations on the Design of the Theatre Royal, Drury Lane* (1813), quoted in Richard Leacroft, *The Development of the English Playhouse,* rev. ed. (London: Methuen, 1988), 167 (original emphasis).

6. Peter Brook, *The Empty Space* (1968; repr. New York: Simon & Schuster, 1996), 44–45.

7. According to information provided by Roger Howells, who worked backstage at the Royal Shakespeare Theatre for many years, the proscenium arch and stage surround were painted a dark color in 1964, with the hope that darkening that area would make the division between stage and auditorium less visible. The darkening was spread to the auditorium walls about 1970. None of these decisions were made by Peter Brook but by the company's artistic directors and heads of design: Peter Hall and John Bury (1964–1967), Trevor Nunn and Christopher Morley (1968–1973), and Trevor Nunn and John Napier (1974–1976). I am grateful to Stanley Wells for bringing my questions to Roger Howells and relaying the answers.

8. Gurr and Ichikawa explain, in *Staging in Shakespeare's Theatres,* the inspiration for these extravaganzas in painting: "Elizabethans loved colour. They painted their house interiors, they hung painted cloths on their walls if they could not afford tapestries, and above all everyone, playgoers or not, who could afford to, dressed as colourfully as they could. Faced with such competition and such an expectation, the players decorated their *frons scenae* with vividly colourful cloths and used their best attire to parade like mannequins" (56). See also 27–28, 36–37.

9. Richard Flecknoe, *Love's Kingdom . . . With a short Treatise of the* English Stage, &c. (London: R. Wood, 1664), sigs. H3–H3v. Further quotations are cited in the text by signature number.

10. Thomas Percy, *Reliques of Ancient English Poetry* (London: Dodsley, 1765), 1:128.

11. Edmund Malone, *Historical Account of the Rise and Progress of the English Stage,* 2nd ed. (Basle: J. J. Tourneisen, 1800), 107–13.

12. The costumes and props of Renaissance London theaters have been subjected to critical scrutiny. Clothing has been studied by Jones and Stallybrass, *Renaissance Clothing and the Materials of Memory* (see chap. 2, n. 7); props, by the contributors to Harris and Korda, *Staged Properties in Early Modern English Drama* (see chap. 2, n. 7). To the best of my knowledge, this chapter presents the first study of arrases and hangings.

13. Smith, *The Poems of Andrew Marvell,* 156 (see chap. 1, n. 1).

14. The distinctive qualities of sound in the two different physical spaces constructed by the Globe and the Blackfriars are mapped out in B. R. Smith, "Within the Wooden O" (see chap. 5, n. 54). In this chapter, I am attempting a similar exploration with respect to vision.

15. Steven Mullaney's descriptions of the area outside Bishopsgate and across the Thames on the South Bank in *The Place of the Stage: License, Play, and Power in Renaissance England* (Chicago: University of Chicago Press, 1988) are apt to be transposed by twenty-first-century readers into the modern, highly urban equivalents of those areas—indeed, into terms that fit Shoreditch and Southwark today. The field sports that John Stow enumerates in *The Survey of London: Containing the Original, Increase, Modern Estate and Government of that City, Methodically set down . . . not only of those two famous Cities, London and Westminster, but (now newly added) Four miles compass,* ed. Antony Munday (London: Nicholas Bourn, 1633), are extended elsewhere in the *Survey* to include play-acting, as witness a play put on by parish clerks at Skinners Well by Smithfield in 1391 (sig. H3). "Of late time," Stow goes on, "in stead of those Stageplayes, have beene vsed Comedies, Tragedies, Enterludes, and Histories, both true and fained: for the acting whereof, certaine publike places have beene erected" (sig. H2v)—implicitly locating those structures in the open outdoor spaces like Skinners Well where amateur plays were once acted on holidays.

16. On the visual evidence presented by Braun and Hogenberg's view, see R. A. Foakes, *Illustrations of the English Stage 1580–1642* (Palo Alto, CA: Stanford University Press, 1985), 2–3. Foakes reproduces on 8–9 an engraving by Adrian Booth, "The View of the Cittye of London from the North towards the Sowth," ca. 1597–99, that shows either the Curtain or the Theatre or both in the open green surroundings like those in Braun and Hogenberg's view of the South Bank.

17. John Marston, *The Scourge of Villanie* (London: James Roberts for John Buzbie, 1598), sig. H4. Further quotations are cited in the text by signature number.

18. Everard Guilpin, *Skialetheia, or A shadowe of Truth* (London: I.R. for Thomas Ling, 1598), sig. D5. Cases for revivals of *Romeo and Juliet* and *The Comedy of Errors* at the Curtain in 1597–1598 are made in Knutson, *The Repertory of Shakespeare's Company 1594–1613,* 182, 202.

19. Reference to the performance of "a Comedy of Errors (like to Plautus his Menechmus)" is included in an account written to commemorate the entire season's festivities (*Gesta Grayorum or The History of the High and Mighty Prince of Purpoole Anno Domini 1594,* ed. Desmond Bland [Liverpool: Liverpool University Press, 1968], 32).

20. On the three practicable "houses" that seem to be called for by the script, see Shakespeare, *The Comedy of Errors,* ed. R. A. Foakes. Arden Shakespeare second series (London: Methuen, 1968), xxxiv–xxxix, where the suggestions of theater historians about the use of the Grey's Inn hall screen are summarized.

21. Shakespeare, *The Comedy of Errors,* in *Mr. William Shakespeares Comedies, Histories, & Tragedies,* sig. I2 (see intro., n. 3); and Shakespeare, *The Complete Works,* 5.1.400 (see chap. 1, n. 35). Further quotations from Shakespeare's scripts are taken from the printing indicated in parentheses (F 1623 or Q+date) and are cited in the text by act, scene, and line numbers from the revised Oxford edition. Folio texts are taken from Charlton Hinman, ed., *The First Folio of Shakespeare* (New York: Norton 1968); quarto texts, from Michael J. B. Allen and Kenneth Muir, eds., *Shakespeare's Plays in Quarto: A Facsimile Edition* (Berkeley: University of California Press, 1981).

22. Sasha Roberts, "'Let me the curtains draw': the dramatic and symbolic properties of the bed in Shakespearean tragedy," in Harris and Korda, *Staged Properties in Early Modern English Drama,* 153–74, closely examines the evidence for beds as stage properties (including an entry in Henslowe's accounts), discusses the larger social meanings of this particular furnishing, and accepts the SD in Q1 of *Romeo and Juliet* as indicating the use of a bed on stage. I am grateful to Leslie Thomson, who shared with me her unpublished paper on "Beds on the Early Modern Stage," which considers almost 90 theatrical uses of beds and remains skeptical about the precise arrangements that these references entailed.

23. In their very full entry on "bed" in *A Dictionary of Stage Directions in English Drama, 1580–1642* (Cambridge: Cambridge University Press, 1999), Alan Dessen and Leslie Thomson leave open the possibility that "curtains" in connection with beds could refer either to the curtains on a practicable stage bed or to the curtains over the central alcove, the space "within" (24–25). See also their entries on "within" (253) and "thrust" (229–30). Further references to Dessen and Thomson's dictionary are cited in the text by entry heading.

24. Malone, *Historical Account of the Rise and Progress of the English Stage,* 94.

25. Ben Jonson, *Everyman in his Humor. As it hath beene sundry times* publickly acted by the right *Honorable the Lord Cham-*berlaine his seruants (1601), in *Ben Jonson,* ed. C. H. Herford and Percy Simpson, vol. 3 (Oxford: Clarendon Press, 1927), 209. Further quotations are cited in the text by act, scene, and line numbers.

26. Ibid., 318.

27. "That within which passeth show" is, of course, Hamlet's phrase (1.2.85).

28. *A Warning for Faire Women. Containing,* The most tragicall and lamentable murther *of Master George Sanders of London Marchant, nigh Shooters hill. Consented vnto By his owne wife....* (London: Valentine Sims for William Aspley, 1599), sig. K3v. Further quotations are cited in the text by signature number.

29. Richard Brathwait, *The Two Lancashire Lovers: or The Excellent History of Philocles and Doriclea* (London: William Griffin for R.B., 1640), sig. o3v. John Dryden, *The Conquest of Granada, The Second Part* (London: T. N. for Henry Herringman, 1672), sig. S3, contains the stage direction for Act 5: "The Scene changes to the Vivarambla; and appears fil'd with Spectators: A scaffold hung with black, &c."

30. *The Merchant of Venice,* 3.2.175–83.

31. Nicholas Ling, *Politeuphuia. Wits commonwealth* (London: I. R. for Nicholas Ling, 1598), sig. H1v.

32. Francis Bacon (attr.), *Apophthegmes New and Old. Collected by the Right Honovrable, Francis Lo. Vervlam, Viscount S*[t]*. Alban.* (London: for Hanna Barret and Richard Whittaker, 1625), sigs. P5–P5v (original emphasis).

33. R. A. Foakes, "Henslowe's Rose/Shakespeare's Globe," in *From Script to Stage in Early Modern England,* ed. Peter Holland and Stephen Orgel (Basingstoke, UK: Palgrave Macmillan, 2004), 11–31, subjects Aernout van Buchel's copy of Johannes de Witt's drawing of the Swan to close scrutiny and points out many reasons why the document should not be taken at face value.

34. John Tatham, *The Fancies Theatre* (London: John Norton for Richard Best, 1640), sig. H3. Further quotations are cited in the text by signature number.

35. Ben Jonson, *Cynthia's Revels,* 147–52 (in the induction), in *Ben Jonson,* ed. C. H. Herford and Percy Simpson, vol. 4 (Oxford: Clarendon Press, 1932), 40.

36. *Ben Jonson,* ed. C. H. Herford, Percy Simpson, and Evelyn Simpson, vol. 9 (Oxford: Clarendon Press, 1950), The editors provide only this commentary on the speech: "*a piece of perspective* in this context can only be a reference to a painted cloth used for scenery, like 'the sittie of Rome' in Henslowe's inventory of properties" (489).

37. Ben Jonson, *Epicoene, or The Silent Woman,* 4.5.28–34, in *Ben Jonson,* ed. C. H. Herford, Percy Simpson, and Evelyn Simpson, vol. 5 (Oxford: Clarendon Press, 1937), 236 (original emphasis).

38. Ben Jonson, *The New Inn,* in *Ben Jonson,* ed. C. H. Herford, Percy Simpson, and Evelyn Simpson, vol. 6 (Oxford: Clarendon Press, 1938), 397 (original emphasis).

39. Gurr and Ichikawa, *Staging in Shakespeare's Theatres,* 6–7.

40. John H. Astington, "The Origins of the *Roxana* and *Messalina* Illustrations," *Shakespeare Studies* 43 (1991): 149–69; Astington, "The *Messalina* Stage and Salisbury Court Plays," *Theatre Journal* 43.2 (1991): 141–56; and Astington, "Rereading Illustrations of the English Stage," *Shakespeare Studies* 50 (1997): 151–70. Astington is cautious in reading Rawlins's image as evidence of the Salisbury Court's stage. More cautious still is Foakes, who advances evidence from Glynne Wickham that the Salisbury Court's stage was an octagonal design not compatible with Rawlins's engraving (*Illustrations of the English Stage 1580–1642,* 80–81).

41. Nathaniel Richards, *The Tragedy of Messallina The Roman Emperesse. As it hath beene Acted With generall Applause divers times, by the Company of his Majesties Revells* (London: Thomas Cotes for Daniel Frere, 1640), sig. A4v (original emphasis). Further quotations are cited in the text by signature number.

42. R. A. Foakes, ed., *Henslowe's Diary,* 2nd ed. (Cambridge: Cambridge University Press, 2002), 308. Further references to this work are cited in the text by page number.

43. Under "canopy," in *A Dictionary of Stage Directions in English Drama,* Dessen and Thomson cite instances where "the *canopy* is opened to reveal seated or reclining figures" (41), suggesting that "canopy" might be a synonym for "curtain" or "arras." Other instances of the term "suggest the use of a recessed space in the tiring-house wall" (41).

44. John Donne, *Iuvenilia* [sic] *or certeine paradoxes and problemes,* 2nd ed. (London: E. P. for Henry Seyle, 1633), sigs. D2–D2v (original emphasis). Further quotations are cited in the text.

45. The *OED* defines "glister" as "to sparkle; to glitter; to be brilliant" (*v., arch.* and *dial.*). Compare the verses that Morocco finds in the leaden casket in *The Merchant of Venice: "All that glisters is not gold"* (F 1623, 2.7.65). The most expensive tapestries were interwoven with gold and silver threads. I am grateful to Bradin Cormack for drawing my attention to this curious word and prompting me to consider what it might mean with respect to color.

46. Lomazzo, *Trattato dell'Arte de la Pittura,* sigs. KK5–KK5v (see chap. 2, n. 55). Further quotations are cited in the text by signature number.

47. Foakes, *Henslowe's Diary,* 317–23.

48. Francis Kirkman, *The Wits, or, Sport upon Sport* (London: Henry Marsh, 1662), sigs. A3–A4. Further quotations are cited in the text by signature number. The story of Bubble figures as Drollery 13 in the anthology and represents a compilation of three separate episodes from John Cooke, *Greene's Tu Quoque, or The City Gallant* (London: for John Trundle, 1614), sigs. D2v–D3, F4–F4v, and L3v–M1v.

49. Edward Reynolds, *A Treatise of the Passions and Faculties of the Soule of Mean* (London: R. H. For Robert Bostock, 1640), sig. D3v.

50. In *Shakespeare's Clown* (Cambridge: Cambridge University Press, 1987), 11–23, David Wiles offers a generously detailed discussion of Tarlton's physical humor, including this citation from Thomas Nashe's *Pierce Pennilesse his supplication to the deuill* (London: Abell Jeffes for I. Busby, 1592) concerning Tarlton's ability to raise laughter—in all but the severe local official who is Nashe's immediate subject—just by suddenly showing his face: "Amongst other cholericke wise Iustices, he was one, that hauing a play presented before him and his Towne-ship, by Tarlton and the rest of his fellowes her Maiesties seruants, and they were now entring into their first merriment (as they call it) the people began exceedingly to laugh, when Tarlton first peept out his head" (sig. D1v).

51. Robert Armin, *A Nest of Ninnies. Simply of themselues without Compound* (London : T. E[ast] for Iohn Deane, 1608), sig. F3. Further quotations are cited in the text.

52. No entry for "rat behind the arras" is to be found in F. P. Wilson, ed., *The Oxford Dictionary of English Proverbs,* 3rd ed. (Oxford: Clarendon Press, 1970) or Morris Tilley, *A Dictionary of Proverbs in England in the Sixteenth and Seventeenth Centuries* (Ann Arbor: University of Michigan Press, 1950).

53. Lucius Annaeus Seneca, *Seneca's Morals Abstracted in Three Parts,* trans. Roger L'Estrange (London: T. N. for Henry Brome, 1679), sigs. N6–N6v (original emphasis).

54. John Fletcher, *Women Pleased,* 4.3.175, 178 in Francis Beaumont and John Fletcher, *The Dramatic Works in the Beaumont and Fletcher Canon,* ed. Fredson Bowers (Cambridge: Cambridge University Press, 1966), 5:511.

55. William Heminge, *The Jewes Tragedy* (London: for Matthew Inman, 1662), sig. I4v.

56. Wright, *The Passions of the Mind in Generall,* sig. F7v (see intro., n. 10).

57. In carrying out my survey, I tracked down all of the nearly 115 references to "arras," "curtain," "hangings," and "traverse" In Dessen and Thomson, *A Dictionary of Stage Directions in English Drama,* 12, 62–63, 110, 235. "Curtain" is by far the commonest term; "traverse," the rarest.

58. Ben Jonson, *Volpone, or The Foxe,* in Herford, Simpson and Simpson, *Ben Jonson,* 5:112 (5.2.83–85). Further quotations are cited in the text by act, scene, and line numbers.

59. Philip Massinger, *The Emperour of the East* (London: Thomas Harper for John Waterson, 1632), sig. C5. Further quotations are cited in the text.

60. Similar uses of the hangings in the King's Men's repertory occur in Francis and Beaumont and John Fletcher's *Philaster* (1609) and William Broome's *The Northern Lass* (1629).

61. A nun directs Calis to perform devotions within the space behind the arras. "Exit *Nun* and draws the Curten Close to *Calis*," says the stage direction at 5.1.28. When Calis's devotions are complete (there is an intervening stretch of dialogue involving other characters), "Enter *Nun*, she opens the Curtain to *Calis*" (5.3.1) and then invites Calis to come to Venus's oracle and pray there. The curtain that defined the outer wall of Calis's oratory now becomes the inner wall of Venus's oracle. Next to Calis's scripted prayer stands the stage direction "Calis *at the Oracle. Arras*" (5.3.21) (*The Mad Lover*, in Bowers, *The Dramatic Works in the Beaumont and Fletcher Canon*, 5:80–81).

62. John Marston's tragedy *Sophonisba*, printed in 1606 "as it hath beene sundry times Acted at the *Black Friers*" calls for music to be played at the end of each act and confirms the testimony of the German visitor Frederic Gerschow, four years earlier, that consort music was as much an attraction at Blackfriars performances as the plays were. See Smith, *The Acoustic World of Early Modern England*, 221 (see chap. 5, n. 54). Andrew Gurr argues that Shakespeare's company preserved these musical traditions when they took over the Blackfriars Theatre and that they even retrofitted a curtained space at the Globe to serve as a musicians' gallery (*The Shakespearean Playing Companies* [Oxford: Oxford University Press, 1996], 367–68).

63. Thomas Kyd, *The Spanish tragedie* (London: Edward Allde for Edward White, 1602), sig. K2v.

64. Plays-within-the-play are one of the motifs cataloged in Charles A. Hallett, *The Revenger's Madness: A Study of Revenge Tragedy Motifs* (Lincoln: University of Nebraska Press, 1980), 89–95. Hallett emphasizes the sealed-off quality of such scenes.

65. Saxo Grammaticus, *Historiae Danicae*, trans. Oliver Elton (1894), in Geoffrey Bullough, ed., *Narrative and Dramatic Sources of Shakespeare*, vol. 7 (London: Routledge, 1973), 69.

66. John Webster, THE TRAGEDY OF THE DVTCHESSE *Of Malfy. As it was Presented priuatly, at the Black-Friers; and publiquely at the Globe, By the Kings Maiesties Seruants. The perfect and exact Coppy, with diuerse things Primed, that the length of the Play would not beare in the Presentment* (London: Nicholas Okes and John Waterson, 1623), sig. I1v (4.1.55).

67. William Davenant, THE VNFORTVNATE LOVERS: *A Tragedie; As it was lately Acted with great applause at the private House in Black-Fryers; By His Majesties Servants* (London: R. H. for Francis Coles, 1643), sigs. G2v–G3.

68. William Hemmings, *The Fatal Contract, a French Tragedy* (London: for J. M., 1653), sig. B4. Further references are cited in the text by signature number.

69. Jasper Mayne, *The citye match* (Oxford: Leonard Lichfield, 1639), sig. H2. Further quotations are cited in the text.

70. John Webster and John Marston, *The Malcontent* (London: Valentine Simmes for William Aspley, 1604), sig. C3v.

71. *Thomas of Woodstock, or, Richard the Second, Part One,* ed. Peter Corbin and Douglas Sedge (Manchester, UK: Manchester University Press, 2002), 5.1.48. Further quotation is cited in the text by act, scene, and line number.

72. William Davenant, *THE CRVELL BROTHER. A Tragedy. As it was presented, at the priuate House, in the Blacke-Fryers: By His Maiesties Seruants* (London: A. M. for John Waterson, 1643), sig. H3v. Further quotation is cited in the text by signature number.

73. Campbell, *The Cabinet of Eros,* 46 (see chap. 1, n. 41).

74. Thomas Dekker, *Satiro-Mastix. Or the Vntrussing of the Humorous Poet* (London: Edward Allde for Edward White, 1602), sig. B4.

75. The portrait of Erasmus is reproduced as plate 78 and the portrait of More as plate 90 in Foister, Roy, and Wyld, *Holbein's "Ambassadors"* (see chap 1., n. 37). The portrait of Erasmus resides at the National Gallery, London; the portrait of More, in the Frick Collection in New York.

76. William Davenant, *News from Plymouth,* in *The Works of Sr. William D'Avenant Kt.* (London: T. N. for Henry Herringman, 1673), sig. CCCC3v.

77. These scripts include *The Merry Devil of Edmonton* (1602) and *The Devil's Charter* (1607).

78. William Davenant, *The Distresses,* in *Works,* sig. GGGG3.

79. William Davenant, *The Platonic Lovers,* in *Works,* sig. DDD1v.

80. The others are John Marston's *What You Will* (Paul's Boys, 1601), in which "*The Curtaines are drawne by a Page, and* Celia *and* Lauerdure, Quadratus, *and* Lyzabetta, Lampatho *and* Meletza Simplicitus, *and* Lucea *displayed sitting at Dinner*" (John Marston, *VVHAT YOV VVILL* [London: G. Edle for Thomas Thorppe, 1607], sig. G3); Dekker, Webster, and Jonson's *Westward Ho* (Paul's Boys, 1604), in which "*The Earle drawes a Curten and sets forth a Banquet*" (*West-Warde Hoe* [London: John Hodges, 1607], sig. F2v; and Thomas Drue's *The Bloody Banquet* (Beeston's Boys, 1639), in which the blindfolded Tymethes is led onstage amid "*Soft musicke, a Table with lights set out. Arras spread*" and exclaims when his hood is taken off, " Ha! The ground spread with Arras? What place is this?/Rich hangings? faire roome gloriously furnish'd?/Lights and luster? riches and their splendor?" (T. D., *The Bloodie Banquet* [London: Thomas Cotes, 1639], sig. D4v.

81. Phillip Massinger, *The Guardian,* in *Three New Playes* (London: Humphrey Mosley, 1655), sig. K6v. Further quotations are cited in the text by signature number.

82. Anthony Munday, Henry Chettle, Thomas Dekker, William Shakespeare, and Thomas Heywood (attr.), *Sir Thomas More* (BL Harleian MS 7368), transcribed in Wells and Taylor, *Complete Works,* 816.

83. E. K. Chambers, *The Elizabethan Stage,* vol. 3 (Oxford: Clarendon Press, 1923), 50–68. Further quotations are cited in the text.

84. Malone, *Historical Account of the Rise and Progress of the English Stage,* 93–94

85. F. G. Fleay, *Introduction to Shakespearian Study* (London: Collins, 1877), 73. Further quotations are cited in the text by page number.

86. Montaigne, *The Essayes or Morall, Politike and Millitarie Discourses of Lo,* trans. Florio, sig. N4 (see chap. 4, n. 49). Further quotations are cited in the text by signature number.

87. Michel de Montaigne, *Essais, Livre 1,* ed. André Tournon (Paris: Imprimerie Nationale, 1998), 418.

88. Michel de Montaigne, *Essais,* trans. Charles Cotton as *Essays of Michael, seigneur de Montaigne in three books,* trans. Charles Cotton (London: T. Basset, M. Gilliflower, and W. Hensman, 1685–1686), sig. KK6.

89. Leacroft, *The Development of the English Playhouse,* 87. Additional evidence, from stage directions as well as surviving elevations, is presented in Bruce R. Smith, *Ancient Scripts and Modern Experience on the English Stage 1500–1700* (Princeton, NJ: Princeton University Press, 1988), 93–97.

90. George B. Bryan, "On the Theatrical Origin of the Expression 'Green Room,'" *Proverbium* (1992): 31–36.

91. *OED,* "baize" *n.,* 1.a. Compare Phillips, *The new world of English words:* "a fine sort of Freeze, from *Baii,* A Citie of *Naples,* where it was first made" (sig. D4v) (see chap. 4, n. 46).

92. Bryan, "On the Theatrical Origin of the Expression 'Green Room,'" 32–33.

93. Thomas Shadwell, *A True Widow* (London: Benjamin Tooke, 1679), sig. A4. Further quotations are cited in the text by signature number. A search of Early English Books Online confirms Bryan's citation as the earliest. The *OED* gives as its earliest citation Colley Cibber's comedy *Love Makes a Man* (1701).

94. W. M. [unidentified], *The Female Wits; or The Triumvirate of Poets at a Rehearsal* (London: William Turner, William Davis, Bernard Lintott, and Thomas Brown, 1704), sig. D1v; Colley Cibber, *Love Makes a Man: or, The Fop's Fortune* (London: Richard Parker, Hugh Newman, and E. Rumbal, 1701), sigs. A1v, G2v.

95. *OED,* "green baize," and "baize," *n.,* 2.

96. Bryan, "On the Theatrical Origin of the Expression 'Green Room,'" 32.

97. The plan by Sir Christopher Wren (1674), reproduced in Leacroft, *The Development of the English Playhouse,* 95, locates the scene room and the green room opening off stage left but suggests that they were also accessible from Vinegar Yard.

AFTERWORD

1. *The Florist: Containing sixty plates of the most beautiful flowers regularly disposed in their succession of blowing. To which is added an accurate description of their colours with instructions for drawing and painting according to nature: being a new work intended for the use & amusement of gentlemen and ladies delighting in that art* (London: Printed for Robert Sayer, T. Bowles, John Bowles and Son, [1760]. The copy I have examined resides in the National Art Library at the Victoria and Albert Museum.

2. *The Florist, or Poetical nosegay and drawing-book. Containing, twenty four copper-plates . . . with a descriptive moral poem to each, to which is annexed their botanical description* ([London?], [1780?]), A1. This example, available through Eighteenth Century Collections Online (ECCO; http:galenet.galegroup.com/servlet/ECCO), is in the collection of the British Library (http://catalogue.bl.uk). What appears to be a later edition with the same title, also available through ECCO, bears the imprint "London: S. Hooper." The ECCO copy was supplied by Cambridge University Library.

3. My searches of the catalogs of the National Art Library at the Victoria and Albert Museum, the British Library, the Library of Congress, and the Huntington Library have turned up about a dozen coloring books dating from before 1900, but no scholarly accounts of the genre.

4. *The Young Artist's Coloring Guide,* No. 12 (New York: Charles Magnus, [1850]), in the Carson Collection, Library of Congress, looks to be an American reissue of a German-designed alphabet book, each plate being accompanied by black-letter type for the German text and Roman type for the English text. Images in *The Little Painter* (Philadelphia, PA: Janentzky and Co., [1860]), also in the Carson Collection, Library of Congress, likewise appear to be German in origin.

5. George Weatherly and Kate Greenaway, *The "Little Folks" Painting Book* (London and New York: Cassell, [1879]), vii. The American edition (copy preserved in the Carson Collection, Library of Congress) bears, inside the front cover, an advertisement for a "Fine Art Moist Colour Box." price 50 cents, with a range of hues approved by the Art Department of the South Kensington Museum: burnt sienna, vandyke brown, crimson lake, sepia, light red, ivory black, vermilion, green bice, yellow ochre, prussian blue, gamboe, and ultramarine. Inside the back cover is a list of other coloring books published by Cassell, including Kate Greenaway's *Painting Book for Little Folks,* which is said to have sold over 60,000 copies in six months.

6. Randle Holme, *The Academy of Armory, Or, A storehouse of armory and blazon* (Chester: Printed for the author, 1688), sig. D1v.

7. Particularly interesting among the hand-colored emblem books in the Sterling Maxwell Collection are a copy of Otto van Veen, *Amorum Emblemata* (Antwerp, 1608) owned in the nineteenth century by Sidney Herbert, 11th Earl of Pembroke, hence possibly a presentation copy to the dedicatee, William Herbert, 1st Earl of Pembroke (SM 1050, 1050.1, 1050.2); a copy of Adriaen de Jonghe, *Emblemata* (Antwerp, 1565) interleaved with blank pages to form a *liber amicorum* in which the original owner Solinus à Sixma, a student at Heidelberg and Louvain in late 1560s and early 1570s—or perhaps his kinsmen Aggaeus à Sixma (inscribed 1654)—collected inscriptions and autographs from friends, along with their fully illuminated coats of arms (SM 658.2); and a copy of the second printing of Michael Maier, *Atalanta Fugiens* (Oppenheim, 1618), a collection of 50 emblems and 53 voice musical canons that illustrate the opposition in alchemical theory whereby volatile mercury (Atalanta) flees forceful sulfur (Hippomenes) before they are united in the golden apple (SM Ar-f.16). I am grateful to David Weston, Keeper of Special Collections at Glasgow University Library, for helping me find my way among the Sterling Maxwell Collection of emblem books.

8. Three signal examples are Robin Meyers, Michael Harris, and Giles Mandebrote, eds., *Owners, Annotators, and the Signs of Reading* (London: British Library, 2005); H. J. Jackson, *Marginalia: Readers' Writings in Books* (New Haven, CT: Yale University Press, 2001); and James Raven, Helen Small, and Naomi Tadmor, eds., *The Practice and Representation of Reading in England* (Cambridge: Cambridge University Press, 1996). On margins more generally, see the essays collected in D. C. Greetham, *The Margins of the Text* (Ann Arbor: University of Michigan Press, 1997), Evelyn Tribble, *Margins and Marginality: The Printed Page in Early Modern England* (Charlottesville, University Press of Virginia, 1993),

and William W. E. Slights, "The Edifying Margins of Renaissance English Books," *Renaissance Quarterly* 42.4 (1989): 682–716.

9. Notes in the Folger Library card catalog of Former Owners mention a third signature, "Joseph S. Woodin," which I was not able to find. The volume bears the bookplates of Edward Dodwell (possibly identifiable with the archeologist Edward Dodwell, 1776–1832) and W. T. Smedley (b. 1851). The card catalog also mentions the bookplate of one "A.W.," which I was also not able to find in the book itself.

10. Middleton and Rowley's source in Reynolds's collection of famous murders was noted as early as 1691 in Gerard Langbaine's *An Account of the English Dramatick Poets* (London: L. L. for George West and Henry Clements, 1691), sig. AA2. Langbaine connects other stories in Reynolds's collection with John Marston's *The Insatiate Countess,* James Shirley's *The Maid's Revenge,* and with a probably fictionalized account of the life of Robert Greene in William Winstanley, *The Lives of the Most Famous English Poets* (1687). Langbaine's citations confirm the continuing popularity of *The Triumphs of God's Revenge,* as do later printings in 1669, 1670, and 1679.

11. John Reynolds, *The Triumphs of Gods Revenge against the Crying and Execrable Sinne of (Wilful and Premeditated) Murther . . . ,* 4th ed. (London: Sarah Griffin for William Lee, 1663), sig. E1. Further quotations are cited in the text.

12. Rei Terada, *Feeling in Theory: Emotion after the "Death of the Subject"* (Cambridge, MA: Harvard University Press, 2001), 156.

13. On the jewel-like qualities of English miniature portraits see Karen Hearn, *Nicholas Hilliard* (London: Unicorn, 2005); Katharine Coombs, *The Portrait Miniature in England* (London: V&A Publications, 1998); and Strong, *The English Renaissance Miniature* (see chap. 2, n. 87). Although portrait miniatures could be wrapped in paper, kept in a cabinet, and brought out for private contemplation or display to others, it was more usual for them to be mounted in gold or silver cases, adorned with precious stones, and worn as pendants. Hilliard's images are of a piece with these bejeweled settings. The background to his portrait of Queen Elizabeth in plate 3, for example, suggests lapis lazuli.

14. Hearn, *Dynasties,* 131 (no. 78) (see chap. 2, n. 2).

15. Michel Serres, *Angels: A Modern Myth,* trans. Francis Cowper (Paris: Flammarion, 1995), 146. Further quotations are cited in the text.

16. Two compelling exemplars are Jonathan Bate, *The Song of the Earth* (Cambridge, MA: Harvard University Press, 2000), which concentrates on the nineteenth century, and Watson, *Back to Nature* (see intro., n. 21), which pushes consideration back to the seventeenth century.

17. "Horizons" figures as a key term in Niklas Luhmann's biologically inspired version of systems theory in *Ecological Communication,* trans. John Bednarz, Jr. (Chicago: University of Chicago Press, 1989). Adapting Humberto Maturana and Francisco Varela's observation that living organisms exist as self-maintain systems ("autopoiesis" is their term), Luhmann proposes that systems in nature, human social systems, and the psychic systems of individuals communicate through greater or lesser degrees of overlap that can be mapped in Venn diagrams.

18. On the pointing index finger as a printer's device and writer's reference marker, see William H. Sherman, *Used Books: Marking Readers in Renaissance England* (Philadel-

phia: University of Prennsylvania Press, 2008), 25–52. I am grateful to Bill Sherman for pointing me in the right direction among the Folger Library's holdings of printed texts with readers' manicules.

19. Edmund Spenser, *The Faerie Queene* (London: H. L. for Matthew Lownes, 1609), sig. M6, in Folger Shakespeare Library copy STC 23084 Copy 1. Further quotations are cited in the text.

Index of Subjects and Names

Numbers in *italics* indicate illustrations.

Index of Images

PLATES IN "A GREEN GALLERY"

FIGURES IN THE TEXT